CHIARA BARBATI

THE CHRISTIAN SOGDIAN GOSPEL LECTIONARY E5 IN CONTEXT

ÖSTERREICHISCHE AKADEMIE DER WISSENSCHAFTEN
PHILOSOPHISCH-HISTORISCHE KLASSE
SITZUNGSBERICHTE, 874. BAND

VERÖFFENTLICHUNGEN ZUR IRANISTIK
HERAUSGEGEBEN VON BERT G. FRAGNER UND FLORIAN SCHWARZ

NR. 81

CHIARA BARBATI

THE CHRISTIAN SOGDIAN GOSPEL LECTIONARY E5 IN CONTEXT

VERLAG DER
ÖSTERREICHISCHEN
AKADEMIE DER
WISSENSCHAFTEN

Angenommen durch die Publikationskommission
der philosophisch-historischen Klasse der ÖAW:
Michael Alram, Bert Fragner, Hermann Hunger, Sigrid Jalkotzy-Deger,
Brigitte Mazohl, Franz Rainer, Oliver Jens Schmitt,
Peter Wiesinger und Waldemar Zacharasiewicz

Cover: The monastery at Bulayïq, Dafusan'gaicun,
Tulufan/Turpan, Xinjiang, PR China (photograph: Chiara Barbati 2015)
Umschlaggestaltung: Bettina Hofleitner

Diese Publikation wurde einem anonymen, internationalen
Peer-Review-Verfahren unterzogen.

This publication has undergone the process of anonymous, international peer review.

Die verwendete Papiersorte ist aus chlorfrei gebleichtem Zellstoff hergestellt,
frei von säurebildenden Bestandteilen und alterungsbeständig.

ISBN 978-3-7001-7904-7

Druck und Bindung: Prime Rate kft., Budapest
http://epub.oeaw.ac.at/7904-7
http://verlag.oeaw.ac.at
Printed and bound in the EU

CONTENTS

PREFACE

In March 2006, during the Ehrencolloquium celebrating the 70th birthday of the late Prof. W. Sundermann, Prof. C.G. Cereti and Prof. D. Durkin-Meisterernst suggested to me that my doctoral thesis should be devoted to a new edition of the Christian Sogdian Gospel lectionary *E5*. It was Prof. W. Sundermann himself who stressed the need for a review of the whole material which he had published because of the numerous points of interest that this material has always shown. I accepted with enthusiasm, gratitude and also with a little fear for the challenge that awaited me. I want to add that my biggest regret is not having published this work before the death of Prof. W. Sundermann, on 12.10.2012.

My doctoral thesis – defended at "Sapienza" University of Rome in September 2009 – was characterized by a distinctly philological and linguistic analysis mainly aimed to restore the text – as far as preserved – of the Christian Sogdian Gospel lectionary *E5* by putting together fragments that had been published separately in different works over the years, i.e. Müller (1913), and Sundermann (1974, 1975, 1981). Yet even with such a clear philological and linguistic outlook there were matters for reflection in different fields, in particular that of translation studies since – as will be discussed in detail later – this particular work, and practically the entire Christian Sogdian literature in general, was translated from Syriac, forming part of the religious heritage of the Syriac-speaking Church of the East.

The present work is based on my doctoral thesis and, at the same time, it goes beyond it. The linguistic analysis of my doctoral thesis, which was the mainstay of the work, has been greatly expanded. The brief synchronic-descriptive analysis – as well as the historical and comparative reflections – are now seen through a magnifying glass consisting of translation studies, language contact and areal linguistics, all of which are indispensable, in my opinion, to a full understanding of Sogdian in general and of the linguistic area of the Turfan oasis between the 8th and the 11th century in particular (this being the time and place from which this material derives). In other words, the interpretation of the linguistic data must first undergo the theoretical rethinking which is strongly required by their context. It is a context in which one language, namely Sogdian, acted as a translation tool for a religious literature conceived and written in another language, namely Syriac, which was neither genealogically related nor typologically similar.

This context, in which multilingualism and multiculturalism played a dominant role, is crucial to a comprehensive understanding of the relevant linguistic material. Nor can this context be ignored when it is a matter of interpreting data related to disciplines other than linguistics, such as codicology or literary, cultural and religious history. The contextualization concerns all of these disciplines, because it is the most suitable tool to bring out the peculiarities and the many facets of what each manuscript is, namely a unique witness to its time and place. Thus, a multidisciplinary approach to the Christian Sogdian Gospel lectionary *E5* has as its ultimate aim that of tying the work itself to its own context in an attempt to return, as far as possible, to the *milieu* that generated it.

In so doing, perhaps I asked myself too many questions compared to the answers that I was able to give. Nevertheless, I hope that the issues discussed in this book may become the basis for further investigations.

I am deeply indebted to Prof. Nicholas Sims-Williams who generously dedicated time to read several versions of this book and offered invaluable advice and criticism. Surely, without his extraordinary help, this work could never have been published. It goes without saying that all remaining faults are mine.

Chiara Barbati, Vienna, January 2016

Acknowledgements

There are many people to whom I am personally and professionally grateful. People for whom a simple "thank you" is not really enough. If each of us is a journey, these are the people without whom I would have been undoubtedly another journey.

To my parents, Loreta and Nicola, and my brother Matteo, for their love and support always beyond all.

To my uncle, Pasquale, let the music play…wherever you are. And to his great family, Maria Grazia and Luca.

To Luca Alfieri, for a friendship that I find hard to define for all that it contains but to which I will always be eternally grateful.

To Natalie Kutzborski and Sarah Bianco for all that we have shared for years.

To Maria Pia Pantano and Francesca Pannoli, two people simply extraordinary.

To Lou for surreal evening conversations on a balcony in Tehran.

To Tiziana Buccico, for her unshakable optimism and a contagious life energy...and for the countless cups of chamomile tea in the most unexpected hours of the day and the night.

To my grandparents and all the people that since 06.04.2009 are no more here.

For L'Aquila.

To Prof. Carlo G. Cereti for believing in me and for being a very stimulating guide.

To Turfanforschung, Berlin-Brandenburgische Akademie der Wissenschaften, in particular to Prof. Desmond Durkin-Meisterernst for all that he has been teaching me for years, and to Dr. Yukiyo Kasai, to Dr. Simone-Christiane Raschmann and Dr. Christiane Reck, for having welcomed and encouraged me.

To Prof. Nicholas Sims-Williams, for being an inexhaustible source of knowledge and for his high willingness in giving precious teachings, advice and suggestions.

To Prof. Pier Giorgio Borbone, Dr. Mark Dickens, Dr. Erica C. D. Hunter, Prof. Emidio Vergani, for having guided me in an area that was not mine, but absolutely essential for me.

To Prof. Mauro Maggi and Prof. Adriano V. Rossi for all the ideas, which – developed during the discussion of my doctoral thesis – have become reasons for growth and maturity while writing the present work.

To Institut für Iranistik of the Österreichische Akademie der Wissenschaften, to Dr. Ulfatbek Abdurasulov, to Dr. Amr Taher Ahmed, to Prof. Bert Fragner, to Vahideh Gandhi, to Bettina Hofleitner, to Prof. Ebba Koch, to Dr. Justine Landau, to Dr. Christine Nölle-Karimi, to Dr. Stephan Popp, to Dr. Giorgio Rota, to Dr. Velizar Sadovski, to Dr. Paolo Sartori, to Hon. Prof. Florian Schwarz, to Dr. Iván Szántó, to Dr. Sibylle Wentker. It was a pleasure and an honour for me working with each of you.
To the series editors, Prof. Bert Fragner and Hon. Prof. Florian Schwarz, for accepting this work for publication in the Veröffentlichungen zur Iranistik.
To Bettina Hofleitner, for her incommensurable help in the layout of this book.
To the Verlag der Österreichischen Akademie der Wissenschaften, for having accepted the book for publication.
To the Berlin-Brandenburgische Akademie der Wissenschaften, for allowing the reproduction of the manuscript fragments in the depositum of the Berlin-Brandenburgische Akademie der Wissenschaften in the Staatsbibliothek zu Berlin – Preußischer Kulturbesitz, Orientabteilung.
To the Niedersächsische Staats- und Universitätsbibliothek Göttingen, for the kind permission to reproduce the photographs of the lost fragments of manuscript *E5* from the bequest of Carl Friedrich Andreas.
To Amalia and Emmanuel, for all the smiles they give me.
To Florian, my husband, for an amazing, exciting journey that I never thought to start.
To Tiziano, my masterpiece.

INTRODUCTION

Text and context are the key words of this book. They are, in fact, the main axes of the theoretical framework built here. The different disciplines applied each time – philology, linguistics, literary history, religious history, cultural history, codicology, translation studies – are nothing more than necessary tools used to shed some light on these two words.

The present text is unique. This is the only Christian Sogdian Gospel lectionary so far discovered, or, to be more precise, the only predominantly monolingual Gospel lectionary – the use of "predominantly" will be specified later – belonging to the only available collection of Christian Sogdian manuscripts, namely the one which is preserved in the Berlin Turfan Collection[1].

The context is that of Late Antiquity and the Early Middle Ages in an oasis, namely Turfan, that has not surprisingly and not unreasonably been defined by Hansen as "midway between China and Iran"[2]. The context is that of the missionary paths of the Church of the East[3] that meet the caravan routes of the Silk Road; of Sogdian communities, of Sogdian traders[4] as well as Christianized Sogdians; of different religious, literary and cultural

---

[1] For an overview of the Christian library of Turfan, ninth to fourteenth century, see: Hunter (2012). For the history of archaeological expeditions which have brought to light around 40,000 documents in more than 20 languages and scripts, see: Durkin-Meisterenst-Raschmann- Wilkens- Yaldiz- Zieme (2004); and Sundermann (2004). For the more specifically Christian Iranian tradition, see above all: Durkin-Meisterernst (2006); Sims-Williams (1992; 1992a; 2009; 2011; 2012); and Sundermann (1974a).

[2] See: Hansen (2012: 83).

[3] The correct modern term is "Holy Apostolic Catholic Assyrian Church of the East": see Baum-Winkler (2003:3-5); and Brock (1996).

[4] See: de la Vaissière (2005). Of course, they were not only traders but also soldiers, diplomats, translators, farmers etc. As amply demonstrated by several scholars the Sogdians played an important role in the social, artistic, economic and political life in Central Asia and China. See: de la Vaissière - Trombert (2005). This volume shows to what extent the Sogdian migrants settled into local cultures and to what extent they maintain close links with the homeland. For instance, with particular regard to the Turfan oasis, the contribution of Skaff to the above mentioned volume entitled "Documenting Sogdian society at Turfan" (during the Tang dynasty) shows that Sogdians were mentioned as "government officials, bronze-smiths, ironsmiths, artists, a painter, leatherworkers, a veterinarian, and an innkeeper. Leatherworking may have been a Sogdian specialty at Turfan because one Tang government list of craftsmen from circa 640 reveals that all of the leatherworkers with visible surnames are Sogdian" (p. 320).

traditions which at the same time are very close one to one another. Here, languages on one hand show instances of internal change, on the other, interference phenomena.

Restoring the text (presented below) to its context means, in my opinion, first trying to answer the following *Fragestellungen*: which were the tools for the development and dissemination of a religious knowledge, typical of the East-Syriac tradition, with a mother Church which has its roots in Edessa (modern Urfa, Turkey) during the second century? How did communities – not only Sogdian communities – located along the Silk Road between Late Antiquity and the Early Middle Ages recognize that knowledge[5]? And how, where and when were those tools modeled? And if we adopt Dickens's description of the role of the Syriac Bible in Central Asia, "The evidence, fleeting as it is, clearly shows that Christianity in Central Asia was not merely a thin veneer over the animistic and shamanistic religious core of the Turkic peoples. There was sufficient spiritual vibrancy and knowledge within the community to support teachers and interpreters of Scripture"[6], what was the role played by issues of translation, transfer of texts, also of images and cultural encounters?

Pinggéra writes about the evangelization practised by the Church of the East in Central Asia: "Es waren in aller Regel christliche Kaufleute, die auf den Handelswegen, namentlich der berühmten „Seidenstraße" ihren Glauben in diese fernen Regionen trugen. Ihnen folgte die Errichtung von Klöstern und Bischofssitzen, die eine fast ganz Asien fast umspannende kirchliche Organisation bildeten. Menschen unterschiedlichster Sprachen und Völker fanden sich so in einer Kirche zusammen. Sie schufen christliche Literaturen und beteten auch in ihren je eigenen Sprachen. Zusammengehalten wurden sie von einem weitmaschigen Kommunikationsnetz mit dem Katholikos-Patriarchen an der Spitze und von dem einigenden Band der syrischen Liturgiesprache, wobei Teile des Gottesdienstes in der Volksprache gehalten werden konnten. Eine eigene Ausbildungsstätte für die Mission errichtete Katholikos Timotheos I. (780-823) im Kloster Bet Abe, wo geeignete Mönche in den Sprachen der verschiedensten Völker Asiens unterwiesen

[5] In this regard, it is suitable to mention the ongoing project on "The transmission of Christian texts at Turfan". The project protagonists, funded by the UK Arts and Humanities Research Council, are the leading specialists in the field, Dr. Erica C.D. Hunter and Prof. Nicholas Sims-Williams, both active at the School of Oriental and African Studies in London.

[6] See: Dickens (2009: 112).

wurden"[7]. Broadly speaking, we can say that the scholarly literature in general, and the aforementioned passage in particular, show that *a)* the patriarchate of Timothy I represents a watershed in the evangelization history relating to the Church of the East, *b)* the monastery is the pre-eminent place for cultural development both religious and secular, and *c)* writing and the book are two powerful dissemination tools for these cultural "products".

a) According to the scholarly literature in this field[8], the Church of the East started from Edessa (present-day Urfa, Turkey) in the second century, separated from the patriarchate of Antioch and broke with the Monophysite Jacobite Church of Syria in the fifth century, becoming the "Church of Persia", and spread to the East reaching Central Asia, China[9] and India[10] between the sixth and the eight century. From the middle of the ninth century on, the missionary advance experiences a setback because of persecutions by the Chinese empire whereas in the eleventh century conversions to Christianity started to flourish again among the Mongol-Turkish tribes. The following centuries, especially the thirteenth and fourteenth, represent

---

[7] See: Pinggéra (2011: 29).

[8] From the extensive literature the most important and most recent studies include the following: Baum-Winkler (2003); Borbone- Marsone (2015); Gillmann-Klimkeit (1999); Hage (1988); Hunter (1996); Lala Comneno (1995); Le Coz (2010), and Moffet (1998). We strongly recommend the *Proceedings of Salzburg International Conference on the Church of the East in China and Central Asia*, the conference that takes place every three/four years at the University of Salzburg thanks to the tireless work of Dr. Li Tang and Prof. Dietmar W. Winkler. It is almost a unique opportunity that brings together Syriacists, Iranists, Sinologists, Turkologists, philologists, historians, art historians, etc. on the theme of the Church of the East in Central Asia and China over the centuries to the present day. Having taken part to the conference in 2013 I can say that this is a unique opportunity for those who care about this issue: experts from different fields are called to share their studies regularly in a continuous and renewed exchange of ideas.

[9] With particular regard to the beginning of evangelization we can recall two dates: 635, when a group of monks from Mosul reaches the capital of the T'ang, and 781, when the stele of Xi'an Fu with a long inscription in Chinese and Syriac is erected commemorating the introduction of the "religion of light" in China. All this, however, would deserve a separate chapter, which goes far beyond this introduction. Similarly, in respect of an extensive bibliography on the subject, only Hunter (2009); Lieu (2007), and Standaert (2001) are cited.

[10] The evangelization of India follows the spice trade routes through the sea. Following a well established tradition, the gospel was first preached in India by the apostle Saint Thomas. For a brief survey, see: Baum-Winkler (2003:51-57); Brown (1956); Le Coz (2010: 242-244). For an overview concerning the Middle Iranian documentation, in India and in Sri Lanka see: Cereti (2003); Gignoux (1995); Gropp (1970); and Hage (1995/6).

another period of strong growth before a downward course. With particular regard to the Turfan oasis, its history can be divided into three periods[11]: prior to the Tang conquest of 640, Tang rule (640-755) when the oasis was one of the three hundred prefectures in the Tang Empire, and after 803 the Uighur Kaghanate. For the purpose of our research, we must stress that Manichaeism was the official state religion of the Uighur Kaghanate until circa AD 1000, when the same Kaghanate choose to patronize Buddhism and not Manichaeism. It means that in Turfan as well as in the Mother Church's region, Christianity was never a state religion. This has been clearly pointed out by Briquel Chatonnet in a volume devoted to the study of the churches within the Church of the East. She writes: "Il faut en effet rappeler que les chrétiens de langue syriaque ne sont presque jamais identifiés avec un royaume ou une structure politique. Dans l'Empire sassanide, ils sont face à un État qui se proclame mazdéen. Du côté byzantin, la communauté syriaque s'affirme très tôt, suite aux controverses christologiques, majoritairement miaphysite, et donc en résistance contre la politique impériale. La conquête arabo-musulmane soumet tous les chrétiens syriaques à un pouvoir musulman, et à un environnement qui finit par devenir majoritairement musulman. De ce fait, ils ne disposent pas d'organisation ou de structure, et donc d'édifice, à nature politique ou culturelle, dans lequel ils pourraient se trouver représentés comme groupe. C'est tout naturellement dans l'église qu'ils peuvent affirmer leur existence en tant que communauté"[12].

Crucial for mapping the links of Christian Sogdian communities within the spread of the Church of the East eastwards are several places like Rew-Ardashīr, Marv, Nishāpur, Herāt, Samarkand including western China during the sixth to the eighth centuries. In 2010 Le Coz writes: "Le mond latin s'est préoccupé de l'évangélisation des peoples barbares seulement à partir du VII siècle, et Byzance ne s'est tournée vers les Slaves que deux cents ans plus tard; en revanche, les chrétiens d'Orient ont entrepris très tôt de propager l'Évangile dans tous les territoires situés à l'est de la Mésopotamie, par la route de la soie, et au sud par la route des épices, qui empruntait la voie maritime. Bien que minoritaire et persécutée, l'Église de Perse a malgré tout fait prevue d'un dynamism missionaire tel, que le nombre élevé de nouveaux évêchés a amené le patriarche Joseph à créer, dès la seconde moitié du VI siècle, les deux premières provinces de l'extérieur, celles du Fars et du Khorasan"[13]. These two provinces are Beit Parsayé with the city of Rew-

[11] According to Hansen (2012: 83-112).
[12] See: Briquel Chatonnet (2013: 11-12).
[13] See: Le Coz (2010: 77).

Ardashīr, as metropolitan seat, and that of Khorasan with the centres of Marv and Nishāpur as metropolitan seats. Marv plays a pivotal role on the Christianization of the Central Asia. To give an idea of its connection within the eastern Iranian area, we can recall – according to Nicholas Sims-Williams[14] –that a legendary bishop of Marv, i.e., Barshabbā, was the founder of the Christian Church in eastern Iran. The complete legend is preserved only in Arabic sources but there is some additional evidence in a few Sogdian and Syriac fragments coming from Xinjiang[15]. Following the Sogdian version, Barshabbā founded several monasteries in a wide area including Fārs, Gorgān, Ṭūs, Abarshahr, Sarakhs, Marw al-Rūd, Balkh, Herāt, and Sīstān. Moreover, the Sogdian Gospel lectionary *E5* commemorates Barshabbā[16]. In so doing, according to Sims-Williams, who in turn quotes Bīrūnī, it agrees with the liturgical calendar of the Melkites Church in Khorezm which includes the commemoration of the priest Barshabbā on the 21st June. At this point, it is also interesting to note three other issues. Two of them link the Christian Sogdians, the Melkite Church and the Turfan oasis[17], while the third links the Church of the East and the Turfan area with the western Iranian area and also with Marv. The first point is that among the Christian Sogdian fragments in East Syriac script from the Turfan oasis, there is a unique fragment[18] containing a part of Psalm 33 (according to the numbering of *Septuaginta*) with Greek quotations as headlines and which accords partly with the *Septuaginta* and partly with the *Peshitta*[19]. The second one – as already pointed out by Sims-Williams[20] – is

---

[14] See: Sims-Williams (1989: 823).

[15] They are now in the Berlin Turfan Collection. According to the new classification system, the corresponding catalogue numbers of the fragments are: *E24/7*, *E24/9* and *E24/11*. See: Sims-Williams (2012: 75-77).

[16] See Chapter 2 of this book. Anyway, according to the new classification system, the corresponding catalogue numbers of the Sogdian fragment which mentions Barshabbā is: *E5/125*. See: Sims-Williams (2012: 40). With particular regard to the Syriac fragments, see: Hunter- Dickens (2014: 59-60).

[17] Another link will be discussed in Chapter 1 from a codicological point of view. It concerns the preference for the format in one column within the Christian (not only Sogdian) manuscript tradition in Turfan just like the Melkites manuscript tradition.

[18] See: Sims-Williams (2004).

[19] Instead of agreeing with the *Peshitta* as testified by the Christian Sogdian biblical texts which in the Turfan oasis are – quoting Sims-Williams (2012: 21) – "almost without exception, those which were required for liturgical use". There are only a few known accordances with Tatian's *Diatessaron* and with the Old Syriac version of the New Testament. With particular regard to the Sogdian Gospel lectionary *E5*, see Chapter 2. For

that an Armenian source from 1307 refers to people living in Khorezm, a "kind of Christians live in these parts, who are called Sogdians, and have their own writing and language; their beliefs are like those of the Greeks, and they are obedient to the Patriarch of Antioch…". The third point is that the so called Pahlavi psalter from the Turfan oasis – consisting of 13 fragmentary pages written in Middle Persian in Pahlavi script – could serve as evidence for the evangelization of the area from Marv. As clearly demonstrated by Durkin-Meisterernst, the Pahlavi psalter looks westward and very probably was not written in Turfan[21].

Two other crucial moments for the presence of the Church of the East in Central Asia, were the foundation of the see of Bactria with the city of Herāt as metropolitan seat and that of Beit Turqayé, i.e., Sogdiana with Samarkand as metropolitan seat. We are in the time of Yshoyahb II (628-644). The Church of the East also reached China in a short time, as we have already seen. At this point it seems apt to quote Le Coz again: "Ainsi, au moment de la conquête musulmane, l'Église d'Orient se trouve-t-elle installée dans la plupart des regions situées à l'est de l'Empire byzantin, organisée en douze provinces qui dependent d'un pouvoir fortement centralisé entre les mains du catholicos-patriarche de Séleucie-Ctésiphon[22]. L'unification de tous les territoires, s'étendant de l'Atlantique jusq'aux frontiers de la Chine sous l'autorité d'un même souverain, le calife de l'Islam, va permettre aux chrétiens de Perse de faire une percée dans le monde syrien……D'autre parte, la sympathie qu'eprouvera le maître musulman, en particulier à partir de son installation à Bagdad, pour la version nestorienne du christianisme, va permettre à l'Église d'Orient, non seulement de survivre, mais encore d'augmenter son influence, principalment en direction de l'Asie"[23].

With particular regard to the Iranian area, we can say that as for Iran

---

a second fragment belonging to the manuscript with Greek lines, see also: Sims-Williams (2011a).

20 See: Sims-Williams (1992b: 46).

21 See: Durkin-Meisterernst (2006). It is a matter of fact that this text is the only Christian text written in Middle Persian in Pahlavi script at Turfan at that time; it is a matter of fact that the Middle Persian was a liturgical language within the Manichaean Church but not for the Christian one, not at Turfan, not in the early Middle Ages; finally, it is a matter of fact that the text sometimes agrees with the Syriac *Peshitta* but sometimes with the *Septuaginta*. See also: Gignoux (1969; 2001).

22 Of course, as Le Coz pointed out in his volume, there are some differences between internal and external provinces with particular regard to the central power. See: Le Coz (2010: 235-247); and also Borbone (2015).

23 See: Le Coz (2010: 81).

proper, as for the Central Asia territories, the secondary – Syriac – sources are to be considered[24] because of a constant lack of direct sources. Despite this, in recent decades fundamental studies have appeared that are essential for understanding these Christian communities in the Iranian area. Consider, for example, the work of Lerner (1977; 1992) and Gyselen (2006) in which each element, linguistic (Syriac-Iranian bilingualism), iconographic etc., is studied in order to understand the role played by Christians in the Sasanian administrative structure, and, consequently, as an attempt to establish the different degrees of the integration of religious minorities within the empire. As for Central Asia, a work that takes the same direction is that of Naymark (1996). Interesting insights are to be expected from the doctoral thesis of Ashurov, "Tarsākyā: an analysis of Sogdian Christianity based on archaeological, numismatic, epigraphic and textual sources"[25], a PhD thesis written at the School of Oriental and African Studies in London, under the guidance of two leading experts in the field, Erica Hunter and Nicholas Sims-Williams. Each work so far mentioned – and any other one, not mentioned for brevity – represents a piece which aims to recreate the entangled puzzle of the East Syriac missionary activities. However, one thing seems to be certain, namely that Patriarch Timothy I (780-823) played a crucial role in the Evangelization of Central Asia, and always provided for the education of missionaries in several fields including theology, languages, bookbinding and calligraphy. When Berti (2009) analyzes the letters of the Patriarch, he gives us an image of Timothy as a man culturally linked to the territory which goes from Mosul and Baghdad to Elam, a Timothy who creates Syro-Oriental cultural elites which peak during the ninth century, the season of scholars and translators. This is the Timothy who establishes the patriarchate seat in Baghdad thereby entering into the heart of the Abbasid dynasty providing the administrative cadres of the Empire to the Arabian

[24] Both for Iranian and non-Iranian peoples (and not just Sogdians), for example, the discovery of ossuaries with crosses dating back to the late seventh-first half of the eighth century, took place at Mizdaxkan, not far from Tokkala, attesting the presence of Christian communities in Khorezm, see: de la Vaissière (2005: 257-258). Consider the work of C. Jullien (2004) for Sasanian Iran starting from sources such as *The acts of the martyrs*. Furthermore, Syriac sources also attest the ordination of a bishop for the Hephthalites around 550 and the conversion of the Kerait in the second half of the seventh century. See: Hunter (1989-1991) and Mingana (1925). These are only very few examples aimed at highlighting the complexity, the extent of the areas involved and the different and multiple empires, peoples, ethnic groups, tribes, etc. involved in a similar scenario.

[25] See: Ashurov (2015).

court[26]. This is the Timothy who was somehow responsible for the transmission of Greek knowledge to the Arab world, who organizes missions to the East, one designed to quell potential internal uprisings and to strengthen and expand the external acquired positions, without ever forgetting their own context. This is the Timothy who carefully watches the issues connected to the translations of texts, the so-called language question[27]. He implements – referring to what I think is a more than brilliant definition by Berti – "il governo della cultura come asse della vita ecclesiale"[28]. Here "monastery" comes into play, because it is the monastery that realizes that "government of culture" so much wanted and promoted by Timothy I.

b) As early as 1958, after two years of field research among the monasteries of the Near East, Leroy wrote, referring in particular to the evangelization of Central Asia "Cette prodigieuse page de l'histoire nestorienne, ce sont les moines qui l'ont écrite pour une grand part, et ce seul fait atteste l'importance de l'institution monastique en Perse. Il en exprime en même temps les traits caractéristiques: à la fois éducateur et missionaire..."[29]. As highlighted by recent studies on Eastern monasticism – especially in the Iranian area – conducted by those who studied this subject for years such as F. Jullien, for about ten centuries the monastery or the monastic community played an indispensable role in the existence, life and the spread of the missions in the Iranian area; this refers, as always, to the geographical area that reaches from Iran proper to China[30]. This phenomenon took place in the fourth century and went through the fifth and sixth century with the first definition of the monastic rules, until its real formulation with subsequent diffusion. So, within the Church of the East, the monastery becomes a

---

[26] Of course, things are never so simple: see, for example, the interpretation given by the scholar on the cultural vibrancy of the large and medium-sized towns vs. the progressive cultural depletion of the small ones that even had played a leading role in past centuries. See, in particular: id.: 363-364.

[27] See: in particular *id.*: 279-351.

[28] See: *id.*: 359.

[29] See: Leroy (1958: 212).

[30] See: F. Jullien (2006; 2011). It is significant that the Christian Sogdian corpus from Turfan also includes the story of Mār Awgen, generally – although not without some doubts – considered the founder of Persian monasticism. See Jullien, F. (2006: 149-51) and Sundermann (1994). According to the new classification system, the corresponding catalogue numbers of the fragments which contain the story are: *E28/9*, *E28/10a-c*. See: Sims-Williams (2012: 131-133).

genuine laboratory of knowledge, an extraordinary center of cultural communication, the place where the range of activities covers copying, translation[31], preservation, production and teaching[32] – not only of the Scriptures but also other disciplines such as medicine[33] and philosophy[34]. Furthermore the Syriac language was of course a liturgical language, or rather, the official language of the Church of the East, but it was also a language of scholarship[35]. Thus, through this language, different kinds of knowledge started to spread along a considerable period of time and space. But how, in detail, did this process of transfer and dissemination occurr?

c) Outlining the expansive policy of Timothy I, and above all the ideology that sustained and promoted it[36], Berti considers three episodes – that of Shuhalisho‘, that of Qardag and Yahbalaha, and that of Elijah – which demonstrate how the missionary monks were chosen according to their most commodious quality for a given context[37]. Sometimes figures more able in languages and in dialectic were singled out, as in the case of Shuhalisho‘, called to sustain the arguments of the Church of the East even against other denominations; sometimes, figures expert in copying and binding, as in the case of Qardag and Yahbalaha, and sometimes, especially for missions in

[31] Leroy speaks explicitly about monks as translators (for example, of Greek works) and as authors (for instances, of ascetical and mystical treaties). See: Leroy (1958: 217).

[32] See: Dagron, G.- Riché, P.- Vauchez, A. (1994: 459), who distinguish two types of schools, "nämlich Kirchliche Bischofsstädten und in den meisten Klosterschulen".

[33] To stay within the Iranian setting, think of the role played by Christians belonging to the Syriac tradition in the transmission of Greek knowledge in Sasanian Iran so well highlighted by Gignoux (2001a). He also points out, rightly in my opinion, that the translations of Syriac knowledge into Middle Persian and Sogdian are a remarkable phenomenon of inculturation (ibid.: 232). Think, for instance, of the fragments in New Persian and in Sogdian from Turfan, both in East Syriac script, of pharmacological texts in the wake of medical knowledge attested in the Syriac tradition. See: Sims-Williams (2011). According to the new classification system, the corresponding catalogue numbers of the mentioned fragments are respectively: *E37*, *E38- E39*. See: Sims-Williams (2012: 186-187).

[34] See: Walker (2006: 164-205).

[35] At least until the ninth century when it began to be partially replaced by Arabic. For an overview, see: Le Coz (2010: 89-125; 185-200).

[36] Very interesting is Berti's consideration on the creation of new metropolitan seats. According to his analysis, they could also depend on Timothy I's will in order to create their own trusted network able to face older and well established metropolitan seats that disapproved him because of his controversial election in 780. See: Berti (2006: 147-148).

[37] See: Berti (2006: 2011).

distant lands that were particularly hard to reach and little known, a simple monk could be singled out, as in the case of Elijah[38]. However, beyond individual skills that are more or less specific, what is indisputable is the importance of being able to read and write. From F. Jullien[39] we learn that the aspirant monk was required to be able to read[40], that his education consisted in carefully listening to the biblical texts read by chapter[41], in learning how to write and that the continuous reading of the Psalms in his cell was one of his fundamental activities. We know that in the first half of the eighth century, in the convent school of Mosul, the education of an aspiring monk was divided into three stages: the first was based on the study of the New Testament, the second focused on the Pentateuch, and the third on readings from the Prophets and the Psalms[42]. Examining the texts from Turfan, Hunter[43] recalls how the Psalms seem to be the first reading tools for the new converts. Dickens (2013), who reaffirms the general importance of the Psalter especially in the monastic context, stresses how this is also true of Turfan – no religious text has been translated into more languages and scripts than the Psalter: in Syriac, in Sogdian language in Sogdian secular script[44], in Syriac and New Persian, in Syriac in Uyghur script[45], in Middle Persian in Pahlavi script. Dickens also noted that the only other text found in different traditions is the legend of St. George, which is in Syriac, Sogdian in East Syriac script and Uyghur Turkic. So, even from this point of view, the Turfan monastery is not an exception but fits perfectly into the East Syriac tradition. In particular, then, the Psalter in Turfan, according to Dickens, seems to attest the very first traditions[46], and is extremely useful to reconstruct the literary and religious history of the Church of the East.

Another important point that F. Jullien highlights in her works and that will have a significant importance in the present argument concerns the

---

38 Berti writes (2006: 147) about Elijah: "Elia infine si portava dietro un vangelo di piccolo formato come segno distintivo e, tra le prime cose che fece, tradusse i Salmi per iniziare alla preghiera le popolazioni da lui convertite".

39 See: F. Jullien (2006; 2011).

40 Rule of Dadīshō': see F. Jullien (2006: 165).

41 This could explain, in my opinion, the reason why in Turfan we have Syriac texts with Sogdian rubrics, i.e. to allow local monks – who probably were not of Syriac mother tongue – to better understand what was read to him.

42 See: F. Jullien (2006: 161).

43 See: Hunter (2012: 82).

44 In particular see: Schwartz (1974); Schwartz- Sims-Williams (2014).

45 In particular see: Dickens- Zieme (2014).

46 It is not the only example, as we will see in the next pages.

existence in the Sasanian Empire of mixed monastic communities, where it frequently happened that each linguistic group led its own ascetic life in a part of the monastery[47]. In other words multilingualism[48] has not been a characteristic of Turfan but of the entire East Syriac tradition over the centuries, throughout a broad geographical area. As already mentioned, Edessa was where the Church of the East began to spread in the second century, and in fact its Aramaic dialect Syriac, despite its continuous role as the official language of the Church[49], was put together with other vernaculars during the religious services. We have some evidence of the controversies between Syriac and Iranian speaking monks with regard to the choice of the language used during the liturgy, in several fragments of a Sogdian version of the life of John of Dailam, an Eastern Syrian saint and founder of monasteries in Fārs[50]. With particular regard to Central Asia[51], it is not surprising that among the vernaculars permitted in the Church service, the main role was played by the Sogdian language which was already the language spoken by the traders along the Silk Road[52] and therefore was adopted by the missionary communities to spread their religious message. In the same way, it seems to me that not only the choice of the language[53] but

---

47 See: F. Jullien (2006: 165-166).

48 See: Dickens (2009a).

49 The use of Syriac along the caravan routes of the Silk Road is testified by literary and archaeological sources. See: Baum-Winkler (2003); Lala Comneno (1995). To give just few examples, in addition to the fragments found in Turfan in several languages – Syriac, Sogdian, Old Turkish, Middle Persian, New Persian – and scripts – East Syriac script, Sogdian secular script, Pahlavi script, Uyghur script – one may mention a clay vessel bearing a Syriac inscription from Jambulin, Kazakstan (fifth-sixth centuries), a clay fragment with the first two psalms in the *Peshitta* version from Penjikent, Tajikistan (seventh-eighth centuries), a stele in Chinese and Syriac (781) recording, as already said, the coming of Christianity to China one and a half centuries earlier; twenty-five Syriac rock inscriptions in the modern-day region of Urgut, Uzbekistan (tenth century), a church (eighth century) excavated in the village of Aq-Beshim, Kyrgyzstan as well as two East Syriac cemeteries (generally dated eleventh - late thirteenth centuries) with 568 gravestones with Syriac inscriptions where over 3.000 people had been buried in the north of the same country. See also: Dickens (2009b); Dickens- Savchenko (2009).

50 See: Sims-Williams (1996; 2014).

51 Taking into account Iran proper, see: Panaino (2007); and Shaked (1990).

52 See: Hansen (2012: 113-139); and de la Vaissière (2005).

53 Sometimes the result was a monolingual text, often a bilingual one, i.e. focusing of course on the Christian Sogdian corpus, Syriac-Sogdian. On the languages alternation Brock stated (2006: 145): "Bilingual Syriac biblical manuscripts are rather more commonly found, and normally the second language is Arabic (it is striking that there are no known bilingual biblical manuscripts providing just Syriac and Greek). Although bilingual

also that of script[54], terminology, images, symbols, and layout[55] is strongly related to the kind of text, its function and its context. Broadly speaking, we can assert that the Christian Sogdian material from the monastery of Bulayïq, dating back from the eight to the eleventh century, perfectly fits within the missionary framework of the Church of the East. Apart from biblical-liturgical texts[56], the Christian Sogdian literature is a monastic and ascetic literature. In fact, this translation literature consists of several biographies including those of St. Serapion, Eugenius, John of Dailam; the legend of St. Barshabbā, bishop of Marv; the story of Daniel; the Wisdom of Aḥiqar; the Dormition of the Virgin Mary; Acts of the Persian martyrs under Shābūr II- Martyrdoms of St. Shahdost, of St. Tarbo, of St. Barbaʿshmin; several martyrdoms such as those of St. Pethion, St. Eustathius, St. Sergius and St. Bacchus, Cyriacus and Julitta, St. George; the legend of the Finding of the Cross by St. Helen, the mother of Costantine; Antirrheticus of Evagrius Ponticus; part of the homily by Bābay of Nisibis; Apostolic Canons; Commentary on the baptismal and Eucharistic liturgies entitled "Explanation of the Mysteries of the Church"; Questions and answers from the Apophthegmata Patrum; Legend of the Sleepers of Ephesus; parts of works of Shem'on d-Taibūtēh and Dādishoʿ Qaṭrāyā; several fragmentary homilies on the ascetic life. Sometimes, the Christian Sogdian literature from Turfan testifies an older tradition in comparison to the Syriac literary tradition[57]. The main examples concern the Sogdian translation of Shem'on d-Taibūtēh[58], the Wisdom of Aḥiqar[59] and the life of John of Dailam[60].

These few pages are aimed at showing that it makes little sense to regard the Christian Sogdian corpus in isolation: the faithful retention of both

manuscripts normally present the two languages side by side, in some biblical fragments from Central Asia a different arrangement is found: here Syriac and a translation into Sogdian are given in alternate lines". Finally, about the idea that the bilingual lectionaries would testify an early liturgical use, see: Baumstark (1921: 11); Sims-Williams (2009: 276, n. 30); and Sundermann (1981: 169).

54 With particular regard to the Sogdian corpus, see: Barbati (2014a) on the use of the East Syriac script; and Reck (2008); Sims-Williams (2013) on the use of the Sogdian secular script.

55 The last issues are still under investigation and are part of my project "Christian Sogdian Book Culture" hosted at the *Institute of Iranian Studies*, *Austrian Academy of Sciences* and funded by the *Austrian Programme for Advanced Research and Technology*.

56 See: Sims-Williams (2012: 21-66).

57 I am referring to the whole Syriac literary tradition, not only that from Turfan.

58 See: Kessel- Sims-Williams (2011).

59 See: Sims-Williams (2014a).

60 See: Debié (2010: 131; 140); and Sims-Williams (2014).

Syriac literary[61] and manuscript[62] tradition shows the strength of the missionary character of the Church of the East.

I would like to end this brief introduction referring to one of the most recent works of the Syriacist Borbone[63] where the scholar, illustrating the structure of the churches of the Church of the East in Central Asia and in China, focuses, among other things, on an illustration in an album of the second half of the fourteenth century, and now preserved in Istanbul. The illustration represents a multi-storey building where several characters are illustrated in their main occupations which seem to be, as pointed out by Borbone, reading and writing. Borbone defines this illustration "scène de monastère"[64] and says: "L'image, qui met côte-à côte des éléments d'origine iranienne et chinoise, ne permet pas une identification précise et ne renvoie probablement à rien de réél. Toutefois, dans cette image se trouvent les éléments caractéristiques d'un monastère, selon le point de vue et les notion du peintre centre-asiatique (parmi lesquelles l'activité de l'étude, les cloches et les simandres, et les peintures murales)"[65].

Therefore, the monastery is the center of religious and secular culture, it is the keystone on which the cultural life turns. It is from a monastery, indeed from the ruins of a monastery, those of Shüï-pang near Bulayïq[66], that the Christian Sogdian corpus mentioned in this introduction comes from, and, of course, also the Christian Sogdian Gospel lectionary which will be discussed in the next chapters from several points of view.

---

61 With different degrees of adherence to the Syriac original. The biblical and liturgical texts are of course the most faithful. Among the ascetic and monastic texts, we have some examples where the Sogdian version agrees with versions in other languages, i.e. readings which were once in the Syriac but which were lost in the later Syriac tradition. For instance, Sims-Williams has demonstrated that the Sogdian version of the Wisdom of Aḥiqar sometimes agrees with the Armenian, Slavonic and Ethiopic versions and not with the Syriac one. See: Sims-Williams (2014a: 108). We can find some differences between the Sogdian and the Syriac versions also with particular regard to the Dormition of the Virgin Mary. See: Sims-Williams (2014b).

62 Even if the last topic is still under investigation, it seems to me that it goes in the same direction of the literary one.

63 See: Borbone (2013).

64 See: Borbone (2013: 450).

65 See: Borbone (2013: 450-451).

66 See: Sims-Williams (1990). About that monastery, many aspects are still unclear. See: Barbati (2015a: 92-97). Concerning the closing date and/or destruction, Hunter is inclined to consider the fourteenth century, the *terminus ad quem*. See: Hunter (2012: 88).

E5[67]: The Manuscript

The Sogdian manuscript *E5* represents one of the largest and best-preserved manuscripts among the Christian Sogdian examples in either East Syriac or Sogdian secular script belonging to the Berlin Turfan Collection. It is well known that in this case, too, only fragments exist[68]; no entire manuscript has been preserved – at least as far as we know. In the case of *E5*, we have more than 30 fragments for a total of about 800 lines of writing. Being a lectionary, it is not difficult to deduce that what has survived is only a small part of the total. Sims-Williams states: "This manuscript is written in a very distinctive hand with full recitation vocalization and accents. Since the gospel texts contained in even the smallest scraps have been identified, there can hardly be any doubt that all the surviving fragments belong to a single manuscript"[69]. Today, most of these fragments are depositum of the Berlin-Brandenburgische Akademie der Wissenschaften at the Staatsbibliothek zu Berlin- Preußischer Kulturbesitz Orientabteilung, while nine of them have been lost – probably during the II World War bombings – although, fortunately, photographic reproductions have been preserved in the Andreas papers in the Niedersächische Staats- und Landesbibliothek in Göttingen[70].

Before analyzing the codicological features related to the Christian Sogdian manuscript fragments *E5*, I consider it worthwhile to voice a few general considerations. The motivation for including a chapter dedicated to codicology comes from my strong conviction that joining the study of the textual as well as that of the material aspects will lead to a better understanding of the manuscript fragments *E5* as a whole. In fact, most previous studies have focused on the content, of course with pioneering exceptions. I am referring, for example, to the interesting annotations made by Sundermann about the number of writing lines regarding this

---

[67] Formerly *C5*. Throughout the present volume the new classification system introduced by Sims-Williams will be adopted. See: Sims-Williams (2012: 11-16; 28; 199-220).

[68] No date and no colophon have been preserved.

[69] See: Sims-Williams (2012: 28). As regards the full vocalization and the recitative accent, they follow the rules belonging to the East Syriac tradition. See: Segal (2003: 7-36; 78-118).

[70] Copies of these were kindly provided by the late Prof. Sundermann and Prof. Durkin-Meisterernst during my study periods in Berlin. These are now available on the Berlin-Brandenburgische Akademie der Wissenschaften and International Dunhuang Project websites under the numbers *n 497* - n 506**. For a general overview of the history of the Berlin Turfan Collection, see: Sims-Williams (2012: 11-16).

manuscript[71], or to those by Sundermann and Sims-Williams about the numbering of the quires in use at the monastery of Bulayïq[72]; or to those by Reck about the use of different kinds of ink found in Christian Sogdian fragments in Sogdian secular script[73]. At present, two new and fundamental publications allow us to take a further step: the catalogue of Iranian manuscripts in Syriac script and the catalogue of Syriac manuscripts of the Berlin Turfan Collection[74]. Both catalogues contain precise and accurate codicological information. It allows us to know much more about each single element and at the same time to adopt that comparative perspective which is necessary and essential to fully understand a material – the Christian Sogdian – that on one hand takes form within the Syriac tradition, proper to the Church of the East, and on the other is set in a *milieu* where other religious traditions play a prominent role, in a process that is both osmosis and differentiation, innovation and conservation; a process which cannot be ignored for the correct understanding of this material.
It is for this reason that in the following pages I will attempt to analyze in detail the main codicological aspects related to the Christian Sogdian manuscript *E5*. I shall meanwhile always consider the general view, i.e., the Christian Sogdian manuscript tradition, which is yet to be defined. And I shall also keep in mind those traditions in contact with it: vertically, as in the case of the Syriac tradition due to its prestige, and horizontally, as in the case of the Manichaean tradition, which mostly stems from the same area and mainly belongs to the same period.

Finally, it is also important to point out that in this study the word codicology is used implying a codicological approach *lato sensu* in order to achieve a broader contextualization[75]. Each element considered here is analyzed according to the traditional codicological investigation but it does

---

[71] See: Sundermann (1975: 87-88).

[72] See: Sims-Williams (1985: 14-16); and Sundermann (1975: 85-86).

[73] See: Reck (2008: 194).

[74] See respectively: Sims-Williams (2012) and Hunter- Dickens (2014).

[75] I do not intend codicology as "archaeology of the book". See for instance: Lemaire (1989). Instead, the theoretical framework I follow is that developed by the Research Networking Programme *Comparative Oriental Manuscript Studies (COMSt)*. See: Bausi- Borbone- Briquel Chattonet- Buzi- Gippert- Macé- Maniaci- Melissakis- Parodi- Witakowski (2015). Finally, in reading this chapter it is important to underline that the research on the Christian Sogdian manuscript tradition is at an early stage; for first results see: Barbati (forthcoming). A detailed paleographical investigation is still missing with very few exceptions. Concerning the manuscript fragments *E5* see: Sundermann apud Reck (2008: 193-194). For Syriac fragments from Turfan see now: Dickens (2013a: 9-10).

not want to be the point of arrival, rather the starting point, not the main aim, but the tool even at the expense of giving fewer answers and to formulate, in contrast, more questions.

1.1. Materials

The manuscript fragments *E5* is written on yellow-brown paper. As recently pointed out by Dickens[76], all Christian fragments from Turfan are written on paper.

Concerning the ink[77], the manuscript fragments *E5* as well as all Sogdian manuscript fragments in East Syriac script are written in black ink, whereas the twenty-eight fragments in Sogdian secular script, which have all been attributed to one scribe, were written in brown ink[78]. To remain in the Turfan oasis, the Pahlavi psalter text is written in black ink too, as happens for Manichaean texts, while in general in the Syriac manuscript tradition the use of black ink is attested – which unlike in Turfan can also be glossy or shiny – as well as of brown ink. Red ink is instead used in titles and sections, not only in Christian Sogdian texts but also in the Pahlavi psalter, in the Manichaean tradition and in the Avestan one which uses it also for marking the beginning and end of a section. Generally speaking, besides red ink, the Syriac manuscript tradition uses green and sometimes blue and yellow ink, often with golden embellishments[79].

With particular regard to the Christian material from Turfan, we are still waiting for a detailed analysis on writing materials[80].

---

[76] See: Dickens (2013a: 5). For a general overview on Syriac manuscripts written on paper see: Borbone- Briquel Chatonnet- Balicka-Witakowska (2015: 253). Quoting these scholars (ibid.): "The oldest Syriac manuscript on paper is a dated copy of the *Book of the Ḥimyarites* finished in April 932, transcribed in Qaryatēn".

[77] In this section, unless otherwise specified, apply the following references: for the Pahlavi Psalter (Durkin-Meisterernst 2006: 3); for the Manichaean manuscript tradition (Gulácsi 2005: 59-104); for the Syriac manuscript tradition (Hatch 1946: 10-11); and, finally, for the Avestan manuscript tradition, (Panaino 2002).

[78] See: Reck (2008: 194).

[79] About the use of the ink in the decorative elements of the *E5* manuscript fragments, see below paragraph *1.4.3. Decorations and verso marks*.

[80] For the first attempt in this direction, see: Durkin-Meisterernst- Friedrich- Han- Helmann-Ważny- Nöller- Raschmann (2015).

1.2. Book form and ordering system

The manuscript fragments *E5*, like the entire available Christian documentation from Turfan, uses the codex as book form[81]. The codex format is the most common among the Manichaean manuscript fragments stemming from Turfan even if it is not the only one[82]. Obviously, owing to the multicultural and multi religious environment, the codex is not the only book format in Turfan during the Early Middle Ages: in this regard, the Christian manuscript tradition from Turfan looks to the Mesopotamian Mother Church.

With particular regard to the ordering system, Borbone- Briquel Chatonnet- Balicka- Witakowska state: "The structure of the quires in Syriac books is remarkably uniform and stable over time, for all geographical areas in which Syriac manuscripts were produced"[83]. Generally speaking, quires in Syriac manuscript tradition are formed from four or five sheets but the latter seems to be the most common[84]. With particular regard to the Christian material from Turfan, Sims-Williams hypothesized a quire of five sheets[85]. Moreover, in accordance with the Syriac tradition, in the Christian Sogdian corpus the quire is numbered with Syriac letters[86].

The manuscript fragments *E5* played a fundamental role in identifying the numbering system of the quires at the monastery of Bulayïq. According to Sundermann and Sims-Williams[87], the same quire-number is placed on the last page of a quire and on the first page of the following quire. We have some examples in the present manuscript fragments[88]: *d* = 4 in *E5/41/r/*, i.e., the first page of the fourth quire; *h* = 5 in *E5/51/r/*, i.e., the first page of the

81 According to Borbone- Briquel Chatonnet- Balicka Witakowska (2015: 255), the Syriac manuscript tradition does not attest the use of horizontal rolls but only that of the vertical rolls, especially in the Melkite manuscript tradition.

82 See: Gulácsi (2005: 59-97).

83 See: Borbone- Briquel Chatonnet- Balicka Witakowska (2015: 255).

84 See: Borbone- Briquel Chatonnet- Balicka Witakowska (2015: 255-256); Dickens (2013a: 12).

85 See: Sims-Williams (1985: 14-16).

86 According to Hatch (1946: 23), in the Syriac tradition sometimes they are numbered with Syriac arithmetical figures, until the ninth century, or letters of the Greek, Coptic or Arabic alphabets.

87 See: Sundermann (1975: 87-90) and Sims-Williams (1985: 14-16; 2012: 28).

88 On the Syriac examples belonging to the Christian Turfan material already pointed out by the scholars above mentioned, see also: Dickens: (2013a: 12).

fifth quire; *t* = 9 *in E5/91/r/*, i.e., the first page of the ninth quire[89]. Other examples are attested in *E5/100/v/*[90] which has *y* =10, i.e., the last page of the ninth quire and in *E5/101/r/* which has *y*=10, i.e., the first page of the tenth quire[91].

Finally, in *E5*, as well as in *E27*, the quire-numbers show a rhomb of four dots as ornaments: it seems to me that the difference between the two manuscripts is that in *E5* they only enclose the quire-number whereas in *E27*[92] "they extend right across the page"[93]. Usually two points are in black ink and two in red ink[94].

1.3. Page layout and spatial organization

According to the best-preserved fragments belonging to *E5*, it can be seen that the width of the manuscript *E 5* is approximately 14.5~15 cm and the length is about 19.5~20 cm. The upper margin size, as well as that of the inner margin, measures approximately 1~1.5 cm, where the lower margin size, as well as that of the outer margin, measures approximately 3 cm. As regards the written area, the width is around 10-11 cm while the length around 16-17 cm. As pointed out by Dickens in analyzing the Christian material from Turfan, "Lectionaries, hagiographies and ascetical literature range from medium to large format"[95].

1.3.1 Columns

The format of the Christian Sogdian manuscript fragments *E5* is one single column. This perfectly reflects the Syriac tradition, if what Hatch reported is true[96], namely that between the seventh and tenth centuries all the Syriac

---

89 Anyway, the quire numbering system in the Christian Sogdian manuscript tradition related to the Syriac manuscript tradition is a very interesting point which I am still investigating.

90 In this book, the fragments belonging to the manuscript *E5* are cited according to the new classification system developed by Sims-Williams (2012: 28).

91 For practical reasons, the numbering system of the quires as well as the decoration points and the cross are not included in my edition but one can easily find all these elements in the photo reproductions of the manuscript fragments *E5* at the end of this work.

92 Formerly *C2*. See: Sims-Williams (1985; 2012: 99-126).

93 See: Sims-Williams (1985: 15).

94 With regard to this alternation in *E5*, see paragraph *Decorations*.

95 See: Dickens (2013a: 6-7). Of course, the size of format is linked to the function of the text. This is another interesting research point which I am still investigating.

96 See: Hatch (1946: 13-14).

manuscript traditions tended to prefer the single or the double column, with a preference for the single one by Melkites. The Christian Sogdian texts are usually dated between the ninth and tenth century, although in the case of *E5* I am inclined to opt for the late tenth to eleventh century for linguistic reasons, which will be discussed in the course of this work. Again, in general, in the Syriac manuscript tradition the number of columns does not seem to be determined either by the content of the manuscript, or by the length of the page. As stated by Hatch[97], the number of columns of a manuscript may, instead, depend on the scribe and, in part, by the local styles that each *scriptorium* develops. While it can be anticipated that the use of a single column characterizes the Bulayïq *scriptorium*[98], it will be interesting to see in detail the reasons for such a claim[99]. Finally, according to a comparative perspective, I think it is appropriate to cite what Durkin-Meisterernst stated: "the use of columns in Syriac manuscripts seems greatly relevant to their use in Manichaean manuscripts not only because of the Christian and the common Jewish background to some aspects of Christian and Manichaean writing: the use of large-column scrolls, mirroring the Torah scroll, in the Christian Acts of the Apostles and in the Manichaean equivalent, the Manichean Church history, seems very likely indeed"[100].

1.3.2 Number of lines

Among the best-preserved fragments belonging to *E5* there is a fluctuation in the number of writing lines. Six fragments are listed as follow – *E5/91*; *E5/100-101*; *E5/125-126* – with 22 lines of writing in both */r/* and */v/*, one fragment – *E5/127/a-c* – with 22 lines of writing in */r/* and 21 lines in */v/*,

[97] See: Hatch (1946: 14).

[98] With very few exceptions where the format consists of two and six columns. See: Dickens (2013a: 7). Another point which still expects exploration is what *scriptorium* would really mean in the context of the medieval Turfan oasis. See: Barbati (2015a: 93); Kotsifou (2012: 326); and Walker (2010: 326).

[99] Another issue which calls for further investigations through a broader contextualization which take into account the Christian material from Turfan, is its relationships with the Mesopotamian Mother Church as well as with other Syriac manuscript traditions such as the Melkite. In the previous chapter, we have seen the literary relationships between the Christian Sogdian material stemming from Turfan and belonging to the Church of the East and the Melkites. Here, we perhaps have evidence from a codicological point of view. Of course, the issue needs to be studied and, even it is so, the next question requiring an answer is to what extent we can establish these relationships. Finally, according to a comparative approach, we should mention that the format of the Pahlavi psalter also consists of one single column.

[100] See: Durkin-Meisterernst (2008: 14).

one fragment *E5/79* – with 20 writing lines in both sides, four fragments – *E5/6a-b*; *E5/19*; *E5/38*; *E5/48* – with 19 lines of writing in both */r/* and */v/* and two fragments – *E5/41*; *E5/72* – with 18 lines of writing in */r/* and */v/*. Sundermann was the first to try to find a *ratio* in the number of writing lines variation[101]. He believes that this could somehow be linked to the place that a particular *folium* occupies within the manuscript. He draws up a scheme demonstrating a gradual increase in writing lines from the beginning to the final part of the manuscript. Following this scheme, up to fragment *E5/41* (excluded), the fragments consist of 19 lines of writing on both sides, then they consist of 20 lines and finally of 22. The progression is undeniable, but there are some exceptions, and if some of them have been highlighted by the scholar, the same cannot be said for all. For example, Sundermann already shows that at the end of the manuscript (the one, according to his reasoning, with 22 lines of writing) there is a fragment – *E5/127a-c* – with 22 lines in */r/* and 21 lines in */v/*, and that *E5/41* should contain, progressively, 19 or 20 lines and instead has 18. I also add that *E5/48* has 19 lines, and *E5/72* has again 18 lines. Therefore, the hypothesis of Sundermann of a gradual variation in the number of writing lines in connection with the place occupied within the manuscript, shows no problems in the beginning part and at the end, but the same cannot be said for the central part where there is an alternation of 18- 19- 18- 20[102]. Obviously, according to the number of writing lines, the distance between a writing line and another also varies: in the fragments with 22 writing lines this amount to around 0.5 cm, while in those constituted by 18 or 19 writing lines it varies between 0.5 and 0.8 cm.

Finally, I should add an observation which is at least worth pointing out here and, later, contextualizing through further investigations. Analyzing this manuscript I realized how sometimes, there is a tendency to go up in writing, for example in *E5/48/v/*; *E5/72/v/*. Now this particularity is recorded in *E5* in conjunction with a lower number of writing lines and a greater distance between one writing line and the other. It may be a coincidence, but might be worth investigating.

---

[101] See: Sundermann (1975: 87).

[102] At the moment I am just describing the peculiarity. It will then be very interesting to consider these data within a broader context that takes into account both the Sogdian and Syriac manuscript traditions. However, I do not think there is any connection between the number of writing lines and the presence of a decorative element: see below paragraph *1.4.3. Decorations and verso marks*.

1.4 The structuring of contents

1.4.1 Titles and rubrics

As in all lectionaries, also in the Christian Sogdian Lectionary *E5*, rubrics indicate what follows and therefore they are considered titled rubrics and are written in red ink. According to Brock[103], the first examples showing the insertion of lectionary headings (sometimes in red ink) as help in locating lections are attested in some Syriac biblical manuscripts dated to the sixth century.

Concerning *E5*, the rubrics are written in the Syriac language in East Syriac script and in red ink, while the following text is in the Sogdian language in East Syriac script and written in black ink. The size of the letters, even of the first, does not change, however it remains the same as those reading letters introduced by the rubrics. Then the manuscript fragments *E5* shows a peculiarity which we do not find in other Christian Sogdian manuscript fragments. There are nine cases in which the titled rubric is immediately followed by the Syriac sentence in black ink, a sentence that represents the first one of the Gospel text, followed by its translation into Sogdian language, afterwards the text continues in Sogdian[104]. The passages involved are attested in the following fragments: *E5/48/v/18-19/*; *E5/75a/Ir/4-6/*; *E5/75a/Ir/6-7/*; *E5/83a-b/r/8-10/*; *E5/91/v/8-9/*; *E5/109/v/1-3/*; *E5/125-126/Iv/15-17/*; *E5/127a-c/r/6-7/*; *E5/127a-c/r/8-10/*[105].

1.4.2 Punctuation

The Christian Sogdian manuscript fragments *E5*[106] entirely retain the marks of punctuation belonging to the manuscript tradition of the Church of the East. Exactly as in the Syriac manuscript tradition[107] a single point or two points (especially from the sixth century) indicate a short pause. One dot can stand directly above the other but often the upper dot is a little to the right or to the left of the lower point.

The manuscript fragments *E5* show single points and double points in

103 See: Brock (2006: 50).

104 Even in the Sogdian Psalter the first verse is in Syriac language (Schwartz 1974: 258-259) and the Pahlavi Psalter presents some letters that remind the reader to read, in that position, the corresponding Syriac verse (Durkin-Meisterernst 2006:2).

105 For a complete discussion, see: Barbati (2010).

106 The same applies to the Pahlavi psalter. See: Durkin-Meisterernst (2006:3).

107 See: Hatch (1946: 42).

which the upper one is a little to the left of the lower point. The full stop is denoted by four small circles and usually one or two of these circles are not only in black ink but in red ink, especially when they are placed at the end of a lesson or of a paragraph. For the alternation of the two inks, see the following paragraph.

With particular regard to the recitation accents, a detailed research on the whole Christian Sogdian material is still a desideratum[108].

1.4.3. Decorations and verso marks

The manuscript fragments *E5*, as well as the entire corpus of the Christians Sogdian manuscripts, whether in East Syriac script or Sogdian secular script, turn out to contain very minimal decorations[109], except for the crosses (if they are considered as a pure decorative element, but this will be discussed later), also for the decoration which adorns the quire number which we have already discussed. So Leroy writes in the chapter on aniconistic Syriac manuscripts that often show only the cross as ornament: "Car bien que l'art des Syriens n'ait pas jeté l'ostracisme sur les répresentations animées – tout le présent travail en témoigne – il faut reconnaître qu'il s'est complu dans la décoration abstraite et qu'il a cherché la beauté des livres surtout dans l'élégance de l'écriture et les ornaments linéaires relevés des couleurs vives. La calligraphie est bien souvent le seul ornament admis"[110].

Obviously, with particular regard to the Christian Sogdian material from Turfan, we are talking about what has been preserved: namely, fragments. For this reason, it seems more appropriate to consider the scarcity of the decorative elements and to advance the most plausible hypothesis about it, more than convincing conclusions.

At any rate, it is not surprising that the cross is "the" decoration. As a matter of fact, according to well established scholarly literature, the cross takes the central position within the symbolism of the Church of the East[111].

---

108 An attempt has been made in this edition to include all punctuation marks, including recitation accents and marks for short pause, for long pause, for end of a passage from a Gospel text. Paratextual elements such as the numbering of quires are not reproduced in the edition but are fully discussed in this chapter. The reader is also referred to the photo reproductions of the manuscript fragments *E5* at the end of this work.

109 The fragments show the so-called "scribal decoration" including "elaborate script, punctuation, attention marks, denotations and text dividers". All quotations are from Borbone-Briquel Chatonnet- Balicka-Witakowska (2015: 259-260).

110 See: Leroy (1964: 106).

111 For an overview, see: Borbone (2006), Hage (1995/1996); Klimkeit (1979), Parry (1996). Moreover, the religious message brought by the missionary activities of the Church of the

Generally speaking, we can assert that the cross visible in the whole Christian Sogdian corpus has two main features: *a)* it is always put in the same position, i.e., the corner of the upper margin of the *verso* side and *b)* it is represented by different forms and, according to the iconography of the Church of the East[112], it never shows the dying Christ because the cross of this Church symbolizes the triumph of the Christ, not his Passion. At this point, taking into account travel literature, we may underline what has been written by William of Rubruk, the Flemish Franciscan missionary and explorer who travelled two years (1253-1255) in Central Asia to convert the Tatars to Christianity by the will of King Louis IX of France: "Ipsi nestoriani et Hermeni numquam faciunt super cruces suas figuram Christi; unde uidentur male sentire de passione, uel erubescunt eam"; and again "Hanc crucem attulerat quidam Hermenus qui uenerat cum monacho, ut dicebat, de Ierusalem et erat argentea, appendens forte quatuor marchas, et habebat IIII gemmas in angulis et unam in medio; ymaginem Saluatoris non habebat quia erubescunt hoc Ermeni et nestorini ut appareat Christus affixus cruci"[113]. In this context, Chiesa rightly pointed out that William of Rubruk does not understand the symbolism behind the use of the cross without the figure of Christ[114].

Finally, it seems to me[115] that the cross attested in the Christian Sogdian corpus does not show elements coming from other traditions, as is often the case in the region nowadays known as Xinjiang. Perhaps the best example is the image of the cross with the lotus flower, an element clearly deriving from

---

East has been disseminated not only through the translation of texts but also through the translation of images and symbols. This last point has in my opinion played an equally important role for the conversion and inculturation of the people they encountered along the Silk Road. From a methodological point of view, I consider it worthwhile to look at this phenomenon embracing the theory of "Kulturbildwissenschaft als Translations-Wissenschaft". See: Mersmann (2004); Bachmann-Medick (2004, 2009).

112 See: Dauvillier (1957); Moule (1931) and Pelliot (1973).

113 For the cited passages see: Chiesa (2011: 76; 186). William of Rubruk resumes this point for the third time when he meets the Uighurs "In predicta ciuitate Cailac habebant ipsi tres ydolatrias, quarum duas intraui ut uiderem stultitias eorum. In prima inueni quendam qui habebat cruciculam de atramento super manum suam; unde credidi quod esset christianus, quia ad omnia que querebam ab eo respondebat ut christianus. Vnde quesiui ab eo: «Quare ergo non habetis hic crucemm et imaginem Iesu Christi?». Et ipse respondit: «Non habemus consuetudinem». Vnde ego credidi quod essent christiani, sed ex defectu doctrine omitterent". See: Chiesa (2011: 116-117).

114 See: Chiesa (2011: 392).

115 Once again, an issue still under investigation.

a Buddhist influence[116]. In the same way, when scrutinizing the missionary activities of the Church of the East, Hage clearly speaks[117] of a Buddhist influence, which is stronger in the Christian texts of Dun-huang[118] than in those of Turfan.

At this point, it would be better to focus on the form and function of the cross as attested in the manuscript fragments *E5*. As regards the form, the cross represented there in black ink would seem to be similar to the Greek cross, i.e., a cross with arms of equal length[119]. At the same time, however, it always shows four decorative dots – in red ink – one in each quadrant, and this element could bring it closer – at least hypothetically – to the pearl cross iconography as it has been outlined by Parry[120], even if there are some differences. Parry's type closest to the cross in *E5*, and dated by him to the sixth to ninth centuries, has the cross arms ending in single dots considered by him as pearls. These pearls are absent in the cross in our lectionary.

While it is still difficult to define a typology of crosses found in the Christian material from Central Asia[121], the characteristics of the cross in *E5* are quite consistent. It is always in black ink with dots in red ink. Moreover I noticed a peculiarity: this kind of cross is always followed in *E5* by a word, or at least by what seems to be a word. The most likely reading is *ḥayyē*, Syriac for "life/salvation"[122]. The term is translated by Brockelmann (1928:

---

[116] See: Parry (1996: 147). On the other hand, however, Parry points out that sometimes – considering the coexistence of different traditions that are very close to each other – it is very difficult to identify and determine the direction of a possible influence from one tradition to another (ibid.: 149 -153). Parry, in the cited work, examines the images of the Church of the East in Central Asia and China focusing more on archaeological material rather than the literary one. Nevertheless I believe that the consideration mentioned above can also be extended to this latter.

[117] See: Hage (1988: 42-54). Some interesting insights for this discussion are offered by Uray (1983) who outlines possible Manichaean and Syro-Oriental traces in the Tibetan manuscripts of the eighth and ninth century from Dun-huang: by means of example, some manuscripts belonging to the Pelliot fund of the National Library of Paris attest the drawing of a cross.

[118] For an overview of the place and its findings, see: Jinshi (2010).

[119] For an overview of the different types of cross, see: Dinkler- v. Schubert (1974: 562-590, in particular pp. 569- 570).

[120] See: Parry (1996: 156; 159).

[121] On the difficulty in defining the type of cross in a Central Asia context, see the interesting reflections of two other scholars, Klein and Reck, in particular regarding the definition of "Nestorian cross" – partially including some ideas of Kol'cenko –, see: Klein- Reck (2004: 153-156).

[122] To the best of my knowledge I do not recognize any Sogdian word.

229) as “1. vita, 2. salvatio (σωτηρία) “, by Pazzini (2004: 130) as “life, saving”, by Payne-Smith (1879-1901 col. 1257) “vita”, by Sokoloff (2009: 444) as “1.life; 2.salvation; 3. nourishment, sustenance”. This reading seems to me very clear in one fragment of *E5*, *E5/91/v/* where not only the letters of the word but also the syāmē are very clearly legible, i.e. two dots placed over a plural form which is in this case required because in Syriac the word for “life, salvation” *ḥayyē*, is plural. In two other fragments, *E5/48/v/* and *E5/126/IIv/*, at least one of the two points forming the syāmē is clearly identifiable. In the fragments *E5/79/v/* and *E5/125-126/Iv/* the letters of the word *ḥayyē* are readable but the part of the fragment where in theory one would expect the syāmē is lost. In the fragment *E5/75-76/IIv/* and in the fragment *E5/130a-b/v/*, only the two last letters of *ḥayyē* are legible, the part where one would expect the syāmē part is lost[123].

The cross followed by the word for “life, salvation” seems not to recur in other Syriac manuscripts according to what the above mentioned Syriacists told me, but it is somehow linked to the manuscript tradition belonging to the Church of the East. Thus Borbone writes: “L’iconografia siriaca della croce trionfante prevede spesso nei manoscritti la presenza di una frase che ne esalta la funzione di strumento di vittoria. Una spesso ricorrente è 'Per mezzo tuo spezzeremo i nemici' (*bak nedqar labeldbabayn*, or *bk ndqr*

---

[123] I proposed the reading *ḥayyē* for the first time during a workshop held in Berlin in 2009 where I highlighted the results of my doctoral thesis, a few months before the actual discussion, and then I proposed this interpretation during my paper at the 4th Salzburg International Conference: Research on the Church of the East in China and Central Asia in June 2013. On that occasion, gleaned from the debate that followed, extremely interesting details emerged which I think are worth reporting. Syriacists Dickens and Hunter, – along with Sebastian Brock – confirmed the presence of something similar also in the Syriac fragments from Turfan. A few months after that conference, Dickens published an article where he notes the Syriac and the Christian Sogdian fragments testifying to this peculiarity. See: Dickens (2013: 12). However, Dickens reads the Syriac adjective “living, alife, life-giving (perhaps to indicate the “life-giving cross”?”, that is without syāmē. With particular regard to the Christian Sogdian fragment *E5* I have clarified why I am inclined to read “life, salvation”, i.e including syāmē. With regard to the Syriac fragments, Dickens (2013:12) cites the following: *Syr HT 45&46*; *SyrHT 48&49*; *SyrHT 75*; *SyrHT 82*; *Syr HT 88*; *SyrHT 96*; *SyrHT 107*; *SyrHT 150*; *SyrHT 181*; and *SyrHT 227*. According to Hunter-Dickens (2014) only *SyrHT 75* (p. 90) and *Syr HT 88* (p. 105) show the adjective “living” (which is reported in Syriac characters); *SyrHT 45&46* shows a “cross with ~ symbol” (p.59); *SyrHT 48&49* attests a cross with decorations (p.62); *SyrHT 82*, *SyrHT 96*, *SyrHT 107*; *SyrHT 150* and *SyrHT 227* show a “black St. Andrew’s cross with four red dots” (p. 98; 114; 122; 160; 226 respectively); finally *SyrHT 181* shows a cross “with surrounding black and red dots” (p. 186).

lbldbbyn); si tratta della citazione di *Salmi 44,6*. In alternativa a quest'espressione alquanto bellicosa compare in certi manoscritti anche la citazione di *Salmi 34,6*, 'Guardate verso di Lui e spate in Lui', la stessa del blocco di Fangshan..."[124]. So, in addition to the ornamental function, our lectionary cross would have a protective function, an apotropaic function, which is also in accordance with the manuscript tradition belonging to the Church of the East[125] and witnessed and emphasized by the term "life, salvation". This term is then followed by four decorative dots forming a rhombus, the same shape of the ornamental element that encloses the quire number and of the point. Similarly, of the four points forming the rhombus, two are in black ink and two in red ink. This is putting things in general terms. In more detail, it seems to me there is a certain correspondence in the alternative use of the ink: in the rhombus placed after the cross and the word which stands for "life, salvation" as well as in the rhombus enclosing the quire number there are the two horizontally opposed black ink dots, while those vertically opposed are in red. The same occurs in the rhombus found in the text between the end of a reading and the beginning of a column; vice versa, in the rhombus placed between the end of the section and the beginning of a new reading, the two horizontally opposed dots are in red ink and those vertically opposed are in black ink. See for example the fragments *E5/48/v/*; *E5/91/v/*.

To summarize, then, the Christian Sogdian lectionary presents a cross in black ink with four dots – one for each quadrant – in red ink and followed by the Syriac word for "life, salvation" and finally by the typical decorative rhombus-shaped element. This is clearly visible in *E5/48/v/*; *E5/79/v/*; *E5/91/v/*; *E5/125-126/Iv/-/IIv/*. With particular regard to *E5/75-76/IIv/* as well as to *E5/130a-b/v/*, I believe that it represents the same sequence even if part of the fragment is missing. What we have in both cases is the final part

---

124 See: Borbone (2006). The scholar in this study examines the Chinese site of Fangshan where some blocks with crosses and a Syriac inscription have been found, already mentioned in the text. I do not wish to offer any conclusion, but it seems to me that somehow there is a correspondence between textual and archaeological material. The fact that the reasoning is based on fragmentary material stemming from different areas requires us to exercise the greatest caution; nevertheless I have dared to put together these scattered elements to see trends belonging to the Turfan Christian community itself (the choice of the word for "life, salvation") with trends well rooted in the Church of the East (as we have already seen, the sentence after the cross, which enhances the value).

125 Especially in the Gospels, the Syriac manuscripts testify to the presence of the cross as having an apotropaic function, often in the first and last page. See: Balicka-Witakowska (1998); Leroy (1964: 113).

of the above sequence, or better, the last two letters of the word *ḥayyē* followed by the decorative element, the same as the most evident cases listed above. The dimensions of this sequence may vary, that is to say, sometimes it extends along the inside top margin, other times, however, it is reduced: see, for example, *E5/48/v/*; *E5/91/v/*.

Yet this is not all. There is another aspect that I think deserves further study, namely the function of the sequence cross + word + decorative element. Also allowing the dual, ornamental and apotropaic function, is it possible to identify a third? It is evident that such a sequence is always located in *verso*. And it is not a coincidence that in his catalogue Sims-Williams defines the *verso mark* exactly with what I have identified as a sequence of cross + word + decorative element[126]. Leafing through the catalogue of Sims-Williams, we note that the *verso mark* appears as a cross in different forms in other Christian Sogdian manuscript fragments in East Syriac script[127]. Moreover, as illustrated by Reck [128], a cross – in various different forms but still in the same position, i.e. the inner edge top of the *verso* side – also appears in Christians Sogdian fragments in Sogdian secular script. Reck writes in this regard: "Werner Sundermann drew my attention to the fragments of the so called C5 manuscript which have also a cross on the corner of the verso sides. There are differences between the form of the crosses, but it is the same system"[129]. Sundermann on this point writes: "Jede Rückseite eines Blattes ist durch ein Zeichen in der rechten oberen Ecke kenntlich gemacht"[130]. As for what Sundermann states, I hope I have shown that in the manuscript fragments *E5* the question is a little more complex than a simple sign used as a *verso mark*.

For example, taking into consideration the definition of the *Lexicon der Christlichen Ikonographie* of the cross as a "sacral initial" marking a text division ("In Texten dient das Kreuz zeichen "als sakrale Initiale" u. zur Trennung")[131], I tried to see if our lectionary cross could be the beginning of a new reading, but if this is valid for *E5/48/v/*; *E5/91/v/*; *E5/125-126/Iv/*; *E5/130a-b/v/*, so that in the text where there is the titled rubric, it is not true for *E5/75-76/IIv/*; *E5/79/v/* and for *E5/125-126/IIv/*.

---

126 See: Sims-Williams (2012: 33; 35; 36; 38; 40; 41; 43).

127 See: Sims-Williams (2012: 48; 54; 80; 93; 94; 103; 105; 107; 108; 110; 114; 115; 117; 118; 123; 127; 130; 132; 137; 138; 140; 146; 151; 165; 166, 167).

128 See: Reck (2008: 200).

129 See: Reck (2008: 194).

130 See: Sundermann (1974: 219).

131 See Dinkler- v. Schubert (1974: 574).

I do not think there is some variation between the presence of the cross + word + decorative element and the fluctuation concerning the number of writing lines, as it is witnessed by another Christian tradition, the *Persian Diatessaron*[132].

I still wonder if there might be some connection to the quire number[133]. If, for example, the cross + word + decorative element was at the end of the quire, it might indicate a binding of the manuscript. For instance, the first page of the fifth quire (*h* = 5 in *E5/51*/r/) notes part of the Gospel for the Sixth Friday of Lent, while *E5/48/v/* containing cross + word + decorative element shows part of the Gospel end for the Fifth Friday of Lent and the beginning of the Gospel for the Sixth Sunday of Lent. Could *E5/48/v/* be the last page of the fourth quire, indicated by *d* = 4 in *E5/41/r/* which notes part of the Gospel for the Fourth Tuesday of Lent? Even if this would be so, I am not sure if this solution can work for all attestations we have.

At any rate, the main question, or what seems to me to be the main question, is still without answer. Why do we find the cross + word + decorative element only in *E5* and in only a few other Syriac manuscript fragments? I would say that the presence is not related to the text genre because we find it in lectionaries – as in the case of *E5* and other Syriac fragments –, as well as in fragments containing Psalter, Ḥudra, Service book, Legend of Barshabbā[134]. Perhaps it is due to the same scribe? Again, it is very difficult to answer since a deep and comparative palaeographical analysis concerning the Christian Sogdian and the Syriac manuscripts is still missing.

Inevitably all the points illustrated in this chapter require a much broader

---

[132] See: Messina (1951: xv). It is an Evangelic harmony; its copy of 1547 has been kept, but Messina already dates it back at least to before the late thirteenth century. The manuscript is currently preserved in Florence at the Biblioteca Medicea Laurenziana (Piemontese, 1989: 104-108). In this manuscript each page is composed by 20 lines except folio 2 in *verso* which has 16 lines, and folio 16 in *verso* which has 18 lines, because in both cases the upper part is occupied by a decoration (frieze). During my work, I have found some contact points with the Sogdian Gospel Lectionary *E5* (see also Chapter 2) and it seemed to me appropriate to quote them in order to give other possible interpretations. Notwithstanding they are different works, coming from different traditions, I think that those contact points may help to delineate some of the characteristics of the East Syriac manuscript and literary tradition in Central Asia among the ninth- eleventh centuries and, for this reason, they will be illustrated.

[133] Hypothesis advanced also by the scholar de Blois – whom I thank – during the debate following my paper at the *4th Salzburg International Conference on the Church of the East in China and Central Asia.*

[134] See: Dickens (2013: 12).

contextualization than the one adopted so far, including the present work. Nevertheless, I hope I have been able to point out the potential of such an approach in the treatment of the Christian manuscript tradition in Bulayïq and in particular the peculiarities of the Christian Sogdian manuscript fragments *E5* hoping to have created, at the same time, new inputs.

E5: THE GOSPEL LECTIONARY

2.1 Previous editions

Found at the beginning of the last century during the second and third German archaeological expedition in the Turfan oasis[135], the Christian Sogdian Gospel Lectionary *E5* has for some time now been a matter of interest for different scholars. Most of the largest fragments belonging to this manuscript have been published for the first time by Müller in 1913[136] and later by Sundermann in three articles (1974, 1975, 1981), which completed Müller's accomplishments and which also added new fragments. Müller printed the text in the original characters followed by a transcription and a translation. He also arranged the fragments according to the New Testament, but more or less at the same time two other scholars, Baumstark (1915) and Burkitt (1925: 124) showed that the order is that of the lectionaries of the Church of the East with one peculiarity, i.e., the presence of a final section constituted by lectures for saints' days and other commemorations. Sundermann accepted this interpretation in his work (1975: 70- 71) referring to three fragments of *E5* which will be discussed a little later. As regards the fragments already published by Müller, most of the time Sundermann does not report the text but provides philological-linguistic comments. Sundermann also published some hitherto unpublished fragments, with the transliteration, translation and commentary in conjunction with others that previously had been erroneously attributed to other texts. Those published for the first time by Sundermann include the fragments *E5/21a-b*, *E5/23*, *E5/51*, *E5/75b*, *E5/76b*, *E5/5*, *E5/127a*. Among those previously attributed to other manuscripts there are *E5/75b*, *E5/76b*, *E5/78* and *E5/130b* fragments. Even today the signature *C58* – which is placed on one of the labels put on the glass used to protect these fragments – demonstrates these were

[135] The four German archaeological expeditions took place between 1902 and 1914. Of these, the first (November 1902 - March 1903) and the third (the entire 1906 up to January 1907) were led by Prof. Grünwedel while the second one (November 1904-August 1905) and the fourth one (June 1913-January 1914) took place under the guidance of Prof. Le Coq. On the history of these and other – Chinese, Japanese, Russian – archaeological expeditions, see: (eds.) D. S. Durkin-Meisterenst-J. Raschmann-M. Wilkens-Yaldiz-P. Zieme (2004) and Sundermann (2004).

[136] Preview in Müller (1907).

attributed to another text by Hansen in 1954, namely *C58*. Sundermann demonstrates that they belong to the lectionary *E5*, after considering the type of writing and paper, both of which correspond exactly to those attested in *E5*.

In 2012, the manuscript is inserted by Sims-Williams[137] in his catalogue of Iranian manuscripts – all in Sogdian except for two in New Persian – in East Syriac script belonging to the Berlin Turfan collection. This catalogue – as already mentioned – generated the new classification system and the sequence with the relative numbering of the fragments which has been established by Sim-Williams[138], who also calculated the missing portion of the text according to the Church of the East Lectionary examined by Maclean in 1894 and Diettrich in 1909. Because the works of Sims-Williams are extremely precise and of great insight, I shall adopt his findings here without feeling the slightest need to add anything. The complete list of fragments identified as belonging to *E5* is available at the end of this chapter. Finally, in 2013 and in 2014, Sims-Williams published together with Pittard[139] some fragments that had been previously published but not yet identified[140]. They prove that the small fragment published and classified by Sundermann as *19c: T II B 38* [141] contains part of the Gospel of Luke 1.44; 55-56 for the Second Sunday of Advent, and is thus the first fragment belonging to the Gospel lectionary *E5*[142]. Again, for the fragment *E5/65*, published by Sundermann as *7b*[143], Pittard and Sims-Williams go beyond the partial identification made by Sundermann himself. Basing the argument on the name "Arimathaea" which always appears in the Passion narratives in the four Gospels, Sundermann had tried to identify */v/* 2-4/ with Matthew 27.64 as part of the Good Friday evening reading. Pittard and Sims-Williams identify in */r/* 1-2/ Matthew 27.54, in */r/* 3-4/ Matthew 27.57 probably as part of the Good Friday evening reading, and in */v/* 5/ Matthew 27.65 probably as part of the reading for Good Friday or Easter Saturday[144]. In a similar way,

137 See: Sims-Williams (2012: 28-43).

138 See: Sims-Williams (2012: 28).

139 Pittard was preparing in the eighties of the last century an edition of this lectionary, which he never finished. His unpublished work was taken into account by Sims-Williams in his catalogue.

140 See: Pittard- Sims-Williams (2013); (2014).

141 See: Sundermann (1975: 82).

142 See: Pittard- Sims-Williams (2013:45); (2014: 58).

143 See: Sundermann (1975: 82-83).

144 See: Pittard- Sims-Williams (2013: 46-47); (2014: 58-59).

E5/75b, published by Sundermann as *19a*[145] – a small fragment with very few legible words – is recognized by Pittard and Sims-Williams again as part of *E5/75a-b*, i.e., of two paper layers that had stuck together and were later separated by the restoration specialists at the Staatsbibliothek zu Berlin – Preussischer Kulturbesitz. According to Pittard and Sims-William's identification, *E5/75b* shows the reading of Matthew 10.19-20, 27 as part of the reading for Friday after Easter[146]. Finally, the fragment *E5/78* published by Sundermann as *19b*[147], identified by Pittard and Sims-Williams as part of the Second Sunday after Easter readings, refers to the Gospel of John 14.11-12 and, for the Third Sunday after Easter, the Gospel of John 16.19[148].

2.2 The Gospel lectionary E5 within the Church of the East

As explained in detail in the introduction, the Christian Sogdian literature – predominantly ascetic and monastic – is a faithful translation – albeit with varying adaptation degrees – of the religious knowledge developed and disseminated by the East Syriac tradition. As a matter of fact, as recently pointed out by Hunter, the material in several languages and scripts, mostly found in the Bulayïq monastery, clearly proves it belongs to the Church of the East. This led Hunter to talk about this monastery as the monastery that – I quote – "served the local Sogdian and Uyghur communities, but its ecclesiastical heritage looked westwards to the hearthland of the Church of the East"[149], defining it "the easternmost library of the Church of the East"[150]. Moreover, as Dickens emphasizes[151], further evidence for the direction which the interpretation and teaching associated with this Church had taken when it settled in Central Asia lies in the terminology attested to by several inscriptions confirming the existence of professional figures processing and disseminating such knowledge. Dickens highlights the attestation of the Syriac word for "interpreter, translator, commentator" *mphašqānā* in the Syriac inscription found in Urgut, Uzbekistan, which probably dates back to between the ninth and tenth centuries, as well as the presence of the Syriac terms for "scholar", "teacher", "interpreter",

---

145 See: Sundermann (1975:81).
146 See: Pittard- Sims-Williams (2013: 47-48); (2014: 59-61).
147 See: Sundermann (1975:81).
148 See: Pittard-Sims-Williams (2013: 49); (2014: 62).
149 See: Hunter (2012:88).
150 See: Hunter (2012: 88).
151 See: Dickens (2009: 99-100).

"exegete", i.e., respectively, *eskulāyā*, *mdrašānā*, *malphānā* and again *mphašqānā*, and also of the much debated Sogdian word for "female teacher", i.e. *xwšt'nc*[152] in inscriptions on tombstones in the Chu Valley, Kyrgyzstan, which can be dated to the thirteenth and fourteenth centuries.

The Christian Sogdian Gospel Lectionary *E5* is no exception. It is well known that the text therein transmitted follows the *Peshitta* text with few exceptions referring to other textual traditions, some more ascribable to a Syro-Oriental context, others less. The task of the following pages will be that of taking stock of the situation in order to briefly summarize what has already been highlighted by previous studies and, on the other hand, to analyze in detail what has emerged as new in the course of the present work.

According to Brock[153], the Syriac Churches attest the existence and use of Syriac lectionary manuscripts not before the ninth century and, from this time on, it would be considered a common practice to have specific lectionaries for the Old Testament readings, for those of the Gospels, for those of the Acts and the Epistles. The selection and arrangement of the readings, says Brock, may vary not only according to the specific Syriac Church – i.e. depending on whether it is the Syrian Orthodox, the Church of the East and the Byzantine Orthodox Church in Syria and Palestine – but even within the same Church. As regards the Church of the East, the scholarly literature[154] about it basically lists two systems: the "Cathedral" system which refers to the Seleucia-Ctesiphon patriarchate, and the system defined as monastic, which developed in the Upper Monastery in Mosul. In our case we are dealing with a Gospel lectionary that, at least according to the attested language, is to be dated back in my opinion to between the end of the tenth and eleventh centuries. This generally refers to the *Peshitta* text and follows the Upper Monastery lectionaries cycle. It is therefore in perfect alignment with the Church of the East, but there are some distinctions. I do not think it is wrong to say that it is the lack of a full adherence to a model which led Kannookadan, in his work to track and trace the history of the formation and development of the Syrian-Oriental lectionaries, to include the Gospel lectionary *E5* between the "Uncategorized Manuscripts"[155], i.e.,

---

152 For the bibliography see Dickens (2012: 100, note 32).

153 See: Brock (2006: 50-51).

154 For an overview, see: Baumstark (1921; 1927), Brock (2006), Burkitt (1923); Desreumaux (1996); Diettrich (1909), Jenner (1997; 2001); Kannookadan (1991), Maclean (1894); Macomber (1967); Parpulov (2012); Rouwhorst (1996).

155 See: Kannookadan (1991: 20), whose remarks need to be clarified in one point: Sogdian is of course not a Middle Persian dialect. On more technical issues, see: Jenner (1997).

between those lectionaries not attributable to a specific tradition. Before attempting to define and discuss the peculiarities of this lectionary, I think it is appropriate to provide an overview of the reading cycle attested therein:

Fragment	*Gospel passage*	*Performing day*
E5/5	Luke 1.44, 55-56	part of the Gospel for the Second Sunday of Advent
E5/6a-b	Luke 1.63-80 and Matthew 1.1	respectively end of the Gospel for the Third Sunday of Advent and beginning of the Gospel for the Fourth Sunday of Advent
E5/19	John 1.19-35	end of the Gospel for the Second Sunday after Epiphany and beginning of the Gospel for the Third Sunday after Epiphany
E5/21a-b	John 1.51; 2.3-5; 2.9-11	part and end of the Gospel for the Fourth Sunday after Epiphany and beginning of the Gospel for the Fifth Sunday after Epiphany
E5/23	John 3.18-21; 3.26-27	respectively part of the Gospel for the Fifth Sunday after Epiphany and part of the Gospel for the Sixth Sunday after Epiphany
E5/28a-b	Matthew 5.30-33; 5.38-41	respectively part of the Gospel for the First Monday of Lent and beginning of the Gospel for the First Tuesday of Lent
E5/34	Luke 13.3-4 and Matthew 20.17-19	respectively part of the Gospel for the Second Friday of Lent and part of the Gospel for the Third Sunday of Lent
E5/38	Matthew 21.28-43	part of the Gospel for the Fourth Sunday of Lent
E5/41	John 5.24-40	part of the Gospel for the Fourth Tuesday of Lent

Fragment	*Gospel passage*	*Performing day*
E5/48	Luke 16.2-15 and John 9.39	respectively end of the Gospel for the Fifth Friday of Lent and beginning of the Gospel for the Sixth Sunday of Lent
E5/51	Matthew 24.24-26; 24.32-33	part of the Gospel for the Sixth Friday of Lent
E5/65	Matthew 27.54(?),57; 27.64-65	respectively part of the Gospel for Good Friday and part of the Gospel for Easter Saturday or for the evening of Good Friday.
E5/72	Luke 24.19-32	part of the Gospel for the Tuesday after Easter.
E5/73	Luke 24.32-35 and John 15.18-20	respectively part of the Gospel for the Tuesday after Easter and part of the Gospel for the Wednesday after Easter
E5/75-76	Matthew 10.14-15; 10.16-26; 10.19-20, 10.27-33 and John 20.19-25	end of the Gospel for the Thursday after Easter, beginning, part and end of the Gospel for the Friday after Easter and beginning and part of the Gospel for the First Sunday after Easter
E5/78	John 14.11-12; 16.19	respectively part of the Gospel for the Second Sunday after Easter and part of the Gospel for the Third Sunday after Easter
E5/79	John 16.19-32	part of the Gospel for the Third Sunday after Easter
E5/80	John 16.32-33; 21.1; 21.5-7	respectively end of the Gospel for the Third Sunday after Easter and beginning of the Gospel for the Fourth Sunday after Easter
E5/91	Luke 10.34-42; 6.12-17	respectively end of the Gospel for the Second Sunday after Pentecost and beginning of the Gospel for the Third Sunday after Pentecost

Fragment	*Gospel passage*	*Performing day*
E5/100-101	John 9.9-38	part of the Gospel for the Third Sunday of Summer, i.e, the Ninth Sunday after Pentecost
E5/109	Matthew 13.17-19; 13.24-25	respectively part of the Gospel for the Second Sunday of Elijah, i.e., the Fifteenth Sunday after Pentecost and beginning of the Gospel for the Third Sunday of Elijah, i.e., the Sixteenth Sunday after Pentecost
E5/125-126	Luke 19.15-27 and Matthew 25.31-33	respectively end of a Gospel for a saint's day and beginning of the Gospel for the commemoration of Saint Barshabbā
E5/127a-c	Matthew 25.45-46; 16.24-28; 17.1-6	end of the Gospel for the commemoration of Saint Barshabbā and beginning of the Gospel for the commemoration of Saint Sergius and Saint Bacchus
E5/130a-b	Luke 12.35-39; 12.42-44 and John 5.19	end of the Gospel for an unidentified day[156] and part of the Gospel for All Saint's Day[157] or probably for the day of Commemoration of the Dead[158].

Previous studies in this regard have shown that the following readings attested in the Gospel lectionary *E5* have no parallel in the Syrian-Oriental lectionaries: *E5/34* = Luke 13.3-4 part of the Gospel for the Second Friday of Lent[159]; *E5/48* Luke 16.2-15 = end of the Gospel for the Fifth Friday of Lent[160]; *E5/51* = Matthew 24.24-26, 24.32-33, part of the Gospel for the

[156] The readings of Luke contained herein are not confirmed in the readings cycle of the liturgical year of the Church of the East. See: Baumstark (1915: 126); Burkitt (1925: 124-125) and Sundermann (1975: 78).

[157] See: Baumstark (1915: 126); Burkitt (1925: 124-125) and Sundermann (1975: 78).

[158] See: Burkitt (1923: 334); Maclean (1894: 268-269) and Sims-Williams (2012).

[159] See: Baumstark (1915: 125) and Sundermann (1974: 231). This passage will be examined further when the absence of the Gospel of Mark in the lectionary *E5* will be discussed.

[160] See: Baumstark (1915: 125) and Sundermann (1974: 236).

Sixth Friday of Lent[161]. A further distinction is then represented by the readings placed at the end of the Gospel lectionary and dedicated to the commemoration of some saints, an element, which, as well highlighted by the literature on the subject, has no counterpart in the East Syrian lectionaries. Therefore over the years it has become common to speak of a Central Asian version attested precisely in our Gospel lectionary[162]. The readings in question are: *E5/125-126* = Luke 19.15-27 and Matthew 25.31-33, respectively end of a Gospel for a saint's day and beginning of the Gospel for the commemoration of Saint Barshabbā[163]; *E5/127a-c* = Matthew 25.45-46; 16.24-28; 17.1-6, i.e., end of the Gospel for the commemoration of Saint Barshabbā and beginning of the Gospel for the commemoration of Saint Sergius and Saint Bacchus[164]; and *E5/130a-b* = Luke 12.35-39; 12.42-44 end of the Gospel for an unidentified day[165].

This is what has already been pointed out but I do not think it includes everything. There are other peculiarities of this Gospel lectionary that I do not think have been treated so far and on which, in my opinion, it is worth reflecting.

In particular, what immediately caught my attention was the *total absence of readings from the Gospel of Mark.* I wonder about the reason of such an absence. Obviously this might be due to a mere fortuity. This is of course always a possibility, considering the fragmentary nature of the material we are dealing with. But should it not be plausible to consider other explanations as well? In general terms, leafing through some Syriac manuscripts catalogues[166], I realized that the Gospel of Mark is the least attested. If we entirely focus our attention on the Christian Sogdian texts from Turfan – since probably a detailed examination of the relationship between the Gospel of Mark, the Syro-Oriental Lectionary cycle and the

---

161 See: Sundermann (1974: 237; 1975: 89-90).

162 Sunderman writes (1975:70): “Da in 18 aber unmittelbar ein Text zum Gedenken des Sergius und Bacchus folgt und auch 19 die Lesung eines Heiligentags ist, so wird man mit Baumastark und Burkitt annehmen dürfen, dass ein Teil des Perikopenbuches – wohl sein letzter – die Lektionen der Heiligengedenktage gesondert zusammenfasste und dass sich in ihnen spezielles Überlieferungsgut einer zentralasiatischen christlichen Kirche erhalten hat”. Just a technical explanation: the numbers 18 and 19 evoked by Sundermann refer to his classification of the fragments belonging to *E5*. See, at the end of this chapter, the section on concordances between all signature systems so far adopted.

163 See: Baumstark (1915: 126); Burkitt (1925: 124); Sundermann (1975: 70-71).

164 See: Sundermann (1975: 75).

165 See: Sundermann (1975: 78).

166 I refer for example to Hatch (1946) and Wright (1901) ones.

Church of the East go beyond the purpose and the tasks of the present work – in the same way we will acknowledge the absence of the Gospel of Mark[167]. According to Hunter- Dickens, the Syriac texts from Turfan attest the following readings of the Gospel of Mark: 6.27-33, 36-41, part of a Gospel but not of a lectionary in *SyrHT326*[168] and Mark 2.10-11 part of a prayer-amulet in *SyrHt114*[169]. It means that Christian Sogdian and Syriac Gospel lectionaries from Turfan do not attest the Gospel of Mark.

And if one sets aside the assumption of pure fortuitousness, I do not think it is unnecessary to dwell on what *E5/34* reports, or Luke 13.3-4, part of the Gospel for the Second Friday of Lent. As we have just seen this passage has already been identified among those that had no correspondence in the Syro-Oriental lectionary cycle. Sundermann [170] writes in this regard, referring in turn to the work of Bamustark[171], I quote "der Lukas-Abschnitt hat jedoch in den bekannten syr. nest. Evangeliaren keine Entsprechung". Now it is time to take a step forward and to ask what lies in the East Syriac tradition. According to Maclean, for the Second Friday of Lent reading, the Eastern Syrian lectionary attests Mark 11:27 and Mark 12:12[172]. In the same way according to Kannookadan's study, the Upper Monastery lectionaries cycle, which the *E5* also refers to, is also the one that – with some exceptions – attests Mark 11:27 and Mark 12:13[173]. So a passage that according to the Eastern Syrian tradition seems in general to attest the presence of Mark's Gospel[174] is replaced in our lectionary by the Gospel of Luke.

Continuing to focus on textual variants and concordance between different traditions, it seems to me an appropriate approach to describing what I have found as concordance between the Gospel lectionary *E5* and

[167] See: Sims-Williams (2012: 22-43; 227) where passages from Gospel of Matthew, Luke and John are listed.

[168] See: Hunter-Dickens (2014: 300-301; 458).

[169] See: Hunter-Dickens (2014: 128-129; 459).

[170] See: Sundermann (1974:231).

[171] See: Baumstark (1915: 125).

[172] See: Maclean (1894: 270-271).

[173] See: Kannookadan (1991: 90).

[174] If we want to add a small note to underline further how the presence of the Gospel of Mark for the Second Friday of Lent is well established in the East Syrian Lectionary cycle, we can also mention its presence in the New Persian lectionary published by Richard, a lectionary that "suit l'année liturgique des Syriens orientaux" and certifies "que les communautés chrétiennes de langue persane -ici, en Crimée au XIVs. - ont utilisé le persan durant les cérémonies du culte". See: Richard (1981: 230; 240).

the *Persian Diatessaron*[175]. These are:

- Matthew 21.30: Sogd. *E5/38/r/3- 4/ (')[t pnt 'γt qw dbtyq] z'ty̱ s'*; Syr. *w-qrb lwt 'ḥrn'*; Gk. *προσελθὼν δέ τῷ δευτέρῳ* ; *Persian Diatessaron āngah badān pesar digar išārat kard.* The Sogdian and New Persian version and are the only ones with the word for "son";
- Matthew 21.32: Sogd. *E5/38/r/10- 11/ p't 'γt qw šm(')[x s' ywḥn]n sn'm θ(br[yn](y̱)*; Syr. *'ṭ' gyr lwt-kwn ywḥnn*; Gk. *ἦλθεν γὰρ Ἰωάννης πρὸς ὑμᾶς*; *Persian Diatessaron šurandah āmad piš šomā.* Only in Sogdian and New Persian language the epithet "Baptist" referring to John is attested;
- Matthew 25.46: *Sogd. E5/127a-c/r/4-5/ 't 'rt'(w)t qw 'yqwncy̱q nw(š)c ž(w)[']n s'*; Syr. *w-zdÿq' l-ḥÿ' d-l'lm*; Gk. *οἱ δὲ δίκαιοι εἰς ζωὴν αἰώνιον*; *Persian Diatessaron va nekān dar zindagāni jāvid va sarmadi beravand.* As I remarked in the course of studying this Gospel lectionary, the Christian Sogdian expression *nwšc žw'n* "eternal life" in the *E5* and other bilingual Sogdian-Syriac fragments becomes a fixed expression which would translate the Syriac *ḥÿ'* "life", and when the Syriac adds the adjective *l'lm* "eternal", this is translated into Sogdian with the adjective *'yqwncyq*. Therefore, both in the Syriac phrase and in the Greek one, the word "life" has only one adjective as attribute, whereas both in the *E5* in the *Persian Diatessaron* two adjectives in hendiadys are recorded.

Another correspondence between this Gospel lectionary and the *Persian Diatessaron* was recorded by Asmussen (1984: 14) and refers to the passage of the Gospel of Matthew 10.29. In this case, the Sogdian text attested in *E5/75-76 /IIr/8/[p]w cn šm'x bγy ptry̱ (r)yž* "without the will of your God the Father" differs from the Syriac text *bl'd ṃn 'bwkwn* "without your Father" and from the Greek one *ἄνευ τοῦ πατρὸς ὑμῶν* "without your Father". According to Asmussen, the presence in Sogdian of the noun *ryž* "will, wish, desire" is part of a textual tradition which is surely Christian but typically Iranian, because of its presence in the Zoroastrian work *Škand Gumānīg Vizār* and, indeed, in the *Persian Diatessaron* where we can read *bē farmān-*

175 Work already mentioned in the last pages of the previous chapter. See: Messina (1951).

i pidar-i šumā[176].

All these observations raise the general question if they are mostly coincidental or rather related, and if so, in what ways. For instance, the total absence of readings from the Gospel of Mark could be due to the hazards of transmission of the manuscript. One may also see here a tradition other than the *Peshitta*, perhaps older – *Old Syriac version*, *Diatessaron* –, a phenomenon that would certainly not be an isolated case within the Christian Sogdian literature[177]. Even when the *Peshitta* was imposed in all the Syriac language dioceses, the ancient versions had the chance to survive, especially in peripheral environments, and one of these may indeed have been the Christian community in Turfan. The absence of the Gospel of Mark may also depend on discretions characteristic for the reception and usage of the Gospel of Mark itself, a phenomenon that is visible in the various cycles of the Syrian-Oriental lectionaries but emerges already from the earliest processes of canonization of the Gospels[178]. Similarly, the correspondences between the Gospel lectionary *E5* and the *Persian Diatessaron* could reveal a Syrian-Oriental circulation of textual traditions which goes beyond the Turfan boundaries to be found in a large area from Iran to Central Asia and down to the Mongol era[179]. These and similar issues discussed by previous studies, above all Sundermann (1974; 1975; 1981) and Asmussen (1984), appear to be related and require further investigations[180] which take the complex and non-linear interaction between textual traditions, discretionary

---

[176] See: Messina (1951: 206).

[177] See for example Parker (2012: 109-112) on the role of the Gospel of Mark in general, and on the Gospel of Mark in relation to the *Codex Sinaiticus*, one of the two manuscripts which constitute the *Old Syriac version*. From a methodological perspective Parker offers an intriguing comparison with musicological research (*id.*: 110). See also: Brock (2006: 48); Burkitt (1904 repr. 2003); Lenzi (2000); Lewis (1910 repr. 2005); Petersen (1994).

[178] This is a very complex phenomenon which – of course – applies not only to the Gospel of Mark. See: Vergani (forthcoming 2016). On the problems related to the sequence of the Gospels, see: Bogaert (1999).

[179] Messina writes (1951: xix) about the copy of the *Persian Diatessaron* which has come down to us, "Il teatro geografico è il Māzandarān a sud del Mar Caspio, e il Chorāsān, la regione nord-orientale del territorio iranico. Il quadro storico poi ci porta in pieno dominio mongolo". Moreover, a small example of the eastern feature of the *Diatessaron* is found precisely in the epithet of John *šurandah* which was mentioned in the text and which corresponds to the Persian *šuyanda*: see Alfieri-Barbati (2010: 35).

[180] I would like to thank Prof. Vergani of the Pontificio Istituto Orientale to encourage my curiosity and support my research within a field that is becoming more and more important for my own work. He has made it even clearer to me how the complexities of these issues defy any simple conclusions.

reception and dynamic context fully into consideration.

Irrespective of any conclusions which one might already draw from the evidence which I have presented above – previously documented as well as new one –, this Gospel lectionary deserves considerable further study, especially in the context of the transmission and reception of the Syrian-Oriental religious legacy in medieval Central Asia[181].

2.3 The signatures of E5. A list of concordances

Since its discovery and to the present day, the Gospel lectionary *E5* and the entire corpus of Christian Sogdian fragments have been the subject of different classification systems. The list of concordances below shows at first the classification system used by Sims-Williams in the catalogue of 2012, which is the one that has been fully adopted by this book, followed by the one available at the Turfanforschung homepage[182], so that anyone can get data directly from the source, and finally by the numbering system (1, 2, 2a, etc..) and the signatures used by Sundermann in 1974, 1975 and 1981[183], as these works continue to be the main reference point for anyone approaching the Gospel lectionary *E5*. In the same way, the lost fragments are listed according to the Sims-Williams's new classification system followed by the numbering that is now used on the homepage of the Turfanforschung, i.e. *n497** - *n506**, and, finally, by Sundermann's classification system. *E* refers to "[Church of the] East"[184], *n* stands for "Nestorian" script, as can be deducted from the previously mentioned Turfanforschung homepage, *T II B* or *T III B* respectively indicate "Turfan", second or third expedition, and Bulayïq; *C* stands for "Christian" and refers to the classification system introduced by Hansen[185].

181 Proof of this is the forthcoming article by Sims-Williams (forthcoming 2016) listing and interpreting the readings in *E5*. I thank Prof. Sims-Williams, with whom I have had the privilege to exchange ideas and opinions on this Gospel lectionary over several years, for sharing a preprint of this article and giving me the opportunity of at least adding this note before I sent the book to the press.

182 See: http://www.bbaw.de/forschung/turfanforschung/dta/n/dta_n_index.html (last accessed on 20 May 2016).

183 See: Sundermann (1974: 218-219).

184 See: Sims-Williams (2012: 16).

185 See: Sims-Williams (2012: 15).

Sims-Williams classification system	*Digital Turfan Archive*	*Sundermann classification system*
E5/5	*n166 [part]*	*19c T II B 38*
E5/6a-b	*n497* + n166 [part]*	*1 T II B 38 + 19c T II B 38*
E5/19	*n 149*	*2 T II B 17[b]*
E5/21a-b	*n413d* + n498*	*2a T III B = C58 + 2a T II B 66*
E5/23	*n150*	*2b T II B 66*
E5/28a-b	*n151 + n409*	*3 T II B 67 + 3 T II B 65= C55*
E5/34	*n152*	*4 T II B x*
E5/38	*n499**	*5 T II B 66*
E5/41	*n500**	*6 T III B 99*
E5/48	*n153*	*7 T II B 12*
E5/51	*n154*	*7a T II B 66*
E5/65	*n501**	*7b T II B 66=C3*
E5/72	*n156*	*8 T II B 16*
E5/73	*n 157*	*9 T II B 66*
E5/75-76	*n158 + n413a*	*10 T II B 71 + 19a B C58*
E5/78	*n413b*	*19b T III B*[186] *= C58*
E5/79	*n502**	*11 T II B 12*
E5/80	*n503**	*T III 99a*
E5/83a-b	*n159b + n504**	*C72+ T II B 66*
E5/91	*n162*	*14 T II B 12*
E5/100-101	*n160+n161*	*15 T II B 34*
E5/109	*n163*	*16 T II B 66*
E5/125-126	*n 505*-n506**	*17 T II B 39*
E5/127a-c	*n164*	*18 T II B 17 + T II B 62 + C3 = T II B 66*
E5/130a-b	*n165+n413c*	*19 T III 52 + T III B = C58*

186 "(less likely *T II B*)": Sims-Williams (2012: 36).

Instructions

In the edition of the Gospel lectionary *E5* the following conventions will be adopted:

xyz = reading certain

(xyz) = reading uncertain but consistent with the suggested one

xyz = readable word deleted by the scribe

{<xyz>} = word added later and generally located along the margins.

[xyz] = completely restored letters

[===] = approximate number of missing letters

[----] = missing letters not hypothesised

[ ] = blank space

< = comes from, the result of

> = gives as a result

However, in the translation, English words in *italics* have been added to enhance the readability of the translation. As a rule, a translation as literal as possible has been adopted.

Transliteration for Sogdian and Syriac: *'bgdh* etc. The transliteration into Latin script has been chosen in order to make the volume more accessible to readers who are not Syriac specialists. As regards the transliteration of Syriac loanwords into the Sogdian language, I follow Sims-Williams[187] in representing "teth, 'e, sade and taw [...] by t, γ, c and θ respectively (rather than by ṭ, ', ṣ and t)".

An attempt to reproduce the punctuation and pointing systems as faithfully as possible – even if not including all recitation accents – has been made[188]. What is already well known is here briefly recalled, i.e., the Christian Sogdian adds the letters *f, x* and *ž*[189] to the 22 signs of Aramaic origin, so similarly it adopts the diacritical points system which is typical of the Syriac script, for which vowels are represented by dots placed above or below the letters: .˙ = *ă* ; .˙[190] = *ā* ; ỵ = *ē̆* ; ỵ = *ī̆* ; ẇ = *ō̆* ; ẉ = *ū̆*.

References **1, 10, 15, 20** etc. recall the numbering with which, in the present work, the writing lines of the whole manuscript are grouped, in order to make any intra text reference easier.

---

187 See: Sims-Williams (1988: 147).

188 Readers are also referred to the photo reproductions of the manuscript fragments at the end of this volume.

189 The presence of these two letters in the bilingual Syriac- New Persian Psalms fragment was attributed by Sundermann (1974a: 450-452) to the influence of the Christian Sogdian writing. The thesis has been recently echoed by Orsatti (2007:132-133).

190 Placed vertically above the letter.

The presentation of the edition has been organized in a way to foreground the character of the lectionary *E5* as a translated text. Therefore, after each Sogdian writing line in transliteration I added the corresponding Syriac text according to the *Peshitta*[191] in order to highlight, also visually, this comparative point of view. The text is then followed by the translation and commentary. Then follow a Sogdian-Syriac glossary and an index of those Syriac terms actually attested in the Syriac parts of the Gospel lectionary *E5*.

Abbreviations

1 : first person
2 : second person
3 : third person
abl. : ablative
acc. : accusative
act. : active
adj. : adjective
adv. : adverb
Aph. : Aphel conjugation
art. cit. : article cited
Av. : Avestan
caus. : causative
col. : column
conj. : conjunction
dir. : direct
dur. : durative
etc. : etcetera
Ethpa. : Ethpaal conjugation
Ethpe. : Ethpeel conjugation
Ettaph. : Ettaphal conjugation
f. : folio; feminine
fut. : future
gen. : genitive
Gk. : Greek
ibid.: ibidem
id. : idem
i.e. : (id est) that is

---

191 See: Pusey-Gwilliam (1901). As one can see, I have not provided a fully pointed text. However, plural forms, omographs (like *ṁn* "who" and *ṃn* "from", *'ṁr* "he says" and *'ṃr* "he said" etc.) have been properly distinguished.

impf. : imperfect
impv. : imperative
indic. : indicative
intr. : intransitive
irr. : irrealis
lit. : literally
loc. : locative
m.: masculine
MP. : Middle Persian
n.: note; neuter
nom. : nominative
NP. : New Persian
num. : numeral
numv.: numerative
obl. : oblique
OP : Old Persian
opt. : optative
Pa. : Pael conjugation
part. : participle
pass. : passive
pers. : person
pf. : perfect
pl. : plural
postp. : postposition
pot. : potential
pp. : past participle
predic. : predicative
prep. : preposition
pres. : present
pret. : preterite
pron.: pronoun
/r/ : recto
sg. : singular
Sogd. : Sogdian
subj.: subjunctive
superl.: superlative
Syr. : Syriac
trans.: transitive
/v/ : verso

vb.: verb
voc. : vocative

Abbreviated references
C2 = Sims-Williams, N. (1985) *The Christian Sogdian Manuscript C2*, Berlin.
GMS = Gershevitch, I. (1954) *A Grammar of Manichean Sogdian Sogdian*, Oxford.

E5: The Language

This chapter is aimed at highlighting the linguistic peculiarities of the Gospel lectionary *E5*. It is generally accepted that the language of *E5* represents, diachronically speaking, the most recent development of Sogdian. Yoshida[192] summarizes the reasons why the language of this Gospel lectionary has come to be considered the last stage of the Sogdian language. They are[193]: the lack of the article; the disappearance of the conjunction *rty* whose functions are resumed by *'t*[194], the use of the conjunction *qt* as relative particle; the strong trend, in nominal inflection, toward the use of the nominative in all cases; and "the new oblique case" which "begins to be formed by adding *-ī* to nom. sg. and to similar generalized forms"[195]. From a purely linguistic point of view, for these and for all the reasons which will be discussed later, and looking at the entire available Sogdian corpus, I am inclined to date this Gospel lectionary around the eleventh century.

Considering the above, it must be taken into account that the language therein attested is the medium of cultural processes resulting from a religious missionary need which has witnessed the ex novo formation of a religious literature, wholly and for the most part faithfully translated from another religious tradition whose medium of transmission was Syriac, not Sogdian. I have already shown how the Christian Sogdian literature, especially with regard to the Gospel lectionary *E5*, aims at very close formal and semantic correspondence and how it satisfies all principles governing a translation oriented toward formal equivalence[196].

Where appropriate, together with phenomena characteristic of translation literature, issues of areal linguistics and language contact are also taken into account in favour of a general presentation which considers all these aspects simultaneously. Only a multiplicity of perspectives can lead to a better understanding of the distribution of linguistic elements in the geographic space and socio-cultural field.

---

192 See: Yoshida (2009).

193 See: Yoshida (2009: 326).

194 On possible cases where *'t* means, in Christian Sogdian, *'rty* or *'r*, see Kessel-Sims-Williams (2011: 298).

195 See: Yoshida (2009: 326). See below 3.3.3 Marking the direct object with singular oblique –y ending.

196 See: Barbati (2015: 447-449).

The linguistic material gleaned from *E5* is divided into five sections: phonology, verbal morphosyntax, nominal morphosyntax, syntax, terminology.

3.1 Phonology

3.1.1 Durative suffix[197]

Alternation between the two forms -*sqn* and -*sq*[198]:

- -*sqn*: *'smsqn* (200); *'štẏt'sqn* (245); *frm'ymsqn* (120; 125; 230); *fš'mmsqn* (325; 390); *γrbt'sqn* (255; 615); *γrbymsqn* (440; 580; 585; 595; 610); *q'mt'sqn* (605); *nm'ymsqn* (190); *ptγwšt'sqn* (360); *sn'm θbr'msqn* (55); *snntqn* (480); *šwyntqn* (520); *w'byntqn* (10; 280; 305; 570); *w'bmsqn* (575); *wdrzt'sqn* (480); *wrnt'sqn* (210); *wrnymsqn* (440); *wrnysqn* (630); *wyc'wqy' θbr'msqn* (195); *wyc'wqy' θbrntqn* (205; 215); *wynmsqn* (600); *wynt'sqn* (485; 635); *wynntqn* (480); *wyntqn* (585); *ž'ytqn* (635); *ž'ẏntqn* (770).
- -*sq*: *brtpθ wn'msq* (470); *frm'ymsq* (130; 145; 200; 320; 350; 400; 420; 675; 715; 735; 755; 795); *γrbtysq* (245); *γrb'msq* (555; 600); *γrbysq* (440); *q'mmsq* (195); *pcqwyrmsq* (660); *ptγwšmsq* (190); *rwpmsq* (670); *sn'm θbrysq* (55); *swx'ẏẏmsq* (670); *w'bysq* (50; 440; 570); *w'bt'sq* (580); *wntysq* (795); *wrn'msq* (635); *z'wrqyn b'sq* (35); *ž'ysq* (440; 775).

The -*sq* form prevails where the verb is immediately followed by the personal pronoun, whose presence is, in turn, the result of a faithful translation from the Syriac[199]. The only exceptions are *wntysq* (795); *z'wrqyn b'sq* (35); and *ž'ysq* (775). For all other cases, I think that the loss of -*n* is to be attributed to the fact that the aforementioned examples – composed by verb + personal pronoun, as *sn'm θbrysq tγw* – constitute a single syntagmatic unit where the presence of four or more consonants between the verb and the pronoun leads to the loss of the final consonant of the first unit

[197] Obviously, the Sogdian durative suffix is used to translate the durative *nuance* of the Syriac verb forms.

[198] I refer to *C2* throughout this chapter because it represents one of the most extensive and best preserved and so far also best studied manuscripts of the entire Christian Sogdian collection and therefore is central to any investigation, whether diachronic, diatopic, diastratic etc. On other Christian Sogdian fragments see most recently Sims-Williamsn (2014a; 2015could).

[199] See: Telegdi (1938).

element thus constituted. This is not a general rule; an opposite example occurs in *wrnymsqn m'x* (440). Further evidence on how these formations composed of verb + personal pronoun must have been perceived by the speakers as a single unit, is offered, in my opinion, by those cases where the pronoun is written attached to the verb[200]. These are the examples: *'yštyw* (220; 225); *'wšnty 'yštyw* (705); *cn'wq 'yštyw* (710); *γw'm- n'fc 'y̤štyw* (710); *wy̤ny̤ qtyštyw* (560). On the other hand, it is undeniable that, from a diachronic point of view, this is a typical development of the Sogdian language. In *E5* the form *-sqwn* is no longer attested, while it is still present in *C2* (p. 65) or better in the first part, *The story of Pethion*, which shows more archaic features than the rest of the manuscript, such as the simultaneous presence of *-sqwn* next to *-sqn* and *-sq*. The vowel of the suffix even disappears completely in Sogdian texts in Brāhmī script dated, according to Sims-Williams[201], around the middle of the ninth century.

3.1.2 Suffix for the future: q'> g'

The most frequently attested form is *-q'*, but there are also examples of voicing *-q'* > *-g'*[202]:

- *''z'ng'* (375); *γwžtg'* (430); *γwžng'* (430); *nm'y̤ngq'* (665); *nyžtwng'* (430); *prycng'* (435); *pstw'ng'* (375); *šwng'* (435); *θbrng'* (510); *w'bng'* (430); *wy̤ng'* (420).

The voicing occurs in cases where *-q-* is preceded by the dental nasal[203] even if there is an example of sonorization after the voiceless dental occlusive in *γwžtg'* (430). Remarkable is also *nm'y̤ngq'* (665), 1 sg. of the future indicative of the verb *nm'y* "to judge" with an unusual suffix for the future *-gq'*. Probably, although not certainly, this form is due to a scribal mistake: the oversight, however, is in my opinion telling. While it attests the form which was supposed to be the regular one, *-q'*, it shows that it must actually have been pronounced *-g'*.

---

200 I exclude any reasons related to the need for having the writing lines with the same length and width.

201 See: Sims-Williams (1996a: 308).

202 See: *GMS* (*§§* 448; 646). No example of the voicing of the suffix for the future is attested in *C2*. This also implies a correction of the Gharib dictionary (1995: 185): Gharib registers as a Sogdian own form *-q'* (*-g'*), rightly quoting *GMS* (*id.*) and *C2*. It should therefore be pointed out that the suffix *-g'* is attested in *E5* and not in *C2*.

203 The same voicing is attested, in *E5*, also in the noun *sng* "stone". *C2* (p. 225) attests *snq*.

3.1.3 Genitive/dative of the pron. 3 pers. m. sg.: xw: wyny ~ wny
In this Gospel lectionary there is an alternation between *wyny* and *wny*, both forms of the genitive/dative pron. of the 3 pers. m. sg. *xw* "he". *wyny*: (15); (30); (40); (50); (55); (70); (75); (110); (130); (140); (145); (160); (165); (170); (185); (190); (210); (220); (230); (225); (295); (355); (390); (395); (440); (505); (510); (520); (525); (560); (675). *wny*: (550); (555); (560); (585); (590); (595); (600); (605); (620); (625); (630); (635); (655); (665); (670); (675); (690); (695); (720); (760); (765); (770); (785); (790); (795). In *C2* (p. 232-233) the form *wyny* is registered[204]. With particular regard to the 3 m. pl. *wyšnt*, in *E5*, both in direct *wyšnt* and in oblique case *wyšnty*, *-y-* is never dropped. In *C2*, however, *-y-* remains constant only in the most conservative text, *The Story of Pethion*, while in other texts, Sims-Williams reported the indiscriminate use of *wyšnt(y)* and *wšnt(y)*[205].

3.1.4 Voicing of the voiceless velar fricative: x > γ
The cases attested in the Gospel lectionary *E5* are: *'γzntq'* (340) < *'xz/'xšt* "to rise up, arise" (265); (305); the deverbative word *'γz'mnty* "resurrection" (190); *'wγẓt* (75) < *'wγẓ/'wxšt* "to go down, descend" (75); (545); *γwšyq m't* (35) < *γwšyq x, sqw, swq/m't* "to grow up" (35); *γwty xwdq'r* "only, alone" (445); (525); (755); *γwty xwtg'r* "alone" (445); and *γwž* "to ask" in all its claims (5); (420); (425); (430). This voicing, a sign of what was to be the real pronunciation of the phoneme, has already been noted by Sims-Williams in *C2* (p. 67) as regards *wγš* < *wxš* "to save", *ptγwsd'rt* < *ptxwsd'rt* "to kill" and *prbγšt* < *prbxšt* "to deliver". The change *x* > *γ* could also provide a dialectological clue: in fact among all the aforementioned forms, those which in *E5* present the voicing, in *C2* result without it and vice versa.

It should be remembered that the alternation between the use of the voiceless and voiced velar fricative is present in secular Sogdian for purely graphic reasons. Resuming the authoritative *excursus* by Sims-Williams on the subject[206], it should be noted that the distinction between *γ* and *x* – which actually was mainly based on their stroke: straight and slightly right curved as in the case of the voiced, left curved with a possible ligature with the

[204] For the distribution of the above mentioned forms in *E5*, see also: Sims-Williams (forthcoming 2016). One remark: with particular regard to *wyny* (675) which is found not in the text but on the inner margin, I am not convinced that it is an addition of a later hand as proposed by Sims-Williams. However, before a thorough study on scribal hands in the entire Christian Sogdian corpus is available one should be very careful about conclusions.

[205] See: *C2* (p. 65).

[206] See: Sims-Williams (1981a).

following word as in the case of the voiceless – only survives in the *Ancient Letters*. Thereafter, except for the final position, such a distinction is lost in secular Sogdian when *γ* starts to be linked to the following letter. According to Sims-Williams, a distinction in the final position is maintained in the Buddhist texts and in the Mount Mugh documents, while in Manichaean, depending on the text, the distinction of *-γ* and *-x* gives way to their confusion. In Christian Sogdian, as already stated by Sims-Williams for *C2* (p. 67), the recurrence of some forms can only confirm the idea that we are dealing with something which goes beyond a purely graphic factor and offers a clue for the real pronunciation, i.e. voiced. The same also applies to the attested forms in *E5*, considering also that compared to the Sogdian secular script, the East Syriac script is less inclined to confusion between the two letters.

3.1.5 'mpd / 'mpst "to fall, precipitate, prostrate"

The present stem is always attested in this Gospel lectionary with the voiced dental occlusive (115); (370) whereas in *C2* (p. 204) the corresponding unvoiced one is attested.

3.1.6 cšm- "eye"

In *E5* only this form is attested: *cšmt'* (175); (300); (550); (560); (565); (570); (585); (615); (620). In *C2* (p. 209) are attested both forms *cšm-* and *cym-*: *cšmw*; *cymw*; *cymt'* (id.)[207]. I have recently shown that, in the Iranian area, the distribution of these two forms leads to interesting insights about the features shared between the north-eastern Iranian linguistic area and the northern-central group of the Central Iranian dialects[208]. This confirms what has been said at the beginning of this chapter about the potentialities of a methodology which looks, simultaneously, in different directions (in this case, diachronic linguistics and areal linguistics).

3.1.7 fcmbd ~ fcmpd "world"

There is an ambivalent use of both forms: *fcmbd* (65); (100); (230); (415); *fcmpd* (310); (315); (410); (435); (450); (465); (695); (750). In *C2* (p. 210) only *fcmbd* is attested.

[207] See also *GMS* (*§* 385).

[208] See: Barbati (2015b: 17-18).

3.1.8 kθ-/ knθ-/ qθ- "city, town"
The plural direct case attested in *E5* refers to the *–t* heavy stems, i.e. *kθt* (655); (660)[209], while in *C2* (pp. 213-214) it is the *-t'* light stems[210].

3.1.9 sng "stone" and "Peter"
In this Gospel lectionary *sng* (175); (540) is attested in the form which shows the voicing *q* > *g*, whereas in *C2* (p. 225) *snq* is attested.

3.2 Verbal morphosyntax

3.2.1 Massive presence of periphrastic formations composed by present participle in -yq + verb "to be" x-, sqw-, swq-/m't
The presence in the Gospel lectionary *E5* is directly proportional to the presence of similar Syriac verb forms composed of a participle + the verb "to be" *hw'*. They are: Sogd. *'bnt d'ryq m't* and Syr. *'ny' hwt* (525); Sogd. *'ndy̤šy̤q m't* and Syr. *msbr hw'* (300); Sogd. *γrby̤q m'ty̤m* and Syr. *yd' hwyt* (70); (75); Sogd. *fry-d'ryq m'tnt* and Syr. *rḥmyn hww* (245); Sogd. *fryd'ryq m't* and Syr. *rḥm hw'* (315)[211]; Sogd. *γrbyq m'tyš* and Syr. *yd' hwyt* (665); Sogd. *pcqwyryq m'tnt* and Syr. *dḥlyn hww* (585); Sogd. *psxnt wnyq m'tnt* and Syr. *mmwyqyn hww* (245); Sogd. *ptγwšyq m't* and Syr. *šm'' hwt* (520); Sogd. *šm'ryq m'tnt* and Syr. *mtḥšbyn hww* (10); Sogd. *šm'ryq m'tnt* and Syr. *sbryn hwyn* (270); Sogd. *šm'ryq m'tnt* and Syr. *sbryn hww* (480); Sogd. *šwyq m'tnt* and Syr. *'zyl hww* (290); Sogd. *šwyqm't* and Syr. *'zl hw'* (290); Sogd. *šwyq m'tnt* and Syr. *'zyl hww* (290); Sogd. *w'by̤q m't* and Syr. *'mr hw'* (550); Sogd. *w'by̤q m'tnt* and Syr. *'mryn hww* (300; 565); Sogd. *wrnyq m'tnt* and Syr. *mhÿmnyn hww* (485).

Gershevitch (*GMS*: §§ 897; 998) had already described this participial formation in *–yq* as typical for Christian Sogdian. According to Gershevitch "it does not seem to occur in Man. or B.[212]". These forms appear to be the result of a "translation" language as a medium of a "translation literature".

---

[209] In *E5* (325) also the singular forms *qθ* (325); (345) and *knθ* (345) are attested. See: *GMS* (§ 340).

[210] See also *GMS* (§ 496).

[211] These last two examples are paradigmatic for a translation literature. It is no coincidence that for the verb "to love", Sogdian uses *fry ny'd'r* to translate the Syriac verbs *rḥm* and *'ḥb*: Sogd. *fry ny'd'rt* and Syr. *rḥm* (435); Sogd. *fry ny'd'ryšt'* and Syr. *rḥmtwnn* (435); Sogd. *fry ny'd'ry* and Syr. *'ḥbtn* (465).

[212] Respectively "Manichaean Sogdian and Buddhist Sogdian".

Therefore, these formations are closely related to their context.

Finally, it should be remembered that in Syriac these formations are used to express, in the present and past tenses, the durative *nuance*, which is maintained in Sogdian through the use of the auxiliary *x-*, *sqw-*, *swq-/m'ṭ*[213]. Other examples of this translation of the Syriac durative *nuance* are: Sogd. *nysty swqnt* and Syr. *ytbyn* (35); *z'wrqyn b'sq* and Syr. *mtḥl* (35)[214].

3.2.2 Sogdian translation of the Syriac medio-passive verbs

The Sogdian uses the past participle + the auxiliary "to be" *b(w)-/qt-* to translate the Syriac medio-passive verbs. Consider the following examples: Sogd. *'yty bwtq'* and Syr. *tštql* (175); Sogd. *'žty̱ bwty̱* and Syr. *'tyld* (620); Sogd. *fšmtyt qtnt* and Syr. *'štdrw* (55); Sogd. *prbxšty̱ bwtq'* and Syr. *mštlm* (140); Sogd. *prm'nty' qty̱ bntq'* and Syr. *nštbqwn* (390); Sogd. *pry̱θtyt bnt* and Syr. *mzdb̈nn* (365); Sogd. *ptγwšty qty* and Syr. *'štm't* (620); Sogd. *spty by* and Syr. *nštlm* (495); Sogd. *spy̱ty̱ qtnt* and Syr. *ḥwrw* (765); Sogd. *swxsty qty* and Syr. *'štql* (300); Sogd. *š'št db'ny bwtq'* and Syr. *ttbdrwn* (445); Sogd. *wγty̱ bwt* and Syr. *mt'mr* (395); Sogd. *wy̱n'wcyq qty̱* and Syr. *'tḥzy* (310); *wy̱n'wcyq qtnt* and Syr. *'tḥzyw* (765); Sogd. *xwycq qty* and Syr. *'tptḥ* (5); Sogd. *xwycq qtnt* and Syr. *'tptḥ* (300); (550); Sogd. *zrγtyt bym* and Syr. *ntprq* (25); Sogd. *žγyrty byq'* and Syr. *ttqr'* (30); Sogd. *žγyrtyt qtnt* and Syr. *'tqryw* (85); Sogd. *žγyrty bwt* and Syr. *'ttlmd hw'* (260); Sogd. *žγyrty bwt* and Syr. *mtqr'* (535).

To this general rule, the following very few examples constitute exceptions. The first concerns the Sogdian verb *wyd's* "to wonder, to be

---

213 About the "durative" value of the auxiliary *m't* in opposition to the "neutral" or "punctual" value of the auxiliary *b'*, see: Durkin-Meisterernst (2007: 31-44). He also recalls the close link between this form and the Sogdian imperfect in *'z-* for the latter, already disused, would be replaced by the first one. Contrary to a diachronic explanation, and in favour of a dialectological distribution between the periphrastic forms with *m't* and the imperfect in *'z-*, is Yoshida (1980). At this point it should be recalled that the almost total disappearance of the imperfect in favour of the periphrastic verb formation (theme of the past and the auxiliary "to be" for the intransitive verbs, theme of the past and the auxiliary "to have" for the transitive verbs) is one of the reasons which led to emphasize the diastratic element within the Sogdian types as they are attested. See, for example, Tremblay (2001: in particular pp. 76-77).

214 The durative imperfect 3sg. *b'sq* is only attested in Christian Sogdian (*GMS*: § 798; Gharib, 1995: 98). I take this also as a result of a faithful translation. The translator had used the mere imperfect *b'*, the durative value of the Syriac *mtḥl* would have been automatically lost, especially considering the punctual value of *b'* (Durkin-Meisterernst: 2007: 41-42). A proper and faithful translation of a sacred text needed, therefore, the addition of the suffix *-sq*.

surprised, to marvel" which translates the Syriac *'tdmr* "id.", medio-passive diathesis of the Ethpeel conjugation: Sogd. *wyd'sd'rnt* and Syr. *'tdmrw* (5); Sogd. *wyd'st'* and Syr. *ttdmrwn* (185); Sogd. *wd's* and Syr. *mtdmrw* (615). The second concerns the Sogdian *ž'tyt byq m'tnt* (10), translation of the Syriac *mtmlln hwy*. So, in Sogdian, there is the plural past participle *ž'tyt* of the verb *ž'y* "to talk, converse, discuss" + *byq* + *x-, sqw-, sqw-/m't* "to be" to translate the Syriac *mtmlln hwy*, past progressive passive composed by the 3 f. pl. part. of the Ethpaal conjugation, i.e., the medio-passive conjugation of Pael *mll* "to talk, speak, converse" + the perfect tense of the auxiliary "to be" *hw'*, 3 f. pl. I believe that in this case the Sogdian uses the auxiliary "to be" *x, sqw, sqw/m't* to faithfully recreate the Syriac past progressive[215] composed exactly by the participle + auxiliary, adding then *byq* < *b(w)-/qt-* for the passive meaning. Interestingly *byq* is registered in *GMS* (§§: 844; 897) and in the Gharib dictionary (1995: 118) only reference to this passage in *E5*[216].

3.2.3 Sogdian translation of Syriac idioms

For the predication of existence Syriac uses the particle *'yt*[217]. The Sogdian translations attested in *E5* are the following: Sogd. *swqyq m't* and Syr. *'ytwhy hw'* (40); Sogd. *'ym* and Syr. *'yty* (45); Sogd. *'yš* and Syr. *'ytyk* (55).

3.2.4 Massive use of periphrastic verbal forms

These are used to create an *ex novo* terminology able to fill lacunae in the Sogdian lexicon. This is the case, for example, in *pr ptcng swx'y/swxswt* "to lift on the cross, crucify"[218], translation of the Syriac *zqp* "1. trans. a. erexit; b. suspendit, crucifixit; c. excitavit; d. divellit, aravit (terram); e. addidit; f. vocali zpql pronuntiavit; 2. intr. a. surrexit; b. horruit; c. crucifixus est"[219]. They serve also to translate the different conjugations of the Syriac language, from the Aphel, i.e. the causative, – this is the case for example of Sogd. *wyc'wqy' θbr* "bear witness, testify" and Syr. *'shd* "id." -; for the three medio- passive/reflexive conjugations as, for example, the Ethpaal conjugation, – this is the case of Sogd. *z'ry sy/sy't* "be merciful, to have compassion" and Syr. *trḥm* from the verbal root *rḥm* and so on.

---

215 As already illustrated in the previous paragraph.

216 With particular regard to Sogd. *z'ry sy' d'rt* and Syr. *'trḥm* (510); and to Sogd. *py'm byrd'rt* and Syr. *'t'sy* (630), see below, *3.2.4*.

217 See: Thackston (1999: 14-15).

218 The verb is not attested in *C2* and is not registered in the Gharib dictionary (1995).

219 See: Brockelmann (1928: 204).

- Sogd. *'frywn ptwyd/ptwyst* or Sogd. *'frywn wn-/qt-* "to bless"[220] as translation for Syr. *brk* "id.": *'frywn ptwysd'rt* and Syr. *ḇrk* (5); Sogd. *'frywn qθ'rt* and Syr. *ḇrk* (295);
- Sogd. *rwxšny'q θbr* "to light up" as translation for Syr. *nhr* "id.": Sogd. *rwxšny'q θbrw* and Syr.*mnhrw* (35); Sogd. *rwxšny'q θbrty* and Syr. *mnhr* (200);
- Sogd. *wyc'wqy' θbr* "to bear witness, testify" and Syr. *'shd* "id.": Sogd. *wyc'wqy' θ'br* and Syr. *'shd* (70); Sogd. *wyc'wqy' θbrd'rm* and Syr. *'shdt* (80); Sogd. *wyc'wqy' θbr'msqn* and Syr. *mshd 'n'* (195); *wyc'wqy' θbrd'rt* and Syr. *'shd* (200); Sogd. *wyc'wqy' θbrntqn* and Syr. *shdyn* (205; 215);
- Sogd. *γwrs prwyd/prwyst* "to put around" and Syr. *'ḥdr* "id.": Sogd. *γwrs prwyd'rt* and Syr.*'ḥdr* (155)[221];
- Sogd. *pcq'w wn/qt* "to reject"[222] and Syr. *sl'* "id.": Sogd. *pcq'w qθ'rnt* and Syr. *'slyw* (175);
- Sogd. *xš'wn wn/qt* "to give authority" and Syr. *'šlṭ* "id.": *xš'wn qθ'rt* and Syr. *'šlṭ* (185);
- Sogd. *pnt prys/pr'γt* "to arrive, go closer" and Syr. *mṭ'* : Sogd. *pnt pr'γt* Syr. *mṭt* (255); Sogd. *pnt pr'γt* and Syr. *ṃṭ'* (415). As evidence of the attention used in translating see: Sogd. *pnt b'w* "to draw near to" as translation of the Syr. *qrb* "id."; Sogd. *pnt b'wd'rnt*[223] and Syr.

---

220 As already shown, this Gospel lectionary knows only the periphrastic form for "to bless" and not the verb *'fryn/ 'fryt* even attested in Christian Sogdian, for example, in *C2* (p. 203). For an overview of this form attestations and its Sogdian related constructions, as well as in the Pahlavi psalter, in the Syro-New Persian fragment, in Manichaean Middle Persian and Parthian and in Inscriptional Middle Persian see: Barbati (2014: 111-112).

221 I think this is an excellent example, but not the only one as we can see leafing through this periphrastic forms list and according to the way in which this Gospel lectionary has tried to create an *ad hoc* terminology following the principle of a faithful translation from the original. The Sogdian *γwrs prwyd/prwyst*, that, as far as I know, is not attested elsewhere, is composed by the adverb *γwrs* "around" (*C2*, p. 212; Gharib, 1995: 176) here used as a pre-verb and the verb *prwyd/prwyst* "to look for, seek" (*C2*, p. 220; Gharib, 1995: 293). The Syriac has *'ḥdrh*, Aphel conjugation, 3sg. from the root *ḥdr* "1. circumdedit, saepsit; 2.a. circumvenit; b. obsedit, inclusit; 3. circumfluxit; 4.a. circumvagatus est; b. ambivit, obivit; 5. mendicavit; 6. iterum fecit; 7. vertigine laboravit" (Brockelmann, 1928: 216). See the glossary: Sogd. *prwyd/prwyst* and Syr. *bs'* "percuisivit, examinavit, scrutatus est" (Brockelmann, 1928: 85).

222 See: Schwartz (1967; 13.17).

223 About the use of the auxiliary *d'r-* for intransitive perfect in Sogdian see: Gharib (2006). Analyzing this kind of formations in Sogdian, Khwarezmian and in some dialects spoken between the Caspian coast and the Alborz Mountain, she suggests interesting insights in

qrbw hww (290); and Sogd. *pnt br* "to drag, put near, bring near" as translation of the Pael conjugation of the Syriac aforementioned verbal root *qrb*: Sogd. *pnt brntq'* and Syr. *mqrbyn* (335).

- Sogd. *pr ptcng swx'y/swxswt* "to crucify" and Syr. *zqp* "id.": Sogd. *pr ptcng swxswd'rnt* and Syr. *zqpw* (270);
- Sogd. *'yzt' wn /qt* "to proclaim" and Syr. *'krz* "id.": Sogd. *'yzt' wnt'* and Syr. *'krzw* (360);
- Sogd. *prm'nty' wn/qt* "to forgive" and Syr. *'štbq* "id.": Sogd. *prm'nty' wnt'* and Syr. *tšbqwn* (390); Sogd. *prm'nty'qtẏ bntq'* and Syr. *nštbqwn* (390);
- Sogd. *bž'xwty' pcγ'z/ pcγšt* "to suffer" and Syr. *ḥš* "id.": Sogd. *bž'xwty' pcγ'z't* and Syr. *nḥš* (500);
- Sogd. *z'ry sy/sy't* "to be merciful, have compassion" and Syr. *'trḥm* "id.": Sogd. *z'ry sy'd'rt* and Syr. *'trḥm* (510);
- Sogd. *py'm byr/byrt* "to find cure" and Syr. *'t'sy* (id.): Sogd. *py'm byrd'rt* and Syr. *'t'sy* (630);
- Sogd. *pcq'md'r* "to be pleased" and Syr. *'ṣṭby* "id.": Sogd. *pcq'md'rm* and Syr. *'ṣṭbyt* (775);
- Sogd. *spyty b(w)/qt* "to become white" and Syr. *ḥwr*: Sogd. *spyty qtnt* and Syr. *ḥwrw* (765)[224].

3.2.5 Tenses and moods in Sogdian and in Syriac[225]

a) Sogd. indic. pres.	= Syr. part. as pres. habitual : Sogd. *ptγwšnt* and Syr. *šm'yn* (180);
b) Sogd. indic. pres. dur.	= Syr. participial inflection as pres. dur. : Sogd. *γrbysq tγw* and Syr. *yd' 'nt* (440);
c) Sogd. indic. fut.	= Syr. impf. (as fut.)[226] : Sogd. *'ẏstq'* and Syr. *n't'*

that area of study. As I have tried to show here and on previous occasions (Alfieri-Barbati: 2010; Barbati: 2015b), the analysis of the relationship between the Middle eastern Iranian area and some dialect areas of contemporary Iran by applying a combination of historical and areal linguistics is a promising field of research.

224 To conclude this paragraph, it is worth mentioning that examples of periphrastic verbs such as "noun + to do" can also be found in Khwarezmian. See: Durkin-Meisterernst (2009:350). Two interesting works by Ciancaglini (2006, 2011) deserve to be noted in this context. After examining such formations in the Middle and New western Iranian area, and after considering them as an Indo-Iranian phenomenon, she looks at the same kind of construction attested in languages that were in contact with Iranian languages, but different in type and genealogy, as a calque on the Iranian type.

225 Each entry is accompanied by an example. For passive forms see the the corresponding paragraph.

	(350);
	= Syr. participial inflection as pres. dur. : Sogd. *θbrng'* and Syr. *yhb 'n'* (510);
	= Syr. part. : Sogd. *'ystq'* and Syr. *'ṫ'* (60; 65);
d)Sogd. fut. dur.	= Syr. participial inflection as pres. dur. : Sogd. *w'bt'sq* and Syr. *'mryn 'ntwn* (580);
e) Sogd. subj.[227] pres.	= Syr. impf. [228]: Sogd. *pstw't* and Syr. *Nkwpr* (375);
f) Sogd. subj. pres.	= Syr. part. pres.[229]: Sogd. *q'ṃ̇nt* and Syr. *ṣb'* (745);
	= Syr. impf.: Sogd. *'xyž't* and Syr. *nqym* (790);
g) Sogd. impv.	= Syr. impv. : Sogd. *ptγwšt'* and Syr. *šm'w* (155); (780);
h) Sogd. opt.	= Syr. impf. (as opt.) : Sogd. *θbry* and Syr. *ntl* (790);
i) Sogd. opt. dur.	= Syr. part. : Sogd. *w'byntqn* and Syr. *'mryn* (10); (280); (305);
	= Syr. participial inflection as pres. dur. : Sogd. *w'byntqn* and Syr. *'mryn hww* (570);
j) Sogd. irr.[230]	= Syr. impf. : Sogd. *wrnwtỵšt'* and Syr. *thymnwn* (150);
	= Syr. part. + past copula as past dur. : Sogd. *'yswty* and Syr. *'t' hwyt* (670);
k) Sogd. impf.	= Syr. pf. : Sogd. *w'bnt* and Syr. *'mrw* (55); (170);
	= Syr. part. + past copula as past dur. : Sogd. *fr'm'y* and Syr. *'mr hw'* (500);
l) Sogd. impf. dur.	= Syr. past copula as past dur.: Sog. *'wštỵ m't* and Syr. *q'm hw'* (80)[231];

[226] In Syriac the imperfect can express the future, the present tense and the optative. See: Thackston (1999: 86-87).

[227] About the subjunctive use in Christian Sogdian see: Telegdi (1938: 222-224).

[228] Exhortation value.

[229] To express possibility as well as in the following case where to a Sogdian subjunctive corresponds a Syriac imperfect.

[230] See: *GMS* (§§: 815-820).

[231] It is worth dwelling on the Sogdian periphrastic form which faithfully follows the Syriac past progressive *q'm hw'* composed by *q'm*, participle of the verb stay" + *hw'* past of the auxiliary "to be". According to Durkin-Meisterernst (2007), in this case, as in all other

m) Sogd. tr. pret. = Syr. pf.[232] : Sogd. *γrbd'rm* and Syr. *yd'ṭ* (215; 465);

n) Sogd. tr. pret. caus. = Syr. pf. Aph. : Sogd. *'ndỵšd'rt*[233] and Syr. *'mtl* (645);

o) Sogd. intr. pret. = Syr. pf. : Sogd. *nyžtym* and Syr. *npqt* (220; 435);

p) Sogd. fut. pot.[234] = Syr. part. act. : Sogd. *qt' wnntq'* and Syr. *mškḥyn* (365);

q) Sogd. opt. pot. = Syr. part.*mškḥ* : Sogd. *qt' wny* and Syr. *mškḥ* (240);

r) Sogd. inf. pres. = Syr. inf. pres. : Sogd. *qrwn* and Syr. *m'bd* (190; 570).

In this Gospel lectionary, the Sogdian infinitive is always preceded by *pr* in the final clauses, and after verbs that indicate "to desire, can/be able to", "to be necessary". With the exception of the final clause, which reflects a construction typical of the Sogdian language, I believe that other cases should be seen as the result of a translation literature. In other words, I believe that the presence of Sogdian *pr* is directly proportional to that of the Syriac *l-*. Therefore:

- final clause: Sogd. *pr* + infinitive and Syr. *l-* + infinitive. Examples: Sogd. *pr rwxšny'q θbrw* and Syr. *l-mnhrw* (35); Sogd. *pr nm'c bry* and Syr. *l-mṣlyw* (535); Sogd. *pr ptbtw* and Syr. *l-mstklw* (500); Sogd. *pr spxšw*[235] and Syr. *l-mšmšw* (525);
- governed by "to wish". Examples: Sogd. *[q](’mt'sqn) šm'x pr ptγwš* and Syr. *ṣbyn 'ntwn l- mšm'* (605); Sogd. *q'mt'sqn pr bw* and Syr. *ṣbyn 'ntwn l-mhw'* (605). In Manichean Middle Persian and Parthian, the verb *k'm-* is often followed by the infinitive[236].
- taken by "can/be able to". Examples: Sogd. *nỵ qt(') wn'nq'zw 'ỵc cn mn'γrỵwỵ rỵž pr (qw)rwn* and Syr. *l' mškḥ 'n' ṃn ṣbwt npšy mdm l-m'bd* (190); Sogd. *qt' wnỵ dw' xypθ'wnt pr spxšỵ* and Syr. *mškḥ l-*

ones found in the Gospel lectionary, and as already mentioned in the previous pages, the durative *nuance* is translated, in Sogdian by the use of the auxiliary *m't*.

232 With some exceptions, for example in (85) the Sogdian preterite, 3 sg. *pcqw'd['rt]* translates the Syriac f. sg. part. *'mr'*.

233 See also: *GMS* (§ 548).

234 On the Sogdian potential see: Sims-Williams (2007).

235 See also: *GMS* (§§ 905; 912).

236 See: Durkin- Meisterernst (2004: 202).

trÿn mrÿwn l-mplḥ (240); Sogd. *nỵ qt' wnt'q' šm'x pr spxšỵ* and Syr. *l' mškḥyn 'ntwn l-mplḥ* (240); Sogd. *pyšt rw'n nỵ qt' wnntq' (pr ptxw')y* and Syr. *npš' dyn l' mškḥyn l-mqṭl* (365); Sogd. *qt' wn(tỵ)q'....pr qrwn* and Syr. *mškḥ.... l-m'bd* (570)[237];

- taken by "to be typical of, necessary, appropriate". Example: Sogd. *s'št pr wyd's* and Syr. *hw l-mtdmrw* (615).

3.3 Nominal morphosyntax[238]

3.3.1 Strong case syncretism and development of a two cases inflectional system[239]

In the singular, an unmarked case functions as nominative, and a marked case with *–y*, i.e. oblique case, could also function as direct object [240]. In the plural there is *-t* for the direct case and *-ty* for the oblique case. This is true not only for the heavy stems, but also for the light stems and the *-ăkă* stems. There are some examples where the nominative of a light stem or an *-ăkă* stem is considered as an uninflected form to which the oblique suffix is added: *rmy-y* (15); (275); (545) and *žwxšqt'y* (535); (545).

With particular regard to light and *-ăkă* stems, we have a drastic decrease of the inflection. The syncretism of cases, in light stems, affects less the basic lexicon and the cultured and religious one. For the first case, the attested examples are: *dst-* "hand" nom. *dsty* (15), loc. *dsty'* (20); (25); (515), dir. pl. *dst'* (385); (400); (480); (485); *dxšt-* "desert", loc. *dxšty'* (40); (265); *ptr-* "father" nom. *ptry* (205); (340); (385); (430), gen. *ptry* (15); (370); (375); (695), abl. *ptr'* (430), voc. *ptr'* (465); *rm-* "people" obl. *rmyy* (15); (545), dir. pl. *rmt'* (335); (505); (690); *žmn-* "time" acc. *žmnw* (155); (170); (795). For the second group, the cultured and religious lexicon, are attested: *by-* "God" nom. *byy* (15); (205); (245); (385); (430); (435); (610); (615), gen. *byy* (15); (30); (180); (270); (370); (375); (630), abl. *by'* (440); (565); (620), voc. *by'* (465); *dwrt-* "peace" nom. *dwrt'* (380); (385); (475), acc. *dwrt'* (450); loc. *dwrty'* (35).

Then few examples of *-ăkă* stems are regularly declined. *bnty* "servant":

---

[237] I think that the infinitive can be reconstructed without much doubt in the following example: Sogd. *nỵ qt' wnỵq m't 'ỵnỵ pr [qrwn]* and Syr. *l' mškḥ hw' hd' lm'bd* (620).

[238] See: Sims-Williams (1982; 1985: 195-200).

[239] The first who noticed it was Sims-Williams (1982: 69- 70; 76, n. 6). For an overview on the Iranian area see: Windfuhr (2009: 23).

[240] See: Chapter 3.3.3. Marking the direct object with oblique -y ending.

dir. sg. (655); (660) and voc. sg. *bnt'* (655), obl. pl. *bntyty* (155); (160); (650); (785); *γr'my* "money, wealth"[241]: dir. sg. *γr'my* (235); (240) and *γr'm'* "possessions, wealth"[242] : dir. sg. *γr'm'* (795).

3.3.2 Use of the nominative singular case instead of the old accusative in the light stems[243]

See the following examples: *qw bγỵ s'* (15); *qw 'brhm m'x ptrỵ s'* (25); *qw xỵpθ rmỵ s'* (30); *qw ysr'yl rmỵ s'* (70); *qw mn'bγỵ ptrỵ s'* (420); *qw bγỵ ptry s'*(435); *qw yw šyr sq'γ[r](ỵ) s'* (765)[244].

Generally speaking, the old acc. sg. m. in *–w* is attested in *E5* only in the following examples: *'nyw* < *'ny* "other": (155); (345); (645); *dstw* < *dst-* "hand": (400); *nyw* < *ny* "other, another"(225); *wyspw* < *wysp* "each, every, all": (420); (430); (650); and *žmnw* < *žmn-* "time" (155); (170); (795).

3.3.3 Marking the direct object with oblique -y ending[245]

The phenomenon is recorded in the scientific literature. Yoshida writes: "Regarding the animacy hierarchy, the latest stage of Sogdian, the language of the Christian Sogdian ms. *C5*[246], employs the oblique case for marking the direct objects which are both human and definite"[247]. Here, I hope to add further elements to the discussion. First, in listing all the attested cases, we can see that the phenomenon, which affects light, heavy and *-ăkă* stems, as well as personal pronouns except for the second person singular, assumes broader contours. Secondly I think that while one can undoubtedly arrive at a morphosyntactic development, on the other hand one must also consider the role played by the context of a translation literature. Without doubt *E5*

---

[241] According to Sims-Williams (forthcoming 2016).

[242] According to Sims-Williams (forthcoming 2016).

[243] This trend also affects the vocalic declension, not only in Christian Sogdian. See: Sims-Williams (1989a: 184). To put it in a wider perspective one should remember that the phenomenon is found in Old Khotanese and in Ossetic. See respectively: Emmerich (1968: 249); Sims-Williams (1990a) and Thordarson (2009). Focusing on the "conflation" (p. 130) of the nominative and accusative in Ossetic, Thordarson asserts that it is a "development in agreement with the general trend of the East Iranian languagues" (id.).

[244] In all the above mentioned cases, we can be certain that they are singular nominative cases of light stems is given by the East Syriac script conventions which allow a full vocalization: in this case, a point under *-y* stands for *i*.

[245] As regards the marking of the direct object in Iranian area, the literature is, as we may well imagine, more than full-bodied. For a general overview see: Haig (2008); and Windfuhr (2009: 33-35). For Bactrian see: Sims-Williams (2011b).

[246] i.e. *E5*.

[247] See: Yoshida (2009: 307).

represents a phase of the language where traditional structures of the nominal morphology disappeared and where, therefore, a strong need to re-categorise certain functions emerges to avoid the risk of the language becoming incomprehensible. Similarly, however, we are also facing with an entirely artificial syntax, completely unknown to the Sogdian language. Such artificiality, combined with a language which no longer has some traditional grammar structures, would have caused the text to become incomprehensible. That is why, in my opinion, sometimes the direct object is marked – in some less clear places – and in others – less ambiguous places – it is not.

The attested cases are the following:

- light stems: Sogd. *ny̨ qt' wnt'q 'šm'x pr spxšy̨ by̨ byyy*[248] "you cannot serve both God ..." and Syr. *l' mškḥyn 'ntwn l-mplḥ l-'lh'* "id."(240); Sogd. *'t c'nw wywsd'rt žyy̨rd'rt xypθ žwxšqt'y̨* "and when was the day he called his disciples" and Syr. *w-kd nght qr' l-tlm̈ydwhy* "id."(535). Finally: Sogd. *qt xw pcp'n m't qt z(r)yncy̨ ysr'yl rmyy* "he was the one to redeem the people of Israel" and Syr. *d-hwyw 'tyd hw' dnprqywhy l-ysryl* "he was the one to redeem Israel" (280), where the noun "people" is an addition of the Sogdian text.
- heavy stems: Sogd. *p't [wyspw 'dy qt žyštwc wnty žyšty d'rt] rwxšny'qy* "[who does wicked things hates] the light" and Syr. *kl gyr dsnÿt' 'bd sn' l-nwhr'* "id."(100); Sogd. *'t ywbd'rt m' xypθ'wnt pd'tqry̨ spncyrspny* "and our master commended the dishonest manager"and Syr. *w-šbḥ mrn l-rb byt' d-'wl'* "id."(225); Sogd. *ny̨ qt' wnt'q 'šm'x pr spxšy̨ by̨ byy̨ 't by̨ yr'my* "You cannot serve God and the wealth" and Syr. *l' mškḥyn 'ntwn l-mplḥ l-'lh' w-l-mmwn'* "id." (240); Sogd. *qt x'ny̨ xypθ'wnty žyy̨rd'rnt b'lz(ḅ)ẇb* "if they have called the master of the house Beelzebul" and Syr. *'n l-mrh dbyt' qrw b'lzbwb* "id."(355); Sogd. *'t tym prycng'zw fcmpdy* "and again I will leave the world"and Syr. *wtwb šbq 'n' l-'lm'* "id." (435); Sogd. *[zw wnyq qθ](')rm fcmpdy* "[I have overcome] the world" and Syr. *'n' zkth l-'lm'* "id."(450); Sogd. *qt pcyqṣnt wy̨šnty̨ xypθ'wnty* "who are waiting for their master" and Syr. *d-mskyn l-mrhwn* "id."(780);
- *-ăkă* stems : Sogd. *fšmd'rt qw wy̨šnt s' xypθ z'ty̨* "he sent his own son to them" and Syr. *šḍr lwthwn l-brh* "id."(165); Sogd. *c'nw šy̨ wy̨d'rnt z'ty̨* "when they saw the son" and Syr. *kd ḥz'why l-br'* (165); Sogd. *'t pt(ry̨) [xy](pθ z't)y̨y* "and the father his own child" and Syr. *w-'b' l-brh* "id." (340);

[248] Here and in all other examples, the underlining is mine.

- personal pronouns. 1 sg.: Sogd. *(m)n'yy žyšty nẏ'd'rt* "…it has hated me" and Syr. *l-y sn'* "id."(310); Sogd. *[qt] (m)n'y (pš)qyrd'rnt* "[If] they persecuted me" and Syr. *'n l-y rdpw* "id." (320)[249]; 3 sg.: Sogd. *['t 'nyd](’rnt) wnyy qt* "and they brought him who" and Syr. *w-'ytywhy l-hw d-*"id." (560); 1 pl.: Sogd. *qt wẋš't m'xy cn m'x s'nt* "that he should save us from our enemies" and Syr. *d-nprqn mn b'ldbbyn* "id."(20); Sogd. *qt pryẇnt .'ḅrz-bry m'xy wyt'p'mnty cn sm'n* "whereby the sunrise shall visit us from on high" and Syr. *d-b-hwn ns'rn dnḥ' mn rwm'* "id."(35); 2 pl.: Sogd. *pcγ'zntq' šm'xy pr wyšnty 'yqwncyq sy'qt* "they may receive you into the eternal dwellings" and Syr. *nqblwnkwn bmṭllyhwn dl'lm* "id."(230); Sogd. *p't zw [wyc]nd'rm šm'xy cn fcmpd c[y]myθy pyd'r žyšt(y)[ny'st šm]'xy fcmpd* "but I chose you out of the world, therefore the world hates you" and Syr. *'n' gyr gbytkwn mn 'lm' mṭl hn' sn' l-kwn 'lm'* "id." (315); Sogd. *zẇ fš'mmsqn šm'xy* "I sent you" and Syr. *'n' mšdr'n' l-kwn* "id."(325); (390); Sogd. *p't prbxšntq' šm'xy qw dtbrt s'* "for they will deliver you over to courts" and Syr. *mšlmyn l-kwn gyr lbyt dyn̈'* "id."(330); Sogd. *ptnwbntq' šm'xy* "beat you" and Syr. *nngdwnkwn* "id."(330); Sogd. *tym wyng' šm'xy* "I will see you again" and Syr. *dyn 'ḥzykwn* "id."(420); Sogd. *fry ny'd'rt šm'xy* "loved you" and Syr. *rḥm l-kwn* "id."(435); 3 pl.: Sogd. *'t ptxwsd'rt wyšnty*" and killed them"and Syr. *w-qṭl 'nwn* "id."(135); Sogd. *nyst wntyq' wyšnty* "He will put them to death" and Syr. *nwbd 'nwn* "id."(170); Sogd. *'brt' wyšnt(y)* "bring them" and Syr. *'ytw 'nwn* "id."(680); Sogd. *'t ywx'ytq' wyšnty yw cn dbtyq* "will separate them one from another" and Syr. *w-nprš 'nwn ḥd mn ḥd* "id."(690); Sogd. *'t synd'rt wyšnty* "and let them up" and Syr. *w-'sq 'nwn* "id"(760); Sogd. *[b]yrt wyšnty* "find them" and Syr. *nškḥ 'nwn*"id."(785);
- demonstrative pronoun *'yny*: Sogd. *(py)[š]t 'ynyy (ny) γrbymsqn m'x cn qw ms'xcy* lit. "but we do not know him where he comes from"

[249] I believe that these examples are particularly significant because, as Yoshida (2009: 306) writes, in Sogdian, "the two highest in the 'agency hierarchy', 'me' and 'you' (sg.), show special forms for the direct object *tāmā* and *tāfā*", forms almost no more attested in this Gospel lectionary (see below under "personal pronouns"). Such cases have already been recorded by the scientific literature (*GMS*: § 1340; Sundermann, 1974: 245), but what has been lacking up to now is, in my opinion, a comprehensive study of the phenomenon which explores, for example, how the disappearance of certain formations, such as *tāmā* etc., is accompanied by the creation of new ones, *(m)n'yy*.

and Syr. <u>*l-hn'*</u>*dyn l'yd'ynn ḥnn ṃn 'ymk'hw* "id." (610);

- numerals: Sogd. *p't qd'*<u>*ywy*</u> *žy̤šty̤ d'rt 't* <u>*dbty̤qy̤*</u> *fry̤* "for either he will hate <u>the first</u> and love <u>the second</u>" and Syr. *'w gyr* <u>*l-ḥd*</u> *nsn' w-*<u>*l-'ḥrn'*</u> *nrḥm* "id."(240).

Therefore, as regards the light stems and those in *ăkă*, we have examples of direct object marked in Sogdian by *-y* and in Syriac by *l-* in post-verbal position. This also applies to the heavy stems, except for (355) where the direct object occurs in preverbal position. The preverbal position and the *-y* marking in Sogdian and *l-* marking in Syriac, can also be found in those examples which concern the demonstrative pronoun *'yny* and the numerals.

As regards the personal pronouns we have the following situation. For the 1 sg. there are direct object cases marked in Sogdian by *-y* and in Syriac by *l-* in preverbal position. For the 3 sg. one direct object case marked in Sogdian by *-y* and in Syriac by *l-* in post-verbal position is attested. For the 1 pl. there are cases where a pronoun/object suffix corresponds to the marking of the Sogdian direct object by *-y* in post-verbal position. For the 2 pl. there is almost an alternation between cases which are similar to those found for the 1 pl. and the cases which attest, always in post-verbal position, a direct object marked by *-y* in Sogdian and by *l-* in Syriac. For the 3 pl., in post-verbal position, there are direct object cases marked by *-y* in Sogdian which correspond to unmarked forms in Syriac. It seems that the word-order does not affect the marking of the direct object.

Furthermore, I have recorded some cases where to an unmarked Sogdian object corresponds an unmarked one in Syriac: Sogd. *xwny '(dy) qt w'c(t) [xypθ db'mn θbr't] qw w(y' s)' (xw)-[ycq](q'ry̤* <u>*p)[w](st)y*</u> "who repudiates his wife gives her the repudiation <u>deed</u>" and Syr. *ṁn d-šr' 'ntth ntl l-ḣ* <u>*ktb'*</u> *d-dwll'* "id."(115); Sogd. *'t* <u>*b'y̤*</u> *pr dwstw wnty̤q' q(w ')[ny]t b'yd'ry̤t s'* "and entrust <u>the vineyard</u> to other vine-dressers" and Syr. <u>*krm'*</u> *nwḥd l-'ḥr̈n' plḥ̈'* "id." (170); Sogd. *p't ny̤ q'mmsq zw m(n)' r*<u>*[yž]*</u> *yw'r xwny̤ 'dy̤* <u>*ry̤ž*</u> *qt fšmd'rt mn'* "because I seek not <u>my</u> own <u>will</u> but the <u>will</u> of him who sent me" and Syr. *l' gyr b'' 'n'* <u>*ṣbyny*</u> *'l'* <u>*ṣbynh*</u> *dmn dšdryny* "id." (195); Sogd. *pyšt c'nw qt znd'rt* <u>*z'ty̤*</u> "but when she gave birth to her <u>son</u>" and Syr. *m' dyldt dyn* <u>*br'*</u> "id" (415); Sogd. *qt šm'x fry ny'd'ryšt'* <u>*mn'*</u> " because you have loved <u>me</u>" and Syr. *d-'ntwn rḥmtwnny̱* "id." (435)[250]; Sogd. *p't šm'ry̤(q) m't(n)t qt* <u>*w't*</u>

[250] This is particulary interesting because the direct object was expressed by a marked form in both the Syriac and the Sogdian in the preceding phrase: Sogd. *p't xw by̤y̤ ptrỵ̇ fry̤ ny'd'rt* <u>*šm'xy̤*</u> *qt šm'x fry ny'd'ryšt'* <u>*mn'*</u> "indeed God the Father loved <u>you</u> because you have loved <u>me</u>" and Syr. *hw̤ gyr 'b' rḥm* <u>*l-kwn*</u> *d-'ntwn rḥmtwn*<u>*ny*</u> "indeed the Father loved <u>you</u> because you have loved <u>me</u>" (435).

wỵnntqn "and thought they saw a spirit" and Syr. *sbryn hww gyr d-rwḥ' ḥzyn* "id." (480).

It is significant what happens in Sogd. *'t c'nw nỵ byrd'rnt (wyn)[y] tmp'ry* "and when they did not find his body"(275). As we can see, the scribe deletes *–y*, requiring us to read *tmp'r*. The deletion of what should have been the oblique case ending, and in this Gospel lectionary also the marker of the direct object, could indicate that this direct object marking is an *in fieri* phenomenon, not yet settled. On the other hand, however, I believe that, contrary to instances, here there is no possibility of confusing the object for the subject and vice versa. The context is clear. If we look at the corresponding Syriac sentence, it sounds: *w-kd l' 'škḥ pgrh* "and how they did not find his body", i.e. an example where the object is not introduced by *l-*. For this reason it may be worthwhile paying briefly attention to other linguistic traditions in the Iranian area. Skjærvø writes: "In the *Psalter* and Manichean Middle Persian, as well as in Parthian, the direct object is often indicated by the preposition *ō*, including in agential constructions, but the use may be restricted to certain verbs, since the verbs such as 'to see, bind', etc., apparently do not take it. It is not clear to what extent this usage may have been influenced by the Aramaic/Syriac use of the preposition *li-*"[251].

It is also true that the following examples show the opposite of what has been said: Sogd. *'t bỵrd'(r)n[t ywnt](s)nw žwxšqt' qt '(w)štyt m'tnt 't x'nt (')dỵt qt dn wỵšntỵ prw (c')[nw] w'byntqn* "and they found the eleven disciples and those who were with them gathered together, saying in the meantime" and Syr. *w-'škḥw l-ḥd'sr d-knyšyn w-l'ylyn d-'mhwn kd 'mryn* "And they found the Eleven and those who were gathered with them saying in the meantime" (305).

3.3.4 Occurrences of cases in the adpositional phrases.

In addition to completely regular forms, the Gospel lectionary *E5* shows cases where prepositions, postpositions and adpositional phrases are indifferently used both in an unmarked case (no ending), and in direct and oblique case, a situation enabled by the substantial cases loss, indeed, of their syntactic value. These are the instances:

- *cn*, prep.[252]: *cn m'x s'nt* "from our enemies"(20); *cn b'γ* "from the

[251] See: Skjærvø (2009: 233). Of course, the main aim of this book is to collect and contextualize data with particular regard to the Sogdian Gospel lectionary *E5*, nevertheless I think that this point calls for further investigations.

[252] As it is well known, it usually governs the ablative or, at least, an oblique case.

vineyard" (175); *cn wyšnt* "from them"[253] (300); *cn mrtxmyt* "from men" (330); *p't w'xš pwxsty m'tnt cn cxwdt* "for it had been agreed by the Jews" (590);

❖ *qw.....s'*, prep. + postp.[254]: *qw wyny s'* "to him"(50);

The Manichaean Sogdian is not exempt from such cases[255]; even Yaghnōbī seems to use prepositions and postpositions both in the direct and in the oblique case[256].

3.3.5 Limited use of post-positions

In the Gospel lectionary *E5* is attested an increased use of prepositions and a lower use of postpositions. These are the postpositions identified: *myd'ny* "among, in the midst of" (60); (165); (250); (330); (380); (475); (570); *nbnt* "with, at, on" (295); (495); (520); (660); (675); *pcrw* "instead of, for"(125); (585); *pšys'* "after" (60); (65); (455); (745); (760); *ptryt* "against" (125); *pyrnm* "before" (150); (275); *pyrnms'* "before, in front of" (25); (245); (270); (335); (370); (375); (675); (680); (680/685); (765); *pyrnms'* correlated with *cn* "formerly, before" (465).

There are also some postpositions which are exclusively attested in adpositional phrases. This is the case, for example, for the postposition *prm* attested only in correlation with *wytwr qw* "up to, as far as, until"(40); (90); (265); (345) as well as in the adpositional phrase *wytwr qw qšy prm* "until now, so far" (425); (485); for the post-position *prw* attested only if correlated with the proposition *dn* with the meaning of "with, together with" (15); (130); (295); (300); (305); (380); (385); (395); (425); (430); (475); (495); (545); (610); (635); (670); (690); (755); (770); for the postposition *pyd'r* attested only in correlation with the preposition *cn* "on, about, concerning, for, because" (280); (290); (345); (350); (380); (405); (415); (430); (495); (750); and with the prepositioned pronouns *cymyθy pyd'r* "for this reason, so, therefore" (175); (315) and *cywyθ pyd'r* "because, since, for, therefore" (70); (210); (245); (295); (585); (590); and, finally, for the postposition *s'r/s'* therein attested only in correlation with the postposition *qw* "to, at" (5); (10);

---

[253] In the text I have adopted a more free translation "from their sight": the phrase sounds "and he disappeared from them".

[254] As it is well known, *qw...s'* generally governs a direct case.

[255] I found instances during my research for my MA thesis on the nominal morphosyntax of Manichaean Sogdian.

[256] Without going into the question of the relationships between Sogdian and Yaghnōbī, particularly interesting from the nominal morphosyntax point of view, is that even in this case the phenomenon here observed embraces a wider perspective.

(20); (25); (30); (35); (40); (50); (55); (65); (70); (110); (115); (120); (125); (130); (135); (140); (145); (150); (155); (160); (165); (170); (175); (180); (185); (190); (195); (200); (220); (225); (230); (235); (240); (245); (250); (255); (270); (275); (280); (285); (290); (295); (300); (305); (310); (325); (330); (335); (340); (345); (350); (385); (390); (395); (410); (405); (420); (425); (430); (435); (440); (445); (450); (455); (460); (475); (480); (495); (500); (505); (510); (515); (525); (535); (550); (555); (560); (565); (570); (585); (595); (605); (615); (625); (630); (635); (645); (650); (655); (665); (670); (675); (680); (685); (695); (700); (715); (720); (735); (740); (755); (765); (770); (775); (780); (785); (795).

Broadly reasoning on these data, it is interesting to note that in *C2* (p. 220, 224) the postpositions *prw* and *s'r/s'* – in *C2* as *s'* form – are still attested while the postposition *pyd'r* is always attested in correlation with the preposition *cn* (*C2*, p. 223). Considering the Manichaean Sogdian, and in particular the *Sogdian Tales*[257] and *Ein manichäisches Bet- und Beichtbuch*[258], all postpositions are still attested alone although there is a predominance, in their use, of adpositional phrases. For example, in the *Sogdian Tales*, the postposition *prw* occurs five times, three of which with the preposition *dn;* the postposition *s'r* occurs twelve times, nine of which with the preposition *kw*. Similarly, in *Ein manichäisches Bet- und Beichtbuch*, the postposition *pyd'r* is attested nine times, six of which in connection with the preposition *cn*. Admitting the necessity of a detailed study which includes all Sogdian varieties and which can yield clear percentages, I am convinced that the progressive decrease in the use of postpositions is an element to be considered from a diachronic perspective[259]. At the same time I am convinced that in this case, too, a factor owed to the translation context comes into the picture. After all, Syriac has not postpositions but prepositions which are translated, in this Gospel lectionary, by prepositions, adpositional phrases and, in some cases, even by postpositions[260]. Moreover, if we turn to other types of Sogdian texts,

---

[257] See: Henning (1945: 1977).

[258] See: Henning (1945: 1977).

[259] Whatever perspective one takes on Yaghnōbī, it is a fact that almost all its postpositions derive from Tajik and that they are mostly used in correlation with prepositions. See: Bielmeier (1989: 486). That means that, regarding the use of prepositions, postpositions and adpositional phrases, Yaghnōbī displays a similar trend as the Gospel lectionary *E5* and therefore of the most recent Sogdian phase, i.e. the eleventh century. Stilo himself (2006: 320), as regards the circumpositions use in the Iranian linguistic area, also cites Yaghnōbī, while admitting, rightly, the need for further studies in this direction.

[260] For all the concordances, see: *Sogdian-Syriac Glossary*.

coming from more or less the same geographical area and roughly coeval, we find a diametrically opposite situation, i.e. an increased use of postpositions against a limited use of prepositions. Cases in point are the Turkish-Sogdians documents coming from Dun-huang and dating to between the ninth and tenth centuries, published by Hamilton and Sims-Williams in 1990, as well as three Manichean letters coming from Bäzäklik that show, according to Yoshida (2009a), a strong Turkish influence. Advancing the Turkish languages influence, Yoshida explains the increased use of postpositions in the aforementioned texts. One might recall at this point the definition given by Stilo concerning the Iranian linguistic area in the following words: "Iranian as buffer zone between the universal typologies of Turkic and Semitic"[261]. In his investigation of several isoglosses within the Iranian speaking areas (position of demonstrative adjectives, numerals, adverb + adjective, object + verb, relative clause + noun, object + adposition), Stilo demonstrates how the mixed typologies found in the Iranian speaking areas go back to the Semitic linguistic contacts in western area and to the Turkic linguistic contacts to the eastern area. Stilo takes into account the modern and contemporary period, but we can apply the same consideration for the bi- and multilingual context in the Turfan oasis in the Middle Iranian linguistic area (with the difference that among the Semitic language we have to consider Syriac instead of Arabic).

3.3.6 Group-inflections

There are cases where in a sequence adjective + noun or adjective + adjective + noun, only the last one has the case and number endings. These are the examples attested in *E5*: *xypθ rmyy* "his people" (15); *pr xypθ zprt byẉnyṭỵ qwc'* "by the mouth of his holy prophets" (20)[262]; *(x)ypθ žwxšqt'(y)* "his disciples" (135); *nỵt bntỵtỵ* "other servants" (160); *xwštr dynd'rt* "chief priests" (270); *'t d't(br)t 't xšywnỵtỵ pyrnms'* "before governors and kings"(330/335); *xyp[θ] p'dyt* "his feet" (485); *xypθ w'(x)št* "his words" (525); *xypθ žwxšqt'ỵ* "his disciples" (535); *'t γrf žwxšqt'ỵ '(w)'zỵ 't γrf rmỵỵ 'w'zỵ* "and a multitude of many disciples and a multitude of many people" (545); *qw xypθ žwxšqt' (s')* "to his disciples" (685); *pr xypθ γwbty'* "in His glory" (685); *zprt frỵštỵt* "holy angels" (690); *xypθ γrywỵ [pcrw]* "for his

[261] See: Stilo (2004: 35).

[262] With particular regard to this example and to *zprt frỵštỵt* "holy angels" (690), Sims-Williams supposes *zprt* for **zprtt*. Personal communication 25.01.2016. However, until there are more examples in the Christian Sogdian manuscript tradition this remains purely hypothetical.

soul" (750); *pr xypθ žmnw* "at the proper time" (795).

This kind of construction is also attested in Manichaean Sogdian[263] and, although it is most frequent with the possessive and quantity adjectives, in this Gospel lectionary it is also attested even with the qualifying adjective[264]. I want to emphasize, finally, that even in this case, we are dealing with a phenomenon not unusual to the eastern Iranian area: cases of group inflections are also attested in Khotanese[265] and in Ossetic[266].

3.3.7 Real "agglutination" clues or tendency to "justify" the lines?

The Gospel lectionary *E5* shows a small number of cases which present a combination between pronoun and/or noun + postposition and a combination between verb + personal pronoun. They are the following, respectively: *qw bγ'[nyq wš]tm'xs'* "into the kingdom of God" (150); *qw šm'xs'* "to you" (320); *qw x'nt b'γd'ṛyts'* "to those vine-dressers" (170); *'ỵštyw* "you are" (220); (225); *šwỵqm't* "he was going" (290); *qtyštyw* "you received" (560). The explanations can be twofold: either they are cases where the handwriting shows how these combinations were actually perceived, or how they began to be actually perceived, i.e. as one single syntagmatic units; or all this is due to the trend, typical of the Christian texts, as well as the Manichaean corpus, of having all writing lines with the same length and width. In the case of verb + personal pronoun combination, *'ỵštyw* (230, 235); *šwỵqm't* (290); *qtyštyw* (560), I am more inclined to consider the first hypothesis; in the case of combination between pronoun + postposition, I am more inclined to the second hypothesis; the same hypothesis is also true for *qw x'nt b'γd'ṛyts'* "to those vine-dresser" (170) but, in this case, I would affirm it with less security.

Surely it would be useful to reflect on data resulting from more substantial material. It would be interesting to note to what extent there are

---

263 See: *GMS* (§ 1639).

264 See: Sims-Williams (1982). In an attempt to explain the factors which determine the choice between a full morphological agreement and a *group inflection*, Sims-Williams says that one of the main distinctions is between qualifying adjectives (which, at least, agree in number, if not in the case) and determining adjectives often in unflexed form. Instead, in this Gospel lectionary, both cases are recorded.

265 See: Emmerick (1968: 258; 2009: 399-400).

266 See: Thordarson, F. (2009: 87; 112). According to Thordarson, this phenomenon "must be seen in connection with the development of the agglutinative morphology of the noun" (ibid.: 112). Thordarson also briefly explains the phenomenon in the Turkic languages, in Tocharian group and in the Caucasian neighbor languages of Ossetic (ibid.: 113).

other similar cases in the Christian Sogdian material[267] and whether such combinations occurred in conjunction with a particular position in the writing line and/or in conjunction with particular combinations of letters and, if so, which ones. For example, taking into consideration the above mentioned Manichaean texts of *Sogdian Tales*, I have observed three similar cases which were more justifiable, in my opinion, by the need to standardize the writing line length and to the particularity, typical of the Manichean handwriting, of combining, indeed, some letters such as *n*, *k*, *s*, *t*, *p*[268].

3.3.8 Personal pronouns.

- *case syncretism also in the inflection of the personal pronouns, especially in adpositional phrases, with resulting alternation of regular and irregular forms.* Below are listed all the examples of the irregular ones[269]. For the 1 sg.: *qw mn's'* (75); (420); (735). For the 2 sg.: *pr tw'* (50); *[qw] t(w') s'* (600). For the 3 sg m. and. f..: *wyny* (505; 520); *qw wyny s'* (50); (65); (130); (295); *qw wy' s'* (115); *-šy̱* (115). For the 1 pl.: *m'x nbnt* (295); for the 3 pl.: *cn wyšnt* (300).
- *disappearance of the prepositional pronominal forms such as t'm', t'f'*[270] etc., still well attested, however, in *C2* (p. 227; 237; 238).
- *exceptions to the Telegdi rule*[271] *about their use after the present and future forms.* As is well known, Telegdi has clearly demonstrated how, in Christian Sogdian, the presence or absence of the personal pronouns after the present and the future depends exclusively on the original Syriac text where they function as personal endings of participial forms[272]. While this Gospel lectionary follows the general rule, there are some exceptions. In most of them the personal pronoun precedes the verb: Sogd. *zw sn'm θbr'msqn* "I baptize" and

[267] With particular regard to noun+ postposition *s'*, Sims-Williams directs my attention on several cases attested in bilingual – Sogdian and Syriac – Gospel lectionaries. Personal communication 25.01.2016.

[268] The passages involved concern: *M 135 /r/8 kww wšṭm'xs''r*; *M 5270 /r/5 kww 'βṭ'myδpr[m]*; *M 5730/1 /v/12 qyr'ns'r*. When I was working on my MA thesis I found, in Manichaean Sogdian, yet another case of this kind: *M 129/v/7/ kww wšṭm'xs'r*.

[269] The oblique direct object cases are excluded because separately discussed.

[270] If we accept the reading of Sims-Williams in (570) we have an example of *t'f'* as attested form in this Gospel lectionary too.

[271] See: Telegdi (1938: 205-211).

[272] See: Thackston (1999: 38-39). In fact, as already explained by Telegdi in the afore-mentioned study, the indicative present to the 3 sg. is not followed by the personal pronoun because, in Syriac, the 3 sg. is an exception.

Syr. *'n' m'md 'n'* "id." (55); Sogd. *zw 'yžnty ny 'ym* "I am not worthy" and Syr. *'n' l' šw' 'n'* "id."(60); Sogd. *zẉ θbrng'* "I will give back" and Syr. *'n' yhb 'n'* "id." (510); Sogd. *tγw ywcẏq'* "you would teach" and Syr. *'nt mlp 'nt* "id.(625)"; Sogd. *tγw wrnẏsqn* "you believe" and Syr. *'nt mhymn 'nt* "id."(630); Sogd. *šm'x wẏnt'-sqn* "you see" (635) and Sogd. *šm'x ptγwšt'* (640) "you listened" are the translation, respectively, of Syr. *ḥzyn 'ntwn* and Syr. *šm'yn 'ntwn*. Telegdi (1938: 211) had already explained such cases by emphasizing the extraneousness of the Sogdian language to the repetition of the personal pronoun in the pre-and post-verbal position. In my view, it is possible that the pre-verbal position has been preferred by the Sogdian, at least in some cases, to emphasize the new sentence compared to what it has been said before[273]. In (635/640) the whole sentence sounds: Sogd. *[q'md'rt qt w](ẏ)[n]((ẏ)[n](t) ['yc qt] šm'x wẏnt'-sqn 't nẏ wẏd'r(n)[t 't] pr ptγwš 'yc qt šm'x ptγwšt' ['t] [ny] [pt](γ)wšd'rnt* "they longed to see, what *you*[274] see, and did not see it, and to hear what *you* hear, and did not hear it", translation of the Syriac sentence *'trgrgw d-nḥzwn mdm d-ḥzyn 'ntwn w-l' ḥzw w-l-mšm' mdm d-šm'yn 'ntwn w-l' šm'w* "id.". These cases seem to be quite unpredictable, as we have also the following examples: Sogd. *t(γ)w cw w'(b)[y](sq t)[γw]* "You, what do you say..." and Syr. *'nt mn' 'mr 'nt* (570); Sogd. *[q]('mt'sqn) šm'x* "you want" and Syr. *ṣbyn 'ntwn* "id."(605); but also Sogd. *q'mt'sqn* "you want" and Syr. *ṣbyn 'ntwn* "id." (605).

3.3.9 Alternation of singular~plural after the cardinal numbers.

This Gospel lectionary presents an alternation of singular and plural forms after the cardinal numbers; this has already been attested in *GMS* (*§§*: 1662-1674) not only for the Christian but also for the Manichaean and Buddhist Sogdian texts. While Gershevitch admits an equivalent alternation of singular~plural after the cardinal numbers, he identifies some guidelines that are also found in *E5*. Thus, for example, Gershevitch recognizes an increased use of the singular with "nouns of time and measure"[275]. Precisely to these two semantic spheres belong the singular nouns *γwdy* "container" (220); (225); *qysrq'n* "denarius" (510); *myθ* "day" (275); *p'r* "measure" (225);

[273] Sims-Williams suggests a function as "contrastive emphasis", a definition which I fully adopt. Sims-Williams, personal communication, 25.01.2016.

[274] The coursive in both cases is mine.

[275] *ibid.*

pcm'r "measure of weight" (650); (655); (660); (675). To Gershevitch's observation that the oblique forms tend to be in the plural after the cardinal, the singular oblique *my[θ]y* (760) is an exception. Another exception is the singular noun *xypθ'wnt* "owner, lord, master" (240) which, as a noun, again according to Gershevitch, "is not so frequently associated with numerals or a given numeral" and, therefore, could also be attested in the plural form. In perfect accordance with Gershevitch's observation are, however, the following plural attestations: *qθt* "cities" (655); 660); *sryt* "heads" (135); *žwxšqt'* "disciples" (305); *x'nt* "those" (540)[276].

3.3.10 The strong productiveness of the Sogdian suffix -'mnty.

According to *GMS* (§: 1100), the Sogdian suffix *-'mnty* is attested in the Manichaean and the Christian tradition. In a previous study[277] I already stressed the presence of deverbative substantives, formed by present stem + deverbative abstract suffix *-'mnty* used to translate Syriac abstracts. I have interpreted the strong and productive development of such formation in Christian Sogdian as a clear attempt to translate the Syriac text source as faithfully as possible. Just to give some examples: Sogd. *'xz'mnty/ 'γz'mnty* (the latter is the form attested in *E5*) "Resurrection" for Syriac *qymt'* "id."; Sogd. *'šty'mnty* "indication, manifestation" translates the Syriac *tḥwty'* "id."; Sogd. *wxš'mnty* "salvation" for Syriac *pwrqn'* "id.".

At this point it is interesting to consider what happen in the so-called Turco-Sogdian. As already pointed out by Hamilton and Sims-Williams[278] and by Yoshida[279] the most salient linguistic feature of the Turco-Sogdian documents (including tree Manichaean letters[280]), is the wide use of non-finite verb forms, the clearest proof of the influence of the Turkish language on the Sogdian one. Among these non-finite verb forms we can find verbal noun ending with the Sogdian suffix *-'mnty*. Yoshida takes as example the Sogdian *tsy'm'nty* "entering", a word which is attested only in the Turco-Sogdian material: *srδy sry pw(šnw nw)[y] myδ tsy'm'nty prnxwnty ZY'my'kcykw wβ'tw* "in the beginning of the year, may the entering of the new day of (the month of) Pušnu (i.e. the first luni-solar month) be fortunate and happy!"[281]. Yoshida compares the Sogdian forms ending with the suffix -

276 As concerns the pronouns, the use of plural is also attested in *C2* (p. 114).

277 See: Barbati (2014: 113).

278 See: Hamilton- Sims-Williams (1990: 10-11).

279 See: Yoshida (2009a: 578).

280 See: Yoshida (2009a).

281 See: Yoshida (2009a: 580).

'mnty with the Old Turkic infinitive ending with *-mäk/-maq* and asserts: "Therefore, the Sogdian construction is most likely to be based on the Turkish idiom"[282]. In other words, a suffix which is attested in the Sogdian language becomes more productive more or less in the same area and at the same time in two Sogdian traditions: in the Christian one in order to translate Syriac abstracts and in the Turco-Sogdian one in order to translate Old Turkic infinitives. Again, this is only another example for the importance of discussing some linguistic phenomena in a broader perspective, in accordance with Jeremiás'observation in her study of the pronominal clitics in Persian, where she writes: "In a descriptive or structurally oriented analysis these variations are themselves meaningless, but in a broader sense or perspective they become historically significant"[283].

3.4 Syntax

The macro-element of immediate visibility and understanding is the exact retention of the Syriac word-order. The result is a completely artificial syntax that puts the verb at the beginning of the sentence, and not at the end as we would expect according to the Sogdian language rules[284]. What we will discuss here are, however, those cases where the Sogdian text, while faithfully translating the sacred text, mainly diverges from the Syriac one because it maintains its grammar structures or because of stylistic choices.

3.4.1 Avoidance of Syriacisms

- the Sogdian text does not adopt the Syriac genitive construction with an additional possessive pronoun[285]. These are the examples: Sogd. *'t pr s't yhwdẏ γrẏ* "and through all the hill country of Judea" and Syr. *w-b-klh ṭwr' d-yhwd* "lit. and for all its mountainous region of Judea" (10); *pr dwyd xẏpθ bntẏ x'nẏ* "on the house of David, his servant" and Syr. *b-byth d-dwẏd 'bdh* "lit. on his house, of David, his servant" (20); Sogd. *ywḥnn-'ẏ wy(c)['w](qy')* "the testimony of John" and Syr. *shdwth d-yḥwhnn* "lit. his testimony, of John" (40); Sogd. *p't 'ẏnẏ fcmbdẏ 'žwnt* "for the sons of this world" and Syr. *bnẅhy gyr d-'lm' hn'* "for, his sons, of this world" (230); Sogd. *cn*

---

[282] *ibid.*

[283] See: Jeremiás (1995: 333).

[284] See: Barbati (2010; 2015).

[285] The same phenomenon is found in the Pahlavi psalter. See: Durkin-Meisterernst (2006: 14). For the Syriac construction see: Thackston (1999: 20)

rwxšny'qy 'žwnt "than the sons of the light" and Syr. *mn bnẅhy d-nwhr'* "than his sons, of the light" (230);

- adjectives maintain their position. For example, the demonstrative adjective continues to precede the noun to which it refers where, in Syriac, it can either precede or follow it[286]: Sogd. *'yny rync'q* "this child" and Syr. *ṭly' hn'* "id."(10); Sogd. *'yny fcmbdy* "of this world" and Syr. *d-'lm' hn'* "id." (230); Sogd. *cn 'yny pd'ty γr'my* "with this dishonest wealth" and Syr. *mn mmwn' hn' d-'wl'* (235). Similarly, the qualifying adjective precedes, as a rule, the noun to which it refers where, in Syriac, it follows[287]: Sogd. *šyry mwd[w]* "good wine" and Syr. *ḥmr' ṭb'* "good wine" (90); Sogd. *qw dwr wy'q s'* "toward a far away place" and Syr. *l-dwk' rḥyq'* "id."(290); Sogd. *qw yw šyr*[288] *sq'γ[r](y) s'* "on a very high mountain" and Syr. *l-ṭwr' rm'* "on a high mountain" (765). So the Sogdian possessive adjective, which often translates a Syriac enclitic, precedes, as a rule, the noun to which it refers: Sogd. *[tw](') qwrθy* "your tunic" and Syr. *kwṭynk* "id." (130); Sogd. *tw'nγwnty* "your tunic" and Syr. *mrṭwṭk* "id." (130); Sogd. *pr wyšnty x'nyt* "in their houses" and Syr. *b-btÿhwn* "id." (220); Sogd. *cn wyny xypθ'wnty pwrc'wnt* "between his master's debtors" and Syr. *mn ḥÿb' d-mrh* "id." (220). The same applies to the numerals: Sogd. *ẏw fṡx* "one mile" and Syr. *myl' ḥd* "id." (130);
- Sogdian also retains its number. The Sogdian noun for "sky, heaven", *sm'n*, for example, is properly singular despite the corresponding Syriac *šm̈y'* which is always plural: (75); (110); (375);
- Sogdian determiner + noun and Syr. noun + determiner. Sogd. *(xw)[ycq](q'ry) p[w](st)y* "repudiation deed" and Syr. *ktb' d-dwll'* "id." (115); Sogd. *nyšqr'n cn (xwr)wny pt[y](rn)* "except on the ground of adultery" and Syr. *mlt' d-znywt'* "id." (120); Sogd. *pr pdq' myθ* "in the day of judgment" and Syr. *bywm' d-dyn'* "id." (325); Sogd. *cn fcmpd 'γ'zy pyr-s'* "before the foundation of the world" and Syr. *mn qdm trm̈yth d-'lm'* "id." (465);
- omission of Syriac pleonastic dative. The Syriac pleonastic dative, often used with the verbs of motion[289], is omitted in the Sogdian

[286] See: Thackston (1999: 30).
[287] See: Thackston (1999: 44).
[288] As it has been noted, the Sogdian *šyr* "very" has no correspondence with the Syriac text.
[289] See: Nöldeke (1898: 224) and Thackston (1999: 58-59).

translation: Sogd. *[γrbt](') (qt) pnt pr'γt qw d(b)[ry s']* "know that it is right at the gates" and Syr. *d'w d-mṭt l-h l-tr'* "id."(255); Sogd. *cywyθ pyd'r qt myθ qšỵ 'wrs{<d'r>}t* "for the day is now far spent" and Syr. *mṭl d-ywm' hš' rkn l-h* "id." (295); Sogd. *b'wnyq xcỵ žwxšqy qt bỵ w'nc'nw wynỵ (x)wštỵ* "it is enough for the disciple to be like his teacher" and Syr. *spq l-ḣ l-tlmyd' d-nhw' 'yk rbh* "id." (350).

3.4.2 Name of the people instead that of the country

Sogd. *qw ysr'ylỵqt s'* "to the Israelites" and Syr. *lwt 'ysryl* "to Israel"(40); Sogd. *nỵ 'y{<m>}sntq' s't ysr'ỵlỵqt(ỵ) kθt* "you will not have gone through all the cities of the Israelites" and Syr. *l' tšlmwn 'nÿn klhyn mdÿnt' d-byt 'ysryl* "you will not have gone through all cities of Israel"(350).

3.4.3 Relative clause

Sogd. *'t yw 'ync' qt šỵ n'm m't' mrθ'*. lit. "and a woman whose name was Martha" and Syr. *w-'ntt' d-šmh mrt'* lit. "and a woman of her name Martha" (520); Sogd. *mrtỵ qt (šy) n'm m't* "lit. a man whose name was" and Syr. *gbr' d-šmh* lit. "a man of his name" (550).

3.4.4 Final clause[290]

Sogd. *qt* + subj. = Syr. *d-* + impf.: Sogd. *qt θbr't qw m'x s'* "to grant us" and Syr. *d-nṫl l-n* "id."(25).

Sogd. *qt* + opt. = Syr. *d-* + impf.: Sogd. *[qt šy] psỵnt* "to ask him" and Syr. *d-nš'lwnyhy* "id."(45).

3.4.5 Expression for possibility, probability

Sogd. *qt* + opt. pot. = Syr. *d-* + part. *mškḥ* : Sogd. *nỵst bntỵ qt qt' wnỵ dw' xypθ'wnt pr spxšỵ* "no servant can serve two masters" and Syr. *lyt 'ḃd' d-mškḥ l-tr̈yn mr̈wn l-mplḥ* "id." (240).

3.4.6 Expression for wish, desire

Sogd. *qt* + subj. = Syr. *d-* + pres. part.: Sogd. *['t xwny 'dy] qt q'ṃ̇[t]*[291] "[and if anyone] would" and Syr. *w-ṁn d-ṣḃ'* "id." (130).

---

[290] The construction *pr* + infinitive has already been discussed in *3.2.5 Tenses and moods in Sogdian and in Syriac*.

[291] The Sogdian subjunctive is easily identifiable thanks to the diacritics placed above and below *m*.

3.4.7 Mechanical translation: the case of qt

qt. Mechanical translation of the Syriac *d-* which however is linked to *'yk* and *'ykn'* in *'yk d-* "as, just as, lik" and in *'ykn' d-* "as", both rendered in Sogdian by *w'nc'nw* "id.": (1); (20); (50); (190); (385).

qt. Mechanical translation of the Syriac *d-* which however is linked to *mṭl* in *mṭl d-* "because, since, for", rendered in Sogdian by *cywyθ pyd'r*: (70); (210); (245); (295); (585);

qt. Mechanical translation of the Syriac *d-* which however is linked to *m'* in *m' d-* "when, at such time", rendered in Sogdian by *c'nw*: (170); (215); (230); (255); (345); (415); (510); (685); (780).

3.4.8 p't "for, but, however, indeed" and pyšt "but, then, afterwards, while"

The Sogdian conjunctions *p't* "for, but, however, indeed" and *pyšt* "but, then, afterwards, while" occur always at the initial position against the corresponding Syriacs which are, respectively, *gyr* and *dyn*, always placed in second position. *p't*: (1); (30); (100); (150); (180); (195); (205); (230); (240); (275); (315); (330); (345); (430); (480); (590); (595); (610); (660); (720); (745). *pyšt*: (35); (115); (130); (140); (150); (165); (205); (245); (270); (280); (330); (335); (345);(370); (375); (385); (395); (415); (425); (465); (515); (525); (530); (550); (560); (565); (575); (580); (600); (605); (635); (640); (680); (685); (765).

3.4.9 w'nw "thus"

In the Sogdian Gospel lectionary *E5* the adverb *w'nw* "thus" is only found in the idiomatic expression such as, for instance, "thus spoke the Lord Jesus" and represents an addition of the Sogdian text which has no correspondence in Syriac[292]: (10); (15); (50); (55); (65); (70); (90); (135); (145); (165); (170); (215); (220); (225); (245); (250); (270); (280); (285); (290); (300); (325); (380); (390); (395); (435); (445); (460); (475); (480); (490); (500); (510); (515); (525); (550); (565); (570); (575); (580); (595); (600); (605); (610); (625); (630); (635); (645); (655); (660); (665); (675); (715); (730); (740); (800).

3.4.10 cwt "whether"

The Sogdian conjunction *cwt* "whether" attested in the Gospel lectionary *E5*, has no correspondence in Syriac: (45); (135); (175); (605).

---

[292] See also the *Sogdian- Syriac Glossary*.

3.5 Terminology

About this Gospel lectionary, in one of my previous studies[293] I discussed the creation of a proper terminology through the following devices: widespread use of generic terms vs. technical terms and loans; creation of *ad hoc* terms and verbal periphrastic forms to replace a lexicon portion missing in Sogdian; their own stylistic choices deviating from the original text. In this section I attempt to point out and explore some aspects of the terminology while taking into account the two essential areas in which we move: accuracy in rendering the original sacred text, and the need for a basic understanding by the community considering the missionary mould of the Church of the East. The following representative examples may serve to highlight these aspects.

3.5.1 Sogd. n'šyrγwzy "the one who hates", "ill-wisher"

The term is not attested in *C2* and is recorded in the Gharib dictionary with the meaning of "enemy (not friend)"[294] according to *E5* where it is attested in plural oblique case as *n'šyrγwzyty̤* (20). In the same passage of *E5*, just one line before, we find the Sogdian *s'n* for "enemy". In my opinion the translator, using *n'šyrγwzy*, wanted to emphasize a precise semantic nuance which, not accidentally, is found in the Syriac text from which the Sogdian one is translated. The Sogdian *n'šyrγwzy*, in plural oblique case *n'šyrγwzyty̤*, translates the 3 m. pl. pres. part., *sn'yn*, from the root *sn* "to hate"[295], while, in the previous line, the Sogdian *s'n*, in plural direct case *s'nt*, translates the Syriac term for "enemy" *b'ldbb'*[296]. For this reason I prefer to translate "the one who hates" and not "the enemy". Sims-Williams suggests "ill-wisher"[297].

3.5.2 Sogd. p'cγny "answer"

The Sogdian term is highly specialized and means "answer": so in *E5* (50), *C2* (p. 218); Gharib[298]. In this Gospel lectionary *p'cγny* translates *ptgm'*, an Iranian loan word entered into the Syriac[299] language. Brockelmann gives

[293] See: Barbati (2014: 111-114).

[294] See: Gharib (1995: 233).

[295] According to Brockelmann "odit". See: Brockelmann (1928: 483).

[296] According to Brockelmann "calumniator, adversaries, hostis, inimicus". See: Brockelmann (1928: 83-84).

[297] Personal communication 25th January 2016.

[298] See: Gharib (1995: 256).

[299] See: Ciancaglini (2008: 242-243).

the following meanings "1. verbum; 2. sententia; 3. versiculus; 4. res"[300]; so also Payne- Smit: "1) dictum, verbum; 2) res, negotium; 3) responsum; 4) ratio; 5) folium; 6) comma, membrum versus, sententia brevior quam versus"[301]. This is a large semantic field covered by the Sogdian term *w'xš*. See: *C2* (p. 229): "word, speech, remark, sentence, verse, thing". In *E5 w'xš* is also used according to the meanings listed above and translates the Syriac *mlt'*[302]: (270); (495); (525). Returning now to the initial passage, (50), the presence of *p'cγny* can be seen as a translator choice who wanted to use the term with the more accurate and appropriate meaning according to the context.

3.5.3 Sogd. qt'ny "sin"

The Syriac word for "sin", i.e. *ḥṭ'*[303], is translated by the Sogdian *γw'n* "id." (30); (390); (505); (625) and once by the Sogdian *qt'ny* "id." (65).

Gharib (1995: 171) considers *γw'n* as common to the three varieties of Sogdian, i.e. Buddhist, Christian and Manichaean, while she considers *qt'ny* as specific to the Christian tradition (1995: 197). *GMS* (§§: 1035; 1038) reports for the Manichaean Sogdian *'kt'ny* and *'krt'ny* for the Buddhist one. Again *GMS* (§: 1032) dates back *γw'n* to a root *γw-* "to lack" (§: 1032) and *qt'ny* to a stem *qt-* < *kṛta* + I quote – "an obscure suffix" – which he identifies as *-āni*[304] whose opposite is that which creates the Buddhist form *pwny'nh* and the Manichaean *pwrny'nyy'* for "piousness, holiness" (§§ 1035, 1038). *C2* (p. 212) records *γw'n* "sin" and *qt'ny-q'ry* "sinful, sinning" (p. 213) which in *E5* means "sinner" (570); (595); (600); (615).

3.5.4 Sogd. b'γ "vineyard" and Sogd. b'γd'ry "vine-dresser"

b'γ is attested with the meaning of "garden" in Gharib[305] and is not attested in *C2*. In *E5* (155); (165); (170) it translates the Syriac *krm'* which has the specific meaning of "vineyard, vineyard"[306]. The Sogdian *b'γd'ry* is attested in *E5* (155); (160); (165); (170) with the meaning of "winemaker" as the translation of the Syriac *plḥ'* "vine-dresser/tenant" according to

---

[300] See: Brockelmann (1928: 616).

[301] See: Payne- Smith (1879-1901: col. 3335-6).

[302] According to Brockelmann, the first meaning is "verbum". See: Brockelmann (1928: 386-387).

[303] According to Brockelmann, "peccatum". See: Brockelmann (1928: 227).

[304] As regarding the suffix, see: Sims-Williams (1981: 16-17).

[305] See: Gharib (1995: 97).

[306] According to Brockelmann, "1. vinea 2. vitis". See: Brockelmann (1928: 347).

Brockelmann (1928: 573): "1. operarius; 2. agricola; 3. cultor (vineae); 4. cultor, adorator". No attestation in *C2* while it is registered by Gharib according to the attestations in *E5* with the meaning of "farmer"[307].

3.5.5 Sogd. z'y "land, ground" and Sogd. fcmbd/fcmpd "world"

In this Gospel lectionary Sogd. *z'y* "land, ground" is systematically used to translate the Syriac *'r'* "id."[308] (320); (370) – in correspondence with the Greek *γῆ* –, while the Sogd. *fcmbd/fcmpd* "world" is used to translate the Syriac *'lm'* "mundus"[309] (65); (100); (230); (310); (315); (410); (415); (435); (450); (465); (695); (750) – in correspondence with the Greek *κοσμὸς* –. Instead, according to Schwartz[310], in the Sogdian fragment of the book of Psalms, *βcmpδ* translates the Syriac *'r'*.

3.5.6 Sogd. w'xš pwx'y "to decide, establish"

In *E5* (590) we read: *p't w'xš pwxsty m'tnt cn cxwdt*: literally, "Indeed, the word has been cut off from the Jews". It renders the Syriac phrase *psqw hww gyr yhẅdy'* "indeed the Jews decided". Sundermann said: "Ich halte diesen Satz für eine falsche Übersetzung von: *psqw hww gyr yhwdy'*"[311]. In my opinion, instead, a Sogdian expression has been coined in an attempt to exactly translate the Syriac verb. Sogdian *w'xš*, as we have already noted, has multiple meanings: *C2* (p. 229): "word, speech, remark, sentence, verse, thing". As concerns the verb *pwx'y* it means "to cut off, amputate"[312]. It occurs in this Gospel lectionary (115) with this meaning to translate the Syriac *psq*. The Syriac verb *psq* has a remarkable semantic range. Brockelmann reports, among others as meaning, "decrevit, constiuit, judicavit"[313]. Because of the semantic extent of this latter, which the Sogdian verb does not have, a periphrastic form has been used, as often happens in such contexts[314].

307 See: Gharib (1995: 97).

308 See: Brockelmann (1928: 51).

309 See: Brockelmann (1928: 527).

310 See: Schwartz (1974: 259).

311 See: Sundermann (1975: 66-67, n. 50).

312 See: *C2* (p. 223).

313 See: Brockelmann (1928: 583).

314 See also the forthcoming Christian Sogdian dictionary of Sims-Williams (Sims-Williams: forthcoming 2016a). I thank Sims-Williams for discussing this point with me in Vienna (25.01.16) and for giving me the PDF version of his new fundamental work. One remark: I do not think that *cn* which precedes *cxwdt* is deleted as proposed by Pittard apud Sims-Williams (forthcoming 2016a). Moreover, with particular regard to preposition *cn* + direct

3.5.7 Sogd. wštm'x "the heavenly kingdom, paradise" and Sogd. xšywnqy' "kingdom"

In this Gospel lectionary the Syriac *mlkwt'* "kingdom, reign"[315] is translated by the Sogdian term *wštm'x* with the meaning of "the heavenly kingdom, Paradise" (150); (645); (695); and with the Sogdian term *xšywnqy'* meaning "the earthly kingdom" (760)[316]. This distinction is also observed in *C2* (respectively p. 230, 234).

3.5.8 Sogd. byy ptry "God the Father"

In the Gospel lectionary *E5* Sogd. *byy ptry* "God the Father" translates Syr. *'b'* "Father" (205); (370); (375); (385); (420); (430); (435); (465); (695); (755) and once Syr. *'lh'* "God": (435)[317].

3.5.9 Sogd. xwt'w "Lord" and Syr. mry' "id."

See the presence of the noun *xwt'w* "Lord" as apposition of "Jesus" never attested in the Syriac text: (65); (175); (245); (250); (265); (285); (325); (380); (385); (395); (445); (455); (475); (480); (515); (525); (535); (545); (560); (625); (630); (645); (740); (760); (765); (770). In *E5*, Sogdian *xwt'w by-* "Lord God" translates Syr. *mry'* "Lord": (15); (30); (175)[318].

3.5.10 Sogd. nwšc žw'n "eternal life"

In *E5*, *nwšc žw'n* becomes, in my opinion, a fixed expression to translate the Syriac word for life *ḥ̈y'* where the Sogdian adjective *'yqwncy̨q* "eternal" always translates the corresponding Syriac *l'lm* (id.): (30); (185); (190); (740)[319].

3.5.11 Sogd. n'y "Lo" and Syr. ḣ' "id."

The Sogdian interjection *n'y* "Lo" translates the Syriac *h'* "id.". And it is, in my opinion, an example of how this Gospel lectionary naturally absorbs, as a

---

case, i.e. *cxwdt*, I do not see any problem: as we have seen in *3.3.4 Occurrences of cases in the adpositional syntagm* we have examples concerning *cn* + direct case. Therefore, I still favour the interpretation I gave in my PhD dissertation (2009) and which I clarified here. At any rate, one can see the photoreproduction: *E5/100/v/*20/.

315 Brockelmann gives as first meaning "regnum". See: Brockelmann (1928: 392).

316 As well as the Syriac *mlk'* is translated by the Sogdian *xšywny* "king, sovereign" (330); (345); (695); (715).

317 See also the *Sogdian- Syriac Glossary* under *by-*.

318 See also the *Sogdian- Syriac Glossary* under *by-*.

319 As I demonstrated for the first time during a conference held in Rome in March 2009. See the Proceedings of this conference: Barbati (2014).

translation vehicle, even those elements prior to *Peshitta* if it is true what Lyon pointed out "…this use of *hā* (Lo!) is one of the single most oustanding features of the Old Syriac, and particularly in the Gospel of John..."[320]. In *E5* the Sogdian *n'y*, as translation of the Syriac *ḣ'*, is attested in the following passages: (1); (135); (255); (275); (325); (440); (445); (660); (775), i.e. respectively, Matthew 20.18; Matthew 24.26; Luke 24.21; Matthew 10.16; John 16.29; John 16.32; Luke 19.20; Matthew 17.5.

Certainly Syriac in relationship to Sogdian stands as the language of prestige, as the official language of the Church of the East, and therefore also as the lexical donor language[321]. On the other hand, the familiarity in translating this language that is manifested in *E5* also points to a remarkable degree of inculturation[322].

The structures and the use of the language as attested in the Gospel lectionary *E5* are the result of the interplay of intralinguistic and extra-linguistic factors: typological internal changes, innovation, preservation, phenomena due to language contact as well as due to a translation literature, historical sociolinguistic context. Without any of these elements we may lose the overview; with each of these elements we can finally talk about a given language also in relation to the historical events, cultural trends and social aspects which went throught it. At this point, I would like to recall what Fragner said about the role of the Persian language within the Islam historical framework: "Ausserdem soll die Frage gestellt werden, in wie weit in bestimmten historischen Situationen auch Sprachen und ihre Verhältnisse zueinander geschichtsmächtig werden können. Ich werde also danach suchen, in welchem Ausmasse linguistische Themen kulturwissenschaftlich und historisch relevant sein können"[323]. If we change the order of the factors, I think we can better understand what I have tried to do, which is to show how the historical-sociocultural factors may, and even must be systematically incorporated into a philological and linguistic analysis. I would say that the language attested in the Gospel lectionary *E5* is a very good example of how a religious process is

[320] See: Lyon (1994: 205).
[321] See: Sims-Williams (1988).
[322] See: Barbati (2014: 116).
[323] See: Fragner (2006: 39).

reflected in linguistic practices[324].

---

324 The idea behind it – an idea that I fully share – is that one can also apply the latest issues of historical sociolinguistics to conceptually written languages, including conceptually written dead languages, See: http://www.oeaw.ac.at/sociolinguistics/.

E5: The Text

E5/5

Part of the Gospel for the 2nd Sunday of Advent. Luke 1.44: /r/1-2/; Luke 1.55: /v/1-2/; Luke1.55-1.56: /v/3/.

/r/

/1/ (p't) n'ẏ˙ [c'nw 'mpst tw' dwrty' wxr pr mn']
44. ḣ' gyr kd ṇpl ql' d-šlmky b-

/2/ (γ)[wš](t) . · p(r)[---------------------------]
-'dn̈y b-ḥdwt' rbt' dṣ 'wl' b-krsy

/v/

/1/ [-------------------------- w'nc]'nw qt
55. 'yk d-

/2/ [ž'd'rt dn m'x ptrty' dn 'b](r)hm 't
-ṃll 'm 'bhÿn 'm 'brhm w-

/3/ [----------------------- pyšt wyžt'] (q)θ'r(t)
-'m zr'h l'lm 56. qwyt dyn

Translation

/r/ /1/ For behold, [when the sound of your salutation fell upon my] /2/ ears, with [great joy the child leapt in my womb]. /v/ /1/ As /2/ [he spoke with our fathers, with Ab]raham and /3/ [with his seed for ever. But *Mary* sta]yed...

Commentary

As already mentioned in Chapter 2[325], the identification of this fragment is the work of Pittard and Sims-Williams. Published in 2013 and in 2014, their reading, identification and, of course, translation are fully accepted with small clarifications. The reconstructions made in /r/1/ and in /v/1-2/ and /v/3/, referring to *pyšt*, are mine on the basis of what is attested in *E5*.

/v/

/2/: The Syriac *'m* is almost always translated in *E5* with the circumposition *dn...prw*. Nevertheless, I have not reconstructed the postposition *prw*

325 See: *2.1 Previous editions*.

because according to Sims-Williams “where dn…pr(w) governs two conjoined noun phrases, dn is repeated before each but pr(’)w is only placed after the last in the series”[326].
/3/: One can conjecture the conjunction *pyšt* “but” (translation of the Syriac conjunction *dyn* “but”) before *wyžt’* which, together with *(q)θ’r(t)*, translates the Syriac *qwyt*. As will be confirmed during the present work, the two conjunctions occupy different positions in the sentence: in *E5 pyšt* always occupies the starting position, whereas the corresponding Syriac conjunction *dyn* is always placed afterwards.

E5/6a-b
End of the Gospel for the 3rd Sunday of Advent. Luke 1.63-80: /r/1-19/; /v/1-18/.
Beginning of the Gospel for the 4th Sunday of Advent. Matthew 1.1: /v/19/.

/r/

/1/(’t) γwžd’rt˙ pyd’r˙ ’t nỵpỵs (’t) [w’nw wγd’rt]
63. w-ṣ̌’l pnqyt’ w-kṭb w-’ṃr

/2/ ywḥnn xcỵ wỵnỵ n’m · ’t wỵd’sd’rnt wỵ(s)[pw]
ywḥnn hẉ šmh w-’tdmrw klnš;

/3/ ’(dỵ) ’t yẇnỵ̇ xwỵcq qtỵ̇ wỵnỵ qwc’ ’t wỵnỵ
64. w-mḥd’ ’tptḥ̇ pẇmh w-lšnḣ

/4/ zb’q. · ’t ž’d’rt. ’frywn ptwysd’rt qw
w-ṃll w-ḅrk l-

10 /5/ bγỵ s’ · ’t qtỵ̇ pcqwỵr˙ pr s’t wỵšntỵ dwsỵt
-’lh’; 65. w-hwt dḥlt’ ‘l klhwn šbbÿhwn

/6/ ’t pr s’t˙ yhwdỵ̇ γrỵ. y’nt ’ỵšt ž’tỵt bỵq˙
w-bklh ṭwr’ d-yhwd hlyn mtmlln hẇy;

/7/ m’tnt · ’t s’t˙ wỵšnt qt ptγwšd’rnt. · ’t
66. w-klhwn d-šm‘w

[326] See: Sims-Williams (forthcoming 2016a, under *prw*).

/8/ šm’ry̤q m’tnt˙ pr˙ wy̤šnty̤ žy’wr˙ ’t w’nw
mtḥšbyn hww b-lbhwn w-

/9/ w’by̤ntqn cw (m)’yš bwtq’ ’y̤ny̤ ry̤nc’q · ’t
-’mryn mn’ ky nhw’ ṭly’ hn’ w-

/10/ xwt’w bγy̤ dsty̤ m’t dn wy̤ny̤ prw ∴ ’t pwrny̤
-’ydh d-mry’ ’yt hwt ‘mh; 67. w-’tmly

/11/ qty̤ zkry’ wy̤ny̤ ptry̤˙ zprt w’t. · ’t bywnqy’
zkry’ ’bwhy rwḥ’ d-qwdš’ w-’tnby

/12/ qθ’rt. · ’t w’nw wγd’rt · pr ’frywn xcy̤
w-’ṃr; 68. mbrk hw̤

/13/ xwt’w ysr’yl bγy̤·˙ qt ’:mbrz brd’rt xy̤pθ
mry’ ’lhh d-’ysryl d-s‘r ‘mh

/14/ rmy̤y̤ ’t qθ’rt qw wy̤ny̤ s’ wẋ̣š’-mnty̤·˙ ’t
w-‘ḅd l-h pwrqn’; 69. w-

/15/ ’xyžd’rt qw m’x s’ wxš’-mnty̤ sry̤ pr dwyd
-’qym l-n qrn’ d-pwrqn’ b-byth d-

/16/ xy̤pθ bnty̤ x’ny̤ · w’nc’nw qt ž’d’rt pr xy̤pθ
-dwyd ‘bdh; 70. ’yk d-ṃll b-pwm’

/17/ zprt by̤wny̤ty̤ qwc’ qt cn ’yqwn ms’ · qt
d-nbÿwhy qdÿš’ d-ṃn ‘lm; 71. d-

/18/ wẋ̣š’t m’xẏ cn m’x s’nt. ’t cn s’t m’x
-nprqn ṃn b‘ldbbÿn w-ṃn ’yd’

/19/ n’šy̤rγwzy̤ty̤ dsty’ · ’t qθ’rt xy̤pθ z’rcnw{<qy’>}
d-klhwn sn’ÿn; 72. w-‘ḅd ḥnnh

/v/

/1/ [dn m’x ptr](t)[y’] (p)rw. · ’t šy’ qθ’rt xy̤pθ zpr(t)
‘m ’bhÿn w-‘hd l-dytqwḧy qdÿšt’;

/2/ [pšt’w]n · (’)t sẇq̇nt qt xwrd’rt qw ’brhm
73. w-mwm̈t’ d-ym’ l-’brhm

/3/ m’x ptry̤ s’ · qt θbr’t qw m’x s’ qt
’bwn d-nṫl l-n; 74. d-

/4/ zrγty̤t bym cn m’x s’nty̤ dsty’ · ’t pw pcq(w)y̤r
-ntprq ṃn ’yd’ d-b‘ldbbÿn w-dl’ dḥl’

/5/ sp’xšym wy̤ny̤ pyrnms’˙ s’t m’x my̤θt. · pr
nplwḥ qdmwḧy; 75. klhwn ywm̈tn b-

/6/ d’tcy̤qy’˙ ’t pr ’rt’wy’ · ’t tγw˙ ry̤ncq’ sm’n-
-k’nwt’ w-b-zdyqwt’; 76. w-’nt ṭly’

/7/ -cyq bγy̤ by̤ẇny̤ žγy̤rty̤ by̤q’ · p’t šwy̤q’˙
nḃyh d-‘ly’ ttqr’ t’zl gy̤r

/8/ xwt’w bγy̤ ptq’rẏ py̤rnms’. qt pšt’ẏy̤ wy̤ny̤
qdm prṣwph d-mry’ d-tṭyb ’wrḥh;

/9/ r’θ · qt θḅr’t nwšc žw’ny̤ ptz’n qw xy̤pθ rmy̤
77. d-nṫl md‘’ d-ḧy’ l-‘mh

/10/ s’˙ pr wy̤šntẏ γwnty̤ prmnty’. · pr m’x z’rcnwq
b-šwbqn’ d-ḥṭḧyhwn; 78. b-rḥm̈’

/11/ bγy̤ z’ry̤sy’-mnty̤ {<qt pry̤ẇnt>}[327] · ’ḅrzbry̤ m’xy̤ wyt’p’-
ḋ-ḥnn’ d-’lhn d-b-hwn ns‘rn dnḥ’

[327] Addition along the inner margin of the fragment.

/12/ -mnty̤ cn sm'n · pr rwxšny'q θbrw qw wy̤šnt
ṃn rwm'; 79. l-mnhrw l-'ylyn

/13/ s' qt pr t'ry̤ 't pr mrcy̤ sy'qt nysty̤
d-b-ḥšwk' w-b-ṭll' d-mwt' ytbyn

/14/ swqnt · qt fry̤ẓ̇t m'x p'dy̤t pr dwrty'
d-ntrwṣ r̈glyn b-'wrḥ' d-šlm';

/15/ r'θ ·⁘· pyšt ry̤nc'q γwšy̤q m't. 't z'wrqy̤n
80. ṭly' dyn rb' hw' w-mtḥyl

/16/ b'sq pr zprt w't · 't dxšty' swqy̤q m't.
b-rwḥ' w-b-ḥwrb' 'ytwhy hw'

/17/ wy̤twr qw wy̤ny̤ 'šty'mnty̤ my̤θ prm qt qw
'dm' l-ywm' ḋ-tḥwyth d-lwt

/18/ ysr'yly̤qt s' ⁘·⁘ (Syriac red) dḥdbšb' d'rb'' dknwn
'ysryl.

/19/ qdym ·⁘ dmty ⁘ ṣḥ ⁘ ' · ktb' dylydwth

Translation
/r//1/ And he asked for a writing tablet and wrote and [so he said]: /2/ "His name is John". And they all wondered /3/ and immediately his mouth was opened and his /3-4/ tongue *loosen*, and he spoke, and blessed /5/ God. And fear came on all their neighbours /6-7/ and all these things were talked about through all the mountain area of Judea, /7/ and all who heard them and /8/ were thinking in their hearts, and so /9/ said: "What then will this child be?" And /10/ the hand of the Lord God was with him. /10-11/ And his father Zechariah was filled with the Holy Spirit and /11-12/ prophesied and so said: "Blessed is /13/ the Lord God of Israel, for he has visited his /14/ people and redeemed it and /15/ has raised up a horn of salvation for us in the /16/ house of His servant David, as he spoke by /16-17/ the mouth of his holy prophets from of old /18/, that he would save us from our enemies and from the hands of all our /19/ ill-wishers; and he performed mercy */v/* /1/ [to our fathers] and he remembered his holy /2-3/ covenant and the oaths which he swore to our father Abraham, /3/ to grant us /4-5/ that we should be delivered from the

hands of our enemies and might serve before him without fear, /5-6/ in fairness and righteousness all our days. /6/ And you, child, /7/ will be called the prophet of the Heavenly God; for you will go /8/ before the face of the Lord God to prepare his /9/ way, to give knowledge of eternal life to his people /10/ in the forgiveness of their sins, through the mercy of our /11/ merciful God; whereby the sunrise shall visit us /12/ from on high to give light to those /13/ who sit in darkness and in the shadows of death /14/ to guide our feet into /15/ the way of peace". But the child grew and became /16/ strong in the Holy Spirit, and he was in the desert /17/ until the day of his public appearance /18/ to the Israelites. (Syriac) of the fourth Sunday of Kānūn /19/ qədēm, from Matthew, chapter 1, Book of the birth[328].

Commentary

/r/

/1/: *pyd'r* "writing tablet"[329]. The word is not attested in Gharib's dictionary (1995). The first person who supposed it had the meaning of "Schreibtafel" was Salemann[330]. According to him, the word represented the Sogdian translation of Syriac *pnqyt'* "πινακίδιον; 1. tabula." [331]. Sundermann[332] accepts this interpretation, and I agree with him. However, Sundermann then refers to a work by Schwartz[333] where the term *pyd'r* would have been attested with the same meaning: *pyd'r • m'(x)[ ] (14) x(yp)θ ('w)nty ẉyn'ncyqy' xcy qy b' (qw žwx)šqt' s'* "*The tablet* (i.e. Diptychs) is the appearance of our Lord unto the disciples". But a few years later, Sims-Williams[334] showed that, in this latter case, we are dealing with the postposition *pyd'r* which is then part of the previous sentence.

Finally, according to Sims-Williams, *pyd'r* "writing tablet" is attested in another Christian Sogdian text, i.e., "The Story of Daniel": in this case, the Sogdian word *pyd'r* refers to the stone tables containing the Ten Commandments[335].

/1/: *[w'nw wγd'rt]*. Sundermann[336] considers that, on the basis of *w-'ṃr* in

[328] See: Sundermann (1974: 225).
[329] See: Sundermann (1974: 223).
[330] See: Salemann (1907: 545).
[331] See: Brockelmann (1928: 580).
[332] See: Sundermann (1974: 223).
[333] See: Schwartz (1967, rev. 1982: 113).
[334] See: Sims-Williams (1985: 116-117).
[335] See: Sims-Williams (1985: 116 n.64 with suggested etymology) and Sims-Williams (2014a: 94).
[336] See: Sundermann (1974: 223).

the Syriac text, the following reconstructions are plausible: *[w'nw w'b]* and *[w'b qt]*. I think it is better to reconstruct *[w'nw wγd'rt]*. As equally seen in /r/12/ and in the entire *E5*, the Sogdian text usually translates the Syriac *w-'ṃr* "and said" with *'t w'nw wγd'rt*, adding the adverb *w'nw* "thus", which has no equivalent in the original Syriac.
/5/: *pcqwyr* "fear". In *C2* (p. 219) the form *pcwqyr* is attested.
/7/: *'t* "and" (at the end of the line). No corresponding word in Syriac, probably a mistake.
/9/: *(m)'yš*. Although this fragment is lost and we must settle for the photographic reproduction, and although it is undeniable that the first letter is not perfectly legible, I still believe that the *ductus* of *m*, as well as that of *y*, is recognizable and not likely to be confused with others such as, for example, *wn-*, *yn-*. Contra Sundermann[337]. In any case, the term is not attested either in Gharib dictionary (1995) or in *C2* glossary. The Syriac text reports the emphatic particle *ky* "now, then, just like". According to Sims-Williams, a variant *m'y* is attested[338].
/9/: *ryn̥c'q* "baby, child". *C2* (p. 224) records *ryncq*.
/11/: *zkry'* "Zechariah". The Sogdian language keeps the Syriac onomastics. See also /r/15/ *dwyd* "David" and, in /v/2/, *'brhm* "Abraham".
/12/: Sogdian translates the Syriac adjective *mbrk* with *pr 'frywn*, i.e. with the preposition *pr* and the noun *'frywn*, although it has the corresponding adjective *'fryty*.
/13/: *ysr'yl* "Israel". Christian Sogdian knows the following forms, namely *ysr'yl* and *ysryl*[339]. In *C2 ysryl* is attested (p. 236), while the Gospel lectionary *E5* contains only the form *ysr'yl*. With regard to the Syriac attestations, Mark Dickens[340] indicates the presence of *'ysryl* and *'ysr'yl* in Jacobite manuscripts, *'ysr'yl* in Melkite manuscripts and *ysryl* next to *'ysr'yl* in the Syro-Oriental manuscripts.
/13/: *'̣mbrz brd'rt*. The verb is composed by *'mbrz* "visit, care" and *br-* "take". In /v/11/ it is recorded as *'brz br*. It is not listed in Gharib dictionary (1995). Instead *GMS* (§§ 654- 657) shows *'mbrz br-* as Christian form and

[337] See: Sundermann (1974: 223).

[338] See: Sims-Williams (2013a: 238). The variant *m'yšt* is also attested. See: Sims-Williams (2015: 95).

[339] See: Gharib (1995: 448).

[340] Oral presentation at the *Christian Manuscripts from Turfan Workshop*, Berlin, March, 27-28 2009. While this observation did not go into the published version of his paper (Dickens: 2013), I am extremely grateful to Dr. Dickens for sending me an earlier and longer draft of his publication (Dickens: 2013) where he pointed out the different spelling of "Israel" within the different Syriac traditions. Personal communication, 23.03.2016.

'nβrz βr as Manichean form. The last form is attested in Turco-Sogdian documents[341].
/15/: *sry̤* "horn". Hapax legomenon[342].
/19/: *z'rcnw-qy'*. The last three letters are placed below the line of writing immediately below *-nw*, reflecting the attention paid by the scribes to justify the text, that is, to ensure that all the lines of writing have the same length.
/v/
/1/: *[dn m'x ptr](t)[y']* "together with our fathers". Sundermann suggests *[ptr](t)[']*[343], which is a nom. acc. pl. I think we can at least assume an ablative plural. The noun is governed by the circumpositional expression *dn....prw* that normally requires the ablative or oblique case and that, despite the collapse of the nominal inflection here witnessed, is a well-preserved construction because it is part of the basic vocabulary and so less subject to typological change.
/6/: *d'tcyqy'* "righteousness, justice". *C2* (p. 209) records *d'cyqy'*.
/10-11/: "Through the merciful goodness of our God". The Sogdian phrase sounds different from the Syriac. The Syriac reads *b-rḥm' d-ḥnn' d-'lhn* "thanks to the kindness of mercy of our God": *rḥm'* and *ḥnn'* are two terms in hendiadys and both mean "mercy", so we could translate "the loving kindness". The Sogdian translation is different because it shows the adjective *z'rcnwq* "merciful", which in my opinion is to be considered an attribute of *βγy̤* "God" because of its position, i.e. preceding the noun to which it refers.
/14/: *swqnt*. See, in Christian Sogdian, the metathesis for *(')skw. (')skw* is a form well attested in both Manichaean and Buddhist Sogdian[344].
/14/: *dwrty'*. Metathesized genitive of the light stem *dwrt* -.
/16/: *pr zprt w't* "in the Holy Spirit". The Syriac text has only *rwḥ'* "Spirit". This is not the only place where the Sogdian translator has understood Syr. *rwḥ'* "Spirit" as implying "Holy Spirit" and therefore inserted the word *zprt* "holy". See also *E5/19/v/12/* and *E5/19/v/16/*[345]. At any rate, the Syriac construction for "Holy Spirit", i.e. *rwḥ' d-qwdš'* is rendered in the Gospel lectionary *E5* as *zprt w't*.
/17/: *qw* "to". The final part of the first letter is lenghthened to make sure that even this writing line is fully aligned with the other ones.
/19/: In this case, and in all other cases attested in *E5*, *(Syriac red)* means

[341] See: Hamilton- Sims-Williams (1990: 60-61).
[342] See: Sunderman (1974: 223).
[343] See: Sundermann (1974: 224).
[344] See: *GMS* (§ 412).
[345] Sims-Williams kindly pointed out to me that we find other examples in *E6/20/r/*; *E27/54/v/15, 21*; and *E27/61/r/23/* (personal communication).

that the following passage is written in the Syriac language in red ink while *(Sogdian black)* indicates that the passage that follows is in the Sogdian language in black ink.

E5/19

End of the Gospel for the 2nd Sunday after Epiphany. John 1.19-28: /r/1-/-/v/2/.

Beginning of the Gospel for the 3rd Sunday after Epiphany. John 1.29-35: /v/2-3/-/19/.

/r/

/1/[xc](ỵ) ywḥnn-'ỵ wy(c)['w](qy') c'nw fšmd'rn(t) [qw wyny s']
19. w-hd' hy shdwth d-ywḥnn kd šdrw lwt-h

/2/ cxwdt [ ] cn 'wršlm dỵnd'rt 't lỵw['yqt qt šy]
yhẅdy' ṃn 'wršlm k̇hn̈' w-lẅy' d-

/3/ psỵnt · tγw . qy · 'ỵš · 't 'z'nd'rt . (')[t ny pstwd'rt]
-nš'lwnyhy 'nt ṁn 'nt; 20. w-'wḍy w-l' kp̣r

/4/ 't 'z'nd'rt · qt nỵ zw 'ym mšyḥ' ['t psd'rnt qw wyny s']
w-'wḍy d-lw 'ṅ' 'n' mšyḥ'; 21. w-š'lwhy

/5/ tỵm · cw nwqr · cwt · 'ly' bỵẇnỵ 'ỵš [tγw 't w'nw wγd'rt]
twb mn' hkyl 'ly' 'nt w-'ṃr

/6/ nỵ '(y)[m] zw · cwt bỵwnỵ 'ỵš tγw . · 't (w)['nw wγd'rt ny]
l' 'yty nby' 'nt w-'ṃr l';

/7/ 't w'nw wγd'rnt qw wỵnỵ s' · '[t qy 'yštγw qt]
22. w-'mrw l-h w-mnw 'nt d-

/8/ θbrỵm p'cγnỵ qw wỵšnt s' (q)[t fšmd'rnt m'x cw]
-nṫl ptgm' l-'ẏlyn d-šdrwn mn'

/9/ w’bỵsq tγw pr tw’ γryw · w’nw [w’b zw ’ym wxr]
’mr ’nt ‘l npšk; 23. ’ṁr ’n’ ql’

/10/ qt žγỵrt dxšty’ · qt mrxỵ wnt[’][xwt’w bγỵ r’θ]
d-qr’ b-mdbr’ d-’šww ’wrḥh d-mry’

/11/ [w’]nc’nw qt wγd’rt ’šγy’ bỵẇnỵ [pyšt wyšnt qt]
’ykn’ d-’ṃr ’š‘y’ nby’; 24. hnwn dyn d-

/12/ fšmtỵt qtnt · cn prỵs’ỵqtỵ m’[tnt ’t šy]
-’štdrw ṃn pr̈yš’ hww; 25. w-

/13/ psd’rnt · ’t w’nw w’bnt qw wỵnỵ s’ cw (nw)[qr sn’m]
-š’lwhy w-’mrw l-h mn’ hkyl

/14/ θbrỵsq tγw · qt tγw nỵ ’ỵš m(š)yḥ’ (’t) [ny ’ly’]
m‘md ’nt ’n ’nt l’ ’ytyk mšyḥ’ w-l’ ’ly’

/15/ ’t nỵ bỵ[wnỵ] · pcγny qθ’rt ywḥnn ’t w’n[w wγd’rt]
w-l’ nby’; 26. ‘ṇ’ ywḥnn w-’ṃr

/16/ qw wỵšnt s’ · zw˙ sn’m˙ θbr’msqn. pr ’p [pyšt šm’xy]
l-hwn ’n’ m‘md ’n’ b-m̈y’ byntkwn dyn

/17/ mỵd’nỵ˙ ’wštỵ stỵ. · xỵd qt šm’x̣ nỵ γr[bt’sqn wyny]
q’m hw d-’ntwn l’ yd‘yn ’ntwn l-h;

/18/ ’ỵnỵ xcỵ xỵd qt mn’ pšỵ ‸{<[s’]>} ’ỵstq’ · ’t [m’t pyrnm]
27. hnw hẉ d-btry ’ṭ’ w-hw’ l-h qdm-

/19/ cn mn’ · xỵd qt zẉ ’ỵžntỵ nỵ ’ỵm qt [------------------]
-y hw d-’n’ l’ šw’ ’n’ d-’šr’ d-‘r̈q’ d-msn̈why

/v/

/1/ [y’nt ’yšt pr] byθγny’˙ qtnt pr [ywrdn]n r[w]tỵ tγ’m
28. hlyn b-byt ‘ny’ hwÿ b-‘br’ d-ywrdnn

/2/ [qw qt sn’m] θbryq m’t ywḥnn (Syriac red) ∴∴ dḥdbšb’
’yk’ d-m‘md hw’ ywḥnn;

/3/ [dtlt’ dbtr dḥn] ’ .:. (Syriac red) dywḥnn .:. bṣḥ .:. ’ .:.:. (Syriac black) (w)lywm’

/4/ (Sogdian black) [’t] dbty̤q my̤θy̤ . wy̤d’rt [ywḥ]nn xwt’w
29. w-l-ywm’ d-btrh ḥẓ’ ywḥnn

/5/ [yšwγ qt ’ysyq] m’t qw wy̤ny̤ s’ ’t w’nw w’b
l-yšw‘ d-’t’ lwt-ḣ w-’ṃr

/6/ [n’y bγy̤ wr’n] xy̤d qt sxwytq’ fcmbdy̤ qt’ny̤
ḣ’ ’mrḣ d-’lh’ ḣw d-šq̇l ḥṭyth d-‘lm’;

/7/ [’yny xcy xyd qt zw wγd]’rm pry̤w qt mn’ pšy̤(s)’ ’[ys]tq’
30. hnw ḣw d-’n’ ’mrt ‘l-why d-btry ’ṫ’

/8/ [mrty ’t m’t pyrn]m cn mn’ . cy̤wy̤θ pyd’r qt
gbr’ w-hw’ l-h qdmy mṭl d-

/9/ [xw xcy cn mn’ pyrnm] ’t zw ny γrby̤q m’ty̤m wy̤ny̤ . .
-qdmy hẉ mny; 31. w-’n’ l’ yd‘ hwyt l-h

/10/ [yw’r qt γrb’ty] b’t qw ysr’yl rmy̤ s’ . . cy̤my̤θy̤
’l’ d-ntyd‘ l-’ysryl mṭl hn’

/11/ [pyd’r ’γtym zw qt] pr ’p sn’m θbrẇ . ’t wy̤c’wqy’
’tyt ’n’ d-b-m̈y’ ’‘md; 32. w-’shd

/12/ [θbrd’rt] (y)[wḥn]n . ’t w’nw w’b . qt wy̤d’rm zprt w’t˙
ywḥnn w-’ṃr d-ḥzyt l-rwḥ’

/13/ [qt] ’wxšt ˙[cn] sm’ny̤ ˙w’ncnw qwpwty̤ç ’t pcprty̤ pry̤w
d-nḥt’ ṃn šm̈y’ ’yk ywn’ w-qwyt ‘l-why;

/14/ [’t zw ny] (γ)rby̤q m’ty̤m wy̤ny̤ . yw’r xwny̤ ’dy qt fšm-
33. w-’n’ l’ yd‘ hwyt l-h ’l’ ṁn d-šdr-

/15/ [-d’rt mn’] qt [s]n’m θbrẇ pr ’p xw fr’m’ẏ qw mn’
-ny d-’‘md b-m̈y’ hẉ ’ṃr l-y

/16/ [s’ qt xwn]ỵ ’dỵỵ qt wỵnỵ tγw ˙qt ’wγẓ̇t zprt w’t
d-’yn’ d-ḥz’ ’nt d-nḥt’ rwḥ’

/17/ [’t pcpr’t] [p]rỵw. · [x]w sn’m θbrtỵq’ pr zprt w’t ·
w-mqwy’ ‘l-why hnw m‘md b-rwḥ’ d-qwdš’;

/18/ [’t zw wyd’r](m) ’t wỵc’wqy’˙˙ θbrd’rm. · qt ’ỵnỵ xcỵ
34. w-’n’ ḥzyt w-’shdt d-hnw

/19/[bγỵ z’ty] ⁘ ’t dbtỵq mỵθỵ. · ’wštỵ m’t ywḥnn.
brh d-’lh’; 35. w-l-ywm’ ’ḥrn’ q’m hw’ ywḥnn

Translation

/r//1/ [And this is] the testimony of John, when the Jews sent /1-2/ [him] priests and Levi[tes] from Jerusalem [to] /3/ ask [him]: “Who are you?”. And he confessed [and did not deny] /4/ and confessed: “I am not the Messiah”. [And they asked him] /5/ again: “What then? Are [you] Elijah, the prophet?” [And so he said:] /6/ “I am not.” “Are you the prophet?” And [so he said: “No.”] /7/And so they said to him: “A[nd who are you? So that] /8/ we may give an answer to those w[ho sent us. What] /9/ do you say about yourself?”. So [he said: “I am the voice] /10/ which cries out in the desert: ‘Make straight [the way of the Lord God],’ /11/ as the prophet Isaiah said”. [But those who] /12/ had been sent were from the Pharisees [and] /12-13/ they asked [him], said thus to him: “[Then] why /14/ are you baptizing, if you are neither the Messiah, [nor] Elijah, /15/ nor the prophet?”. John answered and s[o said to] /16/ them: “I baptize with water, [but] /17/ among [you] stands he whom you do not kn[ow]; /18/ this is the one who will come after me [and was before] /19/ [me], [the strap] of whose [sandal] I am not worthy to [untie]”. /v//1/ [These things] took place in Bethany at the ford [of the river Jordan] /2/ [where] John was [bapt]izing. (Syriac) /2-3/ [the third] Sunday [after Epiphany]; from John in chapter 1. And the day /4/ (Sogdian) [And] the next day John saw the Lord /5/ [Jesus com]ing toward him, and thus said: /6/ [“Behold, the Lamb of God], who will take away the sin of the world! /7/ [This is he] of whom [I sa]id: ‘After me will come /8/ [a man, and he was before] me, because /9/ [he is prior to me].’ And I did not know him, /10/ [but in order that he] should become [known] to the people of Israel; for this reason /11/ [I came to] baptize with water”. /11-12/ And John [bore] witness and thus said: “I saw the Holy Spirit /13/ descending [from] heaven like a dove, and it alighted on him. /14/ [And I] did [not] know him, but he who se[nt] /15/ [me] to baptize with water said to me: /16/ ‘[H]e, on whom you see the Holy Spirit descend /17/ [and alight], he will baptize with the Holy Spirit.' /18/ [And I have seen] and have borne witness that this is /19/[the Son of God]". And the next day John was standing….

Commentary

/r/

/1/: *wy(c)['w](qy')*: Müller[346] reconstructs the word correctly but then he leaves a space, which has no match in the fragment between this and *c'nw* which follows.

/2/: *[ ]*. Between the noun *cxwdt* and the preposition *cn* there is approximately 1cm of space where the paper appears slightly deteriorated, and where, however, no writing signs are detected. On the other hand, it does not seem to miss anything in the text, at least according to the Syriac one.

/3/: *psynt*. Optative *ps*- 3 pers. pl. In the course of the present work I noticed that Sogdian translates the Syriac verb *š'l* "to ask" in two different ways, namely by using now *γwž* than *ps*-. In my opinion that occurs because the Sogdian language distinguishes between a request "to get something" and to ask "to know something", as for the Latin *peto* (ask "to get"), and *quaero* (ask "to know"). In the first case Sogdian uses the verb *γwž*- while in the second, Sogdian uses the verb *ps*-.[347]

/5/: the Syriac *'ly' 'nt* "Are you Elijah?" is translated into Sogdian as *cwt 'yly' byẅny̤ 'y̤š [tγw]* "Are you the Prophet?". Sogdian adds a conjunction *cwt* (as in /r/6/) and *bywny̤* "prophet" as apposition of Elijah, an apposition that is also missing in the Greek text: *Ἠλίας εἶ σύ*[348].

/8/: *wyšnt*. Gharib wrongly attributes[349] – clearly in this case but it is not the only one – *wyš'nd* and *wyšnt* to the Manichaean Sogdian and *wyš'nt* to the Christian and the Secular Sogdian.

/13/: *cw*. The ink is damaged but the *ductus* is perfectly legible.

/18/ : ‸. Reference to a text addition that was probably along the outer margin which, however, has not survived.

/v/

/1/: *pr*. The preposition is quite readable despite the stroke loss of *p* and *r* upper parts.

/1/: *tγ'm*. Sundermann points out[350] that the Sogdian language uses this term with the meaning "Übergang, Furt" to translate the Syriac *'br'* which,

---

[346] See: Müller (1913: 58).

[347] For a list of occurrences of both verbs see the glossary.

[348] See: Soden von (1913:391): textual variants are not attested.

[349] See: Gharib (1995: 426).

[350] See: Sundermann (1974: 225).

according to Brockelmann, means "transitus" and "ripa ulterior"[351].
/3/: *(w)lywm'*. Müller reads one time (once) *lywm'*[352] and another time *w(?)lywm'*[353]. Fluctuation and uncertainty in reading also reported by Sims-Williams[354]. I incline towards *(w)lywm'* since the *w* stroke is not completely effaced.
/5/: *w'nw*. With a magnifying glass the stroke of the last two letters is still distinguishable, although it is almost completely effaced.
/5/: *w'b*. The first two letters, although they have not maintained a well-defined stroke, are still recognizable with the naked eye.
/6/: *fcmbdy*. *fcmbd* "world" is an Indian loan[355].
/6/: *qt'ny*. Certain reading: the stroke of the first two letters is clearly visible with a magnifying glass.
/6/: *sxwytq'*. Defective writing for *sxw'ytq'*, 3 pers. sg. of the present indicative. Here the non-metathesized *sxw-* is attested, but in Christian Sogdian language *swx'y/ swxst-* is more common. The latter is, in fact, the most attested form in *E5*, as deduced from the glossary, and it is the only one recorded in *C2* (p. 226). *GMS* (§ 417) attributes both forms to the Christian Sogdian, to the Manichaean Sogdian and to the Buddhist the one with metathesis, respectively *sxwst-* and *syw(')y-*[356].
/7/: *pšy̨(s)'*. Müller reads[357] *pšy s'* pointing out the uncertain reading of the postposition *s'*. With a magnifying glass, a continuous writing stroke could be seen, so it is appropriate to transliterate *pšy̨(s)'*, considering all as a single syntagmatic unit.
/8/: *mrty* "man" is reconstructed as Syriac has *gbr'* "id.". For the correspondence between Sogd. *mrty* "man" and Syr. *gbr'* "id." and between Sogd. *mrtxmy* "man, person, human being" and Syr. *brnš'* "id." see the *Sogdian-Syriac Glossary*. Furthermore, *mrtxmy* "person" is never used in *E5* to translate the Syriac *npš'* "soul", contrary to what is attested in *C2* (p. 176). In fact, in the Gospel lectionary *E5*, the Syriac *npš'* is mostly translated as *γryw* "himself, soul", and sometimes as *rw'n* "soul".
/10/: *qw ysr'yl rmy̨ s'* "to the people of Israel". In Syriac the noun for "people" is missing.
/11/: *sn'm*. The lower stroke of *-m* is effaced but deducible.

---

351 See: Brockelmann (1928: 508).
352 See: Müller (1913: 59).
353 See: Müller (1913: 60).
354 See: Sims-Williams (2012: 30).
355 See: Sims-Williams (2014a: 45).
356 Also Gharib. See: Gharib (1995: 366-367).
357 See: Müller (1913: 60).

/12/ and */v*/16/ *zprt*. See *commentary* to *E5/6a-b/v*/16/.
/13/: *'wxšt*. The top of *'*- and -*x*- is missing.
/15/: *θbrẇ*. The stroke of the last letter -*w* is no more marked but still readable.
/15/: *fr'm'y* "he said". 3 pers. sg. of imperfect. The verb *frm'y/frm't*, generally "to order, to command"[358], in this Gospel lectionary acquires the meaning of "saying" when Jesus or another important character is speaking[359], as it happens in this case, for John. As a further evidence, we can compare the passage contained in *E5/48/r/7/* where the verb *frm'y/frm't*, referred to a common character, is deleted and replaced by the scribe with the verb *w'b/wγt*- "say, speak".
/16/: *wy̤ny̤*. The *w*- stroke is recognizable but blurred.
/18/: *'̇t*. With particular regard to *'*- the two ends are visible, the upper and the lower one.

E5/21a-b
Part and end of the Gospel for the 4th Sunday after Epiphany. John 1.51; 2.1-3: /r/1-5/; John 2.9-11 /v/1-5/; John 2.3-5: /r/6-9/; John 2.11: /v/6/.
Beginning of the Gospel for the 5th Sunday after Epiphany. John 2.23: /v/8-9/.

/r/
/1/ [c'nw snntqn 't 'wγzntqn qw mrtx]my̤
51. kd slqyn w-nḥtyn lwt brh

/2/ [z'ty̤ s' 't štyq myθy m't bγ'npš]qty̤
d-'nš'; 1. w-lywm' d-tlt' hwt mštwt'

/3/ [pr qtn' glyl'yq kθ 't xwt'w yšwγ m't] (w)d(y̤) m't'
b-qṭn' mdynt' d-glyl' w-'mh d-yšw' tmn ḣwt;

85 /4/ ['t ms xw xwt'w yšwγ 't xypθ žwxšqt](') žγyr(ty)t qtn(t)
2. w-'p hẉ yšw' w-tlmÿdwhy 'tqryw

358 See: *C2* (p. 211) and Gharib (1995:155).
359 See: Telegdi (1938: 231).

/5/ [qw bγ’nypšqty s’ ’t γw’ncyq m’t mwdw ’t w’nw]
l-ḣ l-mštwt’; 3. w-ḥsr hw’ ḥmr’ w-

/6/ pcqw’d[’rt wyny m’t qw xwt’w yšwγ s’ mwdw]
-’mr’ l-h ’mh l-yšw‘ ḥmr’

/7/ nỵst wỵšntỵ · [w’nw fr’m’y qw wy’ s’ xwt’w yšwγ]
lyt l-ḣwn; 4. ’ṁr l-ḣ yšw‘

/8/ (cw) bwt mn’ tw’ [prw ’ync ny tym ’γty sty mn’ nγ’m]
m’ ly w-lky ’ntt’ l’ ‘dkyl ’tt š‘ty;

/9/ w’nw w’b [wyny m’t qw bntyt s’ ’yc qt frm’ytq’]
5. ’mr’ ’mh l-mšṁšn’ mdm d-’ṁr

/v/

/1/ (b)γ’(n)[ypš ’t w’nw w’b qw wyny s’ wyspw ’dy pyrnm]
9. l-ḥtn’; 10. w-’ṃr l-h kl ’nš lwqdm

/2/ šyrỵ mwd[w ’brtq ’t c’nw ’mprt pcšd’rnt wyd’γty]
ḥmr’ ṭb’ myt’ w-m’ d-rwyw hydyn

/3/ [x]wnỵ qt (r)[y]t(r) [xcy pyšt tγw d’ry šyry mwdw]
’yn’ d-bṣyr ’nt dyn nṭrtyhy l-ḥmr’ ṭb’

/4/ [wy]twr q[w] q(š)ỵ [prm ’yny xcy pyrnmcyq qržwrz qt qθ’rt]
‘dm’ l-hš’; 11. hd’ hy ’t’ qdmyt’ d-‘bḍ

/5/ [xwt’w yšwγ pr glyl’yq qtn’ ’t brtpθ qθ’rt xypθ γwbty’]
yšw‘ b-qṭn’ d-glyl’ w-’wḍ‘ šwbḥh

/6/ [’t wrnd’rnt pr wyny xypθ žwxšq](t’) ∵ (Syriac red) dḥd-
w-hymnw b-h tlmÿdwhy.

/7/ [bšb’ dḥmš’ ddnḥ’ dyw](ḥ)nn ∵ bṣ ∵ b ∵

/8/ [kd ’ytwhy hw’ dyn yšw‘ b’wrš](l)m bpṣh’ b‘d(‘)d’ .

/9/ (Sogdian black)[pyšt c’nw m’t xwt’w yšwγ pr ’wr]šlm˘{<[pr]>} pṣh’

Translation
*/r//*1/ [ascending and descending on] /1-2/ [the Son of M]an. [And on the third day there was a wedd]ing /3/ [at Cana, a city of Galilee. And the mother of the Lord Jesus] was there. /4/ [And also the Lord Jesus and his discipl]es were invited /5/ [to the wedding. And the wine ran out, and so] /6/ [sa]id [his mother to the Lord Jesus:] /6-7/ "They have no [wine." So said the Lord Jesus to her:] /8/ "[Woman,] what does this have to do with me and you? [My hour has not yet come"]. /9/ Thus said [his mother to the servants: "Do whatever he tells you"] */v//*1/... the bridegroom [and so said to him: "Everyone] /1-2/ [serves] the good wine [first], [and when they have drunk freely, then] /3/ that which [is] worse. [But you have kept the good wine] /4/ [un]til now". [This is the first sign] /5/ [the Lord Jesus did at Cana in Galilee, and manifested his glory,] /6/ [and his disciple]es [believed in him]. /6-7/ (Syriac) For the [fifth] Sund[ay of Epiphany;] from Joh[n] in chapter 2. /8/ [But when Jesus was in Jerusa]lem for the Feast of Passah. /9/ (Sogdian) [But when the Lord Jesus was in Jeru]salem for the Passah.

Commmentary
/r/
/2/: *bγ'npšqty* "wedding". That form is conjectured because of the presence in *E5/130a /r*/4/ with the meaning "wedding feast" based on its Syriac corresponding form *byt mštwt'*. In *C2* (p. 207) it is recorded as *bγ'nyšpqty*.
/3/: Sogd. *glyl'yq* < Syr. *glyl'* "Galilee" + the Sogdian adjectival suffix *-yq*[360].
/3/: *m't'*. The only attestation of this form of preterite, 3 pers. sg. f. of the verb "to be". Sundermann[361] also refers to other similar forms such as *'γt'* < *'ys/ 'γt* "to come" and *'mpst'*< *'mpd/'mpst* " to fall, to prostrate oneself".
/5/: *'t*. I do not think that the stroke of the first letter of this penultimate word of */r/*5/ is recognizable at all and so I prefer to read it as a conjecture[362].
/v/
/1/: *bγ'nypš* "bridegroom"[363]. The form *bγ'nyšp* is also attested[364].
/2/: *mwdw* "wine". Sundermann already pointed out the metathesis *-wd* for *-dw*[365]. In *C2* (p.215) is in fact attested *mdw*. In this case it is also possible to reconstruct *mwdy*[366].

---

360 See: Sims-Williams (1988: 146).
361 See: Sundermann (1974: 226, n. 5).
362 Contra: Sims-Williams (2012: 30).
363 See: *C2* (p. 207); and Gharib (1995: 101).
364 See: Schwartz (1967, Addendum 1969); and Sundermann (1974: 226-227).
365 See: Sundermann (1974: 227, n. 12).
366 See Sims-Williams (2012: 30).

/3/: *xwnỵ*. The correct reconstruction is by Sims-Williams (2012: 30).
/3/: *rytr̈* “worse”. Christian Sogdian word that seems to be attested only in this manuscript fragments as already pointed out by Sundermann[367]. *C2* (p.224) attests *rytry’* “evil, harm”. *GMS* (A § 1286) records *rytr* in Manichaean Sogdian.
/4/: *prm.* I do not think that the *p* stroke is recognizable at all and so I prefer to consider it as a conjecture[368].
/6/: *žwxšqt’*. The right reading is by Pittard[369].

E5/23

Part of the Gospel for the 5th Sunday after Epiphany. John 3.18-21: /r/.
Part of the Gospel for the 6th Sunday after Epiphany. John 3.26-27: /v/.

/r/

/1/ [qt ny wrnd’rt pr bγy ywt’c z’ty] n’m ·
18. d-l’ hymn b-šmh d-yḥydy ’brh d-’lh’;

/2/ [pyšt ’yny xcy pdq’ qt rwxšny’q ’γt q](w) fcmbd
19. hnw dyn dyn’ d-nwhr’ ’ṭ’ l-‘lm’

/3/ [s’ ’t fry ny’d’rnt mrtxmyt t’ry s](q)’tr cn
w-’ḥbw bnÿnš’ l-ḥšwk’ ytyr ṃn

/4/ [rwxšny’q p’t wyšnt qtyt m’tnt bžy]qt · p’t
d-l-nwhr’ ’ytyhwn hww gyr ‘bdÿhwn bÿš’; 20. kl

/5/ [wyspw ’dy qt žyštwc wnty žyšty d’rt] rwxšny’qỵ
gyr d-snÿt’ ‘bd sṇ’ l-nwhr’

/6/ [’t ny ’yst qw rwxšny’q s’] {<qt>}[ny ’wzmtyt] bnt wỵnỵ
w-l’ ’ṫ’ l-nwhr’ d-l’ ntksswn

[367] See: Sundermann (1974: 227, n. 13).
[368] Contra: Sims-Williams (2012: 30).
[369] See: Sims-Williams (2012: 30).

/7/ [qtyt pyšt xyd qt wnty ršty'q ']y̤st qw
'bdẅhy; 21. ḣw dyn d-'bd šrr' 'ẗ' lwt

/v/

/1/ m'(x) [xwštr xyd qt dn tw' prw m't pr ywrdnn rwty]
26. rbn ḣw d-'mk hw' b-'br' d-ywrdnn

/2/ tγ'm˙ (q)[t tγw wyc'wqy' θbrd'ry cn wyny pyd'r n'y ms xw]
d-'nt shdt 'l-why ḣ' 'p hw̤

/3/ sn'm θ(b)[rtysq 't γrf 'dyt 'ysntqn qw]
m'md w-sg̈y" 'tyn lwt-

/4/ wy̤ny̤ s(') [p'cγny qθ'rt ywḥnn 't w'nw wγd'rt]
-h; 27. 'ṇ' ywḥnn w-'ṃr

/5/ qw wy̤šn[t s' ny qt' wnty mrtxmy pr ny's cn]
l-hwn˙ l' mškḥ brnš' l-msb ṃn

/6/ xypθ γ(r)[ywy ryž 'yc yw'r qt θbrty qty qw wyny]
ṣbwt npšh mdm 'l' 'n 'tyhb l-h

/7/ s' cn sm(')[n --]
ṃn šm̈y'.

Translation
/r//1/ [that he has not believed in] the name [of the only Son of God.] /2/ [But this is the judgment: the light has come into] the world /3/ [and people loved the darkness] more than /4/ [the light because their works were evil.] For /5/ [everyone who does what is hateful hates] the light /6/ [and does not come to the light,] /6-7/ so that his [works] may [not be condemned. But whoever does what is true co]mes to the [light.] /v/ /1/ Our [master, he who was with you at] /1-2/ the ford [of the river Jordan, to whom you bore witness, look, he too] /3/ [is] baptiz[ing and many are coming to] /4/ him. [John answered and so said] /5/ to them: ["A person cannot receive] /5-6/ [anything of his] own [unless it is given him] /7/ from heave[n].

Commentary
/v/
/3/: the present indicative *sn'm θbrtysq* is reconstructed with the durative-

suffix *-sq* according to the durative value proper to the Syriac indicative *m‘md*, from which the Sogdian form is translated.
/5/: *qt’wn-* “to be able to, can” followed by *pr* “to/for” + infinitive *ny’s* has been reconstructed since, in the Syriac text, there is the same construction[370], namely *mškḥ* “to be able to, can”, followed by the particle *l-* + infinitive [371] *msb*.
/6/: in reconstructing *θbrty qty* “was given” < past participle *θbrty* of the verb *θbr-/θbrt* “to give” + *qty*, 3 pers. sg. of the preterite, we used the auxiliary *b(w)-/qt-* because it renders the passive tense in translating, from Syriac, “full” medio-passive diathesis. The Syriac corresponding verb form is *’tyhb*, medio-passive diathesis of Aphel conjugation of the stem *yhb,* “to give”.

E5/28a-b
Part of the Gospel for the 1st Monday of Lent. Matthew 5.30-33: /r/.
Beginning of the Gospel for the 1st Tuesday of Lent. Matthew 5.38-41: /v/.

/r/
/1/ [-----------] ’t qt (t)[w’ xw’rnt dsty bž’xwty’ wnty]
30. w-’n ’ydk d-ymyn’ mkšl’

115 /2/ [tw’ p](w)x’(ẏ) šy̤ pš’[y cn tw’ p’t]
l-k pswq šdyḣ mnk

/3/ [wrq’ry bwt] tw’˙ qt ny̤st [b’t yw cn tw’ ’dmyt]
pqḥ l-k gyr d-n’ḃd ḥd ṃn hdṁyk

/4/ [’](t) [ny s](’t) tw’ tmf’r ’mpd[t tmy’ cyntr]
w-l’ klh pgrk npl b-ghn’;

/5/ [wγty qt]y qt xwny ’(dy)˙ qt w’c(t) [xypθ db’mn θbr’t]
31. ’t’mr d-ṁn d-šr’ ’ntth nṫl

/6/ qw w(y’ s)’ (xw)[ycq](q’ry̤ p)[w](st)y · pyš(t) [zw frm’-]
l-ḣ ktb’ d-dwll’; 32. ’n’ dyn ’ṁr

---

[370] See: *Chapter 3.2.5 Tenses and moods in Sogdian and in Syriac.*
[371] Sometimes, however, *d-* + imperfect is also attested. Even in this case, see: *Chapter 3.2.5 Tenses and moods in Sogdian and in Syriac.*

/7/ -ymsqn (qw) šm’x s’ · qt (wy)[spw x]wny̱ (’)[dy qt w’ct]
’n’ l-kwn d-kl ṁn d-šr’

/8/ xypθ db’ṃ̇n˙ ny̱šqr’n cn (xwr)wny̱ pt[y](rn) [wnty wy’]
’ntth lbr ṃn mlt’ d-znywt’ ‘bd l-ḣ

/9/ (q)[t] (xwrw)ny wn’[t] (· ’t) xwn(y) [’d]y̱ q(t ’)[st prγc’]
d-tgwr w-ṁn d-šq̇l šbyqt’

/10/ (xw)rwny̱ [w](n)ty̱q(’) · t(y̱)m pt[γwšd’ryšt’ šm’x]
g’r; 33. twb šm‘twn

/v/
/1/ [--------------------------------] (Syriac red) dtl(t)[bšb’]

/2/ [qdmyt’ dṣwm’ dmty ⁘ bṣḥ ⁘ h ⁘] (Syriac black) ’ṃr yšw[‘ šm‘twn]

/3/ [w’nw fr’m’y xwt’w yšwγ ptγwš]d’ry̱št’ šm’x q[t wγ]ty̱
38. šm‘twn d-’t’mr

/4/ [qty qt cšmy cšmy̱](y) pcrw ’t dnt’ dnt’ –[372]–pcr – w
d-‘yn’ ḥlp ‘yn’ w-šn’ ḥlp šn’;

/5/ [pyšt zw frm’ym](s)qn˙ qw šm’x s’ ̤ qt n’ ’wšty̱t’
39. ’n’ dyn ’ṁr ’n’ l-kwn d-l’ tqwmwn

/6/ [γnt’qy] (p)try̱t (·) [yw](’r) xwny̱ ’dy̱ qt py̱ẓ̇t tw’ · pr tw’
lwqbl byš’ ’l’ ṁn d-mḥ’ l-k ‘l pkk

/7/ [xw’rnt znw](q) · z[wyr](t) qw wyny̱ s’ ̣ ms d[b](tyq) znẉq
d-ymyn’ ’pn’ l-h ’p ’ḥrn’;

[372] This short line, as well as the next one, is used to level the length of the writing line to all others. Müller (1913: 5) defines it exactly “Zeilenfüller”. An overall analysis carried out according to the Christian Sogdian and Syriac documents from Turfan, has already been inserted in my current project *Christian Sogdian Book Culture*.

/8/ ['t xwny 'dy] qt q'ṃ[t] · qt pdq' wn't (d)n [tw](') pr(w)·
40. w-ṁn d-ṣḃ' d-ndwn ‘mk

/9/ ['t 'st tw](') qwrθy̤. · (p)[ryc] qw [wyny] s'. ms tw' nγwnty
w-nšqwl kwtynk šbwq l-h 'p mrṭwṭk;

/10/ [xwny 'dy qt n](ẏ)'st tw'· ẏw ḟ̣ṣx z'ẏ ·
41. ṁn d-mšḥr l-k myl' ḥd

Translation
/r/ /1/ “and if y[our right hand causes grief] /2/ [to you], cut *it* off *and* throw it away [from you; for] /3/ [it is better] for you that [one of your limbs] should be] destroy[ed] /4/ and [not] *that* your who[le] body should fall [into hell]. /5/ [It was sa]id: ‘Whoever repudiates [his wife, should give] /6/ her a deed of repudiation’. But [I s]ay /7/ to you: everyone [who repudiates] /8/ his wife, except on the grounds of adultery, [makes her] /9/ commit adultery, and whoever mar[ries a repudiated woman] /10/ commits adultery. Again you ha[ve heard]…” (Syriac) for Tues[day] /2/ [of the first week of Lent]. Jesus said: [“You have heard”] /3/ (Sogdian) [The Lord Jesus said thus]: “You have [heard] that [it was] /4/ [said: ‘An eye] for [an eye] and a tooth for a tooth’. /5/ [But I s]ay to you, ‘Do not stand /6/ against [evil]. But if anyone slaps you /7/ [on your right cheek], tu[rn] to him the other cheek also. /8/ [And if anyone] would sue you /9/ [and take you]r tunic, le[t him have] your cloak as well. /10/ [Anyone who] forces you *to go* a one-mile distance...’ ”.

Commentary
/r/
/1/: *'t qt*. The initial part of *'*-, the vertical final stroke of *q*- and the upper part of *-t* are missing. However the overall reading is certain. Müller[373] translates *qt* “dass” following the main meaning of the conjunction, but Sundermann already states that the correct meaning is “wenn” (“if”), as in the Syriac original text there is *'n* “if”[374].
/1/: here it was reconstructed *bž'xwty' wnty* “causes grief” < *bž'xwty'* “suffering, pain” + *wn-/qt-* “to do” at the 3 pers. sg. of the indicative present tense, according to the Syriac *mkšl'*, the f. sg. active participle of the Aphel conjugation from the root *kšl* “to offend”, referred to the f. sg. noun *'yd'* “hand”.

---

[373] See: Müller (1913: 3).
[374] See: Sundermann (1974: 229, n. 30).

/2/: *[p](w)x'(ẏ)* "cut". 2 pers. sg. of imperative, translation of the Syriac imperative *pswq*, 2 pers. sg. from the root *psq* "to cut".
On this verb form reading, several hypotheses have been formulated. Müller[375] identifies a punctuation mark • instead of the letter *-y* here reconstructed and, however, already identified by Sundermann[376]. At any rate, Sundermann himself affirms[377] that between *-x-* and *-'-* there may be *w*, although very small like that, Sundermann continues, found in */r/3/* in *tw'*. For this reason, the scholar reads *[p]x[w]'y*. Actually, it seems to me that where Sundermann reads *w* there is only a stroke that combines a letter to another within the same word. Vice versa I identify *w* before *-x-* instead of the stroke that connects *p-* and *-x* identified by Sundermann: in my opinion, however, it is a round stroke and not an horizontal one that best fits therefore to the *w* letter.
/3/: *nys(t)[b't]* "be destroyed" contra Sundermann *nys(t) [by]* "vernichtet werde"[378]. In the note 32 Sundermann writes: "ich vermute Opt. wie im folgenden Satz" (*ibid.*). The optative of the further sentence is found in */r/4/*: *'mpdy*, read by Müller, with whom I agree, *'mpdt*[379]. The third case is found in */r/5/*: I read *w'ct* while Sundermann *(ibid.)* reads *w'(cy)*. It is worthwhile now dwelling on three verb forms of uncertain reading that I reconstructed as subjunctives and Sundermann (*ibid.*) as optative. Now, in the first case I prefer reconstructing the subjunctive *[b't]* because in Syriac we find the imperfect *n'bd* introduced by *d-* used to indicate a possibility, probability and this is a construction which generally results in Sogdian with the conjunction *qt* followed by the subjunctive, as often found in *E5*[380]. This is the underlying reason even for the second case: the Sogdian *'mpdt* still translates a Syriac imperfect *npl* with the same nuance. Concerning the third case, I prefer assuming the subjunctive *w'c(t)* because the idea of possibility expressed by the context is introduced inter alia, as often happens, by *xwny 'dy qt* (besides *qt*, *c'nw* etc. .): in such cases Christian Sogdian uses the subjunctive[381]. This is supported also by the fact that Syriac has the active participle *šr'*, sometimes used even for a future eventuality. Therefore I find no justification for the hypothesis proposed by Sundermann[382] on the use of

375 See: Müller (1913: 3).
376 See: Sundermann (1974: 229).
377 See: Sundermann (1974: 229, n. 26; n. 31).
378 See: Sundermann (1974: 229).
379 See: Müller (1913: 3).
380 See: *Chapter 3.4.5 Expression for possibility, probability.*
381 About this see also the article by Telegdi (1938: 223-224).
382 See: Sundermann (1974: 229, n. 35).

the parabolic optative *w'c(y)* in Sogdian as narrative tense.
/4/: according to Sundermann[383], the syntagm *tmy' cyntr* is reconstructed although the Syriac text has *bghn'* "in Gehenna". Here a generic term is employed instead of the toponym, because the same syntagm *tmy' cyntr* is attested in *E5* (365) as the translation of the Syriac toponym *ghn'*. The study of the lexicon of this Gospel lectionary led me to prefer generic Sogdian terms instead of technical terms borrowed from Syriac in the attempt, in my opinion, to create their own terminology, while respecting the original text[384].
/4/: *tmf'r* = *tmp'r* "body"[385].
/4/: *'mpdt*: In *E5* the form *'mpd/'mpst* "to fall, prostrate" is attested with the dental sonorization, in *C2* (p. 204), however, the one recorded is the unvoiced dental *'mpt/'mpst*[386].
/5/: *xwny*. *w* and *y* are only partially visible but well recognizable.
/5/: *[wγty qt]y* "It was said". My reconstruction is based on the consideration that Syriac presents *'t'mr*, Ethpeel conjugation – medio-passive diathesis – of the verbal root *'mr* "to say, speak" and that, as we are finding in the course of the present work, Sogdian uses the auxiliary verb *b(w-)/qt-* to translate Syriac medio-passive diathesis[387]. Contra Pittard apud Sims-Williams: *(wγt)[y s](t)y*[388]. Contra Sundermann: *[s' wγty]*[389]. Sundermann reconstructs, as first word, the postposition *s'* considering it as the final part of the previous postposition *cyntr* and then only *wγty*. I believe that the reconstruction of *s'* is superfluous, since, in this Gospel lectionary and in the Christian Sogdian, even the form *cyntr* is well attested and that, when the Syriac Ethpeel conjugation occurs, it is more correct to reconstruct *[wγty qt]y*.
/8/: *db'ṃn* "wife". Typical Christian Sogdian form. The secular Sogdian records *δβ'mn*, and the Manichaean Sogdian *δβ'mbn*[390]. In the Turco-Sogdian documents, *δ'β'm'n* and *dβ'mn* are also attested[391].
/8/: *pt[y](rn)* "cause, ground, reason". About the meaning of this word as a

[383] See: Sundermann (1974: 229).
[384] See: Barbati (2014: 108-110).
[385] See: Müller (1913: 3) and Sundermann (1974: 229, n. 27).
[386] See: *Chapter 3.1.5 'mpd /'mpst* "to fall, precipitate, prostrate".
[387] For a complete list, see: *Chapter 3.2.2 Sogdian translation of the Syriac medio-passive verbs*.
[388] See: Sims-Williams (2012: 31).
[389] See: Sundermann (1974: 229).
[390] See: *GMS* (§§: 304; 453).
[391] See: Hamilton- Sims-Williams (1990: 78; 83).

translation of the Syriac *mlt'* "verbum, res; negotium; causa"[392] previously Sundermann (1975: 84).
/v/
/1/: *[bšb']*. Previously Sundermann (1974: 230).
/2/: *[qdmyt' dṣwm']*. Previously Sundermann (1974: 230).
/2/: (Syriac black) *'ṃr yšw['].* This sentence has no correspondeces with the text of the *Peshitta*. As already pointed out by Sundermann[393] "offensichtlich im Anfang der Lektion ergänzt"[394]. Another example is attested in *E5/48/v/*18-19/.
/2/: *[šm'twn]*. Previously Sundermann (1974: 230).
/5/: *[frm'ym](s)qn*. As regards the suffix *-sqn*, we can see the final part of *s-* where *-q-* and *–n* are perfectly readable with the naked eye. Therefore the confusion made by Müller[395] who reports *w* in East Syriac script with a question mark followed by a blank space, not present in the fragment, followed by *-qn* and then transcribes *–squn*, seems at least curious. What Müller reported in East Syriac script as *-w-* is actually the final part of *-s-*. Sundermann[396] reads *-(s)qwn* but, according to Sims-Williams who reads *-sqn*, it would be a misprint[397]. Either way, the *-sqn* form – together with *–sq*, *-qn*, *-q* – is typical for the Christian Sogdian's durative suffix where the Manichean Sogdian also records *-skwn, -sk, -kn, -k*, the Buddhist Sogdian *-(')skwn* and the ancient Sogdian secular *-skwn*[398].
/5/: *n'* "not". The stroke of the letters is not well defined but it is nevertheless recognizable. It emphasizes the prohibitive meaning of the negation, which justifies its presence instead of *ny* to translate the Syriac *l'*. See: *C2* (p. 216).
/7/: *z[wyr](t)* "turn"; lit. "let turn". Previously Sundermann[399] connects the presence of the Sogdian causative with the Syriac verb *'pn'* Aphel conjugation, i.e. active/causative of *pn'* "1. se vertit; 2. conversus fuit; 3. rediit;"[400].
/7/: *znẉq*. Müller misread *znyq*[401]. However, *znẉq* "cheek" is an addition of the Sogdian translation because it is missing in the Syriac text.

---

392 See: Brockelmann (1928: 386-387).
393 See: Sundermann (1974: 230, n.44).
394 See also: Sims-Williams (forthcoming 2016).
395 See: Müller (1913: 4-5).
396 See: Sundermann (1974: 230).
397 See: Sims-Williams (2012: 31).
398 See: *GMS* (§ 635) and Gharib (1995: 355).
399 See: Sundermann (1975: 85, n. 144).
400 See: Brockelmann (1928: 578).
401 See: Müller (1913: 4-5).

/9/: *qwrθy̤* "tunic". Term registered with the same meaning in *C2* (p. 214)[402].
/10/: *[n](ẏ)'st*. -'- is highly visible. There is no doubt[403], yet Müller does not read it[404].
/10/: *z'y* "distance"[405].

E5/34
Part of the Gospel for the 2nd Friday of Lent. Luke 13.3-4: /r/.
Part of the Gospel for the 3rd Sunday of Lent. Matthew 20.17-19: /v/.

/r/

/1/ m'tnt · pyšt frm'ẏmsq zw˙ qw šm'x s'.. qt ms
3. l' 'mr 'n' l-kwn dyn d-'p

135 /2/ sγtm'n šm'x˙ qt nm'nẏ ny̤˙ ẇnt'. pry̤my̤θ frγn' ny̤st
klkwn 'n l' ttwbwn hkn' t'bdwn;

/3/ bwt'q' · qd' x'nt šts sry̤t qt 'm[p]st pr wy̤šnt
4. 'w hṅwn tmnt'sr d-ṇpl 'l-yhẇn

/4/ s'rb'γ pr šy̤lwḥ' 't ptxwsd'rt wy̤šnty̤ : cwt šm'[rt']
mgdl' b-šylwḥ' w-qṭḷ 'nwn sbryn 'ntwn

/v/

/1/ (x)ypθ žwxšqt'(y̤) [xypθ] 'srty̤˙ 't qw wy̤[šn]t [s'] pr rθ 't
17. tlmÿdwhy bynwhy w-l-hwn b-'wrḥ' w-

---

[402] On the several attestations of this word in Sogdian, as well as in other Iranian languages, see: Sundermann (1975: 85, n. 146).
[403] See: Sundermann (1975: 85).
[404] See: Müller (1913: 4-5).
[405] The meaning "distance" at this point has been suggested by Sims-Williams who pointed out to me that the Sogdian word *z'y* – usually "earth" – may sometimes mean "place" and even "distance". Personal communication 21.01.2016. See also: Sims-Williams (2015: 254).

/2/ w’nw fr’m’ẏ qw wỵšnt s’ · n’ẏ · snỵmq’ ·· m’x . qw ’wršlm
-’ṁr l-hwn 18. ḣ’ slqyn ḥnn l-’wršlm

140 /3/ s’ · ’t mrtxmỵ z’tỵ · prbxštỵ bwtq’ ·· qw xwštrt dỵnd’rt
w-brh ḋ-’nš’ mštl̇m l-rbÿ khn̈’

/4/ ’t qw dpỵrt s’ . · ’t šỵ ’wz’mntq’ qw mrc s’ · ’t šy
w-l-spr̈’ w-nḥybwnyhy l-mwt’ 19. w-nšlmwnyhy

Translation
/r/ /1-2/ They were. But I tell you: unless you repent, you too will all thus /3/ perish. Or those eighteen heads on whom /3-4/ the tower in Siloam fell and killed them: do [you] think whether */v//*1/..his disciples and together with th[em] on the way /2/so, he said to them: “Lo, we are going up to Jerusalem /3/ and the Son of Man will be delivered over to the chief priests /4/ and scribes, and they will condemn him to death; and him…[406].

Commentary
/r/
/1/: Syriac *l’* “no” is not translated in the Sogdian text.
/1/: *frm’ymsq*. The upper part of the first four letters is not preserved, however the well-defined stroke of the entire word does not allow doubts about reading. This also applies to *’* referred to the 2 pers. pl. pron. *šm’x* always attested in this writing line.
Finally see the use of the verb *frm’y* which stands for “to say, speak” and implies that Jesus is speaking. The same use is found in this fragment in */v*/2/.
/2/: *prymyθ frγn’* “thus”. Müller[407] translates literally “in solcher Art”. In the glossary of *C2* (p. 211), Sims-Williams already notes that this expression is used as an adverb meaning “thus”. Indeed *prymyθ frγn’* translates the Syriac *hkn’* “sic, ita”[408].
/3/: *šts* “eighteen”. The reading is by Müller (1913: 41) and it is also accepted by Sims-Williams (2012: 32). Contra Sundermann (1974: 231): *š(t ̣t)s*.
/3/: *sryt*. The Sogdian noun for “heads”, that follows the number “eighteen”, was added in the Sogdian text because, in the Syriac text, there is only the

[406] According to the Syriac text “and they will deliver him…”.
[407] See: Müller (1913: 41).
[408] See: (Brockelmann 1928: 41).

number.
/4/: *šyḷwḥ'* "Siloam". Syriac onomastics.
/4/: *cwt* "whether". The lower part of *c-* and *–t* is missing; however the rest of it is well defined, so the reading is certain. *cwt* is an addition of the Sogdian translation which is not supported by the Syriac text.
At the end of /r/4/ I read *šm'[rt']* "believe" and not *šm'[x]* "you" as Müller does [409]. The Syriac text has a simple present made up of the plural active participle *sbryn*, of the stem *sbr* "to think, believe", followed by the personal pronoun of the 2 pers. pl. used as ending *'ntwn*. As Telegdi demonstrated (1928), these Syriac verb forms imply the personal pronoun translation also in Sogdian but according to the same syntactic order of the original text, so verb + personal pronoun. The sequence pronoun + verb suggested by Müller is not entirely unusual to the Sogdian language but is still an exception. Moreover, a proof of what we have said so far occurs in the same fragment, a little further, in /v/2/ "we are going up": Syr. *slqyn ḥnn* > Sogd. *snyṃq' m'x*. So, probably, the last word of /r/4/ is represented by the present indicative, 2 pers. pl. *šm'[rt']*, followed by the personal pronoun *šm'x* that should be the first word of the following line which, however, has been lost.
/v/
/1/: *žwxšqt'(ỵ)* "disciples". Müller (1913: 17) reads *žwxšqt'* •. Following Müller this is a plural direct case followed by a punctuation mark. In my opinion, however, there is no punctuation mark, but *–y*, usually oblique ending of hard stems which is used here, in my opinion, to mark a direct object[410]. This function can be supposed even if the text has been lost: since it is a Gospel passage, we can run it down and read: "And as Jesus was going up to Jerusalem, he took the *disciples* aside...".
/1/: *'srty* "joined". Müller reads the word correctly but he does not translate it and puts a question mark[411]. It is Sundermann who shows it is a past participle < *āsar-* "(sich) vereinigen mit", and who explains its etymology[412]. The term is also attested in the Turco- Sogdian documents[413].
/1/: *rθ* defective writing of *r'θ* "way".
/2/: The Sogdian *qt* followed by the negative *ny*, placed between the noun *nm'nỵ* "penance" and the verbal form *ẉnt'* "do" means "if not" and translates the Syriac *'n l'* "if not"[414]. Both introduce in their respective

[409] See: Müller (1913: 41). No correspondences in Sundermann.
[410] See: *Chapter 3.3.3 Marking the direct object with oblique –y ending.*
[411] See: Müller (1913: 17).
[412] See: Sundermann (1974: 231-232).
[413] See: Hamilton- Sims-Williams (1990: 73, n. G15.4).
[414] "Nisi" according to Brockelmann (1928: 20).

languages the appropriate verb to express a real possibility: in Sogdian subjunctive, 2 pers. pl. *nm'ny wnt'* "(if not/unless) you repent" and in Syriac imperfect with medio-passive diathesis, 2 pers. pl. *ttwbwn* "*id.*".

E5/38

Part of the Gospel for the 4th Sunday of Lent. Matthew 21.28-43: */r/- /v/.*

/r/

/1/qw wỵnỵ s' m(n)[' z'ty šw' myθqry mr'z šw' pr b'γ]
28. ...l-h bry zl ywmn' plwḥ b-krm';

/2/ pyšt xw˙ p'cγnỵ [qθ'rt 't w'nw] wγd'[rt ny q'mmsq zw]
29. hẉ dyn 'ṇ' w-'ṃr l' ṣb' 'n'

/3/ pyšt '˙yms'˙ nm'nỵ[qyn q]tỵ '[t xr](t ')[t pnt 'γt qw dbtyq]
b-ḥrt' dyn 'ttwỵ w-'zl; 30. w-qrb lwt 'ḥrn'

/4/ z'tỵ s'. 't wγd'rt qw wỵnỵ s' [pry]mỵθ [frγn' pyšt xw]
w-'ṃr l-h hkwt hẉ dyn

/5/ p'cγỵ qθ'rt. 't w'nw w'b · d'p't˙ mn' xyp[θ'wnt' 't]
'ṇ' w- 'ṃr 'n' mry w-

/6/ nỵ xrt · qy cn y'nt dw' [b]r[']t[rt q]θ'rt xỵpθ [ptry ryž]
-l' 'zl; 31. ṃnw mn hlyn tr̈yhwn 'ḅd ṣbyn' d-'bwhy

/7/ w'nw (w')[bnt] qw wỵnỵ s' [xwn]y (pỵr)nmcỵq z'tỵ (w'nw)
'mryn l-h ḣw q̇dmy'

[fr'm'y]
'ṁr

/8/ qw wy[šnt s' xwt'w yšwγ r]št' · frm'ỵmsq [zw qw šm']xs'
l-hwn yšw' 'myn 'mr 'n' l-kwn

/9/ qt bwž[brt 't xry]cqt pyrnm bntq' cn [šm'xỵ] qw
d-mkš' w-znÿt' qdmyn l-kwn l-

/10/ bγ'[nyq wš]tm'xs' · p't 'γt qw šm(')[x s' ywḥn]n
-mlkwt' d-'lh'; 32. 't' gyr lwt-kwn ywḥnn

/11/ sn’m θ(br)[yn](ỵ) pr d’tcỵqỵ r’θ ’t nỵ šỵ w(rnd)[’ryšt’] pyšt
b-’wrḥ’ d-k’nwt’ w-l’ hymntwnyhy

/12/ bwž(b)rt ’t [x](rỵ)cqt š(ỵ) wrnd’rn(t) pyšt šm[’x] ms nỵ
mkš̈’ dyn w-znÿt’ hymnwhy ’ntwn dn ’p l̈’

/13/ (c)’(nw) wỵd’ryšt’ nm’nỵqỵn qtỵšt’ qw ’ym[s’] qt wrnw-
kd ḥzytwn ’ttẇytwn b-ḥrt’ d-thymnwn

/14/ -tỵšt’ prỵ(w) ptγwšt’ ’nyw przbr (yw m)[rt](y) m’t. x’nỵ
bh; 33. šm‘w ’ḥrn’ mtl’ gbr’ ḥd ’yt hw’ mr’

/15/ [f](š)y’w(s) · ’t nyštd’rt b’γ · (’t š)ỵ γ(wr)s prwỵd’rt
byt’ w-nṣḇ krm’ w-’ḥdrh

/16/ (pr)ỵt’ ’t qnd’rt wdỵ crxwšt (’t d)ỵ[s]d’rt wdỵ s’rḇ’γ
syg’ w-ḥpr bḣ m‘ṣrt’ w-ḇn’ b-ḣ mgdl’

/17/ (’t) š(ỵ) pr dst[w] qθ’rt (qw) b’γd’rỵt s’ (’)t xrt p[yšt]
w-’wḥdh l-p̈lḥ’ w-ḥẓq; 34. kd

/18/ c’nw pr’γt bryṫỵ žm(n)[w] fšmd’rt xỵpθ bnt(yt)[y qw b’γ-]
dyn mṭ’ zḃn’ d-p’r̈’ šdr l-‘b̈dwhy lwt plḥ̈’

/19/ -d’rỵt s’ qt f[š’m]ỵnt qw wỵnỵ s’ c(n) [wỵnỵ b’γy bryty]
d-nšdrwn l-h mn p’r̈’ d-krmh;

/v/
/1/ [’t ny’d’rnt b’](γd’rỵt) [wyny bntyty ’t] m’t qt šỵ
35. w-’ḥdw plḥ̈’ l-‘b̈dwhy w-’yt d-

/2/ [pyzd’rnt ’t] m’t qt (š)[ỵ sngs’r qθ]’rnt. ’t m’t qt
-mḥ’why w-’yt d-rgmwhy w-’yt d-

/3/ [šy ptxwsd’rnt ’t tym] fšmd’rt nỵt bntỵtỵ qt γrft xnt
-qṭlwhy; 36. w-twb šḍr ‘b̈d’ ’ḥr̈n’ d-sgÿ’yn

/4/ [cn pyrnmcyq](t) · ’t p(rym)ỵθ frγn’ · qθ’rnt qw wỵšnt
ṃn qdmÿ’ w-hkwt ‘bdw l-ḣwn;

/5/ [s’ pyš]t ’ẏms’ ˙ fšmd’rt qw wy̤šnt s’ . xypθ z’ty̤y̤ ·
37. ’ḥryt dyn šḏr lwt-hwn l-brh

/6/ [c]’nw wγd’rt . · db’t . šfrsntq[’] cn mn’ z’ty̤ · pyšt
kd ’ṃr kbr nbhtwn ṃn bry; 38. plḧ’

/7/ b’γd’ryt c’nw šy̤ wy̤d’rnt ˙ z’ty̤y̤ . w’nw w’bnt (w)y̤šnty̤
dyn kd ḥz’why l-br’ ’mrw bynthwn

/8/myd’[ny ’yn](y) xcy̤ ptrq’n xw’r {<[’yst](’) šy̤ ptxw’y̤m
hnw yrt’ tw nqṭlywhy

’t ny’sy̤m wy̤ny̤ ptr[q’n]>} ’t [n](y’) [d’rn]t šy̤
w-n’ḥwd yrtwth; 39. w-’ḥdw

/9/ ny̤šqwxd’r[nt] by̤qp’r cn b’γ . ’t šy̤ ptxwsd’rnt ·
’pqwhy lbr ṃn krm’ w-qṭlwhy;

/10/ c’nw qt ’γt nwqr ˙ b’γy̤ xypθ’wnt ... cw wnty̤q’ qw
40. m’ d-’ṭ’ hkyl mrh d-krm’ mn’ n‘bd l-

/11/ x’nt b’γd’ry̤ts’ w’nw wγd’rnt qw wy̤ny̤ s’ qt pr
-plḧ’ hnwn; 41. ’mryn l-h d-

/12/ z’ry’(w)[y] mrc ny̤st wnty̤q’ wy̤šnty̤ · ’t b’γ . pr dwstw
-byš byš nwbd ’nwn w-krm’ nwḥd

/13/ wnty̤q’ q(w ’)[ny]t b’γd’ry̤t s’ ˙ · wy̤šnt qt θbrntq’
l-’ḥr̈n’ plḧ’ ’ylyn d-yhbyn

/14/ qw wy̤ny̤ s’ br(yty) [p]r xy̤pθ žmnw ⁘ ·⁘ w’nw fr’m’ẏ qw
l-h p’r̈’ b-zbnhwn; 42. ’ṁr l-

/15/ wy̤šnt s’ xwt’w yšwγ cwt qd’c ˙ ptfs’ty̤ ny̤ ’yš(t’)
-hwn yšw‘ l’ mmtwm qrytwn

/16/ pr pwsty̤ ⁚ qt ṣ̌ng qt pcq’w qθ’rnt dy̤sny̤t xy̤d
b-ktb’ d-k’p’ d-’slyw bnÿ’ hy

/17/ [s](ng) qtỵ qw qrnỵ srỵ s' . · cn xwt'w bγ' m(s)' qtỵ
hwt l-rš' d-zwyt' ṃn lwt mry' hwt

/18/ ['yny 't st]y . wrcwnẏ' pr m'[x] cšmt' cỵmyθỵ pyd'r
hd' w-'ytyḣ tdmwrt' b-'ÿnyn; 43; mṭl hn'

/19/ [frm'ymsq] zw qw šm'x s' q[t] ['y](t)ỵ bwtq' cn
'ṁr 'n' l-kwn d-tštql ṃn

Translation
/r/ /1/ to him: 'My [son], [go today and work in the vineyard']. /2/ But he answer[ed and] sai[d thus]: ['I will n]ot,' /3/ but finally he repented and [we]nt. And [he approached the second] /4/ son and spoke to him [li]kewi[se], [but he] /5/ answered and said thus: 'Yes, my lo[rd', and] /6/ did not go. Which of these two brothers did [the will of] his [father?]" /7/ They said thus: "The first son." Thus [said] /7-8/ the Lord Jesus to th[em], "Truly, I say to [you] /9/: tax collectors and prostitutes will go into /9-10/ the heavenly kingdom of God before [you]. For [Jo]hn /10-11/ the Baptist came to you in the way of righteousness, and you [did] not believe him, but /12/ tax collectors and prostitutes believed him. But you, /13/ even when you saw, did not finally repent that /14/ you might believe in him. Hear another parable. There was a man, /14-15/ the master of a house, and he planted a vineyard and put /15-16/ a fence around it and dug a wine press in it and built a tower there; /17/ and leased it to vine-dressers, and left. But /18/ when the season for fruit drew near, he sent his servants [to the vine-dres]sers /19/ that they might send him some of [the fruit] of [his vineyard]. */v/* /1/ [And the vi]ne-dressers [took his servants and] there was *one* whom /2/ [they beat, and] there was *one* whom they [ston]ed, and there was *one* whom /3/ [they killed. And again] he sent other servants, who were more /4/ [than the first ones] and they did likewise to them. /5/ [Bu]t finally he sent his son to them, /6/ he said thus, 'Perhaps, they will be ashamed at my son.' But /7/ when the vine-dressers saw the son, they said thus /7-8/ among themselves, 'This is the heir. Come, let us kill him and take his inheritance.' And they /9/ took *him and* thr[ew] him out of the vineyard and killed him. /10/ When therefore the owner of the vineyard has come, what will he do /11/ to those vine-dressers?" They said thus to him, /11-12/ "He will kill them with a miserable death and /12-13/ entrust the vineyard to [oth]er vine-dressers who /13-14/ will give him the fruits in their season." Thus said /14-15/ the Lord Jesus to them, "Have you never read /16/ in the Scriptures: 'The stone that the builders rejected, that /17/ stone has become the cornerstone; /17-18/ [this]

was from the Lord God [and] it is a wonder in our eyes'? Therefore /19/ I [tell] you, *[the heavenly kingdom of God]* will be taken from *[you]*...

Commentary

/r/

/4/ and /7/: *z'ty*. Addition of the Sogdian text which, in this case, agrees with the *Persian Diatessaron* as in /r/11/*sn'm θ(br)[yn](ẏ)*. We have already illustrated both cases in the previous chapter.

/5/: *p'cγẏ = p'cγny*.

/5/: *d'p't*. Müller (1913: 94) reports the term in the glossary but puts nearby a question mark, as well as Gharib (1995: 135) who translates "truly". The term is neither in Sundermann glossary (1981) nor in *C2*. My translation, "yes", is based on the corresponding Syriac word *'n'* "yes".

/6/: *qy* "who". The Sogdian text agrees with the Greek text which reports *τίς*. In Syriac we read *mnw* "who is".

/6/: *[b]r[']t[rt]*. It is Sundermann's reading (1974: 232); this Sogdian addition has no confirmation either in Syriac or in Greek. See Sogd. *cn y'nt dw' [b]r[']t[rt]* "of these two brothers" Syr. *ṃn hlyn tṛ̈yhwn* "of these two"; Gk. *ἐκ τῶν δύο* "of these two".

/8/: *[r]št'*. See: Sundermann (1974: 224-225).

/11/: *d'tcẏqẏ*. See: Sims-Williams (1981: 15).

/13-14/: *wrnwtẏšt'*. Verb form typical of the Christian Sogdian used to express unreality, characterized by the inclusion of *-wt-* between the verb stem and the ending. See: *GMS* (§ 820) and Sundermann (1974: 233).

/14-15/: *x'nẏ [f](š)y'w(s)*. Here Sundermann's reading is accepted[415] and not that of Müller[416], i.e., *x'nẏ xẏpθ'wnt* because – although the word is not perfectly legible – there is not a single letter that may be read as, for example, *-p-*, *-θ-*, *-t-*.

Finally, the term *fšy'ws* "lord" has also been attested in Manichaean Sogdian[417].

/v/

/2/: *[sngs'r qθ]'rnt*. This reading is by Sundermann (1974: 233) "sie steinigten".

/8/: *['yn](y)* "This". It is a text portion which is lacking so what I read as *-(y)* is a small stroke on the writing line. Müller (1913: 20-21) reads *-t*, Sundermann (1974: 233) instead reads *-d* as the final letter of *xyd*. I consider

[415] See: Sundermann (1974: 233).

[416] See: Müller (1913: 18).

[417] See: *GMS* (§§ 311; 314) and Gharib (1995: 159).

more correct reconstructing *'yny* [418] "this" as the Syriac has *hn'* "this" always translated, in this Gospel lectionary with *'yny*, whereas *xyd*, "that", translates the Syriac *hw*[419]. In addition Sundermann (*ibid*) reconstructs, before the pronoun, *[qt]*. I consider it superfluous and not necessary for the understanding of the text because the corresponding Syriac *d-* is not present.

/11/: *qw x'nt b'γd'rỵts'* "to those vine-dressers". The postposition *s'* is combined with the term to which it refers to. This is clearly visible to the naked eye ans can not be justified with space problems along the line. It should be emphasized that a little further, in /v/13/, we do not have such a combination. There are two plausible explanations: either it is a purely graphic phenomenon or we are dealing with an agglutinative structure, far from being standardized, and this may explain the presence, even at a short distance one from another, of both forms[420].

/12/: *pr dstw wn/qt* "to hand over, hand down, entrust". See: *C2* (p. 210).

/12-13/: *'t b'γ pr dwstw wntỵq'* "entrust the vineyard". Syntactically, the position of the term *b'γ*, with no ending and in pre-verb position, is ambiguous: according to the Sogdian syntax it may be a subject and not a direct object as it is. The Sogdian strictly follows the Syriac syntax where *w-krm' nwḥd* is read[421].

/15/: *ptfs'tỵ nỵ 'yš(t')*. Perfectum praesens: see *GMS* (§ 851); Sims-Williams (2015: 91); and Sundermann (1974: 234).

/15/: *qd'c* "never". *GMS* (§1569): "ever, only in the negative. Man. *kδ'c...nyy*, Chr. *qd'c..ny*, B. *kδ'c....L'*, "never". Here it translates the Syriac *mmtwm* "semper, inde ab omni tempore, numquam"[422].

/16/: *sng* "stone". In this Gospel lectionary the form that shows the occlusive velar sonorization before the nasal dental is attested, in *C2* (p. 225) the form *snq* is attested[423].

/17/: *sng*. Addition of the Sogdian text that has no confirmation in Syriac which presents only the pronoun *hy* as well as the Greek text which has only *οὗτος*.

/17/: *qrnỵ srỵ*. Sundermann reading is accepted (1974: 234). Contra Müller (1913: 20) *qrγy sry*. About *qrny* see also Sims-Williams (1978: 258).

---

418 The same applies to /v/18/.

419 See the glossary.

420 For a broader discussion, see: *Chapter 3.3.7 Real "agglutination" clues or tendency to "justify" the lines?*

421 For a complete overview, see: *Chapter 3.3.3 Marking the direct object with oblique -y ending.*

422 See: Brockelmann (1928: 409).

423 For a further discussion, see: *Chapter 3.1.2 Suffix for the future: q'> g'.*

/17/: *qtỵ*. As concerns the last word of this writing line, as well as Sims-Williams (2012: 32), I accept the Müller reading (1913: 20) contra Sundermann (1974: 234) *qt(ỵ)*.
/18/: *cšmt'* "eyes'". In this Gospel lectionary this is the only form to be attested while in Christian Sogdian the *cym-* form is also attested (*C2*, p. 209).

E5/41
Part of the Gospel for the 4th Tuesday of Lent. John 5.24-40: */r/- /v/.*

/r/
/1/ ['yqwncyq nwšc žw'n 't qw p](d)q['] (s' ny) ['ystq yw'r xrt]
24. ...ḥÿ' d-l'lm w-l-dyn' l' 'ṫ' 'l' šny l-h

/2/ [cn mrcy qw nwšc žw'n s' r](š)t'˙ ršt'˙ frm['ymsq zw qw šm'x]
ṃn mwt' l-ḥÿ'; 25. 'myn 'myn 'ṁr 'n' l-kwn

/3/ (s') qt 'ỵstq' nγ'm˙ ms qšỵ 'γtỵ [sty wyd'γty]
d-'ty' š't' 'p hš' 'ytyḣ 'mty

/4/ qt mwrtỵt˙ ptγwšntq'˙ bγỵ z'tỵ wxr (')[t x'nt qt]
d-mÿt' nšm'wn qlh d-brh ḋ-'lh' w-hṅwn d-

/5/ ptγwšnt. 'žwntq' · p't w'nc'nw qt [bγy ptry sty]
-šm'yn nḥwn; 26. 'ykn' gyr d-l-'b' 'yt

/6/ nwšc žw'n pr wỵnỵ sty'wỵ. · prỵmỵθ [frγn' θbrd'rt ms]
ḥ̈y' b-qnwmh hkn' yḥb 'p

/7/ qw z'tỵ s' qt bnt nwšc žw'n pr (w)[yny sty'wỵ 't]
l-br' d-nhwwn ḥÿ' b-qnwmh; 27. w-

/8/ p't -xš'wn qθ'rt wỵnỵ qt wn't. m(s) [pdq' pyšt]
-'šlṭh d-nhw' 'ḃd 'p dyn'; 28. d-brh

/9/ qt mrt(x)mẏ z'tỵ (x)cỵ n' (wỵd')st' (p)rỵmỵθ [qt 'ystq']
hẉ dyn d-'nš' l' ttdmrwn b-hd' d-'ty'

/10/ nγ’m · wỵd’[γ](ty) qt s’t wỵšnt qt frwrtqtỵỵ (c)[yntr]
š‘t’ ’mty d-klhwn ’ylyn d-b-qbr̈’ ’nwn

/11/ ptγwšntq’ wỵnỵ wxr ’t nỵžntq’ wỵšnt qt qθ’rnt
nšm‘wn qlḣ; 29. w-npqwn ’ylẏn d-‘bdw

/12/ (šyr)ỵt ’ỵšt qw nwšc žw’[ny] (’γz)’mntỵ s’ · ’t wỵšnt
ṭb̈t’ l-qymt’ dḥ̈y’ w-’yl̈yn

/13/ qt qθ’rnt (γnt’qt) ’ỵšt qw pdq’ỵ ’γz’(mnt)ỵ s’ · nỵ
d-‘bdw bÿšt’ l-qymt’ d-dyn’; 30. l’

/14/ qt(’) wn’nq’ zw ’ỵc cn mn’ γrỵwỵ rỵž pr (qw)rwn yw’r
mškḥ ’n’ mdm ṃn ṣbwt npšy l-m‘bd ’l’

/15/ w’nc’nw qt ptγwšmsq zw ṇm’ẏmsqn · ’(t mn’)
’ykn’ d-šm‘ ’n’ d’n ’n’ w-

/16/ pdq’ d’tcỵq xcỵ p’t nỵ q’mmsq zw m(n)’ r[yž]
-dyny k’yn hẉ l’ gyr b‘’ ’n’ ṣbyny

/17/ yw’r xwnỵ ’dỵ rỵž qt fšmd’rt mn’ qt zw wỵc[’w](qy’)
’l’ ṣbynh d-ṁn d-šdrny; 31. ’n ’n’ mshd

/18/ θbr’msqn pr mn’ γrỵw · mn’ wỵc’wqy’ nỵ qtỵ {<(wy)zrw>}
’n’ ‘l npšy shdwty l’ hẇt šryr’;

/v/

/1/ [’t γrb’msq zw qt wyzrw xcy wyny wyc’wqy’ qt]
32. ...w-yd‘ ’n’ d-šryr’ hy shdwth d-

/2/ [wyc’wqy’ θbrtysq pr mn’ šm’x fšmd’ryšt’ qw]
-mshd ‘l-y; 33. ’ntwn šdrtwn lwt

/3/[ywḥnn sn’m θ]brỵnỵ s’ ’t wỵc’(wqy’ θbrd’rt pr)
ywḥnn w-’shd ‘l

/4/ [ršty’q pyšt zw] nỵ cn mrtxmỵt(y) ’sm[sq](n) [wy](c)’[wqy’]
šrr’; 34. ’n’ dyn l’ hẇ’ ṃn brnš’ nsb ’n’ shdwt’

/5/ [yw'r y'nt 'yšt frm'](y)msq zw qt šm'x [žwt'q']
'l' hlyn 'mr 'n' d-'ntwn tḥwn;

/6/ [xy̱d cr'γ m']t qt fr(θ)y̱pt ['t rwxšny](')q
35. ḣw šrg' hw' d-dl̇q w-mnhr

/7/ [θbrty 't šm'x] (q)'md'ry̱št' qt (š)'nt' qbnq
w-'ntwn ṣbytwn d-tštbhrwn

/8/ [nγ'm pr wyny rwxš]ny'q · pyšt m[n]' (sty̱) mn'˙ wy̱c'wqy'.
d-š't' b-nwhrh; 36. ly dyn 'yt ly shdwt'

/9/ [qt mzy'tr] (cn yw)ḥnn p't '(r)qt (qt θ)brd'rt qw mn'
d-rb' ṃn d-ywḥnn 'b̈d' gyr d-yḥb l-y

/10/ [s' mn](') [bγ](y) [ptry] qt šn ['y'mm x'n](t ')rqt qt
'by d-'šlm 'nwn hnwn 'b̈d' d-

/11/ [wn'msq z](w wy)[c'wqy' θbrntqn pr mn'] (qt) {<[bγ](y̱) ptry̱>}
-'bd 'n' shdyn 'l-y d-'b'
fšmd'rt
šlḥ-

/12/ [mn' 't bγy](ptry) qt [fšmd'rt mn' xw wy̱c'wqy' θbrtysq]
-ny; 37. w-'b' d-šlḥny hw̩ shd

/13/ pr mn' · ny̱ (wyny wxr) q(d)'[c ptγwšd'ryšt' šm'x 't ny]
'ly l' qlh mn mtwm šm'twn w-l'

/14/ wny̱ wy̱n'mn(t)y (wy)d'r(yšt' 't) [wyny w'xš ny 'ncyt]
ḥzwh ḥzytwn; 38. w-mlth l' mqwy'

/15/ [pr šm'x c]ywy(θ) pyd'r qt (pr xw)[ny qt xw fšmd'rt]
b-kwn mṭl d-b-ḣw d-hw̩ šḍr

/16/ [šm'x ny] (w)rnt'sqn · [prwyd]t' [pwstyt qt pr wyšnt]
'ntwn l' mhymnyn 'ntwn; 39. bṣw ktb̈' d-b-hwn

/17/ qt [wr](nt)'s[q] (š)m'(x) [qt 'yqwn]cy̱(q) [nwšc] (ž)w'n˙ sty
msbryn 'ntwn d-ḥ̈y' d-l-'lm 'yt

215 /18/ [pr] (šm)'(xy) ['t wyšnt wyc'wqy'] (θbrntq)n mn' · 't ny̱
l-kwn w-hṇwn shdyn 'l-y; 40. w-l'

Translation

/r/ /1/ [eternal life and] he does not [come] to judgment, [but has passed from death] /2/ [to eternal life. Tr]uly, truly, I say to [you] /3/, an hour is coming, and [is] also now here, [where] /4/ the dead people will hear the voice of the Son of God, and [those who] /5/ hear will live. For as [God the Father has] /6/ eternal life in himself, so [he has also granted] /7/ the Son to have eternal life in [himself and] /8/ then has put him in authority also to execute judgment, [but this] /9/ is the Son of Man. Do not marvel at this, /9-10/ [for] an hour [is coming] when all who *are* in the tombs /11/ will hear his voice and come out, those who have done /12/ good to the resurrection of eternal life, and those /13/ who have done evil to the resurrection of judgment. /13-14/ I can do nothing on my own will. But /15/ I judge what I hear and my /16/ judgment is right, because I do not want my own will /17/ but the will of him who sent me. If I alone bear witness /18/ about myself, my testimony is not true. /v/ /1-2/ [And I know that the testimony that he bears about me is true. You sent to] /3/ [John the Baptist], and he has borne witness to /4/ [the truth. But I] not receive the testimony from man /5/, [nevertheless] I say [these things] to you so that you may be saved. /6-7/ [He] was a burning and shining [lamp and you] were willing to rejoice for a [while] /8/ [in his li]ght. But the testimony that I have is /9/ [greater] than that of John. For the works that /9-10/ God [the Father] has given me to [accomplish], the works that /11/ I [am doing], bea[r] witness [about me] that God the Father /11-12/ has sent [me. And God] the Father who [sent me, has himself borne witness] /13/ about me. His voice [you have] never [heard] /14/, his form you have never seen, and /14-15/[you do not have his word] /15/ abiding in [yo]u, for /15-16/ you do [not] believe the one whom He has sent. [You sear]ch [the Scriptures /16-17/ because you [be]lie[ve] that [in them] you have [eter]nal life; /18/ [well, they] bear [witness] about me and not…

Commentary

/r/

/6/: *sty'wy̱* "essence, being". Contra Müller (1913: 61) and Sundermann (1974: 234) *sty'wyy*. However, even if we accept the reading of *sty'wyy*, the accusative with the *–yy* ending is not "freilich ungewöhnlich" as asserted by Sundermann (*ibid.*), at least for this Gospel lectionary[424].

---

[424] See: Chapter *3.3.3 Marking the direct object with oblique -y ending.*

/7/: *qt bnt nwšc žw'n* "to have eternal life". As already pointed out by Sundermann, Sogdian *qt bnt nwšc žw'n* is a literal translation of the Syriac *d-nhwwn ḥ̈y'* "id." [425]. The Syriac noun for "life", i.e. *ḥ̈y'* is plural and this explains the correspondence with a plural verb form and consequently also explains the reason why of the Sogdian passage, i.e. a plural verb form followed by a singular noun. This sentence had already been mentioned by Telegdi as a good example of a faithful translation from Syriac into Sogdian[426]. The only discrepancy is the addition – as usual in this Gospel lectionary – of the adjective *nwšc* as an attribute of the noun *žw'n* "life" that becomes a sort of fixed expression[427]. Greek agrees with Syriac: that is, in the same cases where Syriac presents only the word for "life", the Greek too only has *ζωή*, and when this noun in Syriac is accompanied by *l'lm,* Greek has *αἰώνιος*.
/8/: *p't-xš'wn qθ'rt* < *p'txš'wn wn-qt-* "to put in authority" as translation of the Syriac Aphel conjugation *'šlṭh* "id."[428].
/8/: *pdq' pyšt*. I reconstruct *pyšt* on the basis of the Syriac *dyn*. Contra Sundermann (1974: 235) *cywyθ pyd'r*. At least in this Gospel lectionary there is no example where the Syriac *dyn* is rendered with the Sogdian *cywyθ pyd'r* which is actually used to translate the Syriac *mṭl d-* or *mṭl hn*[429].
/10/: *wy̤šnt qt frwrtqty̤y̤ (c)[yntr]* "all who *are* in the tombs". See Syr. *'ylyn d-bqbr̈' 'nwn* "those who are in the tombs" and Gk. *οἱ ἐν τοῖς μνημείοις* "those in the tombs".
/13/: *pdq'y̤*. See: Sims-Williams (1981: 14).
/14/: *(qw)rwn*. According to Pittard apud Sims-Williams (2012: 32).
/15/: Sogd. *w'nc'nw qt ptγwšmsq zw ṇm'ẏmsqn* and Syr. *'ykn' d-šm' 'n' d'n 'n'*. In both languages there are two verbal forms, i.e. durative present 1 pers. sg. In the first case, however, Sogdian translates the personal pronoun, 1 pers. sg. *zw*, which follows the verb *ptγwšmsq*, reflecting strictly the Syriac *šm' 'n'* (where the personal pronoun acts as a personal ending). In the second case, instead, the Sogdian translation omits the pronoun after the verb *ṇm'ẏmsqn*, despite the presence in Syriac text of *d'n 'n'*. Probably, while respecting a faithful translation, the repetition of the pronoun may have been considered redundant in Sogdian and, therefore, avoided.
/v/
/2/: *[wyc'wqy' θbrtysq pr mn' šm'x fšmd'ryšt' qw]*. Pittard apud Sims-

[425] See: Sundermann (1974: 235).
[426] See: Telegdi (1938: 206).
[427] For a list of all the cases, see: *Sogdian-Syriac Glossary*.
[428] See: Sims-Williams (forthcoming 2016a).
[429] See: *Sogdian- Syriac Glossary*.

Williams (2012: 32) reads *[wyc’wqy’ θbrtys](q pr mn’. šm’)[x fšmd’ryšt’ qw]*.
/3/: Sogd. *qw ywḥnn sn’m θ]bryṇỵ s’*; Syr. *lwt ywḥnn* and Gk. *πρὸς Ἰωάννην*.
/4/: Sogd. *cn mrtxmỵt(y)*; Syr. *ṃn brnš’* and Gk. *παρὰ ἀνθρώπου*.
/6/: *fr(θ)ỵpt*. The correct reading is by Sundermann (1974: 235).
/7/: *qbnq*. Addition of the Sogdian text which has no correspondence either in Syriac or in Greek.
/10/: *[bγ](y) [ptry]* “God the Father”. When the Sogdian language uses the expression “God the Father", Syriac and Greek have only “Father”, respectively, *’b’* and *πατήρ*.
/16/: *[prwyd]t’*. In the Syriac text one reads *bṣw*. For that reason I reconstruct the Sogdian verb *prwyd/prwyst* “to look for, seek”. See *C2* (p. 220).
/17/: *[wr](nt)’s[q] (š)m’(x) [qt ’yqwn]cỵ(q)*. Pittard apud Sims-Williams (2012:32) reads *[’](w)t[ ](brt’)s(q š)m’(x) [qt ’y](qwn)cỵ(q)*.
/17/: Sogd. *wrnt’sq šm’x* “you believe” and Syr. *msbryn ’ntwn* “you think”. The Sogdian *wrn-* means “to believe (having faith)” and usually translates the Syriac *hymn* which has the same meaning[430]. But in this case, Syriac uses the verb *sbr* whose meanings are, according to Brockelmann (1928: 456): “1. putavit; 2. speravit; 3.exspectavit”[431]. In Greek we read *ὑμεῖς δοκεῖτε*.

E5/48

End of the Gospel for the 5th Friday of Lent. Luke 16.2-15: /r/ and /v/1-17/. Beginning of the Gospel for the 6th Sunday of Lent. John 9.39: /v/18-19/.

/r/

/1/ spncỵrspn qt bỵ mn’ · w’nw w’b xwnỵ spncỵrspn
2. ... rb byt’ d-thẇ’ ly; 3. ’ṁr ḣw rb byt’

/2/ pr xypθ γrỵw · c’nỵ ‸{<cw>} wn’m qt mn’ xypθ’wnt ’stq’ cn
b-npšh mn’ ’‘bd d-mry šql l-ḣ ṃn-

/3/ mn’ spcỵrspny’ · .qt mr’z šw’m nỵ qt’ ẉṇq’ zw · ’t pr
-y rbt bytwt’ d-’ḥpwr l’ mškḥ ’n’ w-l-

[430] With particular regard to the Gospel lectionary *E5*, see: *Sogdian- Syriac Glossary*.
[431] See: Brockelmann (1928: 456).

/4/ θb'rγwž. šfrsmq' zw · γrbd'rm cw wnq' · qt c'nw
-mḥdr bht 'n'; 4. yd't mn' ''bd d-m'

/5/ qt nyẓẓtym˙ cn spncyrspny'. pcγ'zntq' mn' pr wyšnty
d-npqt mn rbt bytwt' nqblwnny b-btÿhwn;

/6/ x'nyt · 't žγyrd'rt ẏw ywtr cn wyny xypθ'wnty pwrc'wnt· .
5. w-qṛ' ḥd ḥd mn ḥÿb' d-mrh

/7/ 't w'nw √fr'm'y wγd'rt qw pyrnmcyq s' c'f ptyqn
w-'mr l-qdmy' km' ḥyb

/8/ 'yštγw qw mn' xypθ'wnt˙ s' · w'nw w'b qw wyny s'˙
'nt l-mry; 6. 'ṁr l-h

/9/ stw γwdy rwγn · w'nw w'b qw wyny s'˙ 's tw' pwsty ·
m'' mtr̈yn mšḥ' 'ṁr l-h sb ktbk

/10/ 't nyd žγrt˙ npys. pnc's γwdy · 't w'nw w'b qw √dbtyq nyw
w-tb b'gl ktwb ḥmšyn mtr̈yn; 7.w-'mr l-'ḥrn'

/11/ s' · 't tγw cw ptyqn 'yštγw qw mn' xypθ'wnt s' ·
w-'nt mn' ḥyb 'nt l-mry

/12/ w'nw w'b qw wyny s'˙ stw p'r γntm · w'nw w'b qw
'ṁr l-h m'' kwr̈yn ḥ̈ṭ' 'ṁr l-

/13/ wyny s'˙ pcγ'z tw' pwsty · 't nyd˙ npys št't p'r ·
-h qbl ktbk w-tb ktwb tmn'yn kwr̈yn;

/14/ 't γwbd'rt m'xypθ'wnt pd'tqrẏ spncyrspny.
8. w-šbḥ mrn l-rb byt' d-'wl'

/15/ qt γrb'q-γwny qθ'rt · p't 'ynẏ fcmbdy 'žwnt· .
d-ḥkym'yt 'ḅd bnẅhy gyr d-'lm' hn'

/16/ γrb'q-str xnt wyšnt cn rwxšny'qy 'žwnt pr 'yny
ḥkymyn 'nwn mn bnẅhy d-nwhr' b-šrbt-

/17/ wy̤šnty̤ qwtr · ’t ms zw˙ frm’ymsqn˙ qw šm’x s’ ⁘
-hwn hd’; 9. w-’p ’n’ ’mr ’n’ l-kwn

/18/ ⁚ qt wnt’ šm’x šy̤rγwzy̤t cn ’y̤ny̤ pd’ty̤ γd’my̤ ·
d-‘bdw l-kwn r̈ḥm’ ṃn mmwn’ hn’ d-‘wl’

/19/ qt c’nw qt ’ẏmst. pcγ’zntq’ šm’xy̤ pr wy̤šnty̤
d-m’ d-gmr nqblwnkwn b-mṭlÿhwn

/v/

/1/ ’yqwn-cy̤q sy’qt · xwny̤ ’dy̤ qt pr qbnq prm’n˙
d-l-‘lm; 10. mn d-b-qlyl mhymn

/2/ ms pr γrf. prm’n xcy̤ · ’t xwny̤ ’dy̤ qt pr qbnq
’p b-sgy mhymn hw w-mn d-b-qlyl

/3/ pd’tqry̤˙ ms pr γrf. pd’tqry̤ xcy̤ · qt nwqr pr pd’ty̤
‘wl ’p b-sgy ‘wl hw;11.’n hkyl b-mmwn’

/4/ γr’my̤˙ py̤rny̤q˙ ny̤ qty̤št’ šm’x⁘ ršty’q˙ qw
d-‘wl’ mhÿmn’ l’ hwytwn šrr’ l-

/5/ šm’x s’. qy̤ py̤rtq’ · ’t qt pr ’y̤c qt ny̤ šm’x
-kwn mnw mhymn; 12. w-’n b-d-l’ dylkwn

/6/ xypθ xcy̤˙ py̤rny̤q ny̤ qty̤št’ ˘‸ {<šm’x>} šm’x xypθ. qy̤ θbrty̤q’
l’ ’štkḥtwn mhÿmn’ dylkwn mnw nṫl

/7/ qw šm’x s’⁙ ⁙ ny̤st bnty̤ qt qt’ wny̤ dw’ xypθ’wnt
l-kwn; 13. lyt ‘bd’ d-mškḥ l-tr̈yn mr̈wn

/8/ pr spxšy̤ · p’t qd’ ywy̤ žy̤šty̤ d’rt˙ ’t dbty̤qy̤. fry̤ ·
l-mplḥ ’w gyr l-ḥd nsn’ w-l-’ḥrn’ nrḥm

/9/ qd’ ywy̱ zpry’q wnty̱˙ ’t dbty̱qy̱ ptyθy’. ny̱ qt’
’w l-ḥd nyqr w-l-’ḥrn’ nšwṭ l’ mškḥyn

/10/ wnt’q’ šm’x pr spxšy̱ by̱ bγy̱y̱ ’t by̱ γr’my̱ ⁘ ⁘
’ntwn l-mplḥ l-’lh’ w-l-mmwn’;

/11/ pyšt pryš’y̱qt˙ c’nw ptγwšd’rnt˙ y’nt s’t. · cy̱wy̱θ
pr̈yš’ dyn kd šm‘w hlyn klhyn mṭl

/12/ py̱d’r qt fry̱ d’ry̱q m’tnt˙ γr’my[432] {<n’-qty̱>} psxnt wny̱q
d-rḥmyn hww ksp’ mmyqyn

/13/ m’tnt pry̱w · pyšt xwt’w yšwγ. w’nw fr’m’y˙ qw wy̱šnt
hww bh; 15. yšw‘ dyn ’ṁr l-hwn

/14/ s’ · šm’x ’y̱št’ qt ’rt’w ’štẏt’sqn xypθ γry̱w
’ntwn ’nwn d-mzdqyn npšhwn

/15/ mrtxmy̱ty̱ py̱rnms’ · pyšt bγy̱ γrbty̱sq šm’x
qdm bnÿnš’ ’lh’ dyn yd‘ lbẅtkwn

/16/ žy’wrt · qt ’y̱c qt ˇ‸mzy̱x {<ptrzty>} xcy̱ mrtxmy̱ty̱ my̱d’ny̱. ·
d-mdm d-rm byt bnÿnš’

/17/ bγy̱ py̱rnms’. pcxwd-γwny̱ xcy̱ ⁘ (Syriac red) dḥd bšb’ dšt’
qdm ’lh’ ndyd hwy̱

/18/ dṣwm’ ⁘ ywḥnn ⁘ bṣḥ ⁘ y ⁘ (Syriac black) w’ṃr yšw‘ lkn̈š’
dyhwd̈y’ ⁘

/19/ (Sogdian black) ’t w’nw fr’m’y xwt’w yšwγ qw cxwd’ny̱ ’w’zy̱t s’ ⁘

[432] This time there is no sign that refers to a correction, but the word is deleted and replaced by *n’-qty̱*, which is vertically placed along the inner margin, close to the corresponding writing line.

Translation
/r/ /1/ ...the manager I had.' And so the manager said /2-3/ to himself: 'What shall I do, since my master is taking the management away from me? I am not able to dig, and I am /4/ ashamed as beggar. I know what to do, so that when /5/ I go forth from management, people may receive me into their /6/ houses.' And he summoned his master's debtors one by one /7/, and thus he said to the first: /7-8/ 'How much do you owe to my master?' Thus he said to him: /9/ 'A hundred containers of oil.' Thus he said to him: 'Take your bill /10/, and sit down quickly and write fifty containers.' And thus he said to another: /11/ 'And how much do you owe to my master?' /12/ And thus he said, 'A hundred measures of wheat.' Thus he said to him: /13/ 'Take your bill, and seat down and write eighty measures.' /14/ "And our master commended the dishonest manager /15/ because he acted astutely. For the sons of this world /16-17/ are more shrewd in dealing with their own generation than the sons of light. And I also tell you /18/: make friends for yourselves by means of unrighteous wealth /19/ so that when it ends, they may receive you into the */v/* /1/ eternal shadows. One who is faithful in a little /2/ is also faithful in much, and one who is dishonest in a little /3-4/ is also dishonest in much. If then /4-6/ you have not been faithful in the unrighteous wealth, who will entrust the truth to you? And if you have not been faithful in that which is another's, who /6-7/ will give you that which is your own? No servant can serve two masters, /8/ for either he hates the one and loves the second, /9/ or he will be devoted to the first and despise the second. /9-10/ You cannot serve both God and wealth". /11/ But as the Pharisees heard all these things, since /12/ they loved money, /13/ they ridiculed him. But thus spoke the Lord Jesus to them: /14/ "You are *those* who showed themselves *to be* righteous /14-15/ before the own soul of men, but God knows your /16/ hearts: what is exalted among men /17/ is an abominable in the sight of God". (Syriac red) for the sixth Sunday /18/ of Lent. John, in chapter 10. (Syriac black) and Jesus spoke to the crowds of Jews /19/ (Sogdian black), and thus spoke the Lord Jesus to the crowds of Jews.

Commentary
/r/
/2/ *c'ny̱*. The correct reading is by Sims-Williams (2012: 33).
/3/: *spcy̤rspny'= spncyrspny'*[433] "management". The word is composed by *spncyrspn* "manager" + abstract suffix *-y'*. See Syriac *rbt bytwt'* "id.", noun

[433] It is the same in */r/5/*.

formed with the abstract -*wt'*.
/7/: *fr'm'y*. Still legible; it is deleted and is replaced by *wγd'rt*, which is vertically placed along the inner margin of the fragment close to /*r*/8/. The substitution which has been made by the scribe, is significant because it proves the semantic sphere of the verb *frm'y/frm't*. The first meaning is "to order, command", but *frm'y/frm't* is used meaning "to say, speak" when someone important is speaking, above all, when Jesus is speaking. In the case here attested, however, the speaker is a simple manager and the scribe – realizing the mistake –, deletes *fr'm'y* and replaces it with the verb *w'b/wγt-* "to say, speak".
/7/: *pyrnmcyq* "first". The form that maintains *r* before -*n*- is here attested, as occurs in Buddhist and Manichaean Sogdian[434]. In Christian Sogdian the word *pynmcyq* can also be found without -*r*-: thus, for example, in *C2* (p. 223).
/7-11/: *ptyqn* "debtor" as translation of the Syriac *ḥyb'* which means – according to Brockelmann[435] – "1. inferiore; 2. noxius; 3. debet (pecuniam); 4. debitor". In /*r/6*/ this Syriac term (plural form) is translated into Sogdian with *pwrc'wnt* (plural form from *pwrc*)[436]. To the best of my knowledge, the Sogdian *ptyqn* is only attested in secular Sogdian – as *ptykn* – meaning "guilty"[437]. Concerning the Sogdian *pwrc'wnt*, *pwrc* meaning "loan" is well attested in Christian, Manichaean and secular Sogdian[438].
/12/: *p'r* "measures". See: *GMS* (§ 1662) which reports the Greek *κόρος*.
/14/: *m'xypθ'wnt*. According to Sims-Williams (2012: 33).
/16/: Sogd. *γrb'q-str* "more shrewd" and Syr. *ḥkymyn* lit."shrewd". Syriac, unlike Sogdian, does not have the comparative and superlative degrees, which can be deduced from the meaning of the sentence, and by *mn* – as in this case – which introduces the second term of comparison in case of a comparative, or by *mn kl* which introduces the second term of comparison in case of superlative[439].
/16/: *wyšnt*. Mechanical translation of the Syriac *'nwn* which is here used as copulas, 3 pers. pl. of the verb "to be", and which is translated in Sogdian with *xnt*, 3 pers. pl. of the present indicative of the verb "to be".
/17/: *qwtr*. Indian loan word. *qwtr* is the Christian Sogdian form. See: Buddhist and Manicheaen Sogdian *kwtr*, secular Sogdian *kwt'r*, Kothanese

434 See: *GMS* (§§ 354; 356).
435 See: Brockelmann (1928: 218).
436 See: *GMS* (§ 1091).
437 See: *GMS* (§ 148); and Gharib (1995: 324).
438 See: Gharib (1995: 330).
439 See: Thackston (1999: 45).

gūttaira and Sanskrit *gotra*[440].

/v/

/1/: *sy'qt* "shadows". Müller reads *sy'qt* but translates "Zelte" whereas Sundermann (1974) makes no comment about it. The Syriac text has the word *mṭl'* which according to Brockelmann[441] means "tectum". The translator might have mistaken *mṭl'* for *ṭll'*, i.e, the Syriac word for "shadow": in this case, we would here expect Sogdian *x'nyt* "dwellings". Or, as pointed out by Sims-Williams[442], the Sogdian *sy'q* means "shadow, shade, shelter, dwelling" and is used to translate Syr. *ṭll'* "shadow" as well as Syr. *mṭl'* "shelter, dwelling".

/1/: *prm'n* "faithful, honest". See Sundermann (1974: 236-237).

/4/: Sogd. *ny qtỵšt' šm'x* and Syr. *l' hwytwn*. The personal pronoun, 2 pl., is attested in Sogdian but not in Syriac[443].

/4/: *ršty'q*. See: Sundermann (1974: 224).

/8/: "hates the one and loves the second". The Syriac text has two imperfects, both indicating a future probability: *nsn'* "will hate" and *nrḥm* "will love". Sogdian translates the first verbal form with *žỵšty d'rt* "he hates" while, in the second case, Sogdian translates only the noun *fry*. The same occurs in the next writing line where Sogdian has the noun *ptyθy'* as translation of the Syriac imperfect used as future, *nšwṭ* "despise".

/10/: *bγỵỵ*. See: Sims-Williams (1981: 14).

/13/: *yšwγ* "Jesus". Syriac onomastics.

/19/: *cxwd'nỵ*. adjective formed by the noun *cxwd* "Jew" + the suffix -*'ny*[444].

E5/51

Part of the Gospel for the 6th Friday of Lent. Matthew 24.24-26: /r/; Matthew 24.32-33: /v/.

/r/

/1/ [----------------- qt] q(t)' b(')[t ms]

24. ...'n mškḥ' 'p

[440] See: *GMS* (§ 483n1).

[441] See: Brockelmann (1928: 275).

[442] See: Sims-Williams (forthcoming 2016a).

[443] See: Chapter *3.3.8 Personal pronouns*.

[444] See: *GMS* (§§ 1040-1041).

255 /2/ [wyctyt n'y pyrnmstr wγ]d'rm qw · šm'[x]
l-gb̈y'; 25. ḣ' qdmt 'mrt l-kwn;

/3/ [s' qt nwqr w'bntq' qw šm](')x s'˙ n'ẏ˙ dxšty' s(t)[y]
26. 'n hkyl n'mrwn l-kwn ḣ' b-ḥwrb' hẉ

/v/
/1/ [γ](rb)t's[qn šm'x qt pnt pr'γt prymyθ frγn']
32..... yd'yn 'ntwn d-mṭ' qyṭ'; 33. hkn'

/2/ ms (š)m'x · c'nw [wyd'ryšt' y'nt s't γrb-]
'p 'ntwn m' d-ḥzytwn hlyn klhyn d'w

/3/ [-t](') (qt) pnt pr'γt qw d(b)[ry s' ršt' frm'ymsq zw]
d-mṭt l-ḣ l-tr''; 34. 'myn 'mr 'n'

Translation

/r/ /1/ [if] will be possible, [even] /2/ [the elect. Lo, I] have told you [beforehand]. /3/ [So, if they will say to y]ou, 'Lo, he is in the desert' ... /v/ /1/ [you k]now [that summer is near. In the same way] /2/ when you too [will see all these things, you kn]ow /3/ that he is near, at the very gat[es. Truly, I say]

Commentary

/r/

/2/: *[wγ]d'rm*. Pittard apud Sims-Williams reads *[w](γ)d'rm*[445]. At any rate, the upper stroke of *-d-* and *-'-* are completely missing, but the lower one is perfectly recognizable and for, this reason, the reading is certain.

/v/

/1/: *[γ](rb)t's[qn]*. Sims-Williams reads *[γ](rb)t's(q)n*[446].

/2-3/: *[γrb—t](')*. The hypothesis of Sundermann is accepted[447]. According to him the 2 pers. pl. ending would be written separately from the verbal stem and it would appear in /v/3/ where two small strokes are preserved – the one below and the upper on e– which let us to suppose -'.

445 See: Sims-Williams (2012: 33).

446 See: Sims-Williams (2012: 33).

447 See: Sundermann (1974: 238, n. 50).

E5/65

Part of the Gospel for Good Friday. Matthew 27.54: */r/*1-2/; Matthew 27.57: */r/*3-4/.

Part of the Gospel for Easter Saturday or for the evening of Good Friday. Matthew 27.64: */v/*2-4/; Matthew 27.65: */v/*4-5/.

/r/

/1/ ['t x'nt 'yšt qt qtnt pcqwyrd]'rnt. [šyr 't w'nw w'bnt]
54. w-'ylyn d-ḧwy dḥlw ṭb w-'mrw

/2/ [pr ršty'q 'yny] (m)'t ∵ [bγy̤ z'ty ------------------------]
šryr'yt hn' brh hw' d-'lh';

/3/ ['γt γ'mqyn mrty c]n rmθ(') [qt šn'm m't ywsp]
57....'t' gbr' 'tyr ' ṃn rmt' d-šmh ywsp

/4/ [qt ms xw žγyr]ty̤ [bwt žwxšqy qw xwt'w yšwγ s']
d-'p hw̤ 'ttlmḋ hw' l-yšw'

/v/

/1/ [------------------------------- wytwr qw šty̤q my̤θy̤]
64...........'dm' l-tlt' yẅmyn

/2/ [p](r)m · qt [ny 'ysynt wyny žwxšqt' -------------------]
d-lm' n'twn tlmÿdwhy ngnbwnyhy

/3/ [p]r xšp'˙ · '(t) [w'nw pcqwyntq' qw rmy s' qt cn mwrty d'm]
b-lly' w-n'mrwn l-'m' d-ṃn byt mÿt'

/4/ ['xš]t˙ · 't [bwtq'--------------bžyqtr cn pyrnmcyq w'nw]
qm w-thw' ṭw'yy 'ḥryt' byš' ṃn qdmyt'. 65.

/5/ [w]'(b) [qw wyšnt s' pylṭws---------------------------------]
'ṁr l-hwn pylṭws

Translation
/r//1/[...and those things which happened,] feared [greatly, and said] /2/[thus: “Truly this] was [the Son of God……..”]. /3/[Came a rich man fr]om Arimathea [whose name was Joseph,] /4/[who had also been call]ed [as a disciple to the Lord Jesus]. */v/* /1-2/[un]til [the third day] that [/3/[his disciples may note come *and steal him* b]y night, and [say thus to the people: /4/”He has [risen from the place of the dead], and [*the latter error* will be worse than former”. Thus] /5/[s]aid [Pilate to them...].

Commentary
/r-v/. As already mentioned[448], the identification of this fragment, following Sundermann[449], is the work of Pittard- Sims-Williams[450] and is here fully accepted. The reconstructions in the text, however, are mine and are based, of course, on the Syriac text, as well as on the correspondences found in this Gospel lectionary between Sogdian and Syriac terminology; where these have failed, I preferred to leave blank spaces considering, however, the uncertainty due to the fragmentary character.

E5/72
Part of the Gospel for the Tuesday after Easter. Luke 24.19-32: */r-v/*.

/r/
/1/ [w’byntqn qw wyny s’ cn xw](t’)[w yšwγ pyd’r xyd]
19... ’mryn l-h ‘l yšw‘ ḣw

270 /2/ [qt cn ncrθ knθ mrt]y̤ qt m’t. bywny̤ · (’t) [z’wrqyn]
d-ṃn nṣrt gbr’ d-hw’ nby’ w-ḥyltn

/3/ [m’t pr w’]xš. ’t pr qty̤t · bγy̤ pyrnms’ ’t mγ[wn]
hw’ b-mlt’ w-b-‘b̈d’ qdm ’lh’ w-qdm

/4/ [rmy] (p)yrnms’ · ’t šy̤ prbxšd’rnt xwštr dynd’rt
klh ‘m’; 20. w-’šlmwhy r̈by khn̈’

448 See: Chapter *2.1 Previous editions*.
449 See: Sundermann (1975: 82-83).
450 See: Pittard- Sims-Williams (2013: 46-47); (2014: 59).

/5/ [’t x]wštrt qw mrcy̱ pdq’ s’. ’t šy̱ pr ptcng
w-qšÿš’ l-dyn’ d-mwt’ w-zqpwhy;

/6/ [s]wxswd’rnt · pyšt m’x w’[nw] šm’ryq̣ m’t˘‸{<ym>}
ḥnn dyn sbryn hwyn

/7/ m’x. · qt xw pcp’n m’t qt z(r)yncy̱ ysr’yl
d-hwyw ‘tyd hw’ d-nprqywhẏ l-’ysryl

/8/ rmy̱y̱ · ’t n’ẏ š(y) myθ xnt n’ẏ cywyθ ms’ qt
w-ḣ’ tlt’ yẅmyn ḣ’ ṃn d-

/9/ y’nt ’y̱št qtnt˙ yw’r ms ’y̱nšt˙ cn m’x wyd’s-
-hlyn klḣyn hwÿ; 22. ’l’ ’p nš̈’ ṃnn

/10/ [-γw]ny̱ prby̱rntqn · p’t py̱r˘{<nm>} qtnt wy̱šnt qw frwrt-
’tmhn qdm hẅy gyr l-byt qbwr’;

/11/ -qty̱ s’ · ’t c’nw ˘‸{<ny̱>} byrd’rnt ˘‸{(wyn)[y]} tmp’ry̱ · ’γtnt
23. w-kd l’ ’škḥ pgrh ’ty

/12/ wγd’rnt qw m’x (s)’ qt (fry)šty̱t wy̱d’ry̱m
’mrn l-n d-m̈l’k’ ḥzyn

/13/ m’x wdy̱ · ’t w’nw w’by̱ntqn cn wyny̱ pyd’r qt
tmn w-’mryn ‘l-why d-

/14/ žwnty̱ xcy̱ · ’t (m)s mrtxmy̱t cn m’x xrtnt
-ḥy ḥw; 24.w-’p ’n̈š’ ṃn-n ’zlw

/15/ [q]w frwrtqty̱ s’. · ’t (byr)d’rnt pry̱my̱θ
l-byt qbwr’ w-’škḥw hkn’

/16/ [frγn’] w’nc’nw qt (wγ)d’rnt ’y̱nšt · pyšt
’yk m’ d-’mr nš̈’ l-h

/17/ [šy ny] (wyd)’rnt ⁘ (wyd)’γty w’nw [fr]’m’y qw
dyn l’ ḥzw; 25. hydyn ’ṃr l-

/18/ [wyšnt s’] x[w]t’w yšwγ · ’ỵ mnt(m)[’](n)ỵt ’t
-hwn yšw‘ ’w ḥsyr̈y r‘yn’ w-

/v/
/1/ [’yšt pcp’n] (m’t) [qt pt’wt mšyḥ’ ’t qt tyst]
26. hlyn ‘tyd hw’ d-nsybr mšyḥ’ w-d-n‘wl

/2/ [qw xypθ] γwbty’ s’ . · ’t [’γ’zyq m’t cn mwš’y]
l-tšbwḥth; 27. w-šry hw’ ṃn mwš’

/3/ [n]wm ’t cn s’t bywnỵtỵ pẇstỵt . · ’[t wycyryq]
w-ṃn klhwn nbÿ’ w-mpšq

/4/ m’t qw wỵšnt s’ cn xypθ γrỵwỵ pyd’r c[n s’t]
hw’ l-hwn ‘l npšh ṃn klhwn

/5/ pwstỵt · ’t pnt b’wd’rnt qw dỵx’w s’ [xyd]
ktb̈’; 28. w-qrbw hww l-qryt’ hy

/6/ qt šwỵq m’tnt ’ws’ · ’t xw ’ndỵšỵq (m)[’t]
d-’zlyn hww l-h w-hw̤ msbr hw’

/7/ qw wỵšnt s’ qt w’nc’nw qt qw dwr wy’q s’
l-hwn d-’yk d-l-dwk’ rḥyq’

/8/ šwỵqm’t · ’t šỵ trγz’y qθ’rnt . ’t w’nw
’zl hw’; 29. w-’lṣwhy w-

/9/ pcqw’d’rnt qw wyny s’ · ’nc’ẏ m’x nbnt ·
-’mryn l-h pwš lwt-n

/10/ cywyθ pyd’r qt myθ qšỵ ’wrs{<d’r>}t pr t’rỵ bỵ
mṭl d-ywm’ hš’ rkn lh l-mḥšk

/11/ ’t tγtỵ qt swqỵ wỵšntỵ nbnt · ’t b’ qt
w-‘l d-nqw’ lwt-hwn; 30. w-hw’ d-

/12/ c’nw ṗšỵd’rt dn wỵšntỵ prw . · ’ỵd’rt nγnỵ ’t
-kd ’stmk ‘mhwn nsb lḥm’ w-

/13/ ’frywn qθ’rt ’t ’wxsd’rt. ’t θbrd’rt
-ḅrk w-qṣ’ w-yḥb

300/14/ qw wy̤šnt s’ · ’t ywny̤ xwycq qtnt wy̤šnty̤
l-hwn; 31. w-mḥd’ ’tptḥ

/15/ cšmt’. ’t šy̤ ptz’nd’rnt · ’t xw swx(sty)
‘ynÿhwn w-’štwd‘why w-hw̤ ’štql

/16/ qty cn wy̤šnt · ’t w’nw w’by̤q m’tnt [yw]
l-h ṃn-hwn; 32. w-’mryn hww ḥd

/17/ qw dbt(y̤q) s’ · cwtny̤˙ m’x žy’wr (γr’)[n]
l-ḥd l’ hw’ lbn yqyr

/18/ m’t m’[x] cy̤ntr : c’nw ž’y̤qm’t (d)[n m’x]
hw’ b-gwn kd mmll ‘m-n

Translation

/r/ /1/ [they said to him: “Concerning the L]or[d Jesus who] /2/ [*was* a ma]n [from the city of Nazareth] *and* was a prophet, and /2-3/ [he was mighty in wor]ds and deeds before God and /4/ before [all the people]. And chief priests and elder delivered him /5-6/ up to be condemned to death, and crucified him. But we had thought in this [way] /7/ that He was going to redeem /7-8/ the people of Israel. And lo, it is the third day since /9-10/ these things happened. Moreover, some of our women told *us* something amazing. Very early indeed in the morning, they were at the sepulchre /11/ and when they did not find His body, they came back /12/ and they said to us: ‘we have seen the angels there’, /13/ and thus they spoke about him that he /14/ was alive. And also the men among us went /15/ to the sepulchre and found *it* just /16/ as the women had said, but /17/ they did [not] see [him]”. Then, thus he said /18/ the Lord Jesus [to them]: “O foolish ones…./*v*/ /1/ [Was it not necessary that the Messiah should suffer these things in order to enter] /2/ [in]to his glory?” And [he began from the] /3/ law [of Moses] and from all the writings of the Prophets, and [he explained] /4-5/ to them *the things* concerning himself i[n all] the Scriptures. And they drew near to the village /6/ to which they were going, and he acted /7/ as /7-8/ if he was going in a place far away. And they compelled him and /8-9/ thus they said to him: “Stay with us, /10/ because now the day is declining and it is becoming

dark". /11/ And he went in to stay with them. And happened that /12/ when he reclined at table with them, he took the bread and /13/ blessed and broke *it*. And he gave *it* to /14/ them. And their /14-15/ eyes were immediately opened, and they recognized him. And he vanished /16/ from their sight. And thus they said to [each] /17/ other: "Or our heart /17-18/ within us was not honoured while he talked t[o us]".

Commentary

/r/

/1/: *[cn xw](t')[w]*. Sundermann, while stating the uncertain reading, proposes *(m')*[451]. I read *(t')* for two reasons. The first concerns the lower stroke of *-t-* which is rounded and put below the writing line (as expected). The second reason is based on the comparison with the Syriac text and its translation into Sogdian. In Syriac, there is *yšwʿ* "Jesus", always accompanied, in the Sogdian text of this Gospel lectionary, by the apposition *xwt'w* "Lord" so that *xwt'w yšwy* "the Lord Jesus" becomes a fixed and idiomatic expression. Therefore, I prefer reading *-(t')-* as part of *xwt'w*. Finally, Pittard apud Sims-Williams (2012: 34) reads *(c)[n xw](t'w)*.

/2/: *[z'wrqyn]* "strong, mighty"[452]. Corresponds to the Syriac *ḥyltn*[453]. Sundermann leaves a blank space and then hypothesizes *m't* as the last word of this writing line; however, according to the Syriac text and calculating the approximate length of this writing line and the number of words possibly contained in it, I prefer to conjecture *m't* as the first word of */r/3/*.

/3/: *qtỵt*. See: Sims-Williams (1981: 16).

/6/: *[s]wxswd'rnt*. Metathesis for *sxws-*. See: *GMS* (§§ 417, 425-426) and Sundermann (1974: 241)[454].

/6/: *m't{<ym>}*. The addition of the personal ending is placed above the writing line, in correspondence with *-t-* and is legible. Sundermann (1974: 241), however, transliterates *m't[ym]*, without reporting the correction which is attested in the fragment.

/7-8/: *ysr'yl rmyy* "the people of Israel". As already seen in *E5/19/v/*10 / where the Syriac text only has "Israel", the Sogdian text adds the word for "people", without any element that might indicate the relationship between the two terms. On the misprinted *ysr'ỵl* apud Sundermann (1974: 241)

---

[451] See: Sundermann (1974: 241, n. 52).

[452] See: *C2* (p. 237).

[453] In (35) the Sogdian verb *z'wrqyn b(w)-/qt-* "to become strong" is attested as translation of the Syriac Ethpaal conjugation *'tḥyl* "id.". See: *Sogdian-Syriac Glossary*.

[454] Sims-Williams underlined that the unexpected feature is the second *–w-*. Personal communication 25.01.2016.

previously Sims-Williams (2012: 34).

/9-10/: *ỵnšt cn m'x wyd's[-γw]nỵ prbỵrntqn* "some of our women told *us* something amazing". Syriac reads *nš̈' mnn 'tmhn* "some of our women have shocked/surprised us" because *'tmhn* is a perfect, 3 pers. pl. of the Aphel conjugation, i.e. the active/causative one, whose meanings are "1. attonitum reddidit; 2. mirari fecit" < *tmh* "miratus est"[455]. The Syriac text, as already noted by Sundermann (1974: 241), agrees with the Greek one *ἐξέστησαν ἡμας*.

/10/ *pỵr˘{<nm>}*. The last two letters *-nm* are added immediately below the writing line in correspondence with *-r*.

/11/: *{(wyn)[y]}*. The correct reading is by Sims-Williams (2012: 34).

/11/: *tmp'ry̱* "body". The scribe deletes *-y*, so it is correct understanding *tmp'r*[456].

/17/: *w'n(w fr)*. After *-n-*, just a little part of the text is missing, but the upper part of *-w* which is related to the previous letter, the upper part of *f-* and the top dot which generally characterizes the letter *r* can be distinguished.

/18/. The interjection *'y* "oh!" is attested only in Christian Sogdian (*C2*: 206)[457]. The corresponding Syriac interjection has two forms: *'w* and *'yw*. According to Brockelmann, *'ẇ* is attested in the *Peshitta*[458].

/v/

/1/: *(m't)*. Now only the lower part of *–t* is recognizable, for the rest the reading is uncertain. Sundermann (1974: 242) reads *(qt)* which is plausible because before the lower stroke of *-t* , there is an horizontal stroke, little distinguishable, that might also be part of *q-*. But considering the lost fragment part, the number of letters that might be contained in it, and the comparison with the Syriac text, I consider *(m't)* the most likely reading.

/3/: *[n]wm* "law" and *pẇstỵt* "writings" are two additions of the Sogdian text. Syriac text has *ṃn mwš' w-ṃn klhwn nbÿ'* "from Moses and from all the Prophets" and it agrees with the Greek text *ἀρξάμενος ἀπὸ Μωϋσέως καὶ ἀπὸ πάντων τῶν προφητῶν* "id."

/8/: *šwỵqm't*. Between *-q* and *m-* a ligature is clearly visible: there is no doubt that this periphrastic verbal form has been written continuously. This is the same for *ž'ỵqm't* in /v/18/.

/10/: *'wrs{<d'r>}t*. Addition placed above the writing line.

---

455 See: Brockelmann (1928: 827).

456 See: *3.3.3 Marking the direct object with oblique -y ending.*

457 As reported by Sims-Williams (1988: 147-148), in the Christian Sogdian fragment *C74* (= *E28*, Sims-Williams: 2012: 213) the Syriac loan *'wh* "ah! alas" is also attested.

458 See: Brockelmann (1928: 14).

E5/73
Part of the Gospel for the Tuesday after Easter. Luke 24.32-35: */r/*.
Part of the Gospel for the Wednesday after Easter. John 15.18-20: */v/*.

/r/

/1/ [prw pr r']θ · 't [prybyrsq]n qw m'x s' pwst(yt)
32. ..b-'wrḥ' w-mpšq l-n ktb̈';

/2/ 't 'xštnt˙ p[r wy'q] 't zy̤wstnt qw '[w]ršlm
33. w-qmw b-ḣ b-š'ṭ' w-hpkw l-'wršlm

/3/ s' · 't by̤rd'(r)n[t ywnt](s)nw žwxšqt' qt '(w)štyt
w-'škḥw l-ḥd'sr d-knyšyn

/4/ m'tnt. 't x'nt (')dy̤t qt dn wy̤šnty̤ prw · (c')[nw]
w-l-'ylyn d-'m-hwn; 34. kd

/5/ w'byntqn. · qt pr ršty'q 'xšt˙ (m)['x xypθ'wnt]
'mryn d-šryr'yt qm mrn

/6/ 't wy̤n'wc[yq] qty̤ qw š[mγwn sng s' 't ms]
w-'tḥzy l-šm'wn; 35. w-'p

/7/ wy̤šnt pry̤by̤(r)[nt x'nt 'yšt qt qtnt pr r'θ]
hṇwn 'št'yw 'ylyn d-ḧwy b-'wrḥ'

/8/ {<'t>} c'nw̤ pt(z˙n)[ty qty qw wyšnt s' c'nw 'wxs-]
w-'ykn' 'tyd' l-hwn kd qṣ'

/9/ -(d)'(r)t [nγny]
lḥm'

/v/
/1/ (m)n'y̤y̤ žy̤šty̤ nẏ'd'rt ['t qt cn f]cm[pd]
18. ...ly ṣn'; 19. w-'lw ṃn 'lm'

/2/ bwtỵšt’ šm’x. · fc(m)[pd wy’ xypθ]tỵ frỵ-d’rỵq
hwytwn ‘lm’ l-dylh rḥm

/3/ m’t. · yw’r nỵ ’ỵšt’ šm[’x cn] fcmpd · p’t zw
hw’ ’l’ l’ hwytwn ṃn ‘lm’ ’n’ gyr

/4/ [wyc]nd’rm š{<m>}’xỵ cn fcmpd. · c[y]myθy pyd’r žỵšt(y)
gbytkwn ṃn ‘lm’ mṭl hn’ sn’

/5/ [ny’st šm]’xỵ fcmpd · šy’ ’brt’ [w’xš] qt
l-kwn ‘lm’; 20. ‘hdw mlt’ d-

/6/ [zw frm’d’rm qw šm’x] s’ · qt (n)[yst] bntỵ qt
-’n’ ’mrt l-kwn d-lyt ‘bd’ d-

/7/ [mzy’tr by cn xypθ xypθ’wnt qt] (m)n’ỵ (pš)qỵrd’rnt
-rb ṃn mrh ’n l-y rdpw

/8/[ms šm’xy pšqyrntq’ ’t qt mn’ w](’)xšt
’p l-kwn nrdpwn w-’n mlty

/9/ [d’rnt ms šm’x xypθy d’rntq’ ---]
nṭrw ’p dylkwn nṭrwn.

Translation
/r/ /1/ on the road, while [he explained] the Scriptures to us?” /2/ And they rose [without delay] and returned to Jerusalem. /3/ And they found [the elev]en disciples who where gathered /4/ and those who together with them, meanwh[ile] /5/ said: “Our [Lord] has risen indeed, /6/ and has appeared to S[imon. And] /6-7/ they [also] told [what had happened on the road], /8-9/ and how he [was] known [to them in the breaking of the bread]… */v/* /1/ “it has hated me. [And If] /2/ you were [of the world], the wor[ld] would love [you as its own]; /3/ but you are not [of the] world. /3-4/ I [ch]ose you out of the world indeed, therefore /4-5/ the world hates you. Remember [the word] that /6/ [I said to you]: ‘A servant is not /7/ [greater than his master.’ If] they persecuted me, /8/ [they will also persecute you. And if they kept my w]ords, /9/ [they will also keep yours].

Commentary

/r/

/1/: *[prw]*. The postposition *prw* is part of *dn m'x* which is attested at the end of *E5/72* /v/18/. Sogdian *dn...prw* "with…" translates Syriac *'m* "id."[459].

/1/: *[pr r']θ*. The correct reading is by Sims-Williams (2012: 34).

/3/: *[ywnt](s)nw* "eleven". This reading is by Schwartz (1967: 60).

/3/: *[ywnt](s(nw) žwxšqt'* "eleven disciples." The Syriac text has only the numeral *ḥd'sr* "eleven" and it agrees with the Greek text which has *τοὺς ἕνδεκα* "eleven".

/5/: *[xypθ'wnt]* "master, sir". Contra Sundermann (1974: 244): *[xwt'w]*. I prefer conjecturing *xypθ'wnt* because I realized that – in this Gospel lectionary – *xwt'w* is exclusively used as apposition of Jesus and without having any corresponding term in Syriac. For all other cases, the Syriac *mr'* is translated by Sogdian as *xypθ'wnt.*

/5/: *w'byntqn*. 3 pers. pl. optative + durative suffix[460].

/6/: *šmγwn*. Syriac onomastics.

/7/: *pry̤by̤(r)[nt]*. 3 pers. pl. imperfect of the verb *prbyr/prbyrt* "to report".

/8/: *'t*. The conjunction *'t* "and" is the first word of /r/8/ and it is put along the inner margin on the same writing line but not vertically, as usual for any additions to the text.

/8/: *c'nw̤*. Pittard apud Sims-Williams (2012: 34) "perhaps *c'nw* altered to *c'ny̤*". Honestly, the stroke seems to me to be more *-w* than *-y*. The latter is generally constituted by a full dot, smaller than that of *w* and similar to an empty circle.

/8/: *pt(z·n)[ty]*. See: Sundermann (1974: 245, note 89) "mit *zeqāpā* über dem *z*, also für *ptz'nty*".

/v/

/2/: *bwty̤št' šm'x* "you were". It translates the Syriac perfect *hwytwn*, and in /v/3/ Sogdian *'y̤št' šm['x]* translates the Syriac *hwytwn*. With particular regard to the use of the 2 pers. pl. pronoun + intransitive verbs, Telegdi records an alternation between "plain" forms and forms with pronoun[461].

/8/: *(pš)qy̤rd'rnt*. The correct reading is by Sims-Williams (2012: 34).

/9/: *[d'rnt ms šm'x xypθy d'rntq'---]*. After those which must have been the last words belonging to John 15.20, we can see three small strokes. This writing line is completely lost and it is in my opinion impossible to conjecture any reading since we can not know what would have been the next Gospel passage.

---

459 See: *Sogdian- Syriac Glossary*.

460 See: Sundermann (1974: 244, n. 87).

461 See: Telegdi (1938: 218).

E5/75-76 = Matthew 10.14-15; 10.16-26; 10.27-33 and John 20.19-25, i.e., End of the Gospel for the Thursday after Easter. Matthew 10.14-15: */Ir/*1-3/. Beginning, part and end of the Gospel for the Friday after Easter. Matthew 10.16-26: */Ir/*3/-*/Iv/*17/.
Matthew 10.26-27: */Iv/*17-20/; Matthew 10.27-33: */IIr/*1-17/.
Beginning and part of the Gospel for the 1st Sunday after Easter. John 20.19-25: */IIr/*17/- */IIv/*20/.

/Ir/

/1/ p'dy̤t · 't ršt'˙ frm'ymsq zw qw šm'xs'..
14....r̈glykwn; 15. w-'myn 'mr 'n' l-kwn

/2/ qt sdwm˙ 't qt γmwr' z'ẏ. · pc'dy̤str bwtq'
d-l'r'' d-sdwm w-d-'mwr' nhw' nyḥ

/3/ pr pdq'˙ my̤θ qd' xyd qθ ·⁛· (Syriac red) d'rwbt'
b-ywm' d-dyn' 'w l-mdynt' hy;

/4/ dmw(d̈)yn' ⁘ dmty ⁘ bṣḥ ⁘ z ⁘ (Syriac black) 'ṃr yšw'

/5/ [ltl](m̈)ydwhy ⁘ (Sogdian black) w'nw frm'ẏ xwt'w yšwγ qw xypθ

/6/ [ž](w)xšqt' s' ⁘ (Syriac) ḣ' 'n'˙ mšdr 'n' lkwn ·⁛· (Sogdian) n'y
16. ḣ'

/7/ zẇ fš'mmsqn šm'xy̤. ·⁛· w'nc'nw wr'(n)t
'n' mšdr 'n' l-kwn 'yk 'mr̈'

/8/ wy̤rqy̤šty̤ my̤d'ny̤ · bwt' nwqr γrb'qt w'nc'nw
byny d'b̈' hww hkyl ḥkÿm' 'yk

/9/ qrmy̤št. 't trn ṅznt w'nc'nw qwpwdy(c)t · pyšt
ḥwẅt' w-tmÿm' 'yk ywn̈'; 17.

/10/ p'ty̤ swqt' cn mrtxmyt p't prbxšntq' ·
'zdhrw dyn ṃn bnÿnš' mšlmyn

/11/ šm’xỵ · qw dtbrt s’ · ’t pr wỵšntỵ ’w’zỵt ·
l-kwn gyr l-byt dyn̈’ w-b-kn̈wšthwn

/12/ ptnwbntq’ šm’xy · ’t d’t(br)t ’t xšywnỵtỵ
nngdwnkwn; 18. w-qdm hgmẅn’ w-m̈lk’

/13/ pyrnms’˙ pnt brntq’˙ šm’xy cn mn’ pyd’r ·
mqrbyn l-kwn mṭlty

/14/ qw wyšnty xypθ˙ w(yc)’wqy’ s’ · ’t qt rmt’ ·
l-shdwt’ dylhwn w-d-‘m̈m’;

/15/ pyš(t) [wy](d)’(γt)ỵ qt prbxšntq’ šm’xỵ. · xw(ys)m
19. ’mty dyn d-nšlmwnkwn

/16/ [n’ brt’ šm’x c]’nỵ qd’ (cw) ž’[yt’q](’) (p’t)
l’ t’ṣpwn ’ykn’ ’w mn’ tmllwn mtyhb

/17/ (θ)[brty bwtq’ qw šm’x s’ pr xypθ nγ’m]
l-kwn gyr b-hy š‘t’

/18/ ’yc q[t ž’yt’q’ p’t ny ’yšt’ šm’x qt]
m’ d-tmllwn; 20. l’ hw’ gyr ’ntwn

/19/ (ž)’ẏt’q(’) [yw’r šm’xy bγy ptry w’t qt]
mmllyn ’l’ rwḥ’ d-’bwkwn

/20/ (ž)’ẏtq(’ p)[r šm’x pyšt prbxštq’ br’t]
mmll’ b-kwn; 21. nšlm dyn ’ḥ’

/Iv/

/1/ xypθ br(’)t(˙) (q)w m(r)c s’ ’t pt(rỵ) [xy](pθ z’t)ỵỵ
l-’ḥwhy l-mwt’ w-’b’ l-brh

/2/ ’t ’γzntq’ ’žwnt (pr) wỵšnt [m](’t) pt(rỵt ’t)
w-nqwmwn bnÿ’ ‘l ’bhÿhwn w-

/3/ šn ptxw’ẏntq’ · ’t bwt’q’ (ž)ỵšt[y](t) (cn)
-nmytwn ’nwn; 22. w-thwwn snÿ’yn ṃn

/4/ wyspw ’dỵ cn mn’ n’mỵ p(y)d’r [pyš](t) xw(nỵ)
klnš mṭl šmy ’yn’ dyn

/5/ ’dỵ qt˙ pt’wt˙ wytwr q{<(w˙)>} (’ym prm xw)[ny]
d-nsybr ‘dm’ l-ḥrt’ ḥw

/6/ žwytq’ ∴ pyšt c’nw qt (p)šqỵ(r)nt š(m’x)[y pr]
nḥ’; 23. m’ d-rdpyn l-kwn dyn b-

/7/ ’yny knθ. · tšt’ šm’x. qw ’(n)yw kθ s’ · p’t
-mdynt’ hd’ ‘rwqw l-kwn l-’ḥrt’

/8/ ršt’˙ frm’ẏmsq zw qw šm’x s’ · qt
’myn gyr ’mr ’n’ l-kwn d-

/9/ nỵ ’y{<m>}sntq’ s’t ysr’ỵlỵqt(ỵ) kθt· ˙ w(y)t(w)r
-l’ tšlmwn ’nÿn klhyn mdÿnt’ d-byt ’ysryl ‘dm’

/10/ qt ’ỵstq’ mrtxmỵ z’tỵ · nỵst žwx(šq)[y]
d-n’t’ brh d-’nš’; 24. lyt tlmyd’

/11/ qt frtr bỵ cn xypθ xwštỵ ’t nỵ bntỵ cn
d-ytyr ṃn rbh w-l’ ‘bd’ ṃn

/12/ xypθ xypθ’w(n)t · b’wnyq xcỵ žwxšqy˙ qt˙
mrh; 25. spq l-h l-tlmyd’ d-

/13/ bỵ˙ w’nc’nw wynỵ (x)wštỵ. ’t bntỵ w’nc’nw wyny
-nhw’ ’yk rbh w-l-‘bd’ ’yk

/14/ xypθ’wnt · qt x’nỵ xypθ’wntỵ žγỵrd’rnt
mrh ’n l-mrh d-byt’ qrw

/15/ bγḷz(ḅ)ẅb. yw c’f wyny x’nycỵqtỵ · n’
b‘lzbwb ḥd km’ l-bnÿ byth; 26. l’

/16/ n(wq)r [pcqw]yrt(’) cn (w)yšnt · p[’t nyst]
hkyl tdḥlwn ṃn-hwn lyt gyr

/17/ [’yc qt ptγwsty bwt qt ny ’št’ty bwtq’]
mdm d-ks’ d-l’ ntgl’

/18/ [’t qt pγwšty bwt qt ny γrb’ty bwtq’] (’y)c( ) qt
w-d-mṭšy d-l’ ntyd‘; 27. mdm d-

/19/ [frm’ymsqn zw qw šm’x s’ t](’)ryỵ.(˙) [šy w’bt’]
-’mr ’n’ l-kwn b-ḥšwk̈’ ’wmrwhy

/20/ [šm’x pr rwxšny’q ’t ’](yc) qt
’ntwn b-nhyr’ w-mdm d-

/IIr/

/1/ pr (šm)’x γwšt ptγwšt’-sqn (š)m’x ’ỵzt’
-b-’dnÿkwn šm‘yn ’ntwn ’krzw

/2/ w[n](t’ pr qw[dwy](t’) ’t n’ p(cq)wỵrt’ cn (w)yšnt qt
‘l ’gr̈’; 28. w-l’ tdḥlwn ṃn ’ylyn d-

/3/ [ptx](w’ynt tmp’r) pyšt rw’n nỵ qt’ wnntq’
qṭlyn pgr’ npš’ dyn l’ mškḥyn

/4/ (pr ptxw’)y · (p)y(št) (p)cqwỵrt’ sq’[try](q)-st(r)
l-mqṭl dḥlw dyn ytyr’yt

/5/ [cn xwny] (’)dỵ (qt’)wntyq’ qt by r[w’n] ’t by
ṃn ṁn d-mškḥ d-l-npš’ w-

/6/ [tmp](’r) (nys)twnt(yq)’ ‸tmy’ cỵnt(r) · cwtnỵ˙ dw’
-l-pgr’ nwbd b-ghn’; 29. l’ tr̈tyn

/7/ sỵc(ỵ)[t] (pr)ỵθt(yt) bnt pr yw bn[t] · ’t ywtr cn
ṣpr̈yn ṁzdb̈nn b-’sr w-ḥd’ ṃn-

/8/ [wyšnt p]w cn šm’x bγy ptrỵ˙ (r)yž. ny ’mp[dt]
-hyn bl‘d ṃn ’bwkwn l’ npl’

/9/ pr (z’)y · pyšt šm’x xypθ ms šm’x sry̤
‘l ’r‘’; 30. dylkwn dyn ’p mn̈’ d-rškwn

/10/ (wrs)y̤ (γžwty) ‸{<s’t>} pcmrty̤t xnt · n’ nwqr pcqwy̤rt’ ·
klhyn mnÿn ’nÿn; 31. l’ hkyl tdḥlwn

/11/ (c)[n γr]f sy̤ctyty (f)r(t)r ’yšt’ šm’x · wyspw
ṃn ṣpr̈’ sgÿ’t’ mytryn ’ntwn; 32. klnš

/12/ ’dy̤ nnqr qt.̈z’nt pr mn’ mrtxmy̤ty̤ py̤r-
hkyl d-nwd’ b-y qdm bnÿnš’

/13/ -nms’ · .̈z’ng’ pryw ms zw mn’ bγ[y] ptry̤ pyr-
’wd’ b-h ’p ’n’ qdm ’by

/14/ -nms’ qt pr sm’(n) · pyšt xwny̤ (’d)y qt pstw’t
d-b-šmy’ ; 33. ṁn dyn d-nkpwr

/15/ pr (m)[n](’) mrtxmy̤ty̤ [pyr]nms’. · ps(t)w’ng(’) (pr)yw
by qdm bnÿnš’ ’kpwr b-h

/16/ [ms zw mn’ bγy] ptr[y] (p)y̤rnms’ q(t) [pr] sm’(n ∴)
’p ’n’ qdm ’by d-b-šm̈y’

/17/ [dḥdbšb’ ḥdt’ ∴] (Syriac red) (d)ywḥnn [bṣḥ ∴] *trace only (red ink)*

/18/ (kd) ḣw’ [dyn rmš’ dywm’ hw dḥd bšb’ (Sogdian black) pyšt]

/19/ c’nw (m)’(t) [xwny xypθ myθy by’ry qt pyrnmcyq -------]
19. kd hw’ dyn rmš’ d-ywm’ ḣw d-ḥd b-šbt’ w-

/20/ (dbrt’) [----------------qw swqyq m’tnt žwxšqt’]
-tr̈’’ ’ḥydyn hww d-’yk’ d-’ytyhwn hww tlmÿd’

/II/v/

/1/ cn cxwdtẏ̤ pcqwy̤ry̤ pyd’r ˇ‸{<’γt [x]wt’w yšwγ˙ [w]’št wyšnty
mṭl dḥlt’ d-yhẅdy’ ’ṭ’ yšw‘ qm bynthwn
mydẏ’ny̤ . ’t w’nw fr’[m’y [qw wyšnt s’] >} · dwrt’ swq’t
w-’ṃr l-hwn šlm’

/2/ dn šm’x prw · ’ỵnỵ w’xš frm’d’rt. · ’št’-
‘m-kwn; 20. hd’ ’ṃr w-ḥwy

/3/ -d’rt wỵšntỵ̇ xypθ dst’. · ’t xypθ qwšỵ · ’t
’ṅwn ’ÿdwhy w-sṭrh w-

/4/ γwšd’rnt žwxšqt’ qt wyd’rnt m’x xypθ-
-ḥdyw tlmÿd’ d-ḥzw l-mrn;

/5/ -’wntỵ · pyšt w’nw fr’m’ẏ qw wyšnt [s’ tym]
21. ’ṃr l-hwn dyn twb

/6/ xwt’w yšwγ · dwrt’ swq’t dn šm’x p(r)[w]
yšw‘ šlm’ ‘m-kwn

/7/ w’nc’nw qt fš̃md’rt mn’ mn’ byγy ptrỵ
’ykn’ d-šdrny ’by

/8/ ms zw. fš̃’mmsqn šm’xỵ · ’t c(’)[nw] fr’m’[y]
’p ’n’ mšdr ’n’ l-kwn; 22. w-kd ’ṃr

/9/ y’nt ’ỵšt. · ftm’d’rṫ pr wỵšnt. ’t w’nw
hlyn ṇpḥ b-hwn w-

/10/ fr’m’y qw wỵšnt s’ · pcγzt’ zprt w’t ·
-’ṃr l-hwn qblw rwḥ’ d-qwdš’;

/11/ qt prm’nty’ wnt’· ’dỵỵ γwn’nt. prm’nty’
23. ’n tšbqwn ḥ̈ṭh’ l-’nš nštbqwn

/12/ qtỵ bntq’ qw wynỵ s’ · ’t qt ny’st’ ·
l-h w-’n t’ḥdwn

/13/ ’dỵỵ γ(w’n)t. nymtỵt bntq’ · pyšt θ’wm’
d-’nš ’ḥydyn; 24. t’wm’ dyn

/14/ ywtr cn dw’[t]snw · xyd qt wγtỵ bwṫ θ’m’. ·
ḥd ṃn tr‘srt’ hw d-mt’mr t’m’

/15/ ny̧ m(’t) d(n) w[y](š)nty prw c’[nw] ’γt xwt’w yšwγ
l̇’ hw’ tmn hw’ ‘mhwn kd ’ṭ’ yšw‘;

/16/ ’t w’[nw w](’)bnt qw wyn[y s](’) [žwxšqt’]
25. w-’mryn l-h tlmÿd’

/17/ [wyd’rym m’x] (x)ypθ’wnt(y) [pyšt xw w’nw w](’)[b]
ḥzyn l-mrn hw̤ dyn ’m̤r

/18/ [qw wyšnt s’ qt ny wynmsqn zw pr wyny d]st’
l-hwn ’n l’ ḥz’ ’n’ b-’ÿdwhy

/19/ [------ ------------------------- pry](w)nt mn’
dwkÿt’ d-ṣṣ̈’ w-rm’ ’n’ b-hyn ṣb̈‘ty

/20/ [------’t ------------------ dst](w̦) pr wyny̧
w-mwšṭ ’n’ ’ydy b-dpnh

Translation
/Ir/ /1/ from your feet. Truly, I say to you /2/ that the land of Sodom and Gomorrah will be more bearable /3/ on the day of judgment than that town. (Syriac) for the Friday /4/ after Easter, from Matthew, in chapter 7. Jesus said /5/ to his disciples (Sogdian) The Lord Jesus thus said to his /6/ disciples: (Syriac) “Behold, I am sending you” (Sogdian) “Behold, /7/ I am sending you out as lambs /8/ in the midst of wolves; so be wise as /9/ serpents, and docile and humble as pigeons. But /10/ beware of men, for they will deliver you /11/ over to judges and /11-12/ will flog you in their assemblies; /12-13/ and you will be dragged before governors and kings for my sake, /14/ to *bear* witness to themselves and the peoples /15/. But [wh]en they will deliver you over, /15-16/ do [not] be conce[rned] about how or what you will s[ay], for /17-18/ wha[t you are to say will be gi]ven to [you in that hour because it is not you who] /19/ speak [but the Spirit of your God the Father who] /20/ will speak through [you. Then the brother will give] */Iv/* /1/ “his own brother to death, and the father his own child, /2/ and sons will rise against their parents /3/ and will them put to death, and you will be hated /4/ by all for the sake of my name. But the one /5/ who endures to the end /6/ will survive. But when they will persecute you in /7/ one town, flee to the next town. /8/ For truly, I say to you: /9/ all the cities of Israel will not be finished until /10/ the Son of Man comes. There is no disciple /11/ who is better than his teacher and nor a servant *better* than /12/ his master. It is

sufficient for the disciple /13/ to be like his teacher, and the servant like his /14/ master. If they have called the master of the house /15/ Beelzebul, how their relatives? /16/ So ha[ve] no fear of them, f[or] /16-17/ [nothing is covered that will not be revealed], /18/ [and hidden that will not be known]. What /19/ [I tell you in the darkness say] /20/ [it in the light, and] what */II r/*1/ you hear in your ears, proclaim *it* /2/ [on the housetops]. And do not fear those who /3-4/ [kill] the body but cannot kill the soul; rather fear much more /5-6/ him who can destroy both soul and body in hell. /6-7/Are not two sparrows sold for a penny? And not one /8/ of them will fall to /8-9/ the ground without the will of your God the Father. /9/ But *as for you* even the hair of your head /10/ is all numbered. So, fear not! /11/ You are better than many sparrows. /11-12/ So everyone who acknowledges me before men, /13/ I also will acknowledge him before my God the Father /14/ who *is* in heaven. But whoever denies /15/ me before men, /15-16/ [I also] will deny him before [my God] the Father who *is* [in] heaven". /17/ (Syriac) [for the ninth Sunday], from John in section 20 /18/ (Syriac) [but] when it was [the evening of the same day, the first after Saturday] /19/ (Sogdian) [but] when it was [the evening of the same day, the first *after Saturday* and] /20/ [*were locked*] the doors [where the disciples were] */IIv/*1/ for fear of the Jews, the Lord Jesus came, stood among them and thus said [to them]: "Peace be /2/ with you". He gaves this speech, /3/ he showed them his hands and his side. And /4/ the disciples rejoiced when they saw our Lord. /5-6/ Then the Lord Jesus thus said to them again: "Peace be with you. /7/ As my God the Father has sent me, /8/ even so I am sending you". And when he had said /9/ these things, he breathed on them and thus /10/ said to them: "Receive the Holy Spirit. /11/ If you forgive the sins of any, /12/ they are forgiven to him; if /13/ you withhold the sins from any, they will withhold". But Thomas, /14/ one of the Twelve, called the Twin, /15/ was not with them when the Lord Jesus came. /16/ And the other disciples th[us] said to him: /17/ "We have seen our Lord". [But he thus said] /18/ [to them: "Unless I see in his h]ands /19/ [the places of the nails, and I put in] them my /20/ [fingers, and I stretch forth my han]d into his

Commentary

/Ir/

/2/: *sdwm ʾt qt γmwrʾzʾẏ* "the land of Sodom and Gomorrah". Syr. *d-lʾrʿʿ d-sdwm w-d-ʿmwrʾ* "id.". Each language maintains its own word order but in so doing the Sogdian loses any element which identifies the morphosyntactic

functions. In the same way, the Sogdian *qt* has to be considered as a mechanical translation of of the Syriac *d-* whose function has been misunderstood by the translator.
/2/: *sdwm* "Sodom" and *γmwr'* "Gomorrah". Syriac toponymy.
/2/: *pc'dy̤*. According to Sundermann (1974: 246). The reading is clear and it also agrees with the Syriac *nyḥ*. Contra Müllller (1913: 5) *pc'yy̤*.
/3-4/: Syriac rubric with reference to the Gospel passage.
/4-7/: In Syriac are reported, after the rubric, the first two sentences of the new Gospel passage, immediately followed by the Sogdian translation.
/4/: *dmw(d̈)yn'*. According to Baumstark (1915: 125) as also pointed out by Sims-Williams (2012: 35).
/5/: *frm'ẏ*. Defective writing for *fr'm'ẏ* that translates, in turn, the Syriac perfect, 3 pers. sg. *'ṃr*.
/7/: *w'nc'nw*. As emphasized by Sims-Williams, the correct reading, *w'nc'nw* indeed, is already present in Müller (1907: 268), while in the subsequent work of the scholar (1913: 6), for a misprint, it is given as *w'ncnw*[462].
/9/: *ṅznt*. The form *nyznt* is attested in *C2* (p. 218) and in the dictionary of Gharib (1995: 255). As has already been explained by Sundermann in a very exhaustive way[463], the writing *-a-* instead of *-e-* is the result of a short pronunciation of *e* in an unstressed syllable.
/9/: *qwpwdy(c)t* "pigeon". Sundermann[464] points out that one would expect **qwpwdyšt* as correct plural form. Although in this point the reading is not clear, the final part of *-c-* is clearly visible. *qwpwtyc* is also attested in this Gospel lectionary in (75)[465]. The form *qrwtyc* is attested in *C2* (p. 213).
/11/: *dtbrt* "judges". Defective writing for *d'tbrt*. We find *d't(br)t* in the next writing line, i.e, */Ir/*12/. Müller (1913: 6) reports *dtbrt* in both cases. With particular regard to *d't(br)t* in */Ir/*12/, Sundermann (1974: 250) notes that Müller gives the correct reading in his first work (1907) and the wrong reading, i.e. *dbrt*, in the next one, but he does not say anything about the form recorded in */Ir/*11/.
/14/: *qt*. A line drawn above *qt* indicates a delation[466].
/17-20/. As I discussed in Chapter 2[467], the identification of */I-IIr/-/I-IIv/*17-

[462] See: Sims-Williams (2012: 35).
[463] See: Sundermann (1974: 246-250).
[464] See: Sundermann (1974: 250).
[465] See also: *GMS* (*§* 1010) and Gharib (1995: 200).
[466] See also: Sims-Williams (2012:35).
[467] See: *2.1 Previous editions*.

20 is thanks to Pittard-Sims-Williams whose work is referred[468]. Instead, the majority of Sogdian reconstructions, which has been made according to the correspondences found in this Gospel lectionary between the Sogdian and the Syriac text, are mine.
/17/:*(θ)[brty bwtq’]*. The reading-reconstruction is by Pittard- Sims-Williams (2013: 47), what follows in the text is my hypothetical reconstruction.
/18/: *’yc q[t*. So Pittard- Sims-Williams (2013: 47). Sundermann reads only *’yc* (1975:81). However, what follows in the text is my reconstruction hypothesis.
/19/: *(ž)’ẏt’q(’)*. The correct reading is by Pittard- Sims-Williams (2013: 47). Sundermann (1975:81) assumes *(’wt’q)*. What follows in the text is my reconstruction hypothesis.
/20/: *(ž)’ẏt’q(’ p)[r*. The correct reading is by Pittard- Sims-Williams (2013:47). Sundermann (1975:81) assumes *(’.t)*. What follows in the text is my reconstruction hypothesis.
/Iv/
/2/: *wỵšnt*. According to Sundermann (1974: 251). Sims-Williams (2012: 35) considers also possible *wỵšnt(y)* which is the reading by Müller (1913: 7).
/2/: *[m](’t) pt(rỵt)* “parents”. Sims-Williams points out two things. The first is considering this compound an **-aka-* stem precisely on the basis of the above plural form here attested. The second concerns the exception of this dvanda compound with respect to what Gershevitch stressed years before, or that the dvanda seem to be attested only as translation of foreign dvanda[469].
/3/: *ptxw’yntq’* “will kill”. Future, 3 pers. pl. < *ptxw’y*. The form *ptwx’y* is also attested in this Gospel lectionary (140). *ptwx’y* is the only one attested in *C2* (p. 222). According to Gharib, the form *ptxw’y* is also attested in Manichaean Sogdian[470].
/4/: *γwšd’rnt*. In this gospel lectionary the verb “ro rejoice” is attested by the metathesis *γw* < *wγ*[471]. See: *C2* (p. 229) *wγš-* “to rejoice” and *GMS* (§§ 213; 517; 1212).
/4/: *xw(nỵ)*. According to Pittard apud Sims-Williams (2012: 35). Sundermann (1974: 251) reads *xw(n)yy*.
/5/: *’dỵ ’-* is still partially legible.
/5/: *q{<(w)>}*. After *q-* the lower stroke of *t*, below the writing line, is recognizable. However this may have been deleted because, immediately above the writing line, *w* is read. For this reason I read *qw*. Pittard apud

[468] See: Pittard- Sims-Williams (2013: 47); (2014: 59-61).
[469] See: *C2*, p.51.
[470] See: Gharib (1995: 322).
[471] See: *Sogdian- Syriac Glossary*.

Sims-Williams (2012 :35) too. Sundermann (1974: 251) instead reads *qt* and Müller (1913: 6-7) *qw*, placing, however, a question mark under *-w*.

/6/: *žwytq'*. According to Müller (1913: 6-7) and Sims-Williams (2012: 35). Sundermann (1974: 251) reads *žw(n)tq'* as mistake for *žwtq'*.

/9/: *'y{<m>}sntq'*. Addition above the writing line between *-y-* and *-s-*.

/10/: *z'ty*. The stroke of the last two letters is still clearly visible.

/11/: *xypθ*. The reading is certain. Nevertheless, with particular regard to the first letter, the upper part is visible, the lower one is missing.

/15/: *by̤lz(ḅ)ẇb*. Syriac onomastics.

/16/: *p['t]*. The upper part of *p-* is well visible and recognizable while the lower one is missing.

/17/: the reconstruction hypothesis is mine.

/18/: *('y)c( ) qt*. The reading is by Pittard- Sims-Williams (2013:48). The reconstruction hypothesis which precedes this reading is mine.

/19/: *t](')ryy̤.(˙)*. The reading is by Pittard- Sims-Williams (2014:60). The reconstruction hypothesis which precedes this reading is mine.

/20/: *'](yc) qt*. The reading is by Pittard- Sims-Williams (2013:48). The reconstruction hypothesis which precedes this reading is mine.

/IIr/

/1/: *ptγwšt'-sqn*. With particular regard to the durative suffix *-sqn*, already read as such by Müller (1913: 8-9), the *-skn* transliteration found in Sundermann (1974: 252) is due to a misprint (Sims-Williams, 2012: 36).

/2/: *pr qw[dwy](t')* "on the roofs". Syr. *'l 'gr̈'* "id.". The reading is by Sundermann[472].

/2/: *pcqwyrt'* "(not) be afraid, do not fear" < *pcqwyr* "to fear". The form *pcwqyr* is attested in this Gospel lectionary[473], while the form *pcwqyr* is recorded in *C2* (p. 219)[474].

/6/: *[tmp]('r) (nys)twnt(yq)'‸ tmy'*. According to Pittard apud Sims-Williams (2012: 36). Contra Sundermann (1974: 253) *[tmp]('r) (nyš)tynt(q)'tmy'*.

/8/ *cn šm'x bγy ptry̤ (r)yž* "without the will of your God the Father". Syr. *bl'd ṃn 'bwkwn* "without your Father" and Gk. *ἄνευ τοῦ πατρὸς ὑμῶν* "without your Father"[475].

/8/: *[wyšnt p]w*. See: Chaudri apud Sims-Williams[476]. Contra Sundermann(1974: 254): *[nyšqr'](n)*.

---

[472] See: Sundermann (1974: 253, n. 135).

[473] See also: *Sogdian- Syriac Glossary*.

[474] See also : *GMS* (§176).

[475] See: *2.2 The Gospel lectionary E5 within the Church of the East.*

[476] See: Sims-Williams (2009: 276, n. 34).

/10/: *(wrs)y̱ (γžwty)*. Sundermann reads *(wrs)y̱ γž(wt')*[477] and Pittard apud Sims-Williams *(wrs)y̱ ˙γž(wy)*[478].
/11/: *sy̱ctyty* = *sycyty*. According to Sundermann (1974: 253, n. 148). The correct form of obl. pl. is attested in the same fragment in */IIr/7/*. As already pointed out by Sims-Williams (2012: 36) *sy̱ctyty* is the only form today readable, but see Müller (1913: 9 -10): *sy̱cty̤ty̱*.
/12/: *nnqr* = *nwqr*.
/12/: *pr mn'*. The ductus of the whole prepositional phrase is not very clear but yet identifiable.
/12/ and /15/: *mrtxmy̤ty̱*. According to Müller (1913: 9-10) and Sims-Williams (2012: 36). Contra Sundermann (1974: 254-255) *mrtxmy̱ty̤*.
/14/: *('d)y*. Almost a centimetre of the fragment is missing, although the upper stroke of the first two letters is quite recognizable.
/17/: *[dḥdbšb' ḥdt' .·.] (d)ywḥnn [bṣḥ .·.]*. The reconstruction is by Sundermann (1974: 255).
/17/: *trace only (red ink)*. According to Pittard- Sims-Williams (2013: 48).
/18-19/: as usual, after the Syriac rubric, we have the first sentence of the new Gospel section in Syriac language followed, in */IIv/19/*, by the Sogdian translation.
/18/: *(kd) ḣw'*. The reading is by Pittard- Sims-Williams (2013: 48). What follows is my hypothesis based on how much text could still be written considering the size of the writing lines in this Gospel lectionary.
/19/: *c'nw (m)'(t)*. The reading is by Pittard- Sims-Williams (2013: 48). What follows is my reconstruction with a clarification. After *[xwny xypθ myθy by'ry qt pyrnmcyq]* and taking into account the Syriac text, we should expect the Sogdian translation of *b-šbt' w-* "after the Shabbath and". I do not think, however, that the writing line could have contained such a large text portion and therefore I prefer stressing the – possible – lack of a text, which was probably added along the inner margin, as already noted other times in this Gospel lectionary.
/20/ *(dbrt')[* . The reading is by Pittard- Sims-Williams (2013: 48). What follows is my reconstruction.
/IIv/
/1/: *[w]'št*. Imperfect, 3 pers. sg. of *'wšt(y̱)/'wšt(y̱)t* "to stay, stand".
/1/: *mydẏ'ny*, postposition "in the middle, between"[479].
/2/: *'y̱ny̤ w'xš frm'd'rt* lit. "he said this speech". Syr. *hd' 'ṃr* "said this" and

---

[477] See: Sundermann (1974: 254).
[478] See: Sims-Williams (2012: 36).
[479] On "Das altertümliche *mydẏ'ny*" see: Sundermann (1974: 255) .

Gk. *καί τοῦτο εἰπὼν* “id.”. The Sogdian text adds *w’xš* “speech”.
/2-3/: *’št’d’rt*. According to Sundermann (1974: 255). Contra Salemann (1907: 536). *’yšt’d’rt*. Müller first reads *’yšt’d’rt* than corrects *’št’d’rt*[480].
/10/: *pcγzt’* = *pcγ’zt’*. Imperative, 2 pers. pl. of the verb *pcγ’z/pcγšt* “to receive, welcome, accept”.
/11/: *γwn’nt* = *γw’nt* “sins”. The scribe already realized the error, considering that there is a small horizontal stroke above *-n-*, which probably indicates a deletion, and that *-n-*, which precedes *-t*, is much smaller than usual; perhaps because it was added later, after indeed having realized the mistake.
/13/: *θ’wm’*. Syriac onomastic.
/14/: *dw’tsnw*. Oblique of the cardinal number *dw’ts* “twelve”.
/17-20/: the identification of these writing lines is due to Pittard- Sims-Williams (2013: 48)[481].
/17/: *w]()[b]*. The reading is by Pittard- Sims-Williams (2013: 48). What comes first is my reconstruction.
/18/: *d]st’*. The reading is by Pittard- Sims-Williams (2013: 48). What comes first is my reconstruction.
/19/: *pry](w)nt mn’*. According to Pittard- Sims-Williams (2013: 48).
/20/ *dst](w.) pr wyny̩*. Reading by Pittard- Sims-Williams (2014: 61).

E5/78

Part of the Gospel for the 2nd Sunday after Easter. John 14.11-12: */r/*.
Part of the Gospel for the 3rd Sunday after Easter. John 16.19: */v/*.

/r/

/17/[q]t (ny̩) [ms c’nw cn ’rqty pyd’r wrnt’ ršt’]
11. ..’n l’ ’pn mṭl ‘b̈d’ hymnw; 12.’myn

/18/ ršt’ (f)[rm’ymsq zw qw šm’x s’ qt]
’myn ’mr ’n’ l-kwn d-

480 Respectively: Müller (1907: 268) and Müller (1913: 78).
481 See: *2.1 Previous editions*.

405 /19/ xwny̤ (')[dy qt wrntyq' pr mn' x'nt 'rqt qt]
-ṁn d-mhymn by 'b̈d' 'ylyn d-

/20/ [z]w (w)n'(m) [ms xw wntyq']
-'n' 'bd 'n' 'p hẉ n'bd

/v/
/18/ ['t w'nw fr'm'y qw wyšnt s' cymyθy p](y)d'r
19.... w-'ṃr l-hwn 'l hd'

/19/ [γwžt'sq šm'x dn dbṯy](q)y
b'yn 'ntwn 'm ḥd̈d'

/20/ [prw qt frm'd'rm qw šm'x s' q](t) qbnq
d-'mrt l-kwn d-qlyl

Translation
/r//17/ "[i]f not [at least believe on account of works. Truly,] /18/ [truly, I] s[ay to you:] /19/ that person who will believe in me, those works which] /20/ I do, [he too will do]". /v/ /18/ [And said thus to them: co]ncerning [this] /19/ [that you are quarelling with one ano]ther /20/[that I said to you: a little....].

Commentary
/r-v/. As already stated in *Chapter 2*[482], the identification of this fragment is the work of Pittard-Sims-Williams whose readings of each writing line are adopted[483]. Some words had already been read by Sundermann as *ršt' (f)[rm'ymsq* in /r/2/; *xwny (')[dy* in /r/3/; *qbnq* in /v/3/[484].
The readings of the missing text are mine and have been carried out, as always, according to the correspondences found among the Syriac and the Sogdian text. Finally, a small clarification about the numbering of the writing lines attested therein. As already pointed out by Pittard-Sims-Williams[485], this fragment belongs to the bottom inner corner of a folio and the last word of /v/ immediately precedes the first word of *E5/79/r/*1/, i.e. the first word of the first writing line of the fragment which follows. For these

---

[482] See: *2.1. Previous editions.*
[483] See: Pittard- Sims-Williams (2013: 49); (2014: 62).
[484] See: Sundermann (1975: 81).
[485] *ibid.*

reasons, and considering that we are in a point of the Gospel lectionary which approximately attests twenty writing lines in */r/* and */v/*, I suppose twenty writing lines for this fragment too, numbering the last as /17/, /18/, /19, /20/ which correspond, respectively, to /1/, /2/, /3/, /4/ in Pittard-Sims-Williams[486].

E5/79

Part of the Gospel for the 3rd Sunday after Easter. John 16.19-32: */r-v/.*

/r/

/1/ 't ny̤ wy̤nt'q' mn'˙ 't tym qbnq 't wy̤nt'q'
19. w-l' tḥzwn-ny w-twb qlyl w-tḥzwn-

/2/ mn'.. ršt' ršt'˙ frm'ymsq zw qw šm'x s'..
-ny; 20. 'myn 'myn 'mr 'n' l-kwn

/3/ qt r'yt'q'˙ šm'x 't mr'wt bwt'q'. · 't
d-tbkwn 'ntwn w-t'lwn w-

/4/ fcmpd˙ γwšty̤q'. 't šm'x 'ntwxcn' ˇ{<q>} bwt'q' ·
-'lm' nḥd' w-l-kwn tkr'

/5/ yw'r šm'x 'ntwxc. qw xwsnty' s' bwtq' ·
'l' krywtkwn l-ḥdwt' thw';

/6/ 'ync c'nw q'my̤ qt zn't. · 'ntwxc bwt˙ wy' qt
21. 'ntt' m' d-yld' kry' l-ḣ d-

/7/ pnt pr'γt wy' zn'mnty̤ my̤θ · pyšt c'nw˙ qt
-ṃṭ' ywm' d-mwldḣ m' d-

/8/ znd'rt z'ty̤. · šy' ny̤ 'brt wy' šqwrθy'˙ · cn
-yldt dyn br' l' 'hd' 'wlṣnḣ mṭl

/9/ xswnty' pyd'r qt 'žt mrtxmy pr fcmbd ·
ḥdwt' d-'tyld brnš' b-'lm';

486 *ibid.*

/10/ ms šm'x· qšy̤. 'ntwxc sty̤ šm'xy · pyšt
22. 'p 'ntwn hš' kry' l-kwn twb

/11/ tym· wy̤ng' šm'xy̤. 't γwšty̤q' šm'x žy'wr ·
dyn 'ḥzykwn w-nḥd' lbkwn

/12/ 't šm'x xwsnty'. ny̤ 'dy̤ 'stq' cn šm'x ·
w-ḥdwtkwn l' 'nš nsb ṃn-kwn;

/13/ 't pr xyd myθ· qw mn' s'. ny̤ γwžt'q' 'y̤c ·
23. w-b-ḣw ywm' l-y l' tš'lwn mḋm

/14/ ršt' ršt'· frm'ymsq zw qw šm'x s'.. qt
'myn 'myn 'mr 'n' l-kwn d-

/15/ wyspw 'y̤c qt γwžt'· qw mn' bγy̤ ptry s'·
-kl mdm d-tš'lwn l-'by

/16/ pr mn' n'm. θbrtyq' qw šm'x s' · wytwr
b-šmy ntl l-kwn; 24. 'dm'

/17/ qw qšy̤ prm ny̤ γwžd'ryšt' 'y̤c pr mn' n'm ·
l-hš' l' š'ltwn mḋm b-šmy

/18/ γwžt'. 't 'st' · qt b't šm'x xwsnty'
š'lw w-tsbwn d-thw' ḥdwtkwn

/19/ spty̤ · y'nt· 'y̤št. pr przbrt ž'd'rm dn
mšmly'; 25. hlyn b-p̈l't' mllt 'm-

/20/ šm'x prw · pyšt 'ystq' nγ'm. · wyd'γt[y]
-kwn 'ty' dyn š't' 'mty

/v/

/1/ qt ny̤ ž'ynq' dn šm'x prw pr przbrt · yw'r
d-l' 'mll 'mkwn b-p̈l't' 'l'

/2/ ryt ’ngm’ny’ nyctwng’ qw šm’x s’ cn bγ’
‘yn b-gl’ ’bdq l-kwn ‘l

/3/ ptr’ pyd’r · pr xỵd mỵθ qt γwžtg’ pr mn’ n’m ·
’b’; 26. b-ḣw ywm’ d-tš’lwn b-šmy

/4/ ’t nỵ w’b˘̭{<ng’>} msq zw qw šm’x s’ qt zw γwžng’
w-l’ ’mr ’n’ l-kwn d-’n’ ’b‘’

/5/ cn bγ’ ptr’ cn šm’x pyd’r · p’t xw bγỵ ptrẏ
ṃn ’b’ ‘l-ykwn; 27. hẉ gyr ’b’

/6/ frỵ ny’d’rt˙ šm’xỵ. qt šm’x fry ny’d’ryšt’
rḥm l-kwn d-’ntwn rḥmtwn-

/7/ šm’x {<mn’>} · ’t wrnwtyšt’ {<wrnd’ryšt’>} · šm’x˙ qt zw. cn bγ’
-ny w-hymntwn d-’n’ ṃn lwt

/8/ ptr’ ms’ nyžtym· nyžtym˙ cn bγ’ ptr’. ’t ’γtym
’lh’ npqt; 28. npqt ṃn lwt ’b’ w-’tyt

/9/ qw fcmpd s’ · ’t tym˙ prycng’ zw˙ fcmpdy.
l-‘lm’ w-twb šbq ’n’ l-‘lm’

/10/ ’t šwng’ zw qw bγỵ ptry s’ · w’nw pcqw’d’rnt
w-’zl ’n’ ly lwt ’b’; 29. ’mryn

/11/ qw wyny s’ wyny žwxšqt’ · n’y˙ qšỵ. pr wyn’wcyqy’
l-h tlmÿdwhy ḣ’ hš’ gly’yt

/12/ ž’ysq tγw · ’t przbrt. ’t nỵ yw-’dỵ w’bỵsq
mmll ’nt w-p̈l’t’ w-l’ ḥd’ ’mr

/13/ tγw · qšỵ γrbỵmsqn m’x qt wỵspw ’ỵc
’nt; 30. hš’ yd‘yn ḥnn d-kl mḋm

/14/ γrbỵsq tγw · ’t ny’zqỵn nỵ ’yš tγw qt ’dỵ
yd‘ ’nt w-l’ snyq ’nt d-’nš

/15/ ps’t tw’ · prymyθ wrnym-sqn m’x qt cn b[γ’]
nš’lk bhd’ mhymnyn ḥnn d-mn ’lh’

445 /16/ nyžtyš · w’nw fr’m’ẏ qw wyšnt s’ xwt’w yšwγ ·
npqt; 31. ’mr l-hwn yšw‘

/17/ wrnt’ qt n’ẏ ’ystq’ nγ’m ’t qšy ’γty
hymnw; 32. d-ḣ’ ’ty’ š‘t’ w-hš’ ’tt

/18/ sty · qt š’št db’ny bwtq’ wyspw ’dy
d-ttbdrwn ’nš

/19/ qw xypθ wy’q s’ ’t pryct’q’ mn’ γwty
l-’trh w-tšbqwnny blḥwdy

/20/ [xw]dq’r · ’t ny ’ym zw γwty xwtg’r qt bγy
w-l’ hwyt blḥwdy d-

Translation

/r/ /1/ “you will not see me, and again a little while and /1- 2/ you will see me? Truly, truly, I say to you /3/: you will weep and lament, and /4/ the world will rejoice. You will be sorrowful, /5/ but your sorrow will turn into joy. /6/ When a woman want to give birth, she has sorrow because /7/ the day of her delivery has come, but when /8/ she has delivered the baby, she no longer remembers the anguish, for /9/ joy that a human being has been born into the world. /10/ So also you have sorrow now, but /11/ I will see you again, and your hearts will rejoice, /12/ and no one will take your joy /13/ from you. In that day you will ask nothing of me. /14/ Truly, truly, I say to you: /15/ whatever you ask to God my Father /16/ in my name, He will give *it* to you. /16-17/ Until now you have asked nothing in my name. /18/ Ask and take, that your joy may be /19/ full. I have said these things to you in similes /20/ but the hour is coming */v/* /1/ when I will no longer speak to you in similes but /2/ will tell you openly about God /3/ the Father. In that day you will ask in my name, /4/ and I do not say to you that I will ask /5/ God the Father on your behalf; for God the Father himself /6/ loves you, because you have loved /7/ me and have believed that I /7-8/ came from God the Father. I came from God the Father and have come /9/ into the world, and again I am leaving the world /10/ and going to God the Father”. /10-11/ Thus his disciples said to him: “Lo, now /11-12/ you are speaking plainly and *as*

for parables, not one do you speak! /13/ Now we know that /13-14/ you know all things and do not need anyone /15/ to question you; this is why we believe that /15-16/ you came from God." The Lord Jesus thus said to them: /17/ "Do you now believe? Behold, the hour is coming, indeed it has come, /18/ when you will be scattered, each /19/ to his own place, and will leave me alone. /20/ Yet I am not alone, for the God

Commentary

/r/

/3/: *fcmpd* and in */r/9/fcmbd*. Both forms are attested in *E5*[487]. *C2* (p. 210) records *fcmbd*.

/6/: Sogd. *'ync c'nw q'my̤ qt zn't* "when a woman want to give birth" and Syr. *'ntt' m' d-yld'* "when a woman gives birth". Sogdian adds the verb *q'm* "to wish, to desire" which is constructed, then, with the conjunction *qt* followed by the 3 pers. sg. subjunctive *zn't*. Syriac, however, agrees with Greek *ἡ γυνή ὅταν τίκτῃ*.

/6-10/. For "have sorrow" Sogdian uses both *'ntwxc b(w)/qt* as *'ntwxc* x, *sqw, swq/m't*[488]. The different use of the two auxiliary verb "to be" has been already discussed by Durkin-Meisterernst: *b(w)/qt* has a "neutral" value or a punctual value, while *x, sqw, swq/m't* has a continuous value[489].

/7/: *šm'x {<mn'>}*. The genitive pronoun for the 1 pers. sg. is added on the same writing line, immediately after *šm'x* which is deleted, in turn, by the scribe himself.

/7/: *wrnwty̤št' {<wrnd'ryšt'>}*. The addition is found on the same writing line, immediately after *wrnwtyšt'* where a delating mark is clearly visible.

/11/: *wy̤ng'* "I will see". I believe that the suffix for the future undergoes a gradual sonorization. In /v/ there are five sonorization examples: four of them are preceded by a dental nasal, and one is preceded by a dental occlusive; then we have an example of an unvoiced syllable maintained, even if preceded by a dental nasal. They are found respectively at: /v/2/; /v/3/; /v/4/; /v/9/ and /v/11/[490].

/v/

/2/: *nyctwng'*. Following Pittard apud Pittard- Sims-Williams (2012: 37) it is a form altered from *nyžyng'*.

/3/: *γwžtg'*. Following Pittard apud Sims-Williams (2012: 37) it is a form altered from *γwžng'*.

---

487 See: *Sogdian-Syriac Glossary*.

488 See: *Sogdian-Syriac Glossary*.

489 See: Durkin-Meisterernst (2007).

490 For a complete list, see: *Chapter 3.1.2 Suffix for the future: q' > g'*.

/11/: *pr wyn'wcyqy'* "openly, plainly". Sogdian uses a periphrasis composed by the preposition *pr* and the noun *wyn'wcyqy'* "revelation, manifestation" to translate the Syriac adverb *gly'yt*[491].
/20/: the last part of John 16:32 attested in this writing line continues – and ends – in *E5/80* /*r*/1/.

E5/80
End of the Gospel for the 3rd Sunday after Easter. John 16.32-33: /*r*/1-4/.
Beginning of the Gospel for the 4rd Sunday after Easter. John 21.1; 21.5-7: /*r*/4/-/*v*/8/.

/*r*/

/1/ [ptry dn mn' prw xcy y'nt 'yš]t. (ž'd'rm) [qw]
32.. -'b' ʿmy hẉ; 33. hlyn 'mrt l-

/2/ [šm'x s' qt pr mn' b't qw šm'x s'] dw(r)t' [pr]
-kwn d-by nhw' l-kwn šlm' b-

/3/ [fcmpd bwt qw šm'x s]' š(qwr)θy' yw'r ·
-ʿlm' hw' l-kwn 'wlṣn' 'l'

/4/ [θty'q byrt' zw wnyq qθ](')rm fcmpdy̤ · (Syriac red) dḥd
'tlbbw 'n' zkyth l-ʿlm'

/5/ [bšb' dḥmš' d](q)ymt' ∵ dywḥnn ∵

/6/ [bṣḥ ∵ k ∵] (Syriac black) [btr hly]n ∵ (Sogdian black) y'n(t) 'yšty̤
1. btr hlyn
pšy̤-

/7/ -[s'] (Syriac black) [ḥwy twb np](š)h yšwʿ ltlm̈ydwhy ∵ (Sogdian black) 'št'-
ḥwy

/8/ -[d'rt tym xypθ γryw xw]t'w yšwγ qw xypθ
twb npšh yšwʿ l-

[491] See: Brockelmann (1928: 116).

/9/ [žwxšqt’ s’ pr tybry]ws swm(tr) [z](m)py
-tlm̈ydwhy ‘l ym’ d-ṭybryws

/v/
/1/ [rync’q]ty [db’t sty šm’xy ’yc pr xwry]
5....ṭlÿ’ lm’ ’yt l-kwn mdm l-ml‘s

/2/ (w’nw) pcqw’d’rnt (q)[w wny s’ ny w’nw]
’mryn l-h l’;

/3/ fr’m’y qw wy̤šnt s’ [pš’yt’ šm’x d’m’]
6. ’ṃr l-hwṅ ’rmw mṣydtkwn

/4/ cn n’wy̤ · xw’rnt qw(š)[y’ ’t byrt’q’ šm’x]
ṃn gb’ d-ymyn’ d-spynt’ w-mškḥyn ’ntwn

/5/ ’t pš’d’rnt ’t ny̤ qt[’ wnnt pr xš d’m’y]
w-’rmyw w-l’̈ ’škḥw l-mgdḣ l-mṣydt’

/6/ cn γrf qpy qt nymty̤ · [’t w’nw wγd’rt]
ṃn swg’’ d-nẅn’ d-’ḥdt; 7. w -’ṃr

/7/ žwxšqy̤ qt (fry)-str d’[rt wny xwt’w]
tlmyd’ ḣw d-rḥm hw’ l-h

/8/ [yšwγ qw] šmγwn sng [s’ ’yny m’x xypθ’wnt]
yšw‘ l-k’p’ hn’ mrn

Translation

/r/ /1/ the Father is with me. I have said these things to /2/ [you, that in me you may have] peace. [In] /3/ [the world you have] tribulation, but /4/ [console yourself; I] have [overcome] the world”. (Syriac red) of the /4/- 5/ [fifth Sun]day of the Resurrection, from John, /6/ [chapter 11] (Syriac black) [After these things] (Sogdian black) after these things /7/ (Syriac black) Jesus [appeared again] to his disciples /7-8/ (Sogdian) [Lo]rd Jesus showed [again] to his /9/ [disciples on the] shore of Lake Tiberias.../v/ /1/ “[Childr]en, [you do not have anything to eat?”] /2/ [So they] answered [him], [“No”.] /2-3/ He [thus] said to them: [“Cast your net] /4/ on the right side of the boat, [and you will find”.] /5/ And they cast *it*, and they [were] not able [to haul the net in] /6/, because of the quantity of fish which was caught. [And so spoke] /7-8/ the disciple whom [the Lord Jesus] loved more [to] Simon Peter: ["This *is* our Lord!]".

Commentary
/r/
/1/: *[ptry dn mn'prw xcy]*. According to Syriac *'my hw*. Sogdian *ptry* recalls *βγy* [492] which is the last word of *E5/79* /v/20/,i.e., the last writing line of the preceding fragment. It is plausible to conjecture that the final part of John 16.32 is represented by the first words of /r/1/ and, therefore, to liste this reading, too, among those reported for this fragment in /r/ and not just John 16.33 and John 21.1[493].
/1/: *ž'd'rm*. For the first time in this Gospel lectionary the verb *ž'y* "to talk, converse" is used, instead of *frm'y-/frm't* even though Jesus is speaking. The Syriac text has *'mr* which is translated, in these cases, by the Sogdian verb *frm'y/frm't*. However, the Sogdian *ž'y* generally translates the Syriac *mll*[494].
/5/: *[bšb' dḥmš']*. According to Baumstark (1915: 125) and Sundermann (1975: 57).
/9/: *[tybry]ws swm(tr) [z](m)py* "Lake Tiberias"[495].
/v/
/4/: *qw(š)[y']* "on the side". See also Sims-Williams (forthcoming 2016a).
/8/: Sogd. *[qw] šmγwn sng [s']* "[to] Simon Peter"[496], Syr. *l-k'p'* "to Peter" and Gk. *τῷ Πέτρῳ* "to Peter". Sogdian therefore diverges from the Syriac text and from the Greek text. However, the Greek text shows a textual variant where *Σιμωνι* "Simon" is added to *τῷ Πέτρῳ*[497].

E5/83a-b
End of the Gospel for the 5th Sunday after Easter. John 17.24-26: /r/1-7/.
Beginning of the Gospel for Ascension Day. Luke 24.36-47: /r/8/-/v/20/.

/r/
/1/ qt fry̤ [n]y'd'ry mn' cn fcmpd 'γ'zy̤ pyr-
24. d-'ḥbtny ṃn qdm tr̈myth d-'lm';

492 See: *3.5.8 Sogd. βγy ptry "God the Father"*.
493 See: Sundermann (1975: 57); and Sims-Williams (2012: 37).
494 See: *Sogdian- Syriac Glossary*.
495 See: Sundermann (1975: 57-58).
496 See: *Sogdian- Syriac Glossary*.
497 See: Soden, von (1913: 488).

/2/ -s' · d'tcyq mn' bγ' ptr'˙ 't fcmpd ny̤
25. 'by k'n' w-'lm' l'

/3/ γr(bd')[rt tw](') · pyšt [z]w · γrbd'rm tw' 't wyšnt
yd'k 'n' dyn yd'tk w-hṇwn

/4/ γr[bd'rnt] (qt) t(γw) fšmd'ry̤ mn' · 't brt(pθ)
yd'w d-'nt šdrtny; 26. w-'wd't

/5/ [qθ'rm wyšnt t]w' n'm˙ 't brtpθ wn'm(sq zw)
'nwn šmk w-mwd' 'n'

/6/ [qt fryt't xyd] qt fry̤ ny'd'ry mn'. b't
d-ḥwb' hw d-'ḥbtny nhw'

/7/ [pr wyšnt 't zw] (b)'m˙ pr wyšnt ·· (Syriac) [ ]
b-hwn w-'n' 'hw' b-hwn.

/8/ [ ] (wkd knÿšyn hww)

/9/ [tlm̈yd'] (m)ḥd' ˙(Sogdian) 't c['nw 'wšt](y)t m'tnt

/10/ žwxšqt' (pr wy'q) ['xšd'rt] xwt'w

/11/ y(šwγ) wy̤šnty̤ myd'ny̤ · 't (w'nw) [fr'm]'ẏ qw
36. yšw' qm bynthwn w-'ṃr l-

/12/ wy̤šnt s' · dwrt' swq't [dn] (šm'x pr)w · zw 'ym˙
-hwn šlm' 'm-kwn 'n' 'n'

/13/ n' pcqwy̤rt' · 't wy̤šnt˙ [wyθrb](d)'rnt. 't qtnt
l' tdḥlkwn; 37. w-hṇwn 'trhbw w-hww

/14/ pr pcqwy̤r p't šm'ry̤(q) m't(n)t. qt w't
b-dḥlt' sbryn hww gyr d-rwḥ'

/15/ wy̤nntqn · w'nw fr'm'ẏ qw (wy̤š)nt s' xwt'w yšwγ
ḥzyn; 38. 'mr l-hwn yšw'

/16/ cw˙ wdrzt'sqn šm'x˙ · 't (c)w snntqn šm'ṛyt
mn' mttzy'yn 'ntwn w-mn' slq̈n mḥšb̈t'

/17/ pr šm'x žy'wrt · wỵnt'˙ mn' [d]st'˙ 't mn' p'dỵt
'l lbẅtkwn; 39. ḥ̇zw 'ÿdy w-ïgly

/18/ qt zw 'ỵm · mr(ws)t' mn' 't γrbt'q' · qt
d-'n' 'n' gwšwnny w-d'w d-

/19/ w'ty y'tỵ˙ 't (st)qỵ. nỵ(st) [wyny] w'(n)c'nw
-l-rwḥ' bsr̈' w-gïm' lyt l-h 'yk

/20/ qt wynt'sqn šm'x (q)t [s](ty) (mn)' · 't c'nw
d-ḥzyn 'ntwn d'yt l-y; 40. w-kd

/v/

/1/ [y]'n(t ')[yšt fr](')m'y.. ('št'd'r)[t qw wyšnt s']
hlyn 'ṃr ḥwy 'nwn

/2/ [xypθ ds](t)[' '](t) xyp[θ] p'dyt · 't [c]'nw [wytwr qw] qšỵ
'ÿdwhy w-ïglwhy; 41; w-kd 'dm' l-hš' ::

/3/ [prm] ny (wrnyq) m'tnt (c)[n wyšnty xwsn](t)y' 't
l' mhymnyn hww ṃn ḥdwthwn w-

/4/ ['d'tyt] (m't)nt · w('nw) f(r'm)['y qw wyšn]t s'
-mttmhyn hww 'ṃr l-hwn

/5/ [sty šm'xy mdy 'yc pr xwrt pyšt wyšnt]
'yt l-kwn tnn mdm l-m'kl; 42. hṇwn dyn

/6/ [θbrd'rnt qw wyny s' ptywfny cn qp' ---]
yhbw l-h mnt' ṃn nwn' d-ṭwy'

/7/ ['t cn 'nqwpyn 't ny'd'rt -----------------]
w-ṃn kkryt' d-dbš'; 43. w-ṇsb

/8/ [x](wrd'rt) [wyšnty pyrnms' 't w'nw fr'm'y]
'kl l-'nÿhwn; 44. w-'ṃr

/9/ qw (wỵšnt)[s' y'nt xnt] (w'xšt qt) [ž'd'rm]
l-hwn hlyn 'nÿn m̈l' d-mllt

/10/ dn š[m'x prw] (c')[nw š](m'x) (nbnt m't)[ym qt]
'mkwn kd lwt-kwn hwyt d-

/11/ s'š(t qt sptỵ) [by wyspw] 'ỵc qt npxštỵ
-wl' hw̱ d-nštlm kl mdm d-ktyb

/12/ stỵ pr (m)[wš'y nwm] 't pr bỵwnytỵ pwstỵt
b-nmws' d-mwš' w-b-nb̄y'

/13/ 't pr m[zmwrty pws](tyt) cn mn' pyd'r · · ·
w-b-mzmwr̈' 'ly;

/14/ [wyd'γty pynd'rt wy]šntỵ m'n pr ptbtw
45. hydyn ptḥ r'ynhwn l-mstklw

/15/ pws(tyt ')[t] (w'nw fr)'m'ẏ qw wyšnt s' qt
ktb̈'; 46. w-'ṃr l-hwn d-

/16/ prym[yθ] (frγn') [np]xštỵ [st]y 't pr[ymyθ] (f)rγn'
-hkn' ktyb w-hkn'

/17/ s'[cyq m']t qt (bž')xwty' pcγ('z't) mšyḥ' · .
zdq hw' d-nḥš mšyḥ'

/18/ ['t qt 'γzt] cn mwrtỵ d'mỵ š(tỵq) mỵθ[ỵ]
w-d-nqwm ṃn byt mÿt' l-tlt' yẅmyn;

/19/ ['t qt 'yzt' qty] bỵ pr wynỵ n'm nm'ṅqrgy'
47. w-d-ntkrz b-šmh tybwt'

/20/ qw (γw'n)tỵ (pr)[m']nty' s'. pr s't rmt' · 't
l-šwbqn' dḥṭḧ' b-klhwn 'm̈m' w-

Translation

/r/ /1/ "because you loved me before the beginning of the world. /2/ O righteous God the Father, the world does not /3/ know you, but I know you; and these ones /4/ know that you have sent me. And /4-5/ [I made them]

know your name, and I will continue to make *it* known, /6/ [that the love with] which you have loved me may be /7/ [in them, and I] in them". /8-9/ (Syriac) And as the disciples were just gathered immediately; (Sogdian)/9-10/and as the disciples were just gathered, /10-11/ immediately the Lord Jesus himself [stood] among them, and said thus /12/ to them: "Peace to you! It is me, /13/ do not be afraid!". But they /14/ frightened as they thought /14-15/ to see a spirit. The Lord Jesus thus said to them: /16/ "What worries you, and what thoughts arise /17/ in your hearts? See my hands and my feet /18/: that it is I myself. Touch me, and you will know that /19/ a spirit does not have flesh and bones as /20/ you see that I have". And when */v/* /1/ he had said these things, he showed [them] /2/ his hands and his feet. And while /2-3/ until now they disbelieved /4/ and were [amazed], thus said [to them] /5/: ["Do you have anything to eat here?" But they] /6/ [gave him a piece of fish], /7/ [and honey and took *them* and] /8/ ate [*them* before them and thus said] /9/ [to them: "These are] the words that [I spoke] /10/ [to] you while I w[as] still with you [:] /11/ it behoves to be fulfil[led all] the things that /11-12/ are written /12-13/ about me in the [Law of] Mo[ses], in the writing of the Prophets and in the books of the P[salms]". /14/ [Then he opened] their mind to understand /15/ the Scriptures, and said thus to them: /16/ "Thus it is written, and thus /17/ it is proper that the Messiah accepts suffering /18/ [and that] on the third day [rise] from the realm of the dead, /19-20/ [and that] repentance for the forgiveness of sins should be proclaimed in his name to all peoples and…

Commentary

/r/

/1-2/: *pyr-s' = pyrnms'*[498]. It is important to note that the *-y-* stroke has been lengthened to make the length of this writing line like that of all other ones.
/7-8/: *[ ]*. As already explained by Sundermann (1975: 59), the blank space that exists between the end of this writing line and the beginning of the next one, evidently had to be filled by the scribe with the column indicating the new Gospel passage; however, this has not occurred and therefore the column is missing. The text begins with the first words of the new passage written in Syriac, immediately followed by the Sogdian translation.
/8-10/: Sogd. *'t c['nw 'wšt](y)t m'tnt žwxšqt' (pr wy'q)* "and as the disciples were just gathered immediately" and Syr. *(w-kd knyšyn hww) [tlm̈yd']*

[498] According to Sundermann (1975: 58).

(m)ḥd' "id". As already explained by Sundermann (1975: 59) the Gospel lectionary shows a perfect correspondence between the Sogdian and the Syriac text but both diverges from the text of the *Peshitta* which reports *w-kd hlyn mmllyn hww* "as they said these things".

Final remarks: In /r/9/ Pittard apud Sims-Williams (2012: 37) reads *'] (k)ḥd'*). I do not agree with this reading because of the Sogdian and Syriac sentences therein attested. In fact, the Syriac *mḥd'* is translated by the Sogdian *pr wy'q* in this Gospel lectionary. In the same way, it seems to be more plausible that -' , which precedes *mḥd'*, is the last letter of *tlm̈yd'* translated by the Sogdian *žwxšqt'* in /r/10/. In /r/10/ I consider *(pr wy'q)* readable as already Sundermann did (1975: 59) and then I reject Müller's reading (1913: 53-54) *(yw wy)'q(y)* which seems to be accepted by Sims-Williams too (2012: 37).

/9/: *'wšt](y)t*. According to Pittard apud Sims-Williams (2012: 37).

/13/: *[wyθrb](d)'rnt*. Pittard apud Sims-Williams (2012: 37) reads *(wyθrb)(d)'rnt*.

/19/: *w'(n)c'nw*. According to Pittard apud Sims-Williams (2012: 37). Contra Müller (1913: 54-55) *(s)' c'nw*.

/v/

/1/: *[y]'n(t ')[yšt]* "these things". Taking into account the Syriac *hlyn*, Sundermann (1975: 59) reads *[x]'n(t ')[yšt]*. I prefer reading *[y]'n(t ')[yšt]* beacause the Syriac *hlyn* is always translated by the Sogdian *y'nt 'yšt*[499] in this Gospel lectionary.

/1-2/: I do not agree with Sims-Williams (2012: 37) but I agree with Sundermann (1975: 59) in believing that there is enough space to conjecture *[s'xypθ ds](t)['*.

/2/: *[wytwr qw]*. Sims-Williams (2012: 37) reads *wyt](w)r (qw)*.

/3/: *(c)[n wyšnty xwsn](t)y'*. Sims-Williams (2012: 37) reads *(c)[n] (wyṣ̌n)[ty xwsn](t)y'*.

/12/: *(m)[wš'y]*. Oblique of *mwš'* "Moses" < Syr. *mwš'* "id."[500].

/12-13/: Sogd. *'t pr bỵwnytỵ pwstỵt 't pr m[zmwrty pws](tyt)* "in the Books of the Prophets and in the books of Psalms" and Syr. *w-b- nb̈y' w-b-mzmwr̈'* "in the Prophets and in the Psalms". Sogdian adds *pwstyt* "books". The Syriac text agrees with the Greek text: *καὶ προφήταις καὶ ψαλμοῖς* "in the Prophets and in the Psalms".

/13/: *m[zmwrty]*. Oblique pl. of *mzmwr-* (f.) "psalm" < Syr. *mzmwr'*.

/17/: *(bž')xwty'*. According to Sundermann (1975: 60).

---

[499] See: *Sogdian- Syriac Glossary.*

[500] See: Sims-Williams (1988: 154).

/18/: *['t qt 'γzt]*. Pittard apud Sims-Williams (2012: 37) reads *(')[t] (q)[t 'γz]t˙*.
/18/: *cn mwrtỵ d'mỵ*. On the use of *mwrty* as a collective noun and on the translation "from the realm of the dead", see: Sundermann (1975: 60). I only add that *mrty-d'm* "realm of the dead" is also attested in *C2* (p. 215), in *E26/23V15f*[501], and in *E29/6R17*[502].
/18/: *mỵθ[ỵ]*. According to Sundermann (1975: 60), it is an accusative indicating time.
/20/: *(γw'n)tỵ*. Sims-Williams (2012: 37) reads *(γw)'nt(y)*.

E5/91
End of the Gospel for the 2nd Sunday after Pentecost. Luke 10.34-42: /r/-/v/6/.
Beginning of the Gospel for the 3rd Sunday after Pentecost. Luke 6.12-17: /v/7/-/v/22/.

/r/
/1/ · 't wrỵcd'rt prỵwnt˙ m(dw) · 't rwγn · 't pcγỵ(n)d'rt
34. w-nṣḷ 'l-yhyn ḥmr' w-mšḥ' w-sm-

/2/ wynỵ˙ pr xypθ xrỵ. 't 'nỵd'rt wynỵ qw tỵm s' ·
-h 'l ḥmrh w-'ytyh l-pwtq'

/3/ 't xwỵsm b' wynỵ pr yw · 't dbtỵq mỵθỵ
w-'tbṭl l-h 'l-why; 35. w-l-ṣprh

510 /4/ fr'q-cšnỵ . · nyšqwγd'rt dw'˙ qỵsrq'n.
d-ywm' 'p̣q tïyn dynïyn

/5/ θbrd'rt qw tỵm-p'šỵ s' · 't w'nw wγd'rt
yḥb l-pwtqy' w-'ṃr

/6/ qw wynỵ s'˙ xwỵsm br' wynỵ xypθ 't qt 'ỵc˙
l-h yṣp dylh w-'n mdm

[501] See: Sims-Williams (2015: 221).
[502] See: Sims-Williams (2014a: 183).

/7/ fy’tr zy’my̤ wy̤ny̤ . · c’nw qt zwrtm˙ zw̤. θbrng’
ytyr tpq m’ d-hpk ’n’ yhb ’n’

/8/ qw tw’ s’˙ · qy̤ nwqr cn y’nt šy̤ xwšty̤q˙ ·
l-k; 36. mnw hkyl m̤n hlyn tlt’

/9/ d’ty̤ sy̤d(t) [tw]’ qt b’ pnt ’dy̤ ndywy̤dy̤ qt
mṫḥz’ l-k d-hw’ qryb̈’ l-hw d-

/10/ ’mps(t) (pr r’θp)’nty̤ dsty’ · pyšt xw̤. w’nw
-n̤pl b-’ÿdy gÿs’; 37. hw̤ dyn

/11/ pcqw’[d](’)rt˙ xy(d) qt z’ry̤sy’ d’rt pry̤w · w’nw
’m̤r ḣw d-’trḥm ‘l-why

/12/ fr’m’y (qw) [wyny s]’ xwt’w yšwγ˙ šw’ · ms
’ṁr l-h yšw‘ zl ’p

/13/ t(γw) pry̤my̤θ frγn’ (qwn’) ·∵ ’t b’ qt c’nw
’nt hkn’ hwyt ‘bd; 38. w-hw’ d-kd

/14/ wy̤šnt˙ šwy̤ntqn pr r’θ. · tγty̤ qw yw dyx(’)w s’ ·
hn̤wn rdyn b-’wrḥ’ ‘l l-qryt’ ḥd’

/15/ ’t yw ’ync˙ qt šy̤ n’m m’t˙ mrθ’. pcγšd’rt
w-’ntt’ d-šmḣ mrt’ qblt-

/16/ wyny̤ xypθ x’ny̤ · ’t m’t wy’ yw xw’r˙ qt šy̤
-h b-bytḣ; 39. w-’yt hwt l-ḣ ḥt’ d-

/17/ n’m m’t. mrym ’t ’γt˙ ny̤sty̤ x’ m’x
-šmḣ mrym w-’tt ytbt l-ḣ

/18/ (x)ypθ’wnty̤ p’dy(ty nbnt · ’)t ptγwš(y̤q) m’t
lwt r̈glwhy d-mrn w-šm‘’ hwt

/19/ x’ wyny̤ xypθ w’(x)št · pyšt mrθ’˙ ’ḃnt d’ṙy̤(q)
mlẅhy; 40. mrt’ dyn ‘ny’ hwt

/20/ m’t˙ x’. pr γrf (sp)’s · ’t ’γt. w’nw pcqw’d’rt
b-tšmšt’ sgy’t’ w-’tt ’mr’

/21/ qw wyny s’ · mn’ xypθ’wnt’: cwt xwysm nyst
l-h mry l’ bṭyl

/22/ tw’˙˙ qt mn’ xw’r prγd’rt mn’ γwty xwdq’r
l-k d-ḥty šbqtny blḥwdy

/v/

/1/ pr spxšw. · frm’ẏ qw wy’ s’˙˙ z’wr θbr’t mn’ ·
l-mšmšw ’ṃr l-ḣ m‘dr’ ly;

/2/ p’cγny̱ qθ’rt˙ xwt’w yšwγ. w’nw fr’m’ẏ qw
41. ‘ṇ’ yšw‘ w-’ṃr l-

/3/ wy’ s’ mrθ’˙˙ mrθ’. · xwy̱sm bry̱nc ’y̱š tγw˙
-ḣ mrt’ mrt’ yṣypty

/4/ ’t wy̱θrbny̱nc. pr γrfty̱št · pyšt yw ’y̱c xcy̱
w-rhybty ‘l sgÿ’t’; 42. ḥd’ hy dyn

/5/ qt γwnty xcy̱ · pyšt mrym˙ šyry̱ ptyfnw wy̱cn-
d-mtb‘y’ mrym dyn mnt’ ṭbt’ gbt

/6/ -d’rt x’. · xyd qt ’yty ny bwtq’ cn wy’ ⁘
l-ḣ ḣy d- -l’ ttnsb ṃn-ḣ

/7/ (Syriac red) dḥdbšb’ d’rb‘’ d[š](ly)[ḥ’] ⁘ d[lw](q)’ ⁘

/8/ (Syriac red) bṣḥ ⁘ w ⁘ (Syriac black) hẉ’ dyn˙ byẅmt’ hnwn ⁘ ⁘
(Sogd. black) pyšt b’˙˙
12. hẉ’ dyn

/9/ pr dy̱wnt˙ my̱θqry̱t. ·· ⁘ nyžty̱ xwt’w yšwγ
b-yẅmt’ hnwn npq yšw‘

/10/ qw γrỵ s’ pr nm’c brỵ · ’t wdỵ (w)ỵn’wd’rt
l-ṭwr’ l-mṣlyw w-tmn ’gh hw’

/11/ pr bγ’nyq nm’c · ’t c’nw wywsd’rt˙ žγỵrd’rt
b-ṣlwth d-’lh’ ; 13. w-kd nght qr’

/12/ xypθ žwxšqt’ỵ . · ’t wycnd’rt˙ cn wy(š)ntỵ . dw’ts ·
l-tlm̈ydwhy w-gḅ’ ṃn-hwn tr‘sr

/13/ x’nt (q)t (p)t(γ’mbr)ỵt n’m ’wstỵd’rt wỵšntỵ ·
hṅwn d-šlÿḥ’ šmy ’nwn;

/14/ šmγwn (x)yd · (q)t n’m ’wstỵd’rt · sng . ’t
14. šm‘wn ḣw d-šmy k’p’ w-

/15/ ’ndr̈’ws wynỵ br’t · ’t yγ(qw)b · ’t ywḥnn ·
- ’ndr̈’ws ’ḥwhy w-y‘qwb w-ywḥnn

/16/ ’t pylypws˙ ’t br θẉlṃy · ’t mθy˙ ’t θ’ẉm’ ·
w-pylypws w-br twlmy; 15. w-mty w-t’wm’

/17/ ’t yγqwb˙ ḥ˙lpyỵ z’ty · ’t šmγwn qt žγ(y)rtỵ
w-y‘qwb br ḥlpy w-šm‘wn d-mtqr’

/18/ bwt ’rsqnỵ · ’t y(h)wd’ yγqwbỵ z’tỵ · ’t
ṭnn’; 16. w-yhwd’ br y‘qwb w-

/19/ skrywt’yq yhwd’ xyd qt (qtỵ) prb(x)šnỵ ∵
-yhwd’ skrywṭ’ ḣw d-hw’ mšlmn’;

/20/ ’t ’wxšt dn wỵšntỵ prẇ xwt’w yšwγ . ’t w’št
17. w-nḥṭ ‘m-hwn yšw‘ w-qṃ

/21/ r’γỵ · ’t γrf žwxšqt’ỵ˙ ’(w)’zỵ ’t γrf
b-pq‘t’ w-knš’ sgy’’ d-tlmÿdwhy w-swg’’

/22/ rmyỵ ’w’zỵ · cn mγwn yhwd ’t cn ’wršlm ·
d-knš’ d-‘m’ ṃn klḧ yhwd w-ṃn ’wršlm

Translation

/r/ /1/ and poured oil and wine on them and set him /2/ on his own donkey and brought him to an inn /3/ and took care of him. /4/ And the morning of the next day he took out two denarii /5/ and gave *them* to the innkeeper, and thus said /6/to him: "Take care of him, and whatever /7/ more you will spend form him, /7-8/ I will give *it* back to you when I come back'. So, which of these three, /9/ according to the law, seems [to you] to be close to the one who /10/ fell among the robbers?" But so he /11/ said: "The one who had mercy on him". And /11-12/ the Lord Jesus thus said [to him]: "Go, and do also /13/ likewise". And it happened that while /14/ they were on the road, he entered a village /15/ and a woman named Martha welcomed him /16/ into her house. And she had a sister /17/ called Mary, and arrived; sat /18/ at the feet to our Lord and listened /19/ to his words. But Martha was engaged /20/ in much serving. And she went up to him and said thus /21-22/ to him: "Oh my Lord! Do you not care that my sister has left me alone */v/* /1/ to serve? Tell her to help me". /2/ The Lord Jesus answered her, and thus said to her: /3/ "Martha, Martha, you worry /4/ and trouble about many things, but one thing /5/ is necessary. But Mary has chosen a good part /6/, which will not be taken away from her". /7/ (Syriac) for the fourth Sunday from the Apostle Luke, /8/ chapter 6. But it was in those days... (Sogdian) But it was /9/ in those days *that* the Lord Jesus went to /10/ the mountain to pray, and there /10-11/ all night he continued in prayer of God. And when day dawned, he called /12/ his disciples and chose *from them* twelve /13/, whom he named apostles: /14/ Simon, whom he named Peter, and /15/ Andrew his brother, Jacobs, John, /16/ Philip, Bartholomew, Matthew, Thomas, /17/ Jacobs, the son of Alphaeus, Simon who was called /18/ the Zealot, and Judas the son of Jacobs, and /19/ Judas Iscariot, who became a traitor. /20/ And Lord Jesus came down with them and stood /21/ in a plain. And a multitude of many disciples and /21-22/ a multitude of many people from all Judea, from Jerusalem…

Commentary

/r-v/: Syriac onomastic.

/r/

/1/: *pcγẏ(n)d'rt*. According to Müller (1913: 35-36) and Sims-Williams (2012: 38). Sundermann (1975: 61) reads *pcγẏzd'rt*.

/3-4/: *'t dbtẏq mẏθẏ fr'q-cšnẏ* "and the morning of the following day". With particular regard to the compound *fr'q-cšnẏ*, Sundermann discussed the

meaning "morning" from a literary meaning of "beim Frühtrunk"[503].
The Syriac text has *w-lṣprh d-ywm'* "and the morning of the day" while the Greek text has *καὶ ἐπὶ τὴν αὔριον* "and the morning".
/4/: *qy̤srq'n* "denarii". The same term is also attested in *E/26/7* as *qysrg'n*[504].
/8-9/: *xwšty̤q d'ty̤*. It is not a clear passage which has no correspondances either in the Syriac or in the Greek text. The problem has been well highlighted by Sundermann (1975: 61), while Müller did not translate it. Sundermann translates "nach dem Gesetz der Lehrer", considering *xwšty̤q* as a denominative < *xwšty̤* "master, teacher" and not a numeral indicator which *GMS* (§ 1325) compares to the New Persian *nafar* and which is attested in this way in the dictionary of Gharib (1995: 439). I suggest to consider *xwšty̤q* as a numeral indicator since it is preceded by "three" and the noun in the oblique case *d'ty̤* meaning "as a rule".
/9/: *sy̤d(t)*. See: Sims-Williams (1985: 85-86, n. 67).
/9/: *[tw]'*. Sims-Williams (2012: 38) reads *(tw)'*. In my opinion, however, the two letters are almost deleted.
/19-20/: *'bnt d'ry̤q m't* lit. "was having ties in", meaning being engaged in, being busy with[505]. With particular regard to *'b.̣nt*, see: Sims-Williams (2012: 38).
/v/
/4/: *wy̤θrbny̤nc*. The reading is by Sundermann (1975: 63). Müller (1913: 37) reads *wy̤θrbγy̤nc* but at the same time, he also assumes *wy̤θrbny̤nc* as a plausible reading. I think that each letter is easily recognizable.
/10/: *(w)y̤n'wd'rt*. According to Pittard apud Sims-Williams (2012: 38)[506].
/19/: *skrywt'yq* "Iscariot" < Syr. *skrywṭ'*. The Sogdian suffix *-'yq* conveys, as demonstrated by Sims-Williams, "…Syriacs gentilics and other adjectival forms in *-āyā* "[507]. (1988: 146; 155). The same applies to *pryš'yqt* "Pharisees" which is attested in the following fragment, i.e., in *E5/100-101/Ir/*18/.
/20/: *w'št*. Imperfect, 3 pers. sg. of the verb *'wšt(y̤)/'wšt(y̤)t* "to stand".

---

503 See: Sundermann (1975: 61).
504 A Christian Sogdian fragment containing the life of John of Dailam. See: Sims-Williams (2012: 82).
505 See: Sundermann (1975: 62).
506 See also: Sims-Williams (2014a: 122).
507 See: Sims-Williams (1988: 146; 155).

E5/100-101
Part of the Gospel for the 3rd Sunday of Summer, i.e, the 9th Sunday after Pentecost. John 9.9-38: */I-IIr/- /I-IIv/.*

/Ir/

/1/ ny̤ xcy̤ · (yw'r) qt (pr) m'nwqy(')[myntq qw wny]
9....l'̈ 'l' mdm' dm' l-h

/2/ s' · pyšt xẇ w'b(y)q m't. q[t zw 'ym w'nw]
hẉ dyn 'mr hw' d-'n' 'n';

/3/ (w)γd'rnt qw wny̤ s' · c'ny̤ xwy̤(c)[qtnt tw']
10. 'mryn l-h 'ykn' 'tptḥ

/4/ cšmt' · p'cγny̤ qθ'rt. 't w'nw wγ(d'rt q)[w]
'ynÿk; 11. 'ṇ' w-'ṃr l-

/5/ [wyšn](t) s' · mrty̤ qt (šy) n'm m't xwt'w
-hwn gbr' d-šmh

/6/ [yšwγ] (q)θ'rt (γ)ry̤(q) 't d'wd'rt pr mn'
yšw' 'ḅd ṭyn' w-ṭš l-y 'l

/7/ [cšmt'] ('t) wγd'(rt q)w m(n)' s' šw' sn'ẏ
'ynÿ w-'ṃr l-y zl 'šyg

/8/ [šylwḥ'y '](py) · 't xrtym sn'd'rm 't wy̤ny̤
b-m̈y' d-šylwḥ' w-'zlt 'šygt w-

/9/ [qtym w'nw] (wγd')rnt qw wny̤ s'· qw sty̤ ·
-'tḥzy l-y; 12. 'mryn l-h 'yk' hẉ

/10/ [w'nw w'b] qw (wyšnt) s'· ny̤ γ(r)b'msq
'm̈r l-hwn l' yd'

/11/ [zw 't 'nyd]('rnt) wny̤y̤ qt cn ftm' smẏnt
'n' ; 13. w-'ytywhy l-hw d-ṃn qdym smy'̈

/12/ [m't q]w pryš'ỵ(qt) s' · pyšt m't myθ šmpd
hw' lwt pr̈yš'; 14. 'ytyḣ hwt dyn šbt'

/13/ [c'nw] (q)θ'rt γ(r)y(q) xwt'w yš(wγ ')t xwỵcq
kd ʻḅd ṭyn' yšwʻ w-ptḥ

/14/ (q)θ'rt w(yny) [xy](pθ) cšmt' ∵ 't tym p(s)d'rnt
l-h ʻynẅhy; 15. w-twb š'lw-

/15/ wnỵ pr[yš]'y(q)t · c'nỵ wỵnỵ qtyštγw · pyšt
-hy pr̈yš' 'ykn' 'tḥzy l-k hẉ

/16/ xẉ w'(n)w wγd'rt qw wỵšnt s' · (γ)rỵq 'wstyd'rt
dyn 'ṃr l-hwn ṭyn' sm

/17/ pr mn' cšmt' · 't s(n)'d'r(m) '(t w)ỵnỵ qtỵm
ʻl ʻynÿ w-'šygt w-'tḥzy ly;

/18/ 't w'nw w'bỵq m'tnt mrtxmỵt (cn pr)yš'-
16. w-'mryn hww 'n̈š' ṃn pr̈yš'

/19/ -ỵqt · 'yn(y m)rtỵ nỵ cn bγ' xcỵ qt šmpd
hn' gbr' l' hw' ṃn 'lh' hẉ d-šbt'

/20/ 'ỵc'(t nỵ) (d)'rtq · pyšt ẏw qwst. w'nw
l' nṭr 'ḥr̈n' dyn

/21/ w'bỵntqn · c'nỵ qt' wn(tỵ)q' qt'ny-(q')rỵ
'mryn hww 'ykn' mškḥ gbr'

/22/ mrtỵ y'nt qržwrzt pr qrwn · 't dw'(ywx'){<q(y)'>}
ḥṭy' hlyn 'tẅt' l-mʻbd w-plgwt'

/Iv/

/1/ [m't wyšnty m]yd'nỵ · [w]('nw) [w](γd)'rt tym qw
'yt hwt bynthwn; 17. 'mryn twb l-

/2/ [xyd smynt s](') t(γ)w cw w'(b)[y](sq t)[γw] (p)ryw q(t)
-hw smy' 'nt mn' 'mr 'nt ʻlwhy d-

/3/ [xwycq qθ](')rt [tw'] (x)[y](p)[θ] tw' cš(mt)'
-pṭḥ l-k 'ynÿk;

/4/ [w](’n)[w] (w)[γd](’r)t q(w w)[yšn]t (s)’ (z)w (w’bmsqn q)t
'ṃr l-hwn 'n' 'mr 'n' d-

/5/ bywny̤ xcy̤ · (p)[y](št) [n](y pyr)y̤q (m')[tn](t pry)[w]
-nby' hw̤; 18. l' dyn hymnw hww 'l-hwy

/6/ c(x)wdt qt (s)[my](nt) [m't] 't (wy̤ny̤) [qty] (w)[ytwr]
yhẅdy' d-smy' hw' w- -ḥz' 'dm'

/7/ qt žγy̤rd'[rnt m't ptryt xy](d) {<'dy̤y̤>} qt
d-qrw l-'bḧwhy d-ḣw d-

/8/ wy̤ny̤ qt(y) ['t] ps(d)'rnt [wyšnty qt 'yny]
-ḥz'; 19. w- š'lw 'nwn 'n hnw

/9/ xcy̤ šm'x z'ty̤ xy(d qt w')[bt'sq šm'x]
brkwn ḣw d-'ntwn 'mryn 'ntwn

/10/ qt c'n(w s)m(ynt) ['žt] (c)'n(y̤) [qšy wyntqn]
d-kd sm' 'tyld 'ykn' hš' ḥz';

/11/ pyšt p'cγny̤ (qθ'rnt) [wny m't ptryt]
20. 'nw dyn 'bhẅhy

/12/ w'nw wγd'rnt γr(by̤)m(s)q(n) [m'x] (qt) ['yny]
w-'mrw yd'ynn d-hnw

/13/ xcy̤ m'x z'ty̤ · 't {<qt>} (c')nw [smynt] '(ž)t (p)[yš](t)
brn w-d-kd sm' 'tyld;

/14/ c'ny̤ qšy̤ w(y̤n)tqn qd' q(y̤ x)w(y̤)c(q q)θ'r(t)
21. 'ykn' dyn hš' ḥz' 'w mnw pṭḥ

/15/ wny̤ wny̤ cšmt' . ny̤ γrb(y)msqn m'[x] · ms
l-h 'ynẅhy l' yd'ynn 'p

/16/ xw tγty̤ xcy̤ qw xypθ srdt s’ ⁚ wny̤ pst’
hẉ ‘l l-h l-šn̈why l-h š’lw

/17/ xw xypθ γrywy̤ p{<c>}rw ž’ẏt · y’nt ’y̤št wγd’rnt
hẉ ḥlp npšh nmll; 22. hlyn ’mrw

/18/ wny̤ m’t[pt]ry̤t · cywyθ pyd’r qt pcqwy̤ry̤q
’bḧwhy mṭl d-dḥlyn

/19/ m’tnt cn cxwdty̤ · p’t w’xš pwxsty̤ m’tnt
hww ṃn yhẅdy’ psqw hww gyr

/20/ cn cxwdt · qt ’dy̤ ’̤z’nt pr {<y̤w>}qt m[šyḥ]’ (xcy̤)
yhẅdy’ d-’n ’nš nwd’ bh d-mšyḥ’ hẉ

/21/ by̤s’ fšqry̤nt ˇ<wny̤> cn ’w’zqty̤ · cy̤(wyθ) py̤d’r
npqwnyhy ṃn knwšt’; 23. mṭl hn’

/22/ wγd’rnt wny̤ m’t (p)try̤t qt tγty̤ xw qw xy̤pθ
’mrw ’bḧwhy d-‘l l-h l-

/IIr/

/1/ (srdt) s’ wny̤ (p)st’ · [’t žγyrd’rnt]
- šn̈why l-h š’lw; 24. w-qr’why

/2/ mrty̤ qt db(ty̤q) pr(wrt)[w xyd qt smynt m’t]
l-gbr’ d-tr̈tyn zbnÿn l-ḧw d-’ytwhy hw’ smy’

/3/ ’t (w)’nw wγd(’rnt qw) wny̤ s[’ γwbty’ ptwyd]
w-’mryn l-h šbḥ

/4/ (q)w (b)[γy] (s’ p’t m’x γ)[rbymsq ’yny mrty]
l-’lh’ ḥnn gyr yd‘yn ḥnn d-hn’ gbr’

/5/ (qt) [qt](’ny-q’ry̤) [x](cy) [p’cγ](n)y̤ (qθ’)[rt]
ḥṭy’ hẉ; 25. ‘ṇ’

/6/ (xw) ’t (w)’[nw w](γd’r)t [qw wy](šnt s’) · qt q(t)’ny-
hẉ w-’ṃr l-hwn ’n ḥṭy’

/7/ -[q’](ry̤ xcy̤ ny) γrb’(msq)n zw · (pyšt yw ’)[yc]
hw̤ l’ yd‘ ’n’ ḥd’ dyn

/8/ [γr]b’m(sq) zw · (q)[t] [smy](nt m)’ty̤(m) ’t q(š)[y]
yd‘ ’n’ d-smy’ hwyt w-hš’

/9/ [n’y wynm](sqn z)[w w](’nw w)[γd](’)[rn]t (qw wny s)’ ty̤m ·
ḣ’ ḥz’ ’n’; 26. ’mryn l-h twb

/10/ [cw qθ](’rt) [qw] t(w’) s’ · c’(n)y̤ xwy̤cq qθ’rt
mn’ ‘ḅd l-k ’ykn’ pṭḥ

/11/ [tw’ tw’ cšmt’ w’](n)w wγd’rt qw wy̤šnt s’ · wγd’rm
l-k ‘ynÿk; 27. ’ṃr l-hwn ’mrt

/12/ [qw šm’x] (s’ ’)t (ny̤ nγw)šd’r(t)’ šm’x ·
l-kwn w-l’ šm‘twn

/13/ [cw tym q](’mt’sqn) šm’x pr ptγwš
mn’ twb ṣbyn ’ntwn l-mšm‘

/14/ [cw db](’t) (m)[s] (š)m’(x) žwxšqt’ q’mt’sqn ·
l-m’ ’p ’ntwn tlmÿd’ ṣbyn ’ntwn

/15/ pr bw (q)w w(ny̤ s)’ · pyšt wy̤šnt ptyθy’ qθ’rnt
l-mhw’ l-h; 28. hnwn dyn ṣḥyw-

/16/ wny̤ ’t w’nw (wγ)d’rnt qw wny̤ s’ · (cwt) tγw ’y̤š
-hy w-’mryn l-h ’nt hw

/17/ xwny̤y̤ žwxšqy̤ · p’t m’x žwxšqt’ ’y̤m
tlmydh d-hw ḥnn gyr tlmÿd’ ḥnn

/18/ mwš’ bywny̤ xypθ · ’t γrbymsqn m’x ·
d-mwš’; 29. w-yd‘yn ḥnn

/19/ qt dn mwš’ prw bγy ž’d’rt · (py)[š]t ’ỵnỵỵ
d-‘m mwš’ ’lh’ ṃll l-hn’ dyn

/20/ (nỵ) γrbymsqn m’x cn qw ms’ xcỵ ·
l’ yd‘yn ḥnn ṃn ’ymk’ hẉ;

/21/ (p’c)γnỵ qθ’rt xwnỵ mrty ’t w’nw wγd’rt
‘ṇ’ ḣw gbr’ w-’ṃr

/22/ qw wỵšnt s’. (pr)ỵmỵθ (nwq)r s’št pr wd’s
l-hwn b-hd’ hw hkyl l-mtdmrw

/IIv/

/1/ [qt šm’x ny γrb](t’)sqn cn qw ms’
d-’ntwn l’ yd‘yn ’ntwn ṃn ’ymk’

/2/ [xcy ’t mn’ xypθ] c(š)mt’ xwycq qθ’rt ·
hẉ w-‘ÿny dyly pṭḥ;

/3/ [pyšt γrbymsq] (m)’x qt bγy pr qt’nỵ-
31. yd‘yn ḥnn dyn d-’lh’ b-ql’

/4/ [-q’ryty wxr ny nγ](w)št · yw’r qw xwnỵ ’dỵ s’
d-ḥṭÿ’ l’ šm‘ ’l’ l-ṁn

/5/ [q](t) [p]c(q)[wyrt] (c)n wnỵ ’t wn’t wnỵ ryž qw
d-dḥl ṃn-h w-‘b̈d ṣbynh l-

/6/ xwnỵ s’ n[γ](wš)t · cn ’yqwn ms’ ptγwštỵ nỵ
-ḣw hẉ šm‘; 32. ṃn ‘lm l’ ’štm‘t

/7/ qtỵ qt x[wy]cq (w)nwtỵ ’dỵ s(m)ynty (cš)[mt’]
d-pṭḥ ’nš ‘ÿn’ d-smy’

/8/ qt smynt ’žtỵ bwtỵ · ’qt nỵ cn bγ’
d-’tyld; 33. ’lw l’ ṃn ’lh’

/9/ bwtỵ ’ynỵ · nỵ qt’ wnỵq m’t ’ỵnỵ pr [qwrwn]
hw’ hn’ l’ mškḥ hw’ hd’ l-m‘bd;

/10/ p’cγny̤ qθ’rnt. ’t w’nw wγd’rnt q[w wny]
34. ‘nw w-’mryn l-h

/11/ s’ · tγ(w) s’t ywp’tqy̤˙ pr γw’n ’žt[yš]
’nt klk b-ḥṭh’ ’tyldt

/12/ ’t tγw ywcy̤q’. m’xy̤. · ’t fšq[rd’rnt wny]
w-’nt mlp̣ ’nt l-n w-’pqwhy

/13/ by̤s’ · ’t ptγwšd’r(t) xwt’w yšw(γ) [qt fšqr]-
lbr̈; 35. w-ṣ̌m‘ yšw‘ d-’pqw-

/14/ -d’rnt wny̤ by̤s’. · ’t šy̤ byrd’rt. ’t (w)[’nw]
-hẏ lbr w-’škḥh w-

/15/ wγd’rt qw wny̤ s’ · tγw wrny̤sqn pr bγy̤
-’ṃr l-h ’nt mhymn ’nt b-brh

/16/ z’ty̤. · p’cγny̤ qθ’rt xwny̤˙ qt py’m by̤rd’rt
d-’lh’; 36. ‘ṇ’ ḣw d-’t’sy

/17/ ’t w’nw pcqw’d’rt · qy̤ xcy̤ mn’ xypθ’-
w-’mr ṁn-ẉ mry

/18/ -wnt’˙˙ qt wrn’m pr wny̤ · w’nw fr’m’ẏ qw
d-’hymn b-h; 37. ’ṁr l-

/19/ wny̤ s’ xwt’w yšwγ˙ šy̤ wy̤d’ry̤ · ’t xy̤d qt
-h yšw‘ ḥzytyḣy w-ḣw d-

/20/ ž’ytqn dn tw’ prw. xw xcy̤ · pyšt xw w’nw
-mmll ‘mk hwyw; 38. hw dyn

/21/ pcqw’d’rt · wrn’msq zẇ mn’ xypθ’wnt’˙
’ṃr mhymn ’n’ mry

/22/ ’t ’mpst nm’c brd’rt qw wny̱ s’ ∴

w-ṇpl sgd l-h

Translation

/Ir/ 1/ “He is not, but he is li[ke him]”. /2/ While he kept saying: “[I am!”. Thus] /3/ they said to him: /3-4/ “How [were your] eyes opened?”. He answered, and thus said /5/ [to them]: “The man who is called the Lord /6/ [Jesus] made mud, anointed my /7/ [eyes] *with it* and said to me: “Go, wash yourself /8/ in the wa[ter of Siloe]. I went, I washed myself and /9/ [I received my sight”.] They [thus] said to him: “Where is he?” /10/ [He thus said] to them: “I do not know *it*”. /11-12/ [And they brou]ght to the Pharisees the man who had formerly been blind. But it was Sabbath /13/ [when] the Lord Jesus had made the mud and /14/ had opened his eyes. /14-15/ And the Pharisees again asked to him: “how did you receive the sight?” But /16/ he thus said to them: “He put mud /17/ on my eyes, I washed myself, and I received my sight”. /18/ Some of the Pharisees thus said: /19-20/ “This man is not from God, for he does not keep the Sabbath”. But one side /20-21/ thus said: “How can a man who is a sinner /22/ do such wonders?” And there was discord */Iv/*1/ among [the]m. So they said again to the /2/ [blind man]: “What do you sa[y] about him, since /3/ he [has opened] your eyes?” /4/ He [thu]s s[ai]d to them: “I say that /5/ he is a prophet”. But the Jews did not believe /6/ that he [had been] blind and [had received] his sight, /7/ until they cal[le]d [the parents] of the man who /8/ had received his sight. [And] asked [them]: “[If is this] /9/ your son, who [you] sa[y] /10/ [was born] blind, how then [does he now see?]” /11/ But [the parents] answered [and] /12/ thus said: “We know that [this] /13/ is our son and that he was born [blind]. But /14/ how he now sees or who opened /15/ his eyes we do not know. /15-16/ He is also of age; ask him! /17-18/ He will speak for himself”. His parents said these things because they /18-19/ feared the Jews. For the Jews had already /20/ agreed that if anyone should recognize him as [Messiah], /21/ he was to be put out of the synagogue. Therefore /22/ his parents said: “He is of age…”*/IIr/* /I/ “*he is* of age; ask him”. /1-2/ [And] for the second time [they called] the man [who had been blind] /3/ and thus said to him: “[Give glory] /4/ to God. For we kn[ow that this man] /5/ is a sinner”. He answered /6/ and thus said to them: “Whether /7/ he is a sinner I do not know *it*. But one [thing] I do /8/ know, that I was blind and now /9/ I see”. They thus said to him again /10/ : “[What] did he do to you? How did he open /11/ [the eyes?]” He thus answered them: /11-12/ “I have already told *it* [to you], and you did not listen. /13/ [What] do you want to hear [again?] /14/ [Perhaps]

do you also want /14-15/ to become his disciples?" But they reviled him /16/ and they thus said: "You are /17/ his disciple, but we are disciples /18/ of the prophet Moses! And we know /19/ that God has spoken to Moses, but /19-20/ we do not know where this one comes from". /21/ The man answered and thus said /22/ to them: "Thus, therefore it is proper to wonder! */IIv/*1/ [You do not kn]ow where he /2/ [comes from, and yet] he opened [my] eyes. /3/ [But] we [know] that God /3-4/ does [not] listen [to the voice of the sin]s, but anyone who /5/ fears him and does his will, /6/ He listens to him. Never has it been heard /7/ that anyone opened the eyes of a blind man /8/ who was born blind. If /8-9/ this man were not from God, he could [d]o nothing". /10/ They answered and said thus [to him]: /11/ "You were born in utter sin /12/ and would you teach us?" And they cas[t him] /13/out. And the Lord Jesus knew [that] /13-14/ they had [cast him] out and he found him /14-15/ and [thus] said to him: "Do you believe /16/ in the Son of God?" He answered that he had found the cure /17/ and he thus said: "Who is he, my Lord, /18/ that I may believe in him?" /18-19/ The Lord Jesus thus said to him: "You have seen him, and it is he who /20/ is speaking to you". But again he /21/ said: "My Lord, I believe!" /22/ And he prostrated himself giving him a prayer.

Commentary

/Ir/

/1/: *qt*. Scribal mistake.

/1/: *(pr)*. Sundermann (1975: 64) prefers reading *xẇ* even considering *pr* a plausible reading. I prefer reading *(pr)*. The stroke of the first letter seems too much rounded at the top to be considered as part of *x*, while it is similar to the ductus of *p*. In the same way, the second letter seems too little rounded to be considered *w* and instead it seems to me like a higher vertically stroke, more similar to *r*.

/11/: *'nyd](’rnt)*. Sims-Williams (2012: 39) pointed out that the reading *'nyd](’rnd)* which we find in Sundermann (1975:64) is due to a misprint.

/11/: *smẏnt* "blind" < Syr. *smy'* "id.". Loan word attested only in this Gospel lectionary. In all other Christian Sogdian texts, the Syriac *smy'* is translated by the Sogdian terms *znt* "blind" and *qwr* "id."[508].

/13/: *[c'nw]*. Sundermann (1975: 64) reconstructs *[qt]*. I prefer reconstructing *[c'nw]* because of the Syriac text which has *kd* "when"

[508] See: Sundermann (1975: 64, n. 22); *C2* (p. 214; 237) and Sims-Williams (1988: 150-151).

always translated as *c'nw* "id." in this Gospel lectionary.
/20/: *'ỵc'(t nỵ) (d)'rtq*. According to Sims-Williams (2012: 39).
/22/: *{<q(y)'>}*. Addition below *(ywx)'*.
/22/: *dw'(ywx'){<q(y)'>}>*. Sundermann (1975: 65) suggests *dw'(pwx')[y] (b')* "Zwei-Teilung entstand". It seems to me that the reading *p* is not warranted because the only visible thing is a point which is put above the writing line, and that, therefore, could be part of *y*. Furthermore, I think that the last letters added below the writing line are three and not two, and the first of them is, more likely, *q*. In this way I reconstruct the verb *[m't]* as the first word of /Iv/1/ highlighting, considering the context, the durative and not the punctual value, which however we might have if we favoured the **b'* reading[509]. Reading *dw'ywx'qy'*, I connect the word to the verb *ywx'y-/ywxst* "to split, to divide" + a suffix that has already been found in *E5/6a-b/r*/19/ in the word *z'rcnwqy'* "mercy"[510]. *dw'ywx'qy'* literally would mean "division into two parts" and then "discord, disagreement". See Syr. *plgwt'*: "1. dimidium, pars; 2. medium; 3. schisma, factio; 4. altercatio, discordia; 5. simulatio, fraus"[511].
/Iv/
/1/: *[w](γd)'rt = wγd'rnt*.
/2/: *w'(b)[y](sq t)[γw] (p)ryw*. Sims-Williams (2012: 39) reads *w'(b)[y](sqn p)ryw*.
/3/: *[tw'] (x)[y](p)[θ]*. Sims-Williams (2012: 39) suggests *(q)[w](t'f' s)[']*. Taking into account the poor condition of this part of the fragment, both readings are plausible[512].
/10/: *qt c'n(w s)m(ynt) ['žt] (c)'n(ỵ) [qšy wyntqn]*. Sundermann (1975: 66) reconstructs *[qt smynt z't]* as last words of /Iv/9/ and then reads *qt c'n(ỵ) [q](šy)* as the beginning of /Iv/10/, leaving then incomplete the rest of this writing line. It seems to me that in /Iv/10/ is quite readable both *qt* and *smynt*, i.e. the two terms reconstructed in the previous line by Sundermann. Therefore I suggest to read */Iv/10/* as *qt c'n(w s)m(ynt) ['žt] (c)'n(ỵ) [qšy wyntqn]*.
/11/: *cn ftm'*. Adverb < prep. *cn* + ablative *ftm'*[513].
/20/: *{<ỵw>}*. Addition put below the writing line.

---

[509] On durative and punctual or "neutral" values of the two auxiliary verbs, see: Durkin-Meisterernst (2007: 31-44).
[510] Even in this case, the suffix is written under *z'rcnw*, considering the Sogdians manuscripts tendency of having (to have) writing lines of the same length and width.
[511] According to Brockelmann (1928: 570).
[512] See: *Chapter 3.3.8 Personal pronouns.*
[513] See: *C2* (p. 211).

/20/: *(xcy)*. Sundermann (1975: 66, n. 45) reads *(tym)*[514]. Surely, this part of the fragment is not very legible, nevertheless I find the ductus of *xcy* very recognizable. This latter reading would be justified also by the Syriac text which has *hw*.
/21/: ˘̣. This sign – which indicates an addition into the text – is clearly visible, then *wny*, placed on the inner margin, is to be inserted between *fšqrẏnt* and *cn*. Sundermann (1975: 67) puts it as the first word of this same writing line.
/21/: *'w'zqtẏ* "synagogue". Hapax legomenon. In my opinion is a calque of the Syriac *byt knwšt'* which is attested not in the *Peshitta* but in the *Vetus Syra*[515].
/IIr/
/2/: *pr(wrt)[w. pr(wrt)[y* is also plausible as already pointed out by Sundermann (1981: 216b) and Sims-Williams (2012: 39).
/5/: *(qt) [qt]('nyq'rẏ)*. Sims-Williams (2012: 39) reads *(q)t (q)t'(n)ẏ q'(r)y.*
/22/: *(pr)ẏmẏθ*. Sims-Williams (2012: 39) reads *(pr dẏ)mẏθ* but I prefer reading *(pr)ẏmẏθ* because of palaeographic reasons and because the Syriac text has *b-hd'* which is translated as *prymyθ* in this Gospel lectionary[516].
/22/: *wd's* = *wyd's*. Infinitive of the verb *wyd's* "to be surprised, wonder".
/IIv/
/7/: *xwycq wnwty*. Sogdian irrealis[517].
/15/: *wγd'rt*. Since Jesus is speaking, the use of the verb *w'b/wγt-* instead of *frm'y/frm't* is quite unusual.

E5/109
Part of the Gospel for the 2nd Sunday of Elijah, i.e., the 15th Sunday after Pentecost. Matthew 13.17-19: */r/*.
Beginning of the Gospel for the 3rd Sunday of Elijah, i.e., the 16th Sunday after Pentecost. Matthew 13.24-25: */v/*.

/r/
/1/ [q'md'rt qt w](ẏ)[n](ẏ)[n](t) ['yc qt]
17. 'trgrgw d-nḥzwn mdm d-

[514] See: Sundermann (1975: 66, n. 45).
[515] See: Barbati (2015a: 102-111).
[516] See: *Sogdian- Syriac Glossary*.
[517] See: *GMS* (§§ 815-816).

/2/ šm’x· wy̤nt’-sqn. ’t ny̤ wy̤d’r(n)[t ’t]
-ḥzyn ’ntwn w-l’ ḥzw w-

/3/ pr ptγwš· ’yc qt šm’x· ptγwšt’ [’t]
-l-mšm‘ mdm d-šm‘yn ’ntwn w-

/4/ [ny] [pt](γ)wšd’rnt ⁘ pyšt šm’x [ptγwšt’]
-l’ šm‘w ; 18. ’ntwn dyn šm‘w

/5/ [*qšy’qry̤ prz](b)r · wyspw ’dy̤ qt pt[γwšt]
mtl’ d-zr‘’; 19. kl d-šm‘

/6/ [wštm’xy̤ w’xš] ’t ny̤ ptbd’t pr[yw]
mtl’ d-mlkwt’ w-l’ mstkl b-h

/7/ [’yst γnt’q]ry̤ šmnw. ’t fc(m)[rzt txmy w’xš]
’t’ byš’ w-ḥṭp mlt’ d-zry‘’

/v/
/1/ (Syriac black) [’ḥrn]’ mtl’ [’mtl] lhwn. w’ṃr ⁘ · (Sogdian black) (’n)[yw]
24.’ḥrn’

/2/ [prz](br) ’ndy̤šd’rt· qw wy̤šnt s’· xwt’w
mtl’ ’mtl l-hwn

/3/ [yšwγ] ’t w’nw fr’m’ẏ ⁘ m’nwq [xcy]
w-’ṃr dmy’

/4/ [sm’ncy]q wštm’x. · qw mrt[y s’ qt]
mlkwt’ d-šmy’ l-gbr’ d-

/5/ [qšt’rt] (š)y̤ry̤ txmy̤ xypθ dy̤[x’w cyntr]
zr‘ zr‘’ ṭb’ b-qryth;

/6/ [’t c’nw ’wbd’rn]t mrtxmy̤t. · ’γt [wny]
25. w-kd dmkw ’nš’ ’ṭ’ b‘ldbbh

Translation

/r/ /1/ [they wanted] to see [what] /2/ you see, and did not see *it*; [and] /3/ to hear what you hear, [and] /4/ did [not] hear *it*. But [hear] /5/ [the para]ble [of the sower]: when anyone he[ars] /6/ [the word of the heavenly kingdom] and does not understand [it], /7/ [the ev]il Satan [comes] and snatch[es] away [the word of the seed in] */v/* /1/ (Syriac) [another] parable [exposed] to them and said. (Sogdian) [another] /2/ [para]ble exposed /2-3/ the Lord [Jesus] to them and thus said: /3-4/ "The heavenly reign looks like to a ma[n who] /5/ [sowed] good seed [in] his vi[llage], /6/ [and while] people [were sleepin]g, [his] *enemy* came…

Commentary

/r/

/1/: [*q'md'rt qt w](ỵ)[n](ỵ)[n](t)*. According to Sundermann (1975: 69) who points out that *[w](ỵ)[n]((ỵ)[n](t)* is an optative. I add that the Sogdian *[w](ỵ)[n]((ỵ)[n](t)* translates the Syriac *nḥzwn*, i.e., imperfect which is used as optative[518].

/5/: *[*qšy'qrỵ prz](b)r*. "the parable of the sower". Syr. *mtl' dzr''* and Gk. *τὴν παραβολὴν τοῦ σπείροντος*. Sundermann (1975: 69) rightly reconstructs the word for "parable", i.e. *przbr*, pointing out the mistake of Müller (1913: 10-11) concerning the reading of the last letter which exactly appears in East Syriac script as *-r*, but then is transliterated as *-t* and therefore it is considered as the final part of the word for "seeder". Müller (id.) translates "des Sämannes" and put the term for "parable" in the preceding line. Instead Sundermann (id.) considers *przbr* as the first word which has to be reconstructed in this writing line and does not mention the possible presence of the word for "sower". I do not agree with either of them. Taking into account the length of each writing line and the missing text at this point, I believe that both words, i.e., "sower" and "Parable", are to be placed at the beginning of this writing line. We should also add that the term for "sower", as far as I know, is not attested in Sogdian and was here reconstructed as **qšy'qrỵ*, considering the noun *qšy'* "sowing" which is in turn attested in *C2* (p. 213). Gharib too (1995: 196) reports only *qšy'* according to *C2* (id.).

/5/: *pt[γwšt]*. According to Sims-Williams (2012: 40).

/6/: *ptbd't.*, 3 pers. sg. of subjunctive. See: Sundermann (1975: 70).

/7/: Sogd. *['yst γnt'q]rỵ šmnw 't fc(m)[-rzt]*; Syr. *'ṫ' byš' w-ḥṭp*; and Gk. *ἔρχεται ὁ πονηρὸς καί ἁρπάζει*. Sogdian adds *šmnw* "Satan", a term absent

[518] See: *3.2.5 Tenses and moods in Sogdian and in Syriac.*

both in Syriac and in Greek[519].

/v/

/1/: *('n)[yw]*. According to Sims-Williams (2012: 40).

/4/: *mrt[y s' qt]*. According to Sims-Williams (2012: 40).

/5/: *xypθ dy̤[x'w cyntr]* "[in] his vi[llage]". As already pointed out by Sundermann (1975: 70), Sogdian misinterprets the Syriac word which, in this case, means "ager" and not "vicus, oppidum". See Brockelmann (1928: 696): "1) vicus, oppidum; 2) ager; 3) possessio; 4) ager urbis.". The Greek text has *ἐν τῷ ἀγρῷ αὐτοῦ*.

/6/: *['wbd'rn]t*. Wendtland[520] reads *w'bd'rnt* without considering that only *-t* has been preserved[521].

E5/125-126

End of a Gospel for a saint's day. Luke 19.15-27: */Ir/*1/- */Iv/*13/.
Beginning of the Gospel for the commemoration of Saint Bar Shabbā.[522] Matthew 25.31-45: */Iv/*13-*/IIv/*.

/Ir/

/1/ [xypθ bnty]ty̤ qt θbrd'rt qw wy̤šnt s'
15. ...'bdẅhy d-yḥb l-hwn

/2/ [n'qty] qt γrbd'rt wyspw yw ywtr cn wy̤šnt
ksp' d-nd' kl ḥd ṃn-hwn

/3/ [cw x](w)'qry' qθ'rt · 't 'γt· py̤rnmcy̤q. 't
mn' 'ttgr; 16. w-'ṭ' qdmy' w-

/4/ [w'nw] pcqw'd'rt · mn' xypθ'wnt'. · tw' pcm'r.
-'ṃr mry mnyk

---

[519] It is worth mentioning that in this case the Sogdian word for "Satan" *šmnw* is "correctly" written but in the Christian – not only Sogdian – material from Turfan it is also attested as up-down writing, a peculiarity which seems to belong to the Syriac manuscript tradition. See: Barbati (2015: 450).

[520] See: Wendtland (2011: 48).

[521] See: Sims-Williams (2012: 40-41).

[522] See: Sundermann (1975-71) and Sims-Williams (2012: 40-41).

/5/ ds' pcm'r wr' qθ'rt · w'nw fr'm'ẏ qw
'sr' mnÿn 'wtr; 17. 'ṁr l-

/6/ wnỵ (s)' · 'ỵ šỵr('q)t' bnt' · qt pr qbnq·
-h 'yw 'bd' ṭb' d-b-qlyl

/7/ bỵrtỵ qtỵš tγw prm'n. · b' p'txš'wn. pr
'štkḥt mhymn thw' šlyṭ 'l

/8/ ds' kθt · 't 'γt · dbtỵq bntỵ. 't w'nw
'sr' kř̈kyn; 18. w-'ṫ' d-tryn w-

/9/ pcqw'd'rt· mn' xypθ'wnt'. · n'ẏ tw' pcm'r.
-'ṃr mry mnyk

/10/ pnc pcm'r wr' qθ'rt · fr'm'ẏ. ms qw 'ỵnỵ
ḥmš' mnÿn 'wtr; 19. 'ṃr 'p l-hn'

/11/ s' · ms tγw· b'· p'txš'wn. pr pnc kθt · 't 'γt·
'p 'nt thw' šlyṭ 'l ḥmš' kř̈kyn; 20. w-'ṭ'

/12/ 'nyw bntỵ. 't w'nw pcqw'd['r]t · mn' xypθ'-
'ḥrn' w-'ṃr mry

/13/ -wnt'. · n'ẏ tw' pcm'r· xyd qt m't mn' nbnt·
h' mnyk ḣw d-'yt hw' lwt-y

/14/ c'nw 'wstỵtỵ. dsprtrỵ cỵntr p't pcqwỵr-
kd sym ḃ-sdwn'; 21. dḥlt gyr

/15/ -msq zw cn tw'· qt mrtỵ 'ỵš· · tγw žwγm'nỵ ·
ṃn-k d-gbr' 'nt qšy'

/16/ 't swx'ẏỵ· tγw. 'ỵc qt ny 'wstỵd'r[y] 't
w-šql 'nt mdm d-l' smt w-

/17/ rwpỵ· tγw. 'ỵc qt nỵ qšd'ry · w'nw fr['m'y]
-ḥṣd 'nt m̈dm d-l' zr't; 22. 'ṁr

/18/ qw wny̤ s’ · cn tw’ qwcy̤ nm’ẏ̤ngq’ tw’ ·
l-h ṃn pwmk ’dwnk

/19/ γnt’q-qr’ ·· bnt’ · γrby̤q m’ty̤š tγw mn’ ·
‘bd’ byš’ yd‘ hwyt l-y

/20/ mrty̤ ’y̤m zw žwγm’ny̤ ⁚ ’t swx’ẏ-ẏmsq zẇ
d-gbr’ ’n’ qšy’ w-šql ’n’

/21/ [’]y̤c qt ny̤ ’wsty̤d’rm ⁚ ’t rwpmsq zẇ ’y̤c
mdm d-l’ smt w-ḥṣd ’n’ mdm

/22/ [qt] ny̤ qšd’rm ⁚ pr cwty̤ ny̤ ’wsty̤d’rẏ mn’
d-l’ zr‘t; 23. l-mn’ l’ yhbt

/Iv/

/1/ n’qty̤ . pr p’n · ’t zẇ ’y̤swty̤ · ’(t) [šy γwžwty]
kspy ‘l ptwr’ w-’n’ ’t’ hwyt w-tb‘ l-h

/2/ dn wr’-’y̤ prw · ’t qw wy̤šnt s’ · qt [’wštytyt]
‘m řbyth; 24. w-l-hṇwn d-qymyn

/3/ m’tnt · wny̤ pyrnms’ . w’nw fr’m’ẏ · ’[st’]
qdmwhy ’ṃr sbw

/4/ cn wny̤ pcm’r . · ’t θbrt’ qw xwny ’dy̤ s’ [qt]
ṃn-h mny’ w-hbw l-hw d-

/5/ sty wny nbnt ds’ pcm’r · {<w’nw pcqw’d’rnt qw wy̤ny̤ s’ m’x
-’yt lwt-h ‘sr’ mnÿn; 25. ’mryn l-h
xypθ’wnt’ . · sty wy̤ny̤ nbnt d(s)[’] pcm’r>} w’nw [fr’m’y] qw
mrn ’yt lwt-h ‘sr’ mnÿn; 26. ’ṁr l-

/6/ wy̤šnt s’ · frm’ẏmsq [zw qw šm’x s’]
-hwn ’mr ’n’ l-kwn

/7/ qt wyspw xwny̤ ’dy̤ qt (sty) [wny θbrty bwt](q’)
d-l-kl ṁn d-’yt l-h ntyhb

/8/ qw wny s’ · pyš(t) [cn xwny ’dy qt nyst]
l-h mn hw dyn d-lyt

/9/ wny. · ms xyd ’yc [qt sty wny ’yty] bwtq’
l-h ’p hw d-’yt l-h ntnsb

/10/ cn wny · yw’r˙ x’[nt mn’] (s’)[nt x’nt q](t ny)
mn-h; 27. brm l-hnwn b‘ldbbÿ ’ylyn d-l’

/11/ qmd’rnt˙ qt p’txš’wn [d’rm pr wyšnt]
ṣbw d-’mlk ‘lyhwn

/12/ ’brt’˙ wyšnt(y). ’t šn (p)[txw’y](t’) [mn’] (p)yr-
’ytw ’nwn w-qṭlw ’nwn qdmy.

/13/ -nm s’ ⁘ (Syriac red) dmry br šb’ [w]š[y]r [mlkt’]

/14/ dmt(y) ⁘ bṣḥ ⁘ yṭ ⁘ (Sogdian black) w’nw (fr’m’y) [xwt’w]

/15/ yšwγ qw xypθ žwxšqt’ (s’) · (Syriac black) m’ d’t’ dyn

/16/ brh [d]’nš’ bšwbḥh : ⁘ (Sogdian black) pyšt č’nw qt ’yṣt˙
31. m’ d-’t’ dyn

/17/ [mr]txmy z’ty˙ pr xypθ γwbty’ : · ’t s’t wny
brh d-’nš’ b-šwbḥh w-klhwn

/18/ zprt fryštyt˙ dn wny prw. · wyd’γty nydtq’
ml’kwhy qdÿš’ ‘m-h hydyn ntb

/19/ pr xypθ γwbty γ’dwq. · ’t ’wzntq’˙ wny
‘l trwnws d-šwbḥh; 32. w-ntknšwn

/20/ pyrnms’. s’t rmt’ · ’t ywx’ytq’ wyšnty
qdmwhy klhwn ‘mm’ w-npršl ’nwn

/21/ yw cn dbtyq. · w’nc’nw xwšp’ny qt ywx’y[t]
ḥd mn ḥd ’yk r‘y’ d-mprš

/22/ stwrt cn bzyַšt · ’t p’dyַ wntyַq’ ˙ stw[rt]
‘r̈b’ ṃn gdÿ’; 33. w-nqym ‘r̈b’

/IIr/

/1/ [cn wny xw](’)rnt qyr’n. ’t bzyַšt cn wnyַ s’pt
ṃn ymynh w-gdÿ’ ṃn smlh;

/2/ [qyr’n] wyd’γtyַ. frm’ẏtq’ xšywnyַ qw wyַšnt
34. hydyn n’mr mlk’ l-hwn

/3/ [s’ qt] (c)n wnyַ xw’rnt qyr’n · ’yַst’ ˙ mn’
d-ṃn ymynh tw

/4/ [b]γyַ ptryַ ’(fr)ytyַtyַ · ptrq’n ny’st’ wštm’x
br̈ykwhy d-’by yrtw mlkwt’

/5/ qt p[cp’n] (m)’t qw šm’x s’ cn fcmpd
d-‘tyd’ hwt l-kwn ṃn tr̈myth

/6/ [’γ’zy----p’t] ’wšntyַ ˙ m’tyַm. ’t xwrt
d-‘lm’; 35. kpnt gyr w-

/7/ θ(brd’)[ryšt’ šm’]x qw mn’ s’ (’t) cn’wq
-yhbtwn l-y l-m’kl w-ṣhyt

/8/ m(’t)[ym ’t cšnt xwyrd’ryšt’ mn’] γw’m-
w-’šqytwnny ’ksny’

/9/ -n(’fc) [m’tym ’t ’wyžd’ryšt’ mn’ bγny]
hwyt w-knštwnny; 36. ‘rṭly’

/10/ m’tym [’t ptmwq nγwsty qθ’rt’ mn’ xwyc-]
hwyt w-ksytwnny kryh

/11/ -n’(q) [m’tym ’t] ’b(r)z brd[’ryšt’ mn’ ’t]
hwyt w-s‘rtwnny w-

/12/ [bntqty] (cyntr m)’tyַm [’t ’γtyšt’ šm’x]
-byt ’syr̈’ hwyt w-’tytwn

/13/ [qw mn’ s’] wyd’γt[y pcqwyntq’ qw wny]
lwt-y; 37. hydyn n’mrwn l-h

/14/ [s’ x’nt ’](rt)’wt · m[’x xypθ’wnt’ qd’]
hṅwn zdÿq’ mrn ’mty

/15/ [wyd’rym] tw’ qt ’wšn(t)[y] (’)[yštγw ’t xwyr]-
ḥzynk d-kpn ’nt w-trsyn-

/16/ -d’rỵm m’x tw’˙ · qd’ cn(’)[wq ’yštγw ’t]
-k ’w d-ṣh’ ’nt w-

/17/ cšnt xwỵ̣(r)d’(rỵ)m tw’˙ · q[d’ wyd’rym tw’]
-’šqynk; 38. w-’mty ḥzynk

/18/ qt γw’m-n’fc ’ỵštγ(w ’)[t ’wyžd’rym tw’]
d-’ksny’ ’nt w-knšnk

/19/ qd’ (xw)[y]cq ’ỵštγw ’(t) [ptmwγd’rym tw’ ’t qd’]
’w d-‘rṭly ’nt w-ksynk; 39. w-’mty

/20/ wỵ̣d’rỵm tw’ [x](w)ỵ̣cn’q [qd’ bntqty cyntr]
ḥzynk kryh’ ’w byt ’syr̈’

/21/ [’]t ’γtỵm m’x [qw tw’ s’ ’t p’cγny qθ’rt]
w-’tyn lwt-k; 40. w-‘ṇ’

/22/ xšywnỵ̣. ’t w(’)[nw frm’d’rt qw wyšnt s’]
mlk’ w-’ṃr l-hwn

/IIv/

/1/ ršt’˙ frm’ymsq zẇ qw šm’[x s’ qt]
’myn ’mr ’n’ l-kwn d-

/2/ c’f qt qθ’ryštq’ šm’x˙ qw [ywtr s’]
-km’ d-‘bdtwn l-ḥd

/3/ cn y’nt mn’ br’trt˙ qštrt’. . qw [mn’ s’ xyd]
ṃn hlyn ’ḥÿ z‘wr̈’ l-y ḣw

/4/ qθ’rt’ ⁛ wyd’γty̤ . frm’ẏtq’ ms · qw w[yšnt]
‘bdtwn; 41. hydyn n’mr ’p l-hnwn

/5/ s’ · qt cn wny̤ s’pt qyr’n · by̤str pxšnt’
d-ṃn smlh zlw

/6/ šm’x cn mn’ · nfry̤ty̤ty̤ ¨ qw ’yqwn-cy̤q
l-kwn ṃn-y lÿṭ’ l-nwr’

/7/ ’tr s’ [xyd] qt ’mty̤ sty̤ · qw γnt’q-
d-l-‘lm hy d-mṭyb’ l-

/8/ -(qry) [šmnw ’t] qw wny̤ žγntt s’ · p’(t) ’wšnty̤
-’klqrṣ’ w-l- m̈l’kwḣy; 42. kpnt gyr

/9/ [m’tym ’t ny θbr]d’ry̤št’ šm’x qw mn’ (s’)
w-l’ yhbtwn l-y

/10/ [pr xwry ’t cn’w]q m’ty̤m . ’t c[šnt] ny̤
l-m’kl w-ṣhyt w-l’

/11/ [xwyrd’ryšt’ mn’] ’t γw’m-n’fc · m’ty̤m
’šqytwnny; 43. w-’ksny’ hwyt

/12/ [’t ny ’wyžd’ryšt’] (m)n’ · ’t bγny̤ m’(t)[y]m
w-l’ knštwnny w-‘rṭly’ hwyt

/13/ [’t ptmwq ny nγwsty qθ’]rt’ m(n’) · ’t (xwy)c-
w-l’ ksytwnny w-kryh’

/14/ [-n’q m’tym ’t bntq]ty̤ cy̤ntr · m’(ty)m ’t
hwyt w-byt ’syr̈’ hwyt w-

/15/ [’brz ny brd’ryšt’ mn](’) ⁛ wyd’ · γty p’cγ(ny)
-l’ s‘rtwnny; 44. hydyn n‘nwn

/16/ [wnntq’ ’t ms] (w)y̤šnt. . ’t w’nw pc[q](w)yntq’
w-’p hnwn w-n’mrwn

/17/ [m'x xypθ'wnt'] qd' wyd'rym tw' 'wšnty
mrn 'mty ḥzynk kpn'

/18/ [qd' cn'wq qd' γw]'m-n'fc qd' bγny
'w ṣhy' 'w 'ksny' 'w 'rṭly'

/19/ [qd' xwycn'q qd' bntqty] cyntr 't ny spxšd'rym
'w kryh' 'w byt 'syr̈' w-l' šmšn-

/20/ [tw' wyd'γty p'cγny wnt]yq'. 't frm'ẏtq'
-k; 45. hydyn n'n' w-n'mr

/21/ [qw wyšnt s' ršt' frm'ym]sq zw qw šm'x {<s'>}
l-hwn 'myn 'mr 'n' l-kwn

Translation
/Ir/ /1/ [his se]rvants to whom he had given /2/ [the money] to know /2-3/ [what] each of them had gained. And the first came and /4/ [thus] said: "My Lord, your *pcm'r* /5/ has made ten *pcm'r* more". Thus said to /6/ him: "Oh good servant! Because /6-7/ you showed yourself to be faithful in a very little, you shall have authority over /8/ ten cities". And the second servant came, and thus /9/ said: "My Lord, your *pcm'r* /10/ has made five *pcm'r* more". And he also said to him: /11/ "And you will also be over five cities". And /11-12/ another servant came and thus said: "My Lord, /13/ lo, is your *pcm'r*, which I kept /14/ laid away in a handkerchief. For I was /15/ afraid of you, because you are a severe man /16/ and you take what you did not deposit and /17/ reap what you did not sow". He thus said /18/ to him: "I will judge you for your own mouth, /19/ wicked servant! You knew that /20/ I am a severe man and I take /21/ what I did not deposit and I reap what I /22/ did not sow. Why did not you put my */Iv/* /1/ money on the table? I might have come back and [I might have collected it] /2-3/ with interest". And he thus said to those who /3/ stood in front of him: /4/ "T[ak]e the *pcm'r* from him, and give *it* to the one [who] /5/ has the ten *pcm'r*". And they thus said to him: "Our Lord, he has ten *pcm'r*!". [He] thus [said] /6/ to them: "I tell /7/ you that to everyone who has, more [wi]ll be [given] /8/ but [from the one who has not], /9/ even [what he has] will be [taken away]. /10/ But as for these [enemies of mine, who did not] /11/ want me to reign [over them], /12/ bring them here and k[il]l them [before me]". /13/ (Syriac) of my lord Bar Shabbā and the sovereign Shir. /14/ In Matthew, chapter 19. (Sogdian) /14-15/ The Lord Jesus thus said to his disciples: (Syriac) "But when the Son of

Man will come /16/ in his glory (Sogdian) “But when the Son of Man /17/ will come in his glory, and all /18/ the holy angels with him, then he will sit /19/ on the throne of his glory, and /19-20/ before him all the peoples will be gathered, and he will separate them /21/ one from another just as a shepherd separates /22/ the sheep from the goats. And he will place the sheep */IIr/* /1/ [on his] right side, and the goats on his /1-2/ left [side]. Then the king will say to those /3/ [who] *stand* on his right: “Come, /4/ *you who are* blessed by my God the Father, inherit the heavenly kingdom /5/ prepared for you /5-6/ from the [foundation] of the world. [For] I was hungry and /6-7/ you gave me food, /7-8/ I was thirsty [and you gave me drink], /8-9/ [I was] a stranger [and you welcomed me], /9-10/ I was [naked and you clothed me], /11/ si[ck and you visited me], /12/ I was in [prison and you came to] /12-13/ [me]”. Then /13-14/ the righteous [will answer him]: “O[ur Lord, when] /15/ [did we see] you hungry [and] /15-16/ [feed] you, or thir[sty and] /17/ give you drink? Wh[en did we see you] /18/ a stranger and [welcome you?] /19/ When naked and [clothe you? And when] /20/ did we see you sick? [When in prison] /21/ and visit [you]?”. /21-22/ [And] the king [answered] and [said] th[us to them:] */IIv/* /1/ “Truly, I say t[o y]ou [:] /2/ as you did *it* [to one] /3/ of the least of these my brothers, /3-4/ you did it to [me]”. Then he will also say to th[ose] /5/ on his left side: /5-6/ “Depart from me, *you* cursed, /6-7/ into the eternal fire prepared for the ev[il] /8/ [Satan and] for his messengers. For /8-9/ I [was] hungry [and] you gave /9-10/ me [no] food, and I was [thi]rsty and /10-11/ [you gave me] no [drink], and I was a stranger /12/ [and] you did [not welcome] me, I was naked /13/ [and] you [did not clothe] me, /13-14/ [I was] sick [and] I was in prison and /15/ [you did not visit me]”. Then /15-16/ they [also] [will] answer and said thus: /17/ ‘[Our Lord], when did we see you hungry, /18/ [when thirsty or a stran]ger or naked /19/ [or sick or] in prison, and did not /19-20/ assist [you]?”. [Then he will answ]er and will say /20/ [to them: ‘Truly, I sa]y to you…

Commentary

/Ir/

/4/: *pcm’r*. A unit of weight translating the Syriac *mny’*. See *GMS* (§1662) “pound”.

/8/: *’t ’γt dbtyq bnty* “and the second servant came”. Syr. *w-’ṫ’ dtryn* “and the second came” and Gk. *καὶ ἦλθεν ὁ δεύτερος* “and the second came”.

/8-9/: *mn’ xypθ’wnt’ n’ẏ tw’ pcm’r* “my Lord, your *pcm’r*”. *n’ẏ* “here” has been deleted as pointed out by Sims-Williams[523].

/Iv/

/1/: *p'n*. See: Hamilton-Sims-Williams (1990: 30) and Schwartz- Sims-Williams (2014: 42-43).

/1/: *zw 'ẏswtẏ*. First clause irrealis characterized by putting *-wt-* between the present stem and the endings which are *-y* for the 1 pers. sg. and for the 3 pers. sg., and *-yšt'* for the 2 pers. pl.[524].

/2/: *dn wr'-'ẏ prw*. *wr'-'ẏ* is an oblique form. See also: Sims-Williams (1981: 14). In Sundermann (1975: 71) we read that it is an accusative form but this is surely due to a misprint.

/11/: *wyšnt]*. Pittard apud Sims-Williams (2012: 41) reads *wy](šnt)*

/13/: *dmry br šb' [w] š[y]r [mlkt']* "of my lord Bar Shabbā and the sovereign Shīr." The reconstruction was made by Sundermann (1975: 73).

/19/: *γwbtẏ*. Oblique case of *γwbty'* "glory". See: Sims-Williams (1981: 15).

/20/: *wẏšntẏ*. See: Pittard apud Sims-Williams (2012: 41).

/IIr/

/1/: *xw](')rnt*. According to Sims-Williams (2012:41).

/5/: *qt p[cp'n] (m)'t*. Pittard apud Sims-Williams (2012: 41) reads *qt p(cp')n] (m)'t*.

/6/: *['γ'zy p't]*. According to the Syriac text, I think this is the most plausible reconstruction. It is true, however, that the portion of the text – which is now unreadable – takes up more space. It might, therefore, suggest an extra word, as *pyrnms'*. This is because the phrase "from the foundation of the world" can also be accompanied by *pyrnms'* by meaning "from before the foundation of the world" as it indeed occurs in *E5/83a-b /r/*1/. See: Syr. *mn qdm tr̈myth d'lm'*, according to Brockelmann (1928: 733) "ab (ante) initio mundi". The Sogdian text would thus have been able to add *pyrnms'*, although there is no correspondence with the Syriac text.

/10-11/: *[xwyc]-n'(q)*. According to Pittard apud Sims-Williams (2012: 41). The same applies to /IIv/13-14/.

/19/: *xw[y]cq*. See Sundermann (1975:74).

/IIv/

/10/: *c(š)[nt]*. So previously Sundermann (1975: 74). At the same time, Sundermann states that it is a correction for *c(y)-*, where *-y-* would be the letter actually written in the fragment. Müller (1913: 25-27) also reads *cy-*. Now, it is true that what we have on the fragment could be read as *-y-* but I believe that, taking into account the size and the shape, we can consider it as

---

523 Personal communication 25.01.2016.

524 See: *GMS* (§§ 815- 821).

the initial part of *-š-*.
/16/: *pc[q](w)yntq'= pc[q](w)'yntq'*.
/20/: *[p'cγny wnt]y̤q'* "he will respond". Future indicative, 3 pers. sg. that I reconstructed according to the Syriac *n'n'*, 3 pers. sg. of imperfect which is used as future < *'n'* "to answer"[525]. Sundermann (1975: 75) considers *[pcqwy](t)q'* a plausible reading. I prefer reconstructing *[p'cγny wnt]y̤q'* because – with particular regard to *E5* – this is the Sogdian verb which is used to translate the Syriac *'n'* whereas *pcqw'y/pcqw'd'r* "to say" translates the Syriac *'mr* "id."[526].
/21/: *{<s'>}*. Addition put below the writing line in correspondence with *šm'x*.

E5/127a-c

End of the Gospel for the commemoration of Saint Bar Shabbā. Matthew 25.45-46: /*r*/1-5/.
Beginning of the Gospel for the commemoration of Saint Sergius and Saint Bacchus. Matthew 16.24-28; 17.1-6: /*r*/5/-/v/21/.

/*r*/

/1/ qt c'[f qt ny qθ'rt]' šm'x · (q)[w ywtr]
45. d-km' d-l' 'bdtwn l-ḥd

/2/ (s)' c(n) [y](')nt (q)[štrt' ms] (n)y̤ qw mn' [s']
ṃn hlyn z'wr̈' 'p l' l-y

740 /3/ qθ'rt' · 't š(wn)t[q'] (m)y̤šnt · qw 'yqwn-[cyq]
'bdtwn; 46. w-n'zlwn hlyn l-tšnyq'

/4/ z'r(y)'(w)y̤ s' . · 't 'rt'(w)t qw 'yqwn-cy̤q nw(š)c
d-l-'lm w-zdÿq' l-ḥ̈y' d-l-'lm

/5/ ž(w)[']n s' ∴ (Syriac red) dmry srg[y]s wmry bkws ∴ ∴

/6/ dmty ∴ bṣ · yb (Syriac black) 'ṃr yš[w'] ltlmyd̈w(hy) (Sogdian black) w'nw
24. hydyn

525 See: *3.2.5 Tenses and moods in Sogdian and in Syriac.*
526 See: *Sogdian- Syriac Glossary.*

/7/ fr’m’ẏ xwt’w y(š)wγ qw xypθ žwxšqt[’] s’ ··
’ṃr yšw‘ l-tlm̈ydwhy

/8/ (Syriac black) ṁn [dṣb’ dn](’)t’˙˙ btry nkpẇr bnpš(h) ⁘ (Sogdian black) xwn)ỵ
ṁn-

/9/ ’dỵ [qt q](’)ṛṃt (qt ’)ỵṩt mn’ p(š)ys’. pstw’t
-dṩb’ d-n’t’ btry nkpẇr

/10/ [pr xypθ γ](r)yw ⁘ ’t sw[x](’)ẏt xypθ pcng d’rwq.
b-npšh w-nšqwl zqyph

/11/ [’t ’ys]t mn’ pšys’ · p’t xwnỵ ’dỵ qt
w-n’t’ btry; 25. ṁn d-ṣb’ gyr

/12/ [q’mt qt] ’ž’(ẇ)t xypθ γryw. šy pnyšt · xwnỵ
d-nḥ’ npšh nwbdyḣ w-ṁn

/13/ [’dy qt pnyšt xypθ] γryw˙ cn mn’ (p)yd’r. šỵ
d-nwbd npšh mṭlty

/14/ [byrt p’t cw wr’] w(n)t[yq’ mr](txmỵy).
nškḥyḣ; 26. mn’ gyr mthn’ brnš’˙˙

/15/ [qt s’t f](c)mpd tbyžt˙ ’[t] (x)[ypθ γr]ỵw γšỵp
’n klh ‘lm’ nqn’ w-npšh nḥsr

/16/ [wn’t qd’ c](w) θbrtỵ[q]’ mrtxmỵ xypθ γrywỵ
’w mn’ ntl brnš’˙ tḥlwp’

/17/ [pcrw p’t p](c)p’n [xcy] mrtxmỵ z’tỵ qt
d-npšh; 27. ‘tyd hẉ gyr brh d-’nš’ d-

/18/ [’ystq’] pr xypθ [b]γy [ptry] γ(wb)ty’˙ dn xypθ
-n’t’ b-tšbwḥt’ d-’bwhy ‘m

/19/ [zprt fr]yštỵtỵ prw. · . ’t [wyd]’γtỵ twžtq’
ml’k̈why qdÿš’ w-hydyn nprw‘

/20/ [qw wyspw] yw yw ’dy̤ s’ w’nc’[nw wny] qty̤t
l-’nš ’nš ’yk ‘bdẅhy;

/21/ [ršt’ frm]’ẏmsq zw qw [šm]’x s’..
28. ’myn ’mr ’n’ l-kwn

/22/ [qt xnt] mrtxmy̤t˙ qt ’wšty̤ty̤ sw[q]nt {<mdy̤. .>}
d-’yt ’ñš’ d-qymyn tnn

/v/

/1/ [qt ny] pcšntq’ [mrc wytwr qt wyn]ntq’
d-l’ nṭ‘mwn mwt’ ‘dm’ d-nḥzwn

/2/ [mrtx]my̤ z’ty̤ (q)[t ’ystq’ p](r) xy̤[p]θ
l-brh d-’nš’ d-’ṫ’ b-

/3/ [xšy](w)nqy’ ⁘ ’t xwšw m[yθ]y̤ (p)šys’. · prẏ̤(p)d’rt
-mlkwth; 1. w-btr št’ yẅmyn ḍbr

/4/ xwt’w yšwγ šmγwn sng · ’t yγqwb
yšw‘ l-k’p’ w-l-y‘qwb

/5/ ’t ywḥnn wny̤ br’[t] · ’t sy̤nd’rt wy̤šnty̤
w-l-ywḥnn ’ḥwhy w-’sq̣ ’nwn

/6/ qw yw šyr sq’ γ[r](y̤) s’ γwty̤ xw[d]q’r ·
l-ṭwr’ rm’ blḥwdyhwn;

/7/ ’t (p)cywfs xwt’w yšwγ wy̤šnty pyrnms’ ·
2. w-’šṭḥlp yšw‘ qdmyhwn

/8/ ’t wyr(w)[x]šd’rt˙ wny̤ ry̤t w’nc[’nw xwr] (py)št
w-ṇhr prṣwph ’yk šmš’

/9/ wny̤ nγwdnt˙ spy̤ty̤ qtnt. ˙ w’nc’n[w rwx]šny’(q)
nḧtwhy dyn ḥwrw ’yk nwhr’;

/10/ ’t wy̤n’wcy̤q qtnt qw wy̤šnt s[’ mwš’]
3. w-’tḥzyw l-hwn mwš’

/11/ ’t ’ly’ c’nw ž’ẏntqn dn wnẏ [prw pyšt]
w-’ly’ kd mmllyn ‘mh; 4.

/12/ p’cγn[y q](θ’)rt šmγw[n sng ’t w’nw pcqw’-]
‘ṇ’ dyn k’p’ w-’ṃr

/13/ -d’rt qw xwt’w yšw[γ s’ mn’ xypθ’wnt’]
l-yšw‘ mry

/14/ šyr[y xcy m]’xẏ (q)[t mdy ’ym]
špyr hẉ l-n d-tnn nhw’

/15/ ’t qt [q’](m)ẏ (t)[γw] wnẏmq’ [mdy šy sy’qt]
w-’n ṣb’ ’nt n‘bd tnn tlt mṭllyn

/16/ yw tw’ ’t yẇ m(w)[š](’)ẏ [’](t) [yw] ’l[y’y ’t c’nw]
ḥd’ lk w-ḥd’ l-mwš’ w-ḥd’ l-’ly’; 5. w-‘d

/17/ xw ž’ysq (n)’y [y](w r)[wxšn]y p[r](ẏ)[by]
hẉ mmll ḣ’ ‘nn’ nhyrt’

/18/ m’γwnt p[r] wẏ[šnt] ’t [w]xr qt[y cn pryby]
’ṭlt ‘l-yhwn w-ql’ hw’ ṃn ‘nn’

/19/ qt mẏθ fr’m’y ’ẏnẏ xcy [mn’ fry]
d-’ṃr hnw bry

/20/ z’tẏ qt [pryw] pcq’md’rm (q)[w wny s’]
ḥbyb’ d-bh ’ṣṭbyt l-h

/21/ ptγwšt’ ⁘ ’t c[’]nw ptγwšd’r[nt žwxšqt’]
šm‘w; 6. w-kd šm‘w tlmÿd’

Translation

/r/ I/ every time you [did not d]o /1-2/ it to one of the least, [so] you did not /2-3/ do it to me. And they will go away, these ones into /3-4/ eternal punishment and the righteous ones into /4-5/ eternal life. (Syriac) of my lord Sergius and my lord Bacchus /6/ from Matthew, chapter 12. Jesus said to his disciples: (Sogdian) /6-7/ The Lord Jesus thus said to his disciples: /8/

(Syriac) “Who wants to come after me, let him deny himself”. (Sogdian) “Who /9/ wants to come after me, let him deny /10/ hi[ms]elf, /10-11/ take up the wood of his cross /11/ [and] follow me. For whoever /12/ [would] give life to his soul, will lose it. /12-13/ [But] whoever [loses his] soul for my sake /14/, [will find it. For, what will profit a m]an [if] /15/ he will gain the [whole] world and /15-16/ [will forfeit] his soul? [Or, what] will a man /16-17/ give [in return] for his soul? [For] /17-18/ the Son of Man [is go]ing to come to the glory [of God his Father] with his /19/ [holy] angels and [th]en he will repay /20/ each person according to what [he] has done. /21/ [Truly], I say to you: /22/ [there are] men standing here */v/* /1/ [who] will [not] taste [death until they s]ee /2/ the Son of [M]an coming in his /3/ [kin]gdom”. And after six d[ay]s /3-4/ the Lord Jesus took with him Simon Peter, Jacobs, /5/ and John, his brother, and led them up /6/ a very high mountain by themselves. /7/ And the Lord Jesus was transfigured before them; /8/ and his face shone like [the sun], /9/ and his clothes became white as light. /10-11/ And [Moses] and Elijah appeared to them while talking [with] him. [But] /12-13/ Simon [Peter] answered [and thus spo]ke to Lord Jesus: “[Oh my Lord], /14/ [it is] good that we [are here]; /15/ and if yo[u] wish, I will make [three tents here], /16/ one for you and one for Mo[s]es and [one] for Eli[jah].” [And while] /17/ he was speaking, behold, [a] b[r]ig[ht] c[loud] /18/ overshadowed them, and a voice *from* [the cloud] /19/ thus said: “This is /19-20/ [my dearest] Son, wi[th whom] I am well pleased. /20-21/ Listen [to him]!”. And when [the disciples] heard…

Commentary

/r/-/v/: Syriac onomastic.

/r/

/6/: *tlmydໍ̈w(hy)*. As already pointed out by Sims-Williams (2012: 41), Müller (1913: 12-13) correctly reads *tlmyd̈w(hy)*, while what we find in Sundermann (1975: 76), i.e., *tlmyḍ ẇ(hy)*, is due to a misprint.

/6/: Sims-Williams underlines[527] that Sogdian does not translate the first word of the new Gospel passage, i.e., Syr. *hydyn* because it would not make sense: the Sogdian translates the preceding Syriac sentence which start with *’ṃr* and not with *hydyn*.

/10/: *’t sw[x](’)ẏt xypθ pcng d’rwq* “and take up the wood of his cross”. See Syr. *w-nšqwl zqyph* “and take up his cross” and Gk. *καὶ ἀράτω τὸν σταυρὸν αὐτοῦ* “id.”.

[527] Personal communication, 23.01.2016.

/10/: *sw[x](')ẏt*. According to Müller (1913: 12-13). Sims-Williams (2012: 41) is also inclined to the same reading. Contra Sundermann (1975: 76) *sw[x](')y·̇t*.
/14/: *wr'] w(n)t[yq' mr](txmy̤y̤)* I agree with the reading suggested by Sims-Williams (2012: 41).
/22/: *{<mdy̤ . ·>}*. Addition immediately below the writing line in correspondence with *-t*, i.e., the last letter of the last word *sw[q]nt*.
/v/
/3/: *pry(p)d'rt*. I agree with Sundermann reading *-(p)-* and not *-f-*[528].
/4/: Sogd. *šmγwn sng* "Simon Peter". See Syr. Syr. *k'p'* "Peter" and Gk. *τὸν Πέτρον*. However, the Sogdian text agrees with a textual variant of the Greek text: *Σιμωνα Πετρον*[529].
/6/: *γwtỵ*. As already pointed out by Sims-Williams (2012: 42), *γtwỵ* in Sundermann (1975: 77), is due to a misprint.
/14/: *šyr[y xcy m]'xỵ (q)[t mdy]*. Sims-Williams (2012: 42) reconstructs *šy(r)[y xcy m]'xỵ (q)[t (mdy̤)*.
/15/: *[mdy*. Sims-Williams (2012: 41) reconstructs *(m)[dy*.
/16/: Taking into account the features of the manuscript fragments *E5* as well as the Syriac text, I read *yw tw' 't yw m(w)[š](')ỵ ['](t) [yw] 'l[y'y 't c'nw]* "one for you, one for Moses and one for Elijah; and while". Sundermann (1975: 78) reads *yw tw' 't yw m(w)[š' (?) x](c)ỵ ['](t) [yw] 'l[y'y xypθ (?) 't c'nw]* and translates "eine dir und eine dem M[oses i]st und [eine] dem El[ia eigen(?). Und als]". Sundermann points out that, as for the verb *x(c)y*, *-c-* "ist nur der linke Teil mit Ansatz des unterzeiligen Teiles bewahrt" (*id.*). I think that the readings *xcy* and *xypθ* are quite unlikely, and this is for two reasons. The first concerns the size of both blanks: in the first case, after *m(w)-* there are about 0.5 cm before a stroke which, in my opinion, may be well identified as the lower part of *'*, immediately followed by *ỵ*[530]. From the reading of the whole Gospel lectionary, I can state that 0.5 cm is a space usually occupied by two letters at most and, therefore, I consider it unlikely to read *m(w)[š' (?) x](c)ỵ* with *[š' (?) x](c)ỵ*, written in just 0.5 cm. Furthermore, I see no reasons to reconstruct *c* since there is not any stroke that goes below the writing line, as instead for the above-mentioned letter, and because the stroke before *y* has a *ductus* which is much more similar to the upper part of *'*. According to my interpretation, *-y* would be the ending of

528 See: Sundermann (1975: 77, n. 105).

529 See: Soden, von (1913: 60).

530 It is to be remembered that the oblique ending *-'y* in Syriac loans is attested in this Gospel lectionary as well as in other Christians Sogdian texts. See: Sims-Williams (1998: 148; 150).

the oblique case used as dative. Last consideration: *xcy* has no correspondence within the Syriac text.
Same reasons for *xypθ*: after *l-*, the last letter preserved from this complicated writing line, and according to the fragment size, approximately 2.3 cm should be missing, the right proportion for *[y'y 't c'nw]*. Furthermore, in this case too, *xypθ* has no correspondence within the Syriac text.
/17/: *(n)'y [y](w r)[wxšn]y p[r](ỵ)[by]*. According to Sundermann (1975: 78).
/18/: *m'γwnt*. Imperfect, 3 pers. pl. pers. < *'γwnt* "to overshadow, cover".

E5/130a-b
End of the Gospel for an unidentified day. Luke 12.35-39; 12.42-44: */r/1/-/v/7/*.
Part of the Gospel for All Saint's Day or probably for the day of Commemoration of the Dead. John 5.19: */v/7-12/*.

/r/

/1/ bnt˙ bỵstỵt šm'x myd'nt. 't ptswγtỵt
35. hwwn 'syryn ḥṣÿkwn w-mnhryn

/2/ šm'x cr'γt · 't bwtq̱'˙ m'nwq. qw
šr̈gykwn; 36. w-hww dmyn l-

/3/ mrtxmỵt s' qt pcỵqṣnt wỵšntỵ xypθ'wntỵ˙ ·
-'nš' d-mskyn l-mrhwn

/4/ qt qd' zwrtq' cn bγ'npšqtỵ · qt c'nw
d-'mty npn' ṃn byt mštwt' d-m'

785 /5/ qt '(γt) ['t tw]md'rt. · ywnỵ pỵnntq' dbrỵ qw
d-'ṭ' w-ṇqš mḥd' nptḥwn l-

/6/ wny [s' fwx'r] (x)'nt bntỵtỵ˙ · x'nt qt 'ỵṣt
-h; 37. ṭwbyhwn l-'b̈d' hnwn 'ylyn d-n't'

/7/ [wyšnt xypθ'wnt 't b]ỵrt wỵšntỵ c'nw γwr'tỵt ·
mrhwn w-nškḥ 'nwn kd 'yryn

/8/ [ršt’ frm’ymsq] zw qw šm’x s’ ∴ qt
’myn ’mr ’n’ l-kwn d-

/9/ [byntq’ xypθ myd’n ’t pšy](d)tq’ wy̰šnty̰ ·
-n’swr ḥṣ̈why w-nsmk ’nwn

/10/ [’t ftyrtyq’ spxštyq’ wyšnty] · ’t qt dbty̰q ·
w-n‘br nšmš ’nwn; 38. w-’n b-mṭrt’

/11/ [qd’ štyq γwr’tqy’ ’yst ’t b]yrt · pry̰my̰θ
d-ṫr̈tyn ’w d-tlt n’t’ w-nškḥ hkn’

/12/ [frγn’ fwx’r x’nt bntyty pyšt ’yny] γrbt’ ·
ṭwbyhwn l-‘b̈d’ hnwn; 39. hd’ dyn d‘w d-’lw yd‘

/v/

/1/ ’t γrb’q spncy̰rspn · qt šy̰ ’xy̰ž’t
42. …rb byt’ mhymn’ w-ḥkym’ d-nqymywhy

/2/ wny̰ xypθ’wnt pr xypθ sp’s · qt θbry̰
mrh ‘l tšmšth d-ntl

/3/ pd’(r)ty’ pr xypθ žmnw · fwx’r xwny̰ bnty
prs’ b-zbnh; 43. ṭwbwhy l-hw ‘bd’

/4/ qt ’y̰ṣ̌t wny̰ xypθ’wnt šy̰ byrt qt wnty̰sq
d-n’t’ mrh nškḥywhy d-‘bd

/5/ prymyθ frγn’ · pr ršty’q [frm’y]msq
hkn’; 44. šryr’yt ’mr

/6/ zw qw šm’x s’ ∴ qt p’t(x)[š’wn wntyq’ w]ny̰
’n’ l-kwn d-nqymywhy

/7/ pr s’t wny̰ γr’m’ ∴ (Syriac red) ’[ḥrn’------(Syriac black) ’ṃr yšw‘ dl’
‘l klh qnynh.
mškḥ]

800 /8/ br’ ‛bd mdm ⁘ (Syriac red) ‘d ⁘ [------------------------]

/9/ ḥ(zy) · bm‘ly · ṣ · [------------------------------------]

/10/ (Syriac black) dwkrn’ d(y)[--------------.]{<’ṃr yšw‘ l>}[---------]

/11/ (Sogdian black) w’nw fr’[m’y xwt’w yšwγ qw ====]

/12/ s’ · (t)[--]

Translation

/r/ 1/ “your belts will have fastened /1-2/ and your lamps alight. Be like /3/ men who are waiting for their master /4/ when he comes back home from the wedding feast /4-5/ and when he comes and knocks, immediately /5-6/ they open the door [to him]. [Blessed *are*] those servants whom /6-7/ [their master] finds awake when he comes. /8/ [Truly, I say] to you: /9/ [he will dress himself and] [ha]ve them [recline at table], /10/ [and he will come to serve them]. And if /10-11/ [he comes] in the second [or in the third watch], and thus finds *them*, /12/ [blessed *are* those servants! But] know [this]… */v/* 1/ and the wise manager, whom /2-3/ his master will set over his household, to give /3/ their sustenance at the proper time. Blessed *is* that servant /4/ whom his master will find /4-5/ working when he comes. /5-6/ Truly, I sa[y] to you: ‘he [will set] him /7-8/ over all his wealth’. (Syriac) “[Another………… Jesus said:] ‘the Son [is not able] to do anything’. As far as..... /9/ See at the opening *of* section [5…………….]. /10/ Commemoration of [......] said Jesus to […….] /11- 12/ (Sogdian) [The Lord Jesus] thus spo[ke t]o [............

Commentary

/r/

/2/: *bwtq̱’*. The scribe himself deleted *-q-*. So *bwt’* and not *bwtq’*.

/3/: *pcỵqṩnt*. Imperfect, 3 pers pl.

/5/: *tw]md’rt*. According to Sims-Williams (1995: 61; 2012: 43).

/5-6/: *pỵnntq’ dbrỵ qw wny [s’]* “they open the door to him”. *dbr* “door” is an addition of the Sogdian text and it corresponds neither with the Syriac *nptḥwn lh* nor with the Greek *ἀνοίξωσιν αὐτῷ*.

/v/

/3/: *pd’(r)ty’* “sustenance”. The diacritic point that distinguishes *r*, which is

usually placed above it, is missing[531].
/6/: *p't(x)[šw'n wntyq' w]ny*. Lit. "he will give him power". Sundermann has already showed that the Sogdian text agrees with a textual variant which is attested in the *Codex Sinaiticus*, i.e., *nšlṭyhy* "he will give him power"[532] and not with the *Peshitta* text which has *nqymywhy* "he will raise as head".
/7/ *γr'm'*. Feminin noun according to Sims-Williams[533] who distinguishes *γr'm'* (f.) "possessions, wealth" and *γr'my* (m.) "money, wealth".
/7-12/: These writing lines are quite complicated to reconstruct and interpret, as already demonstrated by Sims-Williams in a very exhaustive way (2012: 43). The following notes, then, point out the main aspects.
/7/: *'[ḥrn' --------'ṃr yšw' dl' mškḥ]*. In so doing, I accept the reconstruction made by Sims-Williams (2012: 43). Sundermann (1975:80) reads *'[mr 'n' lkwn dl' mškḥ]* "I tell you: he can't". The objection – in my opinion correct – raised by Sims-Williams (2012: 43) is that if this had really been the opening sentence of another reading, it would have been written in black ink as occurred in */v/8/*.
/10/: *(w){<'ṃr yšw' l>}*. Vertical addition put along the inner margin in correspondence with *v/8-12/*. Sims-Williams (2012: 43) points out that this sentence, whose Sogdian translation is found in */v/11/*, has been added by the scribe along the margin after realizing the mistake and being aware that each new reading begins with the Syriac reading followed by the Sogdian translation. Sundermann (1975: 80), while identifying in */v/11/* the Sogdian translation of this addition, suggests that it should be placed in */v/8/*, after the Syriac *'d*.
/10/: Syr. *dwrkn'*. See: Brockelmann (1928: 153- 154) "1. memoria; 2. dies festus; 3. epulum funebre; 4. sacrificii pars".
/10/: *d(y)[*. I agree with Sims-Williams (2012: 43) in considering also plausible the following readings: *d(ḥ)[* ; *d(c)[* ; *dš[* .

---

531 As regards the word, already Sundermann (1975: 79, n. 115) refers to Benveniste (1959).
532 See: Sundermann (1975: 80, n. 117).
533 See: Sims-Williams (forthcoming 2016a). See also: *Sogdian-Syriac Glossary*.

SOGDIAN-SYRIAC GLOSSARY

This glossary contains all Sogdian words occurring in the *E5* text except those which are wholly restored (i.e. including those which are partially restored but certain). Each Sogdian entry is followed by its English translation and by its Syriac parallel according to the *Peshitta* (Syriac ø means that we do not have the Syriac form that corresponds to the Sogdian one).

This is a basic glossary: all informations on nominal and verbal morphosyntax are given in the chapter focused on linguistics features of *E5*. Exceptions, if deemed necessary, will be reported from time to time.

’bnt d’ryq x-, sqw-, swq-/m’t “to be engaged in, be busy with”. Syr. **‘ny’ hwt** : 525.
    ’ḅṅt d’ṙỵq m’t Syr. *‘ny’ hwt* : 525.
’br “to bring”. Syr. **’yty** : 680.
    ’brt’ Syr. *’ytw* : 680.
’brhm “Abraham”. Syr. **’brhm** : 1; 25.
’dy “someone, anyone, one”. Syr. **’nš’** : 390; 420; 440; 590; 620.
    ’dyy Syr. *l-’nš* : 390.
’dy : see *xyd.*
’fryty “blessed”. Syr. **bryk** : 695.
    ’frytyty Syr. *brÿk’*: 695.
    pr ’frywn “blessed”. Syr. **mbrk** : 15.
’frywn ptwyd/ptwyst “to bless”. Syr. **brk** : 5.
    ’frywn ptwysd’rt Syr. *ḅrk*: 5.
’frywn wn-/qt- “to bless”. Syr. **brk** : 295.
    ’frywn qθ’rt Syr. *ḅrk* : 295.
’γ’z “beginning”. Syr. **tr̈myt’** : 465.
    ’γ’zy : 465.
’γwnt “to overshadow, cover”. Syr. **’ṭl** : 775.
    m’γwnt Syr. *’ṭlt* : 775.
’γz’mnty “Resurrection”. Syr. **qymt’** : 190.
’qt “if”. Syr. **’lw** : 620.
’ly’ “Elijah”. Syr. **’ly’** : 45; 770; 775.
    ’ly’y Syr. *l-’ly’* : 775.
’(m)brz br “to visit”. Syr. **s‘r** : 15; 35; 705.
    ’mbrz brd’rt Syr. *s‘r* : 15.
    .’ḅrz-bry̤ Syr. *ns‘ r* : 35

'brz brd'ryšt' Syr. *s'rtwnn* : 705.
'mpd/'mpst "to fall, prostrate oneself". Syr. **npl** : 115; 135; 370; 515; 635.
'mpdt Syr. *npl* : 115.
'mpdt Syr. *npl'* : 370.
'mpst Syr. *ṇpl* : 135; 515; 635.
'mty x-, sqw-, swq- /m't "to be prepared". Syr. **'tṭyb** : 720.
'mty sty Syr. *mṭyb'* : 720.
'ndr̈'ws "Andrew". Syr. **'ndr̈'ws** : 540.
'ndyš "to act". Syr. **sbbr** : 290.
'ndyšyq m't Syr. *msbr hw'* : 290.
'ndyš "to expose". Syr. **'mtl** : 645.
'ndỵšd'rt Syr. *'mtl* : 645.
'ngm'ny' : see *ryt 'ngm'ny'*.
'ntwxc "sorrow, grief, sadness". Syr. **krywt'** : 410.
'ntwxc b(w)-/qt- "to have sorrow". Syr. **kr'** : 415.
'ntwxc bwt Syr. *kry'*: 415.
'ntwxcn'q b(w)-/qt- "to be sorrowful". Syr. **kr'** : 410.
'ntwxcn'q bwt'q' Syr. *tkr'* : 410.
'ntwxc x-, sqw-, swq-/m't "to have sorrow". Syr. **kr'** : 415.
'ntwxc sty Syr. *kry'*: 415.
'ny "other". Syr. **'ḥrn'** : 155; 170; 345; 645.
'nyw: 155; 345; 645.
'nyt Syr. *'ḥr̈n'* : 170.
'ny/'nyt "to bring". Syr. **'yty** : 505; 560.
'nyd'rt Syr. *'yty* : 505.
'nyd'rnt Syr. *'ytyw* : 560.
'p "water". Syr. **m̈y'** : 55; 70; 75; 555.
'py : 555.
'rq "work". Syr. **'bd'** : 205.
'rqt Syr. *'b̈d'* : 205.
'rsqny "Zealot". Syr. **ṭnn'** : 545.
'rt'w "righteous". Syr. **zdyq** : 705; 740.
'rt'wt Syr. *zdÿq'* : 705; 740.
'rt'w 'št'y/'št't "to show oneself to be righteous". Syr. **'zdq** : 245.
'rt'w 'štẏt'sqn Syr. *mzdqyn* : 245.
'rt'wy' "righteousness". Syr. **zdyqwt'** : 30.
's/'yt "to take, receive". Syr. **šql** : 175; 215.
'yty bwtq' Syr. *tštql* : 175.
'stq' Syr. *šql* : 215.
's/'yt "to marry". Syr. **šql** : 120.

'st Syr. *šql* : 120.
's/'yt "to take, receive". Syr. **nsb** : 200; 220; 420; 425; 530; 675.
'smsqn Syr. *nsb 'n'* : 200.
's Syr. *sb* : 220.
'stq' Syr. *nsb* : 420.
'st' Syr. *tsbwn* : 425.
'yty bwtq' Syr. *ttnsb* : 530.
'st' Syr. *sbw* : 675.
'srty "joined, together with". Syr. **byn** : 135.
'šγy' "Isaiah". Syr. **'š'y'** : 50.
'št'y/'št't "to show, indicate". Syr. **ḥwy** : 380; 455; 485.
'št'd'rt Syr. *ḥwy*: 380; 455; 485.
'štÿt'sqn Syr. *ø*: 245.
'šty'mnty "appearance". Syr. **tḥwty'** : 40.
't "and". Syr. **w-** : 1; 5; 10; 15; 20; 25; 30; 35; 40; 45; 50; 55; 60; 65; 70; 75; 80; 85; 95; 110; 120; 125; 135; 140; 145; 150; 155; 160; 165; 170; 180; 190; 200; 210; 215; 220; 225; 230; 235; 240; 250; 265; 270; 275; 280; 285; 290; 295; 300; 305; 310; 320; 330; 335; 340; 345; 350; 355; 360; 365; 380; 385; 390; 395; 410; 420; 425; 430; 435; 440; 445; 460; 465; 475; 480; 485; 495; 500; 505; 510; 515; 520; 525; 530; 535; 540; 545; 550; 555; 560; 565; 570; 575; 580; 595; 600; 605; 610; 620; 625; 630; 635; 640; 645; 650; 655; 660; 665; 670; 675; 680; 685; 690; 695; 700; 710; 725; 730; 735; 740; 745; 750; 755; 760; 765; 770; 775; 780; 790.
't "and". Syr. *ø*: 140.
'tr "fire". Syr. **nwr'** : 720.
'w'zqty "synagogue". Syr. **knwšt'** : 590.
'w'zy "assembly, multitude". Syr. **knš'** : 250; 545.
'w'zyt Syr. *kn̈š'* : 250.
'w'zy "meeting, assembly". Syr. **knwšt'** : 330.
'wfs/'wbt "to sleep". Syr. **dmk** : 650.
'wfd'rnt Syr. *dmkw* : 650.
'wγẓ/'wxšt "to go down, descend". Syr. **nḥt** : 75; 545.
'wxšt Syr. *nḥt'* : 75.
'wγẓt Syr. *nḥt'* : 75.
'wxšt Syr. *nḥt* : 545.
'wrsd'r "to decline". Syr. **rkn** : 295.
'wrsd'rt Syr. *rkn* : 295.
'wršlm "Jerusalem". Syr. **'wršlm** : 45; 95; 135; 305; 545.
'ws' "there". Syr. *ø*: : 290.
'wst(y)/'wst(y)t "to put, place, set, lay, lay away". Syr. **sm** : 565; 660; 665;

670.
'wstyd'rt Syr. *sm* : 565.
'wstyty Syr. *sym* : 660.
'wstyd'ry Syr. *smt* : 665.
'wstyd'rm Syr. *smt* : 670.
'wst(y)/'wst(y)t "to put, deposit". Syr. **yhb** : 670.
'wstyd'ry Syr. *yhbt* : 670.
'wšnty x-, sqw-, swq-/ m't "to be hungry". Syr. **kpn** : 700; 705; 720; 730.
'wšnty m'tym Syr. *kpnt* : 700; 720.
'wšnty 'yštyw Syr. *kpn 'nt* : 705.
'wšnty Syr. *kpn'* : 730.
'wšt(y)/'wšt(y)t "to stand". Syr. **q'm** : 60; 80; 125; 380; 545; 755.
'wšty sty Syr. *q'm* : 60.
'wšty m't Syr. *q'm hw'* : 80.
'wštyt' Syr. *tqwmwn* : 125.
w'št Syr. *qm* : 380; 545.
'wštyty swqnt Syr. *qymyn* : 755.
'wxsd'r "to break". Syr. **qṣ'** : 295; 310.
'wxsd'rt Syr. *qṣ'* : 295; 310.
'wxšt : see *'wxz, 'wzγz/ 'wxšt*.
'wxz, 'wzγz/'wxšt "to go down". Syr. **nḥt** : 545.
'wxšt Syr. *nḥṭ* : 545.
'wz/'wšt "to gather, come together, be collected". Syr. **knš** : 305; 475; 690.
'wzntq' Syr. *ntknšwn* : 690.
'wštyt m'tnt Syr. *knyšyn* : 305.
'wšt m'tnt Syr. *knyšyn hww*: 475.
'wz'm "to condemn". Syr. **ḥyb** : 140.
'wz'mntq' Syr. *nḥybwn* : 140.
'xšt : see *'xz*.
'xyž "to raise, put, place". Syr. **'qym** : 20; 790.
'xyžd'rt Syr. *'qym* : 20.
'xyž't Syr. *nqym* : 790.
'xz/'xšt "to rise up, arise". Syr. **qwm** : 265; 305.
'xštnt Syr. *qmw* : 305.
'xšt Syr. *qm* : 265; 305.
'γz- : 340.
'γzntq' Syr. *nqwmwn* : 340.
'y "oh!". Syr. **'w** : 285.
'y "oh!". Syr. **'yw** : 655.
'yc "something, anything, thing, what". Syr. **mdm** : 190; 250; 360; 420;

440; 495; 510; 640; 665.

'yc Syr. **dl'** : 235.

'yc Syr. *ø* : 190; 530; 600; 680.

'yc "what?". Syr. **m'** : 340.

'yc't d'r "to keep, guard". Syr. **nṭr** : 565.

'yc't d'rtq Syr. *nṭr* : 565.

'yd'r "to take". Syr. **nsb** : 295.

'yd'rt Syr. *nsb* : 295.

'yqwn "ever". Syr. **'lm** : 20; 620.

'yqwncyq "eternal". Syr. **l'lm** : 210; 235; 720; 740.

'ym : see *x*.

'ym "end". Syr. **ḥrt'** : 345.

'yms' "finally". Syr. **b-ḥrt'** : 140; 150.

''yms' Syr. *b-ḥrt'* : 140;

'yms' Syr. *b-ḥrt'* : 150.

'yms' "finally". Syr. **'ḥryt** : 165.

'yms "to end". Syr. **gmr** : 230.

'ẏmst Syr. *gmr* : 230.

'yms "to be finished". Syr. **šlm** : 350.

'ymsntq' Syr. *tšlmwn* : 350.

'ync "woman". Syr. **'ntt'** : 275; 280; 415; 520.

'ynšt Syr. *nš̈'* : 275; 280.

'nc'y/'nc't "to stay". Syr. **pwš** : 295.

'nc'y Syr. *pwš* : 295.

'yny "this". Syr. **hn'** : 10; 60; 80; 165; 230; 565; 610; 620; 660; 775.

'yny Syr. *hd'* : 230; 345; 380; 620.

'nyy Syr. *l-hn'* : 610.

y'nt Syr. *hlyn* : 145; 245; 510; 570; 715; 735.

y'nt 'yšt "these things". Syr. **hlyn** "these" : 10; 275; 390; 425; 450; 485; 585.

y'nt 'yšty : 455.

'ys/'γt "to come". Syr. **'t'** : 60; 65; 105; 150; 165; 170; 180; 275; 350; 380; 395; 425; 435; 445; 520; 525; 650; 655; 660; 670; 685; 695; 715; 745; 785; 795.

'ystq' Syr. *'ṫ'* : 60; 65.

'ystq' Syr. *'ty'* : 180; 425; 445.

'yst' Syr. *tw* : 165; 695.

'ystq' Syr. *n't'* : 350.

'yst Syr. *'ṭ'* : 105.

'yswty Syr. *'t'hwyt* : 670.

'y̤ṣt Syr. *'t'* : 685.
'y̤ṣt Syr. *n't'* : 745; 785; 795.
'yst Syr. *n't'* : 745.
['ysyq] m't Syr. *'t'* : 65.
'yty̤ [sty] Syr. *'ytyh* : 180.
'yty sty Syr. *'tt* : 445.
'ytnt Syr. *'ty* : 275.
'yt Syr. *'ṭ'* : 150; 170; 380; 395; 650; 655; 660; 785.
'yt Syr. *'tt* : 520; 525.
'ytym Syr. *'tyt* : 435.
'ytym Syr. *'tyn* : 715.

'yš : see *x*.

'yzt' wn- /qt- "to proclaim". Syr. **'krz** : 360.
'yzt' wnt' Syr. *'krzw* : 360.

'yžnty x-, sqw-, swq-/m't "to be worthy". Syr. **šw'** : 60.
'yžnty 'ym Syr. *šw'* : 60.

'z'n "to confess, acknowledge". Syr. **'wdy** : 45; 370; 375; 590.
'z'nd'rt Syr. *'wḍy* : 45.
.'z̈'nt Syr. *nwd'* : 370; 590.
.'z̈'ng' Syr. *'wd'* : 375.

'ž'w " to live, cause to live, give life to". Syr. **nḥ'** : 180; 745.
'žwntq' Syr. *nḥwn* : 180.
'ž'ẇt Syr. *nḥ'* : 745.

'žt "born". Syr. **'tyld** : 415; 580.

'žty b(w)-/qt- "to be born". Syr. **'tyld** : 415; 580; 620; 625.
'žt Syr. *'tyld* : 415; 580.
'žty bwty Syr. *'tyld* : 620.
'žt[yš] Syr. *'tyldt* : 625.

'žwn "son". Syr. **br'** : 230; 340.
'žwnt Syr. *bnÿ'* : 230.
'žwnt Syr. *bnÿ'* : 340.

b(w)-/qt- "to become, happen, be". Syr. **hw'** : 10; 15; 60; 150; 175; 185; 195; 215; 235; 275; 285; 295; 315; 320; 330; 350; 410; 425; 470; 475; 515; 535; 545; 605; 620; 655; 660; 775; 780.
bwtq' Syr. *nhw'* : 10; 320.
bwtq' Syr. *thw'* : 410.
bntq' Syr. *-yn* : 150.
bnt Syr. *nhwwn* : 185.
bwt' Syr. *hww* : 330.

bwtq̱' Syr. *hww*: 780.
bwty Syr. *hw'* : 620.
by Syr. *thw'* : 215.
by Syr. *ø* : 350.
by Syr. *nhw'* : 350.
b' Syr. *hw'* : 295; 515; 535.
b' Syr. *thw'* : 655; 660.
b't Syr. *thw'*: 425.
b't Syr. *nhw'* : 470.
b'm Syr. *'hw'* : 470.
bwty̱št' Syr. *hwytwn* : 315.
bw Syr. *mhw'*: 605.
qty Syr. *hwt* : 10; 175; 195.
qty Syr. *–w* : 15.
qty Syr. *hw'*: 545; 775.
qtnt Syr. *hwÿ* : 60; 275.
qtnt Syr. *hww* : 475.
qtyšt' Syr. *hwytwn* : 235.

b(w)-/qt- "to be able, can". Syr. **mškḥ** : 190; 215; 240; 250; 365; 460; 570; 620.
qt(') wn'nq'zw Syr. *mškḥ 'n'*: 190.
qt'ẉṇq' zw Syr. *mškḥ 'n'* : 215.
qt'wny Syr. *mškḥ* : 240.
qt'wnt'q'šm'x Syr. *mškḥyn 'ntwn* : 240.
qt'b't Syr. *mškḥ'* : 250.
qt'wnntq' Syr. *mškḥyn* : 365.
qt['wnnt] Syr. *'škḥw* : 460.
qt'wntyq' Syr. *mškḥ* : 365; 570.
qt'wny̱q m't Syr. *mškḥ hw'*: 620.

b'γ "vineyard". Syr. **krm'** : 155; 165; 170.
b'γy : 170.

b'γd'ry "vine-dresser". Syr. **plḥ'** : 155; 160; 165; 170.
b'γd'ryt Syr. *plḧ'*: 155; 160; 165; 170.

b'wnyq x-, sqw-, swq-/m't "to suffice, be sufficient". Syr. **spq** : 350.
b'wnyq xcy Syr. *spq* : 350.

bγ- "God". Syr. **'lh'** : 10; 15; 35; 180; 240; 245; 270; 425; 440; 565; 595; 610; 615; 620; 630.
bγy̱ : 10; 180; 245; 270; 595; 610; 615; 630.
bγyy Syr. *l-'lh'* : 240.
bγ': 440; 565; 620.

bγ- ptr- "God the Father". Syr. **'b'** "Father": 205; 370; 375; 385; 420; 430; 435; 465; 695; 755.
bγy ptry : 205; 370; 375; 385; 430; 435; 695; 755.
bγ' ptr': 430; 435.
bγ' ptr': 465.
bγ- ptr- "God the Father". Syr. **'lh'** "God": 435.
bγ' ptr': 435.
xwt'w bγ- "Lord God". Syr. **mry'** "Lord" : 15; 30; 175.
xwt'w bγy : 15; 30.
xwt'w bγ' : 175.
sm'ncyq bγ- "Heavenly God". Syr. **'ly'** "Supreme": 30.
sm'ncyq bγy : 30.
bγ'npšqty "wedding". Syr. **mštwt'** : 80.
bγ'npšqty "wedding feast". Syr. **byt mštwt'** : 780.
bγ'nyq "divine, of God". Syr. **d-'lh'** : 150; 535.
bγ'nypš "bridegroom". Syr. **ḥtn'** : 90.
bγny "naked, nude". Syr. **'rṭly'** : 730.
bγny x-, sqw-, sqw-/ m't "to be naked". Syr. **'rṭly' hw'** : 725.
bγny m'tym Syr. *'rṭly' hwyt* : 725.
bntqty "prison". Syr. **'syr'** : 730.
bntqty Syr. *'syr̈'* : 730.
bnty "servant, slave". Syr. **'bd'** : 20; 155; 160; 240; 315; 355; 650; 655; 785; 795.
bntyty Syr. *'b̈d'* : 155; 160; 650; 785.
bnt' : 655.
bnty Syr. *ø* : 655; 660.
bγlzbwb "Beelzebul". Syr. **b'lzbwb** : 355.
br : see *pnt br*.
br't "brother". Syr. **'ḥ'** : 340; 540; 715; 760.
br'trt Syr. *'ḥ̈'* : 715.
br'trt Syr. ø : 145.
brtpθ wn-/qt- "to inform, make known". Syr. **'wd'** (Aph.) : 470.
brtpθ qθ'rm Syr. *'wd't* : 470.
brtpθ wn'msq zw Syr. *mwd' 'n'* : 470.
br θwlmy "Bartholomew". Syr. **br twlmy** : 540.
bry "fruit". Syr. **p'r'** : 155; 170.
bryty Syr. *p'r̈'*: 155; 170.
bwžbr "tax collector". Syr. **mks'** : 150.
bwžbrt Syr. *mks̈'* : 150.
by "both". Syr. *ø* : 240; 365.

byqp'r "out, outside". Syr. **lbr** : 165.
bynt/bst- "to fasten". Syr. **'sr** : 780.
bnt bystyt Syr. *nhwwn 'syryn* : 780.
byr/byrt "to find". Syr. **'škḥ** : 275; 280; 305; 625; 785; 790.
byrd'rnt Syr. *'škḥ* : 275.
byrd'rnt Syr. *'škḥw* : 280; 305.
byrd'rt Syr. *'škḥ* : 625.
byrt Syr. *nškḥ* : 785; 790.
byrty b(w)-/qt- "to show oneself to be". Syr. **'štkḥ** (Ethpe.) : 655.
byrty qtyš tyw Syr. *'štkḥt* : 655.
bys' "out". Syr. **lbr** : 625.
bys' fšqr "to put out". Syr. **npq** : 590.
bys'fšqrynt Syr. *npqwn* : 590.
bystr pxšn "to depart". Syr. **zl** : 720.
bystr pxšnt' Syr. *zlw* : 720.
byθγny' "Bethany". Syr. **byt'ny'** : 60.
bywnqy' wn-/qt- "to prophesy". Syr. **'tnby** (Ethpa.) : 15.
bywnqy' qθ'rt Syr. *'tnby* : 15.
bywny "prophet". Syr. **nby'** : 20; 30; 45; 50; 55; 270; 285; 495; 575.
bywnyty Syr. *nbÿ'*: 20; 285.
bywnyty Syr. *nby'*: 495.
bywny Syr. ø : 610.
bzyšt "goats". Syr. **gdÿ'** : 690; 695.
bž'xwty' pcγ'z/pcγšt "to suffer". Syr. **ḥš** : 500.
bž'xwty'pcγ'z't Syr. *nḥš* : 500.
bžyq "evil, bad". Syr. **byš** : 100.
bžyqt Syr. *bÿš'* : 100.

c'f "how, how much, how many, just as". Syr. **km'** : 220; 355; 715; 735.
c'nw "how, as, while, when, although". Syr. **kd** : 40; 150; 155; 165; 245; 275; 295; 300; 305; 380; 390; 475; 470; 485; 495; 515; 535; 580; 660; 770; 780; 785.
c'nw "when, at such time". Syr. **m' d-** : 170; 215; 230; 255; 345; 415; 510; 685; 780.
c'nw "how". Syr. **'ykn'** : 310.
cn'wq x-, sqw-, sqw-/m't "to be thirsty, thirst". Syr. **ṣhy** : 700; 710; 725.
cn'wq m'tym Syr. *ṣhyt* : 700; 725.
cn'wq 'yštyw Syr. *ṣh''nt* : 710.
c'ny "how". Syr. **'ykn'** : 550; 570; 580; 600.
cn "from, out of, of, than, by". Syr. **mn** : 20; 25; 35; 45; 55; 100; 110; 145;

160; 165; 175; 190; 200; 205; 215; 220; 260; 275; 280; 285; 290; 300; 315; 330; 345; 350; 355; 360; 365; 370; 395; 420; 430; 440; 460; 485; 500; 510; 530; 535; 545; 565; 590; 610; 620; 650; 665; 675; 680; 690; 695; 715; 720; 735; 780.
cn "to, before". Syr. **l-** : 150.
cn "from". Syr. **ṃn lwt** : 435.
cn ftm' "before, previously". Syr. **ṃn qdym**: 560.
cn…ms' "from". Syr. **ṃn** : 20; 620.
cn…ms' "from". Syr. **ṃn lwt** : 175; 435.
cn qw ms' "from where". Syr. **mn 'ymk'** : 615.
cn...pyd'r "on, about, concerning". Syr. **'l** : 280; 290; 405; 430; 495.
cn...pyd'r "for, because". Syr: **mṭl(t)** : 345; 350; 380; 415; 750.
cn...pyrnm "before". Syr. **ṃn qdym** : 70.
cn...pyrs' "formerly, before". Syr. **ṃn qdym** : 465.
cr'γ "lamp". Syr. **šrg'** : 780.
cr'γt Syr. *šr̈g'* : 780.
crxwšt "wine press". Syr. **m'ṣrt'** : 155.
cšm- "eye". Syr. **'yn'** : 175; 300; 550; 560; 565; 570; 585; 615; 620
cšmt' Syr. *'ynÿ* : 175; 300; 550; 560; 565; 570; 585; 615; 620.
cšnt xwyr "to cause to drink, to give to drink". Syr. **'šqy** (Aph.) : 710; 725.
cšnt xwyrd'rym Syr. *'šqyn* : 710.
cšnt xwyrd'ryšt' Syr. *'šqytwnn* : 725.
cw "what? why". Syr. **mn'** : 10; 45; 55; 170; 215; 225; 335; 480; 570; 750.
cw "what?". Syr. **m'** : 85.
cwt "whether". Syr. **ø** : 45; 135; 175; 605.
cwtny "or not". Syr. **l'** : 300; 365; 525.
cxwd "Jew". Syr. **yhwdy'** : 45; 380; 575; 590.
cxwdt Syr. *yhẅdy'* : 45; 575; 590.
cxwdty Syr. *yhẅdy'* : 380; 590.
cxwd'ny "Judaic, of Jews". Syr. **d-yhwd̈y'** : 250.
cymyθy "for this reason, therefore". Syr. **mṭl hn'** : 70.
cymyθy pyd'r "for this reason, so, therefore". Syr. **mṭl hn'** : 175; 315.
cyntr "in, at, inside, within". Syr. **b-** : 185; 365; 660.
cyntr "in". Syr. **byt** : 705; 730; 735.
cyntr "inside". Syr. **b-gw** : 300.
cywyθ pyd'r "because, since, for". Syr. **mṭl d-** : 70; 210; 245; 295; 585.
cywyθ pyd'r "therefore". Syr. **mṭl hn'** : 590.
cywyθ ms' "since". Syr. **ṃn** : 275.

d'm : see *mwrty d'my.*

d'p't "yes". Syr. **'n'** : 145.
d'rwq "wood". Syr. **ø** : 745.
d't "law". Syr. **ø** : 515.
d'ty : 515.
d'tbr "judge". Syr. **dyn'** : 330.
dtbrt Syr. *dyn̈'* : 330.
d'tbr "governor". Syr. **hgmwn'**: 330.
d'tbrt Syr. *hgmẅn'* : 330.
d'tcyq "just, righteous". Syr. **k'n'** : 195; 465.
d'tcyqy' "righteousness, justice ". Syr. **k'nwt'** : 30.
d'tcyqy' Syr. *k'nwt'* : 30.
d'w "to anoint, smear". Syr. **ṭš** : 555.
d'wd'rt Syr. *ṭš* : 555.
db'm'n "wife". Syr. **'ntt'** : 120.
db'ny : see *š'št db'ny b(w)-/qt-*.
db't "perhaps". Syr. **kbr** : 165.
dbr- "door, gate" Syr. **tr'** : 255; 380.
dbry: 255.
dbrt': 380.
dbr- "door, gate" Syr. **ø** : 785.
dbry: 785.
dbtyq "next, other". Syr. **'ḥrn'** : 80; 130; 240.
dbtyqy Syr. *l-'ḥrn'* : 240.
dbtyq "second". Syr. **tr̈tyn** : 595; 790.
dbtyq "other, another". Syr. **ḥd** : 300; 690.
dbtyq "next". Syr. **dbtr'** : 65.
dbtyq "one another". Syr. **ḥdd'**: 405.
dbtyq "next". Syr. **ø**: 505.
dn...prw : "with, together with". Syr. **'m** : 15; 130; 295; 300; 305; 380; 385; 395; 425; 430; 475; 495; 545; 610; 635; 670; 690; 755; 770.
dnt' "tooth". Syr. **šn'** : 125.
dpyr "scribe". Syr. **spr'** : 140.
dpyrt Syr. *spr̈'* : 140.
ds' "ten". Syr. **'sr'** : 655; 675.
dsprtr "handkerchief". Syr. **sdwn'** : 660.
dst- "hand". Syr. **'yd'**: 15; 20; 25; 385; 400; 480; 485; 515.
dsty: 15.
dsty': 20; 25.
dstw: 400.
dst' Syr. *'ÿd'* : 385; 400; 480; 485.

dsty' Syr. *'ÿdy* : 515.
pr d(w)stw wn-/qt- "to entrust, lease, hand over, hand down ". Syr. **'wḥd** (Aph.) : 155; 170.
pr dstw qθ'rt Syr. *'wḥd* : 155.
pr dwstw wntẏq' Syr. *nwḥd* : 170.
dw' "two". Syr. **tryn** : 145; 240; 365; 510.
dw'ts "twelve". Syr. **tr'sr / tr'srt'** : 395; 535.
dw'tsnw : 395.
dw'ywx'qy' "division". Syr. **plgwt'** : 570.
dwr "far, distant". Syr. **rḥyq'** : 290.
dwrt- "peace". Syr. **šlm'** : 35; 450.
dwrty' : 35.
dwrt' : 450.
dwrt' swq't "peace be". Syr. **šlm'** "peace!" : 380; 385; 475.
dwstw : see *pr d(w)stw wn-/qt-*.
dwsy "neighbour". Syr. **šbb'** : 10.
dwsyt Syr. *šbbÿ* : 10.
dwyd "David". Syr. **Dwyd** : 20.
dxšt- "desert". Syr. **ḥwrb'** : 40; 265.
dxšty' : 40; 265.
dxšt- "wilderness". Syr. **mdbr'** : 50.
dxšty' : 50.
dynd'r "priest". Syr. **khn'** : 45; 140; 270.
dynd'rt Syr. *khn̈'* : 45; 140; 270.
dys/ dysd'r "to build". Syr. **bn'** : 155.
dẏsd'rt Syr. *ḅn'* : 155.
dysny "builder". Syr. **bny'** : 175.
dysnyt Syr. *bnÿ'* : 175.
dywnt, dywyd : see *xyd*.
dyx'w "village". Syr. **qryt'**: 290; 520; 645.

fcmbd "world". Syr. **'lm'** : 65; 100; 230; 415.
fcmbdy : 65; 230.
fcmpd "world". Syr. **'lm'** : 310; 315; 410; 435; 450; 465; 695; 750.
fcmpdy Syr. *l-'lm'* : 435; 450.
fcmrz "to snatch". Syr. **ḥṭp** : 640.
fcmrzt Syr. *ḥṭp*: 640.
fr'q-cšny "morning". Syr. **ṣpr'** : 510.
frγn' : see *prymyθ frγn'*.
frm'y/frm't "to speak, say, order, command". Syr. **'mr** : 75; 120; 125; 130;

135; 145; 170; 200; 230; 245; 250; 285; 320; 325; 350; 380; 385; 390; 400; 420; 445; 460; 475; 480; 485; 490; 500; 515; 525; 630; 645; 655; 660; 665; 675; 685; 695; 715; 720; 735; 740; 755; 775; 795.

fr'm'y Syr. *'m̈r* : 135; 170; 245; 250; 480; 515; 630; 655; 665; 685.

frm'ymsqn zw Syr. *'mr 'n'* : 120; 125.

zw frm'ymsqn Syr. *'n' 'mr 'n'* : 230.

frm'ymsq zw Syr. *'mr 'n'* : 130; 145; 200; 320; 350; 400; 420; 675; 715; 735; 755; 795.

fr'm'y Syr. *'ṃr* : 75; 285; 380; 445; 460; 385; 390; 475; 485; 490; 500; 525; 645; 660; 675; 740; 775.

frm'y Syr. *'ṃr* : 325.

frm'd'rt Syr. *'ṃr* : 380.

fr'm'y Syr. *'mr hw'* : 500.

frm'y Syr. *'ṃr* : 525.

frm'ẏtq' Syr. *n'mr* : 695; 720; 735.

frtr "better". Syr. **ytyr** : 350.

frtr "better". Syr. **mytr** : 370.

frθyp "to burn". Syr. **dlq** : 200.

frθypt Syr. *dl̇q* : 200.

frwrtqty "tomb, sepulchre". Syr**. qbwr'** : 185; 275; 280.

fry d'r "to love". Syr. **rḥm** : 240.

fry Syr. *nrḥm* : 240.

fry ny'd'r "to love". Syr. **rḥm** : 435.

fry ny'd'rt Syr. *rḥm* : 435.

fry ny'd'ryšt' Syr. *rḥmtwnn* : 435.

fry ny'd'r "to love". Syr. **'ḥb** : 465.

fry ny'd'ry Syr. *'ḥbtn* : 465.

fryd'ryq x-, sqw-, swq-/m't "to love". Syr. **rḥm hw'** : 245; 315.

fry-d'ryq m'tnt Syr. *rḥmyn hww* : 245.

fryd'ryq m't Syr. *rḥm hw'* : 315.

frystr d'r "to love". Syr. **rḥm hw'** : 465.

frystr d'rt Syr. *rḥm hw'* : 465.

fryšty "angel". Syr. **ml'k'** : 280; 690; 755.

fryštyt Syr. *m̈l'k'* : 280; 690.

fryštyty: 755.

fryž/fršt "to guide". Syr. **rwṣ** : 35.

fryẓ̌̇'t Syr. *ntrwṣ* : 35.

ḟṣx "mile". Syr. **myl'**: 130.

fš'm/fšmt "to send". Syr. **šdr** : 45; 55; 75; 155; 160; 165; 195; 325; 385; 390; 470.

fš'mynt Syr. *nšdrwn* : 160.
fšmd'rm Syr. *šdr* : 75.
fšmd'rnt Syr. *sdrw* : 45.
fšmtyt qtnt Syr. *'štdrw* : 55.
fšmd'rt Syr. *šḍr* : 155; 160; 165 ; 195.
fš'mmsqn Syr. *mšdr'n'* : 325; 390.
fšmd'rt Syr. *šdrn* : 385.
fšmd'ry Syr. *šdrtn* : 470.
fš'm/fšmt "to send". Syr. **šlḥ** : 205.
fšmd'rt Syr. *šlḥ* : 205.
fšqr "to cast out". Syr. **'pq** : 625.
fšqrd'rnt Syr. *'pqw* : 625.
fšy'ws "master". Syr. **mr'** : 155.
ftm "to breathe". Syr. **npḥ** : 390.
ftm'd'rt Syr. *ṇpḥ* : 390.
fwx'r "blessed". Syr. **ṭwb** : 795.
fy'tr "more". Syr. **ytyr** : 510.

γ'dwq "throne". Syr. **trwnws** : 690.
γmwr' "Gomorrah". Syr. **'mwr'** : 320.
γnt'q "evil". Syr. **byš** : 190.
γnt'qt Syr. *byšt'* : 190.
γnt'qry "bad, evil, wicked". Syr. **byš** : 640; 665.
γnt'q-qr': 665.
γnt'qry "bad, evil, wicked". Syr. **ø** : 720.
γntm "wheat". Syr. **ḥ̈ṭ'** : 225.
γr "mountain". Syr. **ṭwr'** : 10; 535; 765.
γry : 10; 535; 765.
γr'm' "wealth, possessions, wealth". Syr. **qnyn'** : 795.
γr'm' Syr. *qnyn'* : 795.
γr'my "money, wealth". Syr. **mmwn'** : 235; 240.
γr'my Syr. *l-mmwn'* : 240.
γr'n "honoured". Syr. **yqyr** : 300.
γrb/γrb't "to know". Syr. **yd'** : 70; 75; 215; 245; 255; 440; 465; 480; 555; 580; 585; 595; 600; 610; 615; 650; 665 ; 790.
γrbyq m'tym Syr. *yd' hwyt* : 70; 75.
γrbyq m'tyš Syr. *yd' hwyt* : 665.
γrb'ty b't Syr. *ntyd'* : 70.
γrbd'rm Syr. *yd't* : 215; 465.
γrbtysq Syr. *yd'* : 245.

γrbt'sqn šm'x Syr. *yd'yn 'ntwn* : 255.
γrbd'rt Syr. *yd'* : 465.
γrbd'rt Syr. *nd'* : 650.
γrbd'rnt Syr. *'yd'w* : 470.
γrbt'q' Syr. *d'w* : 480.
γrbt'sqn Syr. *yd'yn 'ntwn* : 615.
γrb'msq zw Syr. *yd' 'n'* : 555; 600.
γrbymsqn m'x Syr. *yd'ynn* : 580; 585.
γrbymsqn m'x Syr. *yd'ynn ḥnn* : 440; 595; 610.
γrbysq tγw Syr. *yd' 'nt* : 440.
γrbt' Syr. *yd'* : 790.

γrb'q "wise". Syr. **ḥkym** : 230; 330; 790.
γrb'qstr Syr. *ḥkymyn* : 230.
γrb'qt Syr. *ḥkÿm'* : 330.

γrb'q-γwny "astutely". Syr. **ḥkym'yt** : 230.

γrf "much, more, many". Syr. **sgy** : 160; 235; 370; 525; 545.
γrft Syr. *sgÿ'* : 160.
γrftyšt Syr. *sgy't'* : 525.

γrf "many, quantity". Syr. **swg"** : 460.

γryq "mud". Syr. **ṭyn'** : 555; 560; 565.

γryw "soul, own, oneself". Syr. **npš'** : 50; 110; 190; 195; 215; 245; 290; 585; 745; 750.
γrywy : 190; 290; 585; 750.

γšyp wn-/qt- "to forfeit". Syr. **ḥsr** : 750.
γšyp wn't Syr. *nḥsr* : 750.

γw'm- n'fc "stranger". Syr. **'ksny'** : 730.

γw'm- n'fc x-, sqw-, sqw-/m't "to be a stranger". Syr. **'ksny' hw'** : 700; 710; 725.
γw'm- n'fc m'tym Syr. *'ksny' hwyt* : 700; 725.
γw'm- n'fc 'yštyw Syr. *'ksny' 'nt* : 710.

γw'n "sin". Syr. **ḥṭh'** : 30; 390; 505; 625.
γw'nty : 30; 505.
γwn'nt Syr. *ḥ̈ṭh'* : 390.

γwb/γwbt "to commend". Syr. **šbḥ** : 225.
γwbd'rt Syr. *šbḥ* : 225.

γwbty' "glory". Syr. **šwbḥ'** : 685; 690.
γwbty: 690.

γwbty' "glory". Syr. **tšbwḥt'** : 285; 755.

γwdy "container". Syr. **mtryn** : 220; 225.

γwnty x-, sqw-, swq-/m't "to be necessary". Syr. **mtb''** : 530.

γwnty xcy Syr. *mtb'y'* : 530.
γwr'ty "awake". Syr. **'yr'** : 785.
γwr'tyt Syr. *'yryn* : 785.
γwrs prwyd/prwyst "to put around". Syr. **'ḥdr** : 155.
γwrs prwyd'rt Syr. *'ḥdr* : 155.
γwš "ear". Syr. **'dn'** : 1; 360.
γwšt Syr. *'dn̈y*: 1; 360.
γwš "to rejoice". Syr. **ḥd'** : 385; 410; 420.
γwšd'rnt Syr. *ḥdyw*: 385.
γwštyq' Syr. *nḥd'* : 410; 420.
γwšyq x-, sqw-, swq-/ m't "to grow up". Syr. **rb' hw'** : 35.
γwšyq m't Syr. *rb' hw'* : 35.
γwty xwdq'r "alone". Syr. **lḥwd** : 445; 525; 755.
γwty xwtg'r "alone". Syr. **lḥwd** : 445.
γwž "to ask". Syr. **š'l** : 5; 420; 425; 430.
γwžd'rt Syr. *ṣ'l* : 5.
γwžt'q' Syr. *tš'lwn* : 420.
γwžt' Syr. *tš'lwn* : 420.
γwžd'ryšt' Syr. *š'ltwn* : 425.
γwžt' Syr. *š'lw* : 425.
γwžtg' Syr. *tš'lwn* : 430.
γwž "to ask". Syr. **b''** : 430.
γwžng' Syr. *'b''* : 430.

ḥ.lpyy̤ "Alphaeus". Syr. **ḥlpy** : 540.

knθ- "town". Syr. **mdynt'** : 345.
kθ- "city". Syr. **k'rk'** : 655; 660.
kθt Syr. *kr̈kyn* : 655; 660.

q'm "to want, wish". Syr. **ṣb'** : 130; 200; 605; 680; 745; 770.
q'ṃt Syr. *ṣb̈'* : 130; 745.
q'md'ryšt' Syr. *ṣbytwn* : 200.
q'mt'sqn šm'x Syr. *ṣbyn 'ntwn* : 605.
q'mt'sqn Syr. *ṣbyn 'ntwn* : 605.
qmd'rnt Syr. *ṣbw* : 680.
q'my̤ tγw Syr. *ṣbyt* : 770.
q'm "to want, wish". Syr. **b''** : 195.
q'mmsq zw Syr. *b'n'* : 195.
q'm "to want, wish". Syr. . **ø** : 415.

q'my : 415.
qbnq "little, few". Syr. **qlyl** : 235; 405; 410; 655.
qbnq "for a while". Syr. **ø** : 200.
qd' "or, nor, ". Syr. **'w** : 135; 240; 325; 335; 585; 710; 730.
qd' "when". Syr. **'mty** : 710; 730; 780.
qd'c "ever, never". Syr. **mmtwm** : 175; 210.
qn/qnd'r "to dig". Syr. **ḥpr** : 155.
qnd'rt Syr. *ḥpr* : 155.
qp "fish". Syr. **nẇn'** : 460.
qpy Syr. *nẅn'* : 460.
qrm "serpent". Syr. **ḥwy'** : 330.
*qrmyš*t Syr. *ḥwẅt'* : 330.
qrny sry "cornerstone". Syr. **rš' dzwyt'** : 175.
qržwrz "miracle, wonder". Syr. **'t'**: 570.
qržwrzt Syr. *'ẗẅt'* : 570.
qš/qšt "to sow". Syr. **zr'** : 665; 670.
qšd'ry Syr. *zr't* : 665.
qšd'rm Syr. *zr't* : 670.
qštr "smaller, least". Syr. **z'wr** : 715; 735.
qštrt' Syr. *z'wr̈'* : 715; 735.
qšy̭ "now". Syr. **hš'** : 90; 180; 295; 415; 440; 445; 585; 600.
qt "that, so that, in that, because". Syr. **d-** : 1; 10; 15; 20; 25; 30; 35; 40; 45; 50; 60; 65; 70; 75; 80; 105; 115; 120; 125; 130; 150; 160; 170; 175; 180; 185; 190; 195; 200; 205; 210; 215; 220; 230; 235; 240; 245; 250; 255; 265; 270; 275; 280; 290; 295; 305; 310; 320; 335; 345; 350; 355; 360; 365; 370; 375; 385; 395; 405; 410; 415; 420; 425; 430; 435; 440; 445; 460; 465; 470; 480; 485; 500; 515; 520; 525; 530; 540; 545; 550; 560; 565; 570; 575; 580; 585; 590; 595; 600; 610; 615; 620; 630; 640; 650; 655; 660; 665; 670; 675; 680; 690; 695; 705; 710; 720; 735; 740; 745; 750; 755; 760; 765; 770; 775; 780; 785; 795.
qt "that, so that, in that, because". Syr. **ø** : 190; 550.
qt "if". Syr. **'n** : 55; 110; 195; 235; 355; 390; 510; 590; 595; 790.
qt ny "unless, if not". Syr. **'n l'** : 135; 400.
qt'ny "sin". Syr. **ḥṭ'** : 65.
qt'nyq'ry "sinner". Syr. **ḥṭy'** : 570; 595; 595/600; 615.
qt'nyq'ryty Syr. *ḥṭÿ'*: 615.
qtnt : see *b(w)-/qt-*.
qty : see *b(w)-/qt-*.
qty' "deed, action, work". Syr. **'bd'** : 270; 755.
qtyt Syr. *'b̈d'* : 270; 755.

qθ- "town". Syr. **mdynt'** : 325.
qθ'rt : see *wn-/qt-*.
qw "where". Syr. **'yk'** : 555.
qw 'ÿms' "in the end, finally,". Syr. **b- ḥrt'** : 150.
qw "to". Syr. **l-**: 75; 110; 645.
qw "to". Syr. **lwt** : 105.
qw…s' "to". Syr. **l-** : 5; 10 ; 20; 25; 30; 35; 50; 55; 70; 110; 115; 120; 125; 130; 135; 140; 145; 150; 155; 160/165; 170; 175; 185; 190; 220; 225; 230; 235; 240; 245; 250; 255; 270; 285; 290; 295; 300; 305; 310; 325; 335; 340; 345; 350; 385; 390; 395; 410 ; 420; 425; 430; 435; 440; 445; 450; 455; 460; 475; 480; 495; 500; 505; 510; 515; 525; 535; 550; 555; 565; 570; 585; 595; 605; 615; 625; 630; 635; 645; 650; 655; 665; 670; 675; 680; 685; 695; 700; 715; 720; 735; 740; 755; 765; 770; 775; 780; 785; 795.
qw…s' "to". Syr. **lwt** : 40; 65; 155/160; 165; 195/200; 435; 560.
qw…s' "at, to". Syr. **lbyt** : 275; 280; 330.
qwc' "mouth". Syr. **pwm'** : 5; 20; 665.
 qwcy : 665.
q(w)rwn: see *wn-/qt-*.
qwpwtyc "pigeon". Syr. **ywn'** : 75; 330.
 qwpwdy(c)t Syr. *ywn̈'* : 330.
qwrθy "tunic". Syr. **kwtyn'** : 130.
qws "side". Syr. **ø** : 565.
 qwst : 565.
qwšy "side". Syr. **sṭr'** : 385.
qwšy "side". Syr. **gb'** : 460.
qwtr "generation". Syr. **šrbt'** : 230.
qy "who, which?". Syr. **mnw** : 145; 250; 510; 585; 630.
qy "who?". Syr. **ṁn** : 45.
qyr'n "side". Syr. **ø** : 695; 720.
qysrq'n "denarius". Syr. **dynr'** : 510.
 qysrq'n Syr. *dynr̈yn* : 510.

m'n "mind". Syr. **r'yn'** : 500.
m'nwq "like, similar". Syr. **dmy'** : 645; 780.
m'nwqy' "likeness". Syr. **mdm'** : 550.
m'r'wt b(w)-/qt- "to lament". Syr. **'ly** : 410.
 mr'wt bwt'q' Syr. *t'lwn* : 410.
m't : see *x*.
m't ptryt "parents". Syr. **'bhÿ** : 340; 585; 590.
m'x : see *zw*.

m'yš "then". Syr. **ky** : 10.
mdw/mwd "wine". Syr. **ḥmr'** : 90; 505.
mdy "here". Syr. **tnn** : 755.
mγwn "all". Syr. **kl** : 270; 545.
mn' : see *zw*.
mntm'ny "foolish". Syr. **ḥsyry r'yn'** : 285.
mntm'nyt Syr. *ḥsyr̈y r'yn'* : 285.
mrc "death". Syr. **mwt'** : 35; 140; 270; 340.
mrcy: 35; 270.
mrtxmy "man, person". Syr. **brnš'** : 200; 250; 330; 370; 375; 415; 750.
mrtxmyty Syr. *brnš'* : 200.
mrtxmyty Syr. *bnÿnš'* : 250; 370; 375.
mrtxmyt Syr. *bnÿnš'*: 330.
mrtxmy "man, person". Syr. **'nš'** : 280; 565; 650; 780.
mrtxmyt Syr. *'n̈š'* : 280; 565; 650; 780.
mrtxmy "man". Syr. **gbr'** : 645.
mrtxmy z'ty " Son of Man ". Syr. **brh d-'nš'** : 140; 185; 350; 685; 750; 760.
mrty "man". Syr. **gbr'** : 155; 550; 565; 570; 595; 610; 670.
mrθ' "Martha". Syr. **mrt'** : 525; 530.
mrθ': 530.
mrws "to touch". Syr. **gš** : 480.
mrwst' Syr. *gwšwnn* : 480.
mrxy wn-/qt- "to make straight". Syr. **'šw** : 50.
mrxy wnt' Syr. *'šww* : 50.
mrym "Mary". Syr. **mrym** : 520; 530.
ms "also, even". Syr. **'p** : 130; 150; 180; 185; 230; 235; 255; 275; 280; 370; 375; 390; 415; 515; 585; 605; 660; 680; 720.
mšyḥ' "Messiah". Syr. **mšyḥ'** : 45; 55; 500; 590.
mθy "Matthew". Syr. **mty** : 540.
mwd : see mdw/mwd.
mwrty "dead person". Syr. **myt'** : 180.
mwrtyt Syr. *mÿt'* : 180.
mwrty d'm "realm of the dead". Syr. **byt mÿt'** : 500.
mwrty d'my : 500.
mwš' "Moses". Syr. **mwš'** : 610; 775.
mwš'y Syr. *l-mwš'* : 775.
myd'n "bealt". Syr. **ḥṣ'** : 780.
myd'nt Syr. *ḥṣÿ* : 780.
myd'ny "among". Syr. **byt** : 250.

myd'ny "among". Syr. **bynt** : 60; 165; 380; 475; 570.
mydẏ'ny̧ : 380.
myd'ny "in the midst of". Syr. **byny** : 330.
myšnt "these". Syr. **hlyn** : 740.
myθ "so". Syr. **ø** : 775.
myθ "day". Syr. **ywm'** : 25; 40; 65; 80; 275; 295; 325; 415; 420; 430; 500; 505; 760.
myθt Syr. *yẅmt'*: 25.
myθy : 65; 80; 505.
myθ Syr. *yẅmyn* : 275.
myθy Syr. *yẅmyn* : 500; 760.
myθ "day". Syr. **ø** : 560.
myθqry "day". Syr. **ywm'** : 535.
myθqryt Syr. *yẅmt'* : 535.
mzmwr "Psalm". Syr. **mzmwr'** : 495.
mzmwrty Syr. *mzmwr̈'* : 495.

n' "not". Syr. **l'**: 125; 185; 355; 360; 370; 475.
n'qty "money, silver". Syr. **ksp'** : 245; 670.
n'm "name". Syr. **šm'** : 5; 100; 345; 425; 430; 470; 505; 520; 550.
n'm 'wst(y)/'wst(y)t "to name". Syr. **šmy** : 540.
n'm 'wstyd'rt Syr. *šmy* : 540.
n'šyrγwzy "the one who hates". Syr. **sn'** : 20.
n'šyrγwzyty Syr. *sn'yn* : 20.
n'w "boat". Syr. **spynt'** : 460.
n'wy : 460.
n'y "lo, behold". Syr. **ḣ'** : 1; 135; 255; 275; 325; 440; 445; 660; 775.
n'y "lo, behold". Syr. **ø** : 655.
nbnt "with, at, on". Syr. **lwt** : 295; 495; 520; 660; 675.
ndywy̧d "that". Syr. **hw** : 515.
ndywydy Syr. *l-hw*: 515.
nγ'm "time, hour". Syr. **š't'** : 180; 185; 425; 445.
nγn "bread". Syr. **ḥm'** : 295.
nγny : 295.
nγwdn "clothing, garment". Syr. **nḥt'** : 765.
nγwdnt Syr. *nḥ̈t'* : 765.
nγwnty "tunic". Syr. **mrṭwṭ'** : 130.
nγwš "to listen, to hear". Syr. **šm'** : 605; 615; 620.
nγwšd'rt'šm'x Syr. *šm'twn* : 605.
nγwšt Syr. *šm'* : 615; 620.

nfryty "cursed". Syr. **lyṭ'** : 720.
nfrytyty Syr. *lÿṭ'* : 720.
nm'c "prayer". Syr. **ṣlwt'** : 535.
nm'c br/ brt "to pray". Syr. **ṣl'** : 535.
nm'c bry Syr. *mṣlyw* : 535.
nm'c br/ brt "to pray". Syr. **sgd** : 635.
nm'c brd'rt Syr. *sgd* : 635.
nm'nqrgy' "repentance". Syr. **tybwt'** : 505.
nm'ny wn-/qt- "to repent, to regret". Syr. **'ttyb** : 135.
nm'ny wnt' Syr. *ttwbwn* : 135.
nm'nyqyn b(w)-/ qt- "to repent". Syr. **'ttwy** : 140; 150.
nm'nyqyn qty Syr. *'ttwy* : 140.
nm'nyqyn qtyšt' Syr. *'ttwytwn* : 150.
nm'y "to judge ". Syr. **d'n** : 190; 665.
nm'ymsqn Syr. *d'n 'n'* : 190.
nm'ỵngq' Syr. *'dwn* : 665.
npys/npxšt "to write". Syr. **ktb** : 5; 225; 495; 500.
nypys Syr. *kṭb* : 5.
npys Syr. *ktwb* : 225.
npxšty sty Syr. *ktyb* : 495; 500.
nšyd/nyštd'r "to plant". Syr. **nṣb** : 155.
nyštd'rt Syr. *nṣb* : 155.
nwqr "then, thus, therefore, so". Syr. **hkyl** : 45; 55; 170; 235; 330; 355; 370; 510; 615.
nwm "law". Syr. **ø** : 285.
nwšy "eternal, immortal". Syr. **ø** : 30; 185; 190; 740.
nwšc Syr. *ø* : 30; 185; 190; 740.
ny "not". Syr. **l'** : 45; 55; 60; 70 ; 145 ; 150; 175; 180; 190; 195; 200; 210; 215; 235; 240; 275; 300; 315; 350; 370; 395; 400; 410; 415; 420; 425; 430; 440; 445; 460; 465; 485; 530; 550; 555; 565; 575; 585; 600; 605; 610; 620; 635; 665; 680; 725; 735.
ny "other, another". Syr. **'ḥrn'** : 160; 225.
nyt Syr. *'ḥr̈n'* : 160.
nyw Syr. *'ḥrn'* : 225.
ny's/ny't "to take, seize, catch". Syr. **'ḥd** : 165; 390; 395; 460.
ny'sỵm Syr. *'ḥdw* : 165.
ny'st' Syr. *t'ḥdwn* : 390.
nymtyt bntq' Syr. *'ḥydyn* : 395.
nymty Syr. *'ḥdt* : 460.
ny'zqyn x-, sqw-, swq-/m't "to need". Syr. **snyq hw'** : 440.

ny'zqyn 'yš tγw Syr. *snyq 'nt* : 440.
nyd/nst "to sit". Syr. **ytb** : 35; 225; 520; 690.
nysty swqnt Syr. *ytbyn* : 35.
nyd Syr. *tb* : 235.
nysty Syr. *ytbt* : 520.
nydtq' Syr. *ntb* : 690.
nyst : see x.
nyst b(w)-/qt "to be destroyed, perish". Syr. **'bd** : 115; 135.
nyst b't Syr. *n'bd* : 115.
nyst bwt'q' Syr. *t'bdwn* : 135.
nyst wn-/qt- "to kill". Syr. **'wbd** : 170.
nystwntyq' Syr. *nwbd* : 170 ; 365.
nyšq'w/nyšqwγt "to throw out, take out ". Syr. **'pq** : 165; 510.
nyšqwxd'rnt Syr. *'pqw* : 165.
nyšqwγd'rt Syr. *'pq* : 510.
nyšqr'n cn "except on". Syr. **lbr mn** : 120.
ṇznt "humble". Syr. **tmym'** : 330.
ṇznt Syr. *tmÿm'* : 330.
nyž, nyžy/nyžt "to come out, go forth". Syr. **npq** : 190; 220; 435; 445; 535.
nyžntq' Syr. *npqwn* : 190.
nyžtym Syr. *npqt* : 220; 435.
nyžtyš Syr. *npqt* : 445.
nyžty Syr. *npq* : 535.

p'cγny "answer". Syr. **ptgm'** : 50.
p'cγny wn-/qt- "to answer". Syr. **'n'** : 55; 140; 145; 525; 550; 580; 595; 610; 625; 630; 730; 735; 770.
pcγny qθ'rt Syr. *'ṇ'* : 55.
p'cγny qθ'rt Syr. *'ṇ'* : 140; 525; 550; 595; 610; 630; 770.
p'cγy qθ'rt Syr. *'n'*: 145.
p'cγny qθ'rnt Syr. *'nw* : 580; 625.
p'cγny wnntq' Syr. *n'nwn* : 730.
p'cγny wntyq' Syr. *n'n'* : 735.
p'd "foot". Syr. **rgl'** : 35; 320; 480; 485; 520.
p'dyt Syr. *r̈gly'* : 35; 320; 480; 485.
p'dyty Syr. *r̈gly'* : 520.
p'dy wn/ qt "to place". Syr. **'qym** : 690.
p'dy wntyq' Syr. *nqym* : 690.
p'n "table". Syr. **ptwr'** : 670.
p'r "measure". Syr. **kwr̈yn** : 225.

p’t “for, but, however, indeed”. Syr. **gyr** : 1; 30; 100; 150; 180; 195; 205; 230; 240; 275; 315; 330; 345; 430; 480; 590; 595; 610; 660; 720; 745.
p’t “for, but, however, indeed”. Syr. **ø** : 185.
p’txš’wn “authority”. Syr. **šlyṭ** : 655; 660.
p’txš’wn d’r “ to reign”. Syr. **’mlk** : 680.
p’txš’wn d’rm Syr. *’mlk* : 680.
p’txš’wn wn-/qt- “to put in authority”. Syr. **’šlṭ** : 185.
p’txš’wn qθ’rt Syr. *’šlṭ* : 185.
p’txšw’n wn-/qt- “to set over”. Syr. **’qym** : 795.
p’txšw’n wntyq’ Syr. *nqym* : 795.
p’ty: see p’y.
p’y/p’t “to beware”. Syr. **’zdhr** : 330.
p’ty swqt’ Syr. *’zdhrw* : 330.
pc’dy “bearable”. Syr. **nyḥ** : 320.
pc’dystr: 320.
pcγ’z/pcγšt “to welcome, receive, get”. Syr. **qbl** : 220; 225; 230; 390; 520.
pcγ’zntq’ Syr. *nqblwnn* : 220.
pcγ’zntq’ Syr. *nqblwn* : 230.
pcγ’z Syr. *qbl* : 225.
pcγzt’ Syr. *qblw*: 390.
pcγšd’rt Syr. *qblt* : 520.
pcγyzd’r “to set”. Syr. **sm** : 505.
pcγyzd’rt Syr. *sm* : 505.
pcq’md’r “to be pleased”. Syr. **’ṣṭby** : 775.
pcq’md’rm Syr. *’ṣṭbyt* : 775.
pcq’w wn-/qt- “to reject”. Syr. **sl’** : 175.
pcq’w qθ’rnt Syr. *’slyw* : 175.
pcqs “to wait”. Syr. **sk’** : 780.
pcγqṣnt Syr. *mskyn* : 780.
pcqw’y/pcqw’d’r “to say, tell”. Syr. **’mr** : 85; 295; 435; 460; 515; 525; 630; 635; 650; 655; 660; 675; 730.
pcqw’d’rt Syr. *’ṃr* : 515; 630; 635; 650; 655; 660.
pcqw’d’rnt Syr. *’mryn* : 295; 435; 460; 675.
pcqw’d’rt Syr. *’mr’* : 85; 525.
pcqwyntq’ Syr. *n’mrwn* : 730.
pcqwyr “fear, fright”. Syr. **dḥlt’** : 5; 380; 480.
pcqwyry : 380.
pcqwyr “to fear”. Syr. **dḥl** : 260; 360; 365; 370; 475; 620; 660.
pcqwyrd’rnt Syr. *dḥlw* : 260.
pcqwyrt’ Syr. *tdḥlwn* : 360; 370.

pcqwyrt' Syr. *tdḥlkwn* : 475.
pcqwyrt' Syr. *dḥlw* : 365.
pcqwyrt Syr. *dḥl* : 620.
pcqwyrmsq Syr. *dḥlt* : 660.
pcqwyryq x-, sqw-, sqw-/m't "to be afraid". Syr. **dḥl hw'** : 585.
pcqwyryq m'tnt Syr. *dḥlyn hww* : 585.
pcm'r "measure of weight". Syr. **mny'** : 650; 655; 660; 675.
pcm'r Syr. *mnÿn* : 655; 660; 675.
pcmr "to number". Syr. **mn'** : 370.
pcmrtyt xnt Syr. *mnÿn 'nÿn :* 370.
pcng "cross". Syr. **zqyp'** : 745.
pcp'n "imminent". Syr. **'tyd** : 275; 750.
pcp'n x-, sqw-, swq-,/m't "to be prepared". Syr. **'tyd hw'** : 695.
pcp'n m't Syr. *'tyd'h* : 695.
pcpr "to remain". Syr. **qw'** : 75.
pcprty Syr. *qwyt* : 75.
pcrw "instead of, for". Syr. **ḥlp** : 125; 585.
pcš "to taste". Syr. **ṭ'm** : 760.
pcšntq' Syr. *nṭ'mwn* : 760.
pcywfs "to be transfigured". Syr. **'štḥlp** : 765.
pcywfs Syr. *'štḥlp* : 765.
pcxwd-γwny "abominable". Syr. **ndyd'** : 250.
pd'rty' "sustenance". Syr. **prs'** : 795.
pd'ty "dishonest". Syr. **'wl'** : 235.
pd'tqry "dishonest". Syr. **'wl'** : 225; 235.
pdq' "judgment". Syr. **dyn'** : 180; 190; 195; 270; 325.
pdq'y : 190.
pdq' wn-/qt- "to sue". Syr. **dwn** : 130.
pdq'wn't Syr. *ndwn* : 130.
pnc "five". Syr. **ḥmš'** : 660.
pnc's "fifty". Syr. **ḥmšyn** : 225.
pnt "close, near". Syr. **qryb'** : 515.
pnt b'w "to draw near to". Syr. **qrb** : 290.
pnt b'wd'rnt Syr. *qrbw hww* : 290.
pnt br "to drag, put near, bring near". Syr. Pa. conj. **qrb** : 335.
pnt brntq' Syr. *mqrbyn* : 335.
pnt prys/pr'γt "to arrive, go close(r)". Syr. **mṭ'** : 255; 415.
pnt pr'γt Syr. *mṭt* : 255.
pnt pr'γt Syr. *mṭ'*: 415.
pnyš "to lose". Syr. **'wbd** : 745.

pnyšt Syr. *nwbd* : 745.
pr "at, in, on, upon, for, to, by, with". Syr. **b-** : 1; 10; 20; 25; 30; 35; 40; 55; 60; 70; 75; 135; 150; 175; 185; 210; 215; 230; 235; 255; 265; 270; 325; 330; 340; 360; 365; 370; 375; 390; 400; 415; 420; 425; 430; 470; 480; 495; 505; 515; 520; 535; 590; 615; 625; 630; 655; 685; 755; 760; 795.
pr "on, over". Syr. **'l-** : 10; 50; 125; 135; 195; 200; 210; 340; 360; 370; 480; 505; 530; 555; 565; 655; 660; 670; 690; 775; 790; 795.
pr "to, for". Syr. **l-** : 35; 190; 215; 240; 295; 365; 500; 525; 535; 570; 605; 615; 620; 640.
pr "with". Syr. **ø** : 170; 550.
pr'γt : see prys.
prbxš/prbγt, prbxšt "to deliver". Syr. **'šlm** : 140; 270; 330; 335.
prbxšty̱ bwtq' Syr. *mštlm* : 140.
prbxšd̈'rnt Syr. *'šlmw* : 270.
prbxšntq' Syr. *mšlmyn* : 330.
prbxšntq' Syr. *nšlmwn* : 335.
prbxšny "traitor". Syr. **mšlmn'** : 545.
prbyr/prbyrt "to announce". Syr. **'tmh** : 275.
prbyrntqn Syr. *'tmhn* : 275.
prbyr/prbyrt "to tell". Syr. **'št'y** : 310.
prybyrnt Syr. *'št'yw* : 310.
pr cwty "why?". Syr. **lmn'** : 670.
prm: see wytwr.
prm'n "faithful". Syr. **mhymn** : 235; 655.
prm'nty' "forgiveness". Syr. **šwbqn'** : 30; 505.
prm'nty' Syr. *šwbqn'* : 30.
prm'nty' wn/qt "to forgive". Syr. **'štbq** : 390.
prm'nty' wnt' Syr. *tšbqwn* : 390.
prm'nty' qty̱ bntq' Syr. *nštbqwn* : 390.
pr ptcng swx'y/swxswt "to crucify". Syr. **zqp** : 270.
pr ptcng swxswd'rnt Syr. *zqpw* : 270.
prw : see dn...prw.
prwrtw "time". Syr. **zbn'** : 595.
prwyd/prwyst "to search". Syr. **bṣ'** : 210.
prwydt' Syr. *bṣw* : 210.
pryby "cloud". Syr. **'nn'** : 775.
pryc/ prγt "to leave". Syr. **šbq** : 435; 445; 525.
prycng'zw Syr. *šbq 'n'* : 435.
pryct'q' Syr. *tšbqwnn* : 445.
prγd'rt Syr. *šbqtn* : 525.

prymyθ "at this, for this, therefore". Syr. **b-hd'** : 185; 440; 615.
prymyθ frγn' "thus". Syr. **hkn'** : 135; 185; 280; 500; 790; 795.
prymyθ frγn' "likewise". Syr. **hkwt** : 145; 160.
prymyθ frγn' "likewise". Syr. **hkn' hwyt** : 515.
pryp/ pryft "to lead, take". Syr. **dbr** : 760.
pryֹpd'rt Syr. *ḍbr* : 760.
prys/pr'γt "to draw near, come". Syr. **mṭ'** : 155; 415.
pr'γt Syr. *ṃṭ'* : 155; 415.
pryֹš'yq " Pharisee". Syr. **pryš'** : 55; 245; 560 ; 565.
prys'yqty Syr. *prÿš'* : 55.
pryš'yqt Syr. *prÿš'* : 245; 560 ; 565.
pryt' "fence". Syr. **syg'** : 155.
pryθty b(w)-/qt- "to be sold". Syr. **'zdbn** : 365.
pryθtyt bnt Syr. *mzdb̈nn* : 365.
pryw : see xw.
prywnt : see xyd.
przbr "parable". Syr. **mtl'** : 155; 640; 645.
przbr "simile". Syr. **pl't'** : 425; 430; 440.
przbrt Syr. *p̈l't'* : 425; 430; 440.
ps "to ask, question". Syr. **š'l** : 45; 55; 440; 560; 575; 585; 590.
psynt Syr. *nš'lwn* : 45.
psd'rnt Syr. *š'lw* : 55; 560; 575.
ps't Syr. *nš'l* : 440.
pst' Syr. *š'lw* : 585; 590.
pstw "to deny". Syr. **kpr** : 375; 745.
pstw't Syr. *nkpwr* : 375; 745.
pstw'ng' Syr. *'kpwr* : 375.
psxnt wnyq x-/m't "to ridicule". Syr. **mmyq(-w)** : 245.
psxnt wnyq m'tnt Syr. *mmwyqyn hww* : 245.
pṣh' "Passah". Syr. **pṣh'** : 95.
pš'y "to throw away". Syr. **šd'** : 115.
pš'y Syr. *šd'*: 115.
pš'y "to cast". Syr. **'rm** : 460.
pš'd'rnt Syr. *'rmyw* : 460.
pšqr/pšqrt "to persecute". Syr. **rdp** : 320; 345.
pšqyrd'rnt Syr. *rdpw* : 320.
pšqyrnt Syr. *rdpyn* : 345.
pšt'y/pšt't, pšt'yt "to prepare". Syr. **ṭyb** : 30.
pšt'yy Syr. *tṭyb* : 30.
pšyd/pšyd'r "to recline at table". Syr. **'stmk** : 295.

pšyd'rt Syr. *'stmk* : 295.
pšyd/pšyd'r "to recline at table". Syr. **smk** : 785.
pšydtq' Syr. *nsmk* : 785.
pšys' "after". Syr. **btr** : 60; 65; 455; 745; 760.
pt'w "to endure". Syr. **sybr** : 345.
pt'wt Syr. *nsybr* : 345.
ptbd/ptbst "to understand". Syr. **'stkl** : 500; 640.
ptbtw Syr. *mstklw* : 500.
ptbd't Syr. *msktl* : 640.
ptfs/ptfs't "to read". Syr. **qry** : 175.
ptfs'tỵ 'yšt' Syr. *qrytwn* : 175.
ptγ'mbr "apostle". Syr. **šlyḥ'** : 540.
ptγ'mbryt Syr. *šlÿḥ'* : 540.
ptγwnt/ptγwst "to hide". Syr. **kssy** : 105.
ptγwstyt bnt Syr. *ntksswn* : 105.
ptγwš "to hear, listen". Syr. **šm'** : 10; 155; 180; 190; 245; 360; 520; 605; 620; 625; 640; 780.
ptγwšntq' Syr. *nšm'wn* : 180; 190.
ptγwšnt Syr. *šm'yn* : 180.
ptγwšmsq Syr. *šm' 'n'* : 190.
ptγwšt'-sqn Syr. *šm'yn 'ntwn* : 360.
ptγwšyq m't Syr. *šm'' hwt* : 520.
ptγwšt' Syr. *šm'w* : 155; 780.
ptγwšt' Syr. *šm'yn 'ntwn* : 640.
ptγwš Syr. *mšm'* : 605; 640.
ptγwšty qty Syr. *'štm't* : 620.
ptγwšd'rt Syr. *ṣm'* : 625.
ptγwšd'rnt Syr. *šm'w* : 10; 245; 640; 780.
ptq'ry "person". Syr. **prṣwp'** : 30.
ptnwb "to flog, beat". Syr. **ngd** : 330.
ptnwbntq' Syr. *nngdwn* : 330.
ptr "father". Syr. **'b'** : 15; 25; 205; 340; 370; 375; 385; 420; 430; 435; 465; 695.
ptry (nom.) : 205; 340; 385; 430.
ptry (acc.) : 25; 420; 435.
ptry (gen.) : 15; 370; 375; 695.
ptr' (abl.): 430.
ptr' (abl.) Syr. *ø* : 455.
ptr' (voc.): 465.
ptrq'n " inheritance". Syr. **yrtwt'** : 165.

ptrq'n ny's/ny't " to inherit ". Syr. **yrt** : 695.
ptrq'n ny'st' Syr. *yrtw* : 695.
ptrq'n xw'r "heir". Syr. **yrt'** : 165.
ptryt "against". Syr. **lwqbl** : 125.
ptrzty "exalted". Syr. **rm** : 250.
ptswc/ptswγt "to be light". Syr. **nhr** : 780.
ptswγtyt Syr. *mnhryn* : 780.
ptwx'y/ptxwst "to kill". Syr. **qṭl** : 135; 165; 365; 680.
ptxwsd'rt Syr. *qṭl* : 135.
ptxwsd'rnt Syr. *qṭlw* : 165.
ptxw'ym Syr. *nqṭlyw* : 165.
ptxw'ynt Syr. *qṭlyn* : 365.
ptxw'y Syr. *mqṭl* : 365.
ptxw'yt' Syr. *qṭlw* : 680.
ptwx'y/ptxwst "to kill, put to death". Syr. **myt** : 345.
ptxw'yntq' Syr. *nmytwn* : 345.
ptxw'y : see ptwx'y.
ptyfn "part". Syr. **mnt'** : 530.
ptyfnw : 530.
ptyqn "debtor". Syr. **ḥyb'** : 220; 225.
ptyrn "cause, ground, reason". Syr. **mlt'** : 120.
ptyθy' wn-/qt- "to despise". Syr. **šwṭ** : 240.
ptyθy' Syr. *nšwṭ* : 240.
ptyθy' wn/qt "to revile". Syr. **ṣḥy** : 605.
ptyθy'qθ'rnt Syr. *ṣḥyw* : 605.
ptz'n "knowledge". Syr. **md‘'** : 30.
ptz'n "to recognize". Syr. **'štwd‘** : 300.
ptz'nd'rnt Syr. *'štwd‘w* : 300.
pw "without". Syr. **dl'** : 25.
pwrc'wnt "debtors". Syr. **ḥÿb'** : 220.
pwrny "filled". Syr. **'tmly** : 15.
pwsty "Scriptures, writing, bill". Syr. **ktb'** : 175; 220; 225; 290; 305; 500.
pwstyt Syr. *ktb̈'* : 290; 305; 500.
pwsty "writing". Syr. **ø** : 285; 495.
pwstyt : 285; 495.
pwx'y/pwxst "to cut off". Syr. **psq** : 115.
pwx'y Syr. *pswq* : 115.
py'm byr/byrt "to find the cure". Syr. **'t'sy** : 630.
py'm byrd'rt Syr. *'t'sy* : 630.
pyd'r "writing tablet". Syr. **pnqyt'** : 5.

pyd'r: see cn...pyd'r
pyd'r : see cywyθ pyd'r
pyn "to open". Syr. **pṯḥ** : 785.
pynntq' Syr. *npthwn* : 785.
pyr "to entrust". Syr. **hymn** : 235.
pyrtq' Syr. *mhymn* : 235.
pyrnm "before". Syr. **qdm** : 150; 275.
pyrnmcyq "first, ". Syr. **qdmy'** : 145; 160; 220; 650.
pyrnmcyqt Syr. *qdmÿ'* : 160.
pyrnms' "before, in front of ". Syr. **qdm** : 25; 245; 270; 335; 370; 375; 675; 680/685; 765.
pyrnyq "faithful". Syr. **mhymn** : 235; 240.
pyrnyq Syr. *mhÿmn'* : 235; 240.
pyrs': see cn...pyrs'
pyrỵq x-, sqw-, sqw-/m't "to believe". Syr. **hymn hw'** : 575.
pyrỵq m'tnt Syr. *hymnw hww* : 575.
pyšt "but, afterwards, then, while". Syr. **dyn** : 35; 115; 130; 140; 150; 165; 205; 245; 270; 280; 330; 335; 345; 370; 375; 385; 395; 415; 425; 465; 515; 525; 530; 550; 560; 565; 575; 580; 600; 605; 635; 640; 680; 685; 765.
pyz/pyšt "to slap". Syr. **mḥ'** : 125.
pỵẓ̇t Syr. *mḥ'* : 125.
pyšd'rt Syr. *nqš* : 775.

r'γ "plain". Syr. **pq't'** : 545.
r'γy : 545.
rmθ' "Arimathea". Syr. **rmt'** : 260
r'θ "way, road". Syr. **'wrḥ'** : 30; 35; 135; 150; 305; 520.
rθ : 135.
r'θp'n "robber". Syr. **gys'** : 515.
r'θp'nty Syr. *gÿs'* : 515.
r'y "to weep, cry". Syr. **bk'** : 410.
r'yt'q' Syr. *tbkwn* : 410.
rm "people". Syr. **'m'** : 15; 30; 335; 505; 545; 690.
rmỵỵ : 15; 545.
rmỵ: 30.
rmt' Syr. *'m̈m'* : 335; 505; 690.
rm "people". Syr. **ø**: 70; 275.
rmỵ : 70.
rmyy : 275.
ršt' "truly". Syr. **'myn** : 145; 180; 320; 350; 400; 410; 420.

ršty'q "true". Syr. **šrr'** : 235.
  pr ršty'q "indeed, truly". Syr. **šryr'yt**: 305; 795.
rw'n "soul". Syr. **npš'** : 365.
rwγn "oil". Syr. **mšḥ'** : 220; 505.
rwp "to reap". Syr. **ḥṣd** : 665; 670.
  rwpy tγw Syr. *ḥṣd 'nt* : 665.
  rwpmsq zw Syr. *ḥṣd 'n'* : 670.
rwt "river". Syr. **'br'** : 60.
  rwty : 60.
rwxšn "bright". Syr. **nhyrt'** : 775.
  rwxšny : 775.
rwxšny'q "light". Syr. **nwhr'** : 100; 205; 230; 765.
  rwxšny'qy : 100; 230.
rwxšny'q θbr "to give light, shine". Syr. **nhr** : 35; 200.
  rwxšny'q θbrw Syr. *mnhrw* : 35.
  rwxšny'q θbrty Syr. *mnhr* : 200.
rync'q "child". Syr. **ṭly'** : 10; 30; 35; 455.
  ryncq': 30.
  rync'qty Syr. *ṭlÿ'* : 455.
ryt "face". Syr. **prṣwp'** : 765.
ryt 'ngm'ny' "openly". Syr. **'yn b-gl'** : 430.
rytr "worst". Syr. **bṣyr** : 90.
ryž "will". Syr. **ṣbwt** : 190.
ryž "will". Syr. **ṣbyn'** : 195; 620.
ryž "will". Syr. **ø** : 370.

s'c "to be proper, behove". Syr. **wl' hw'** : 495; 615.
  s'št Syr. *wl' hw* : 495; 615.
s'cyq x-, sqw-, swq-/m't "to be proper". Syr. **zdq hw'** : 500.
  s'cyq m't Syr. *zdq hw'* : 500.
s'n "enemy". Syr. **b'ldbb'** : 20; 25; 680.
  s'nt Syr. *b'ldbbÿ*: 20; 680.
  s'nty Syr. *b'ldbbÿ*: 25.
s'pt "left". Syr. **sml'** : 695; 720.
s'rb'γ "tower". Syr. **mgdl'** : 135; 155.
s't "all, whole, utter". Syr. **kl** : 10; 20; 25; 115; 185; 245; 350; 370; 505; 625; 685; 795.
sdwm "Sodom". Syr. **sdwm** : 320.
sγtm'n "all". Syr. **kl** : 135.
sq' "high". Syr. **rm** : 765.

sq'tr "more". Syr. **ytyr** : 100.
sq'tryqstr "much more". Syr. **ytyr'yt** : 365.
skrywt'yq "Iscariot". Syr. **skrywṭ'** : 545.
sm'n "sky, heaven". Syr. **šm̈y'** : 75; 110; 375.
sm'ny Syr. *šm̈y'* : 75; 110.
sm'n "height". Syr. **rwm'** : 35.
sm'ncyq "heavenly". Syr. **ø** : 30.
sm'ncyq "heavenly". Syr. : **d-šmy'** : 645.
smynt "blind". Syr. **smy'** : 580; 620.
smynty : 620.
smynt "blind". Syr. **ø** : 620.
smynt x-, sqw-, swq-/m't "to be blind". Syr. **smy' hw'** : 560; 575; 600.
smyṇt m't Syr. *smy' hw'* : 560; 575.
smynt m'tym Syr. *smy' hwyt* : 600.
sn/st "to go up, arise". Syr. **slq** : 135; 480.
snymq' Syr. *slqyn ḥnn* : 135.
snntqn Syr. *slq̈n* : 480.
sn'm θbr "to baptize". Syr. **''md** : 55; 60; 70; 75; 105.
sn'm θbrw Syr. *''md* : 70; 75.
sn'm θbrysq Syr. *m'md tyw* : 55.
sn'm θbr'msqn Syr. *m'md 'n'* : 55.
sn'm θbryq m't Syr. *m'md hw'* : 60.
sn'm θbrtỵq' Syr. *m'md* : 75.
sn'm θbrtysq Syr. *m'md* : 105.
sn'm θbr "to baptize". Syr. **ø** : 150; 200.
sn'm θbrynỵ: 150; 200.
sn'y "to wash". Syr. **'šyg** : 555; 565.
sn'ẏ Syr. *'šyg* : 555.
sn'd'rm Syr. *'šygt* : 555; 565.
sng "stone". Syr. **k'p'** : 175.
sng "stone". Syr. **ø** : 175.
sng "Peter". Syr. **k'p'** : 540.
sngs'r wn-/qt- "to stone". Syr. **rgm** : 160.
sngs'r qθ'rnt Syr. *rgmw* : 160.
sp's "service, ministration". Syr. **tšmšt'** : 525; 790.
sp'xš "to serve". Syr. **plḥ** : 25; 240.
sp'xšym Syr. *nplwḥ* : 25.
spxšy Syr. *mplḥ* : 240.
sp'xš "to serve, assist". Syr. **šmš** : 525; 735.
spxšw Syr. *mšmšw* : 525.

spxšd'rym Syr. *šmšn* : 735.
spncyrspn "manager, caretaker". Syr. **rbyt'** : 215; 225; 790.
spncyrspny: 225.
spncyrspny' "management". Syr. **rbt bytwt'** : 215; 220.
spty "full". Syr. **mšmly'** : 425.
spty b(w)-/qt- "to be fulfilled". Syr. **'štlm** : 495.
spty by Syr. *nštlm* : 495.
spyty b(w)-/qt- "to become white". Syr. **ḥwr** : 765.
spyty qtnt Syr. *ḥwrw* : 765.
sr "head". Syr. **ø** : 135.
sryt : 135.
srd "year". Syr. **šnt'** : 585; 590.
srdt Syr. *šn̈'* : 585; 590.
sry "horn". Syr. **qrn'** : 20.
stq "bone". Syr. **gr̈m'** : 485.
stqy : 485.
stw "hundred". Syr. **m''** : 220; 225.
stwr "sheep". Syr. **'rb'** : 690.
stwrt Syr. *'r̈b'* : 690.
sty: *see x*.
sty'wy "being, self". Syr. **qnwm'** : 185.
swq : *see x*.
swqnt xwr "to swear". Syr. **mwmt' ym'** : 25.
swqnt xwrd'rt Syr. *mẅmt'ym'* : 25.
swqyq x-, sqw-, swq-/m't "to live, be". Syr. **'yt hw'** : 40.
swqyq m't Syr. *'ytwhy hw'* : 40.
swxsty b(w)-/qt- "to vanish". Syr. **'štql** : 300.
swxsty qty Syr. *'štql* : 300.
swx'y/swxst "to take away, take up". Syr. **šql** : 65; 665; 670; 745.
sxwytq' Syr. *šq̇l* : 65.
swx'yy Syr. *šql 'nt* : 665.
swx'ÿÿmsq Syr. *šql 'n'* : 670.
swx'ÿt Syr. *nšqwl* : 745.
sy'q "shadow". Syr. **ṭll'** : 35.
sy'qt Syr. *ṭl̈l'*: 35.
sy'q "shadow, shelter, dwelling". Syr. **mṭll'** : 235.
sy'qt Syr. *mṭlÿ* : 235.
sycy "sparrow". Syr. **ṣpryn** : 365; 370.
sycyt Syr. *ṣpr̈yn* : 365.
syctyty Syr. *ṣpr̈'* : 370.

syd "to appear, seem". Syr. **'tḥzy** : 515.
sydt Syr. *mtḥz'* : 515.
syn "to lead up". Syr. **'sq** : 760.
synd'rt Syr. *'sq* : 760.

š'n "to rejoice". Syr. **'štbhr** : 200.
š'nt' Syr. *tštbhrwn* : 200.
š'št db'ny b(w)-/qt- "to be scattered". Syr.**'ttbdr** : 445.
š'št db'ny bwtq' Syr. *ttbdrwn* : 445.
šfrs "to be ashamed". Syr. **bht** : 165; 215.
šfrsntq' Syr. *nbhtwn* : 165.
šfrsmq' Syr. *bht 'n'* : 215.
šqwrθy' "anguish, tribulation". Syr. **'wlṣn'** : 415; 450.
šm'r/šm'rt "to think". Syr. **sbr** : 270; 480.
šm'ryq m'tnt Syr. *sbryn hwyn* : 270.
šm'ryq m'tnt Syr. *sbryn hww* : 480.
šm'r/šm'rt "to lay up, think". Syr. **'tḥšb** : 10.
šm'ryq m'tnt Syr. *mtḥšbyn hww* : 10.
šm'r' "thought". Syr. **mḥšbt'** : 480.
šm'ryt Syr. *mḥšb̈t'* : 480.
šm'x : see tyw.
šmnw "the devil, Satan". Syr. **ø** : 640.
šmpd "Sabbath, Saturday". Syr. **šbt'** : 560; 565.
šmγwn "Simon". Syr. **šm'wn** : 540.
šmγwn sng "Simon Peter". Syr. **k'p'** : 465; 760; 770.
šn : see xw.
št't "eighty". Syr. **tmn'yn** : 225.
šts "eighteen". Syr. **tmnt'sr** : 135.
štyq "third". Syr. **tlt'** : 500.
šw-/yt "to go". Syr. **'zl** : 30; 290; 435; 515; 555; 740.
šwyq' Syr. *t'zl* : 30.
šwyq m'tnt Syr. *'zlyn hww* : 290.
šwyqm't Syr. *'zl hw'* : 290.
šwng' Syr. *'zl 'n'* : 435.
šw' Syr. *zl* : 515; 555.
šwntq' Syr. *n'zlwn* : 740.
šw-/yt "to go, proceed". Syr. **rd'** : 520.
šwyntqn Syr. *rdyn* : 520.
šy : see xw.
šy "three". Syr. **tlt'** : 510.

šy’ ’br/’brt “to remember”. Syr. **‘hd** : 315; 415.
šy’ ’brt’ Syr. *‘hdw* : 315.
šy’ ’brt Syr. *‘hd’* : 415.
šy’ qt “to remember”. Syr. **‘hd** : 25.
šy’qθ’rt Syr. *‘hd* : 25.
šy̤lwḥ’ “Siloam”. Syr. **šy̤lwḥ’** : 135.
šyr “very”. Syr. **ø** : 765.
šyrγwzy “friend”. Syr. **rḥm’**: 230.
šyrγwzyt Syr. *r̈ḥm’* : 230.
šyr “good”. Syr. **ṭb’** : 90; 190; 530; 645.
šyry : 90; 645.
šyryt Syr. *ṭb̈t’* : 190.
šyry Syr. *ṭbt’* : 530.
šyr “good”. Syr. **špyr** : 770.
šyr’qty “good, honest”. Syr. **ṭb’** : 655.
šyr’qt’ : 655.

t’ry “darkness”. Syr. **ḥšwk’** : 35; 360.
t’ry bw-/qt- “to become dark, grow dark”. Syr. **ḥšk** : 295.
t’ry by Syr. *mḥšk* : 295.
tbryws swmtr “Lake Tiberias”. Syr. **ym’ dṭybrys** : 455.
tbyž “to gain”. Syr. **qn’** : 750.
tbyžt Syr. *nqn’* : 745.
tγ’m “ford”. Syr. **ø** : 60; 105.
tyt : see tys.
tγw “you”. Syr. **’nt** : 30; 45; 50; 55; 75; 225; 440; 470; 515; 570; 605; 625; 630; 660; 665.
tw’ Syr. *–k* : 50; 110; 115; 125; 130; 220; 225; 440; 465; 510; 570; 600; 35; 650; 655; 660; 665; 710; 730.
tw’ Syr. *l-k* : 115; 130; 515; 525; 775.
tw’ Syr. *l-ky* : 85.
tw’ Syr *ø* : 655.
šm’x “you” Syr. ***’ntwn*** : 60; 150; 200; 210; 240; 255; 360; 410; 415; 435; 480; 485; 605; 635; 640.
šm’x Syr. *-kwn* : 120; 125; 135; 150; 175; 230; 235; 245; 255; 320; 350; 360; 370; 380; 385; 410; 420; 425; 430; 475; 480; 495; 580; 695; 715; 735; 755; 780; 785; 795.
šm’x Syr. *l-kwn* : 230; 345; 720.
šm’xy Syr. *-kwn* : 215; 230; 330; 335; 420.
šm’xy Syr. *-lkwn* : 325; 330; 345; 390; 415; 435.

šm'x Syr. *ø* : 235; 315; 435; 700; 715; 725.
tm "hell". Syr. **ghn'** "Gehenna" : 365.
tmy' : 365.
tmf'r: see *tmp'r*.
tmp'r "body". Syr. **pgr'** : 115; 275; 365.
tmf'r : 115.
tmp'ry : 275.
trγz'y wn-/qt- "to compel". Syr. **'lṣ** : 290.
trγz'y qθ'rnt Syr. *'lṣw* : 290.
trn "docile". Syr. **tmym'** : 330.
tš "to flee". Syr. **'rq** : 345.
tšt' Syr. *'rwqw*: 345.

twmd'rt "he knocked". Syr. **ṇqš** : 785.

twž "to repay". Syr. **pr'** : 755.
twžtq' Syr. *nprw'* : 755.
txm "seed". Syr. **zr''** : 645.
txmy : 645.
tym "again". Syr. **twb** : 45; 120; 410; 420; 435; 560; 570; 600.
tym "inn". Syr. **pwtq'** : 505.
tymp'šy "innkeeper". Syr. **pwtqy'** : 510.
tys/tγt "to go in". Syr. **'l** : 295; 520; 585; 590.
tγty Syr. *'l* : 295; 520; 590.
tγty xcy Syr. *'l* : 585.

θ'm' "Twin". Syr. **t'm'**: 395.
θ'wm' "Thomas". Syr. **t'wm'** : 395; 540.
θb'rγwž "beggar". Syr. **mḥdr** : 215.
θbr-/θbrt "to give, grant". Syr. **yhb** : 25; 30; 50; 170; 205; 240; 295; 425; 510; 650; 675; 700; 725; 750; 790.
θbr't Syr. *nṫl* : 25; 30.
θbrym Syr. *nṫl* : 50.
θbrntq' Syr. *yhbyn* : 170.
θbrtyq' Syr. *nṫl* : 240; 425; 750.
θbrd'rt Syr. *yḥb* : 205; 295; 510; 650.
θbrng' Syr. *yhb 'n'* : 510.
θbrt' Syr. *hbw* : 675.
θbrd'ryšt' Syr. *yhbtwn* : 700; 725.
θbry Syr. *ntl* : 790.

w'b/wγt- "to say, speak, call". Syr. **'mr** : 10; 15; 50; 55; 65; 70; 90; 125;

140; 145; 165; 170; 215; 220; 225; 255; 265; 280; 300; 305; 395; 430; 440; 510; 550; 555; 565; 570; 575; 580; 585; 590; 595; 600; 605; 610; 625; 630.

w'byntqn Syr. *'mryn* : 10; 280; 305.
w'byntqn Syr. *'mryn hww* : 570.
w'bng' Syr. *'mr 'n'* : 430.
w'bysq Syr. *'mr 'nt* : 50; 440; 570.
w'bnt Syr. *'mrw* : 55; 170.
w'bnt Syr. *'mryn* : 145; 395.
w'b Syr. *'ṃr* : 65; 70; 145; 225; 395.
w'b Syr. *'mr'* : 90.
w'b Syr. *'ṁr*: 215; 220; 225; 265.
w'bmsqn Syr. *'mr 'n'* : 575.
w'bt'sq Syr. *'mryn 'ntwn* : 580.
w'byq m'tnt Syr. *'mryn hww* : 300; 565.
w'byq m't Syr. *'mr hw'* : 550.
wγty bwt Syr. *mt'mr* : 395.
wγd'rt Syr *'ṃr* : 15; 50; 140; 165; 220; 510; 550; 555; 565; 575; 595; 600; 610; 630.
wγd'rt Syr *'mryn* : 570.
wγd'rm Syr. *'mrt* : 255; 600.
wγd'rnt Syr. *'mryn* : 170; 550; 555; 595; 600; 605; 625.
wγd'rnt Syr. *'mrw* : 50; 580; 585; 590.
wγd'rnt Syr. *'mrn* : 280.
wγd'rnt Syr. *'mr* : 280.
wγty qty Syr. *'t'mr*: 125.

w'c "to repudiate". Syr. **šr'** : 115.
w'ct Syr. *šr'*: 115.

w'nc'nw "as, just as, like". Syr. **'yk (d-)** : 1; 20; 75; 280; 290; 325; 330; 355; 690; 755; 765.

w'nc'nw "as". Syr. **'ykn' d-** : 50; 190; 385.

w'nc'nw "as". Syr. **'ykn'** : 180.

w'nw "so, in this way, thus". Syr. **ø** : 10; 15; 50; 55; 65; 70; 90; 135; 145; 165; 170; 215; 220; 225; 245; 250; 270; 280; 285; 290; 300; 325; 380; 390; 395; 435; 445; 460; 475; 480; 490; 500; 510; 515; 525; 550; 565; 570; 575; 580; 595; 600; 605; 610; 625; 630; 635; 645; 655; 660; 665; 675; 715; 730; 740; 800.

w'št : see 'wšty.

w't "spirit". Syr. **rwḥ'** : 40; 480; 485.
w'ty : 485.

w'xš "word, speech ". Syr. **mlt'** : 270; 495; 525.

w'xšt Syr. *m̈l'* : 495; 525.
w'xš "speech". Syr. **ø** : 380.
w'xš pwx'y "to decide, establish". Syr. **psq** : 590.
w'xš pwxsty m'tnt Syr. *psqw hww* : 590.
wd's: see wyd's
wdrz "to worry". Syr. **zy'** : 480.
wdrzt'sqn Syr. *mtzy'yn 'ntwn* : 480.
wdy "there". Syr. **tmn** : 80; 280; 535.
wdy "there, in it". Syr. **bh** : 155.
wn-/qt- "to do, to make, to act, to perform, to cause". Syr. **'bd** : 20; 170; 185; 190; 215; 230; 405; 515; 555; 560; 570; 600; 620; 715; 720; 740; 770; 795.
wntyq' Syr. *n'bd* : 170.
wn'm Syr. *''bd* : 215.
wn'm Syr. *'bd 'n'* : 405.
wnq' Syr. *''bd* : 215.
wnt' Syr. *'bdw* : 230.
wn't Syr. *'b̈d* : 185; 620.
wnymq' Syr. *n'bd* : 770.
wntysq Syr. *'bd* : 795.
qθ'rt Syr. *'ḅd* : 20; 230; 550; 555; 600.
qθ'rnt Syr. *'bdw* : 190.
qwn' Syr. *'bd* : 515.
qwrwn Syr. *m'bd* : 190.
qrwn Syr. *m'bd* : 570.
qθ'ryšt' Syr. *'bdtwn* : 715.
qθ'rt' Syr. 'bdtwn : 720; 740.
wny : see xw
wnyq wn-/qt- "to conquer, overcome". Syr. **zk'** : 450.
wnyq qθ'rm Syr. *'n'zkt* : 450.
wr' "interest". Syr. **rbyt'** : 670.
wr''y : 670.
wr' wn-/qt- "to increase". Syr. **ytr** : 655; 660.
wr'qθ'rt Syr. *'wtr* : 655; 660.
wr'n "lamb". Syr. **'mr'** : 325.
wr'nt Syr. *'mr̈'* : 325.
wrcwny' "wonder, prodigy". Syr. **tdmwrt'** : 175.
wrn "to believe". Syr. **hymn** : 150; 210; 435; 440; 445; 485; 630; 635.
wrnd'ryšt' Syr. *hymntwn* : 150; 435.
wrnd'rnt Syr. *hymnw* : 150.

wrnwtyšt' Syr. *thymnwn* : 150.
wrnt'sqn Syr. *mhymnyn 'ntwn* : 210.
wrnymsqn Syr. *mhymnyn ḥnn* : 440.
wrnt' Syr. *hymnw* : 445.
wrnyq m'tnt Syr. *mhymnyn hww* : 485.
wrnysqn Syr. *mhymn 'nt* : 630.
wrn'm Syr. *'hym*n : 630.
wrn'msq Syr. *mhymn 'n'*: 635.
wrn "to think". Syr. **sbr** : 210.
wrnt'sq Syr. *msbryn 'ntwn* : 210.
wrycd'r "to pour". Syr. **nṣl** : 505.
wrycd'rt Syr. *nṣḷ* : 505.
wštm'x "heavenly kingdom, Paradise". Syr. **mlkwt'** : 150; 645; 695.
wxr "voice". Syr. **ql'** : 180; 190; 210; 775.
wxš "to save, redeem". Syr. **prq** : 20.
wxš't Syr. *nprq* : 20.
wxš'mnty "salvation". Syr. **pwrqn'** : 20.
wxš'mnty wn-/qt- "to save, redeem". Syr. **pwrqn' 'bd**: 15.
qθ'rt wẋš'mnty Syr. *'bd pwrqn'*: 15.
wy' : see xw.
wy'q "place". Syr. **dwk'** : 290.
wy'q "place". Syr. **'tr'** : 445.
pr wy'q "immediately". Syr. **mḥd'** : 475.
wyc'wqy' "testimony". Syr. **shdwt'** : 40; 195; 200; 205; 335.
wyc'wqy' θbr "to bear witness". Syr. **'shd** : 70; 80; 195; 200; 205; 215.
wyc'wqy' θ'br Syr. *'shd* : 70.
wyc'wqy' θbrd'rm Syr. *'shdt* : 80.
wyc'wqy' θbr'msqn Syr. *mshd 'n'* : 195.
wyc'wqy' θbrd'rt Syr. *'shd* : 200.
wyc'wqy' θbrntqn Syr. *shdyn* : 205; 215.
wycn/ wyct "to choose". Syr. **gb'** : 315; 530; 535.
wycnd'rm Syr. *gbyt* : 315.
wycnd'rt Syr. *gbt* : 530.
wycnd'rt Syr. *gḇ'* : 535.
wyd'γty "then". Syr. **hydyn** : 285; 690; 695; 705; 720; 730; 755.
wyd'γty "when". Syr. **'mty** : 185; 335; 425.
wyd'rt : see wyn.
wyd's "to wonder, be surprised, marvel". Syr. **'tdmr**: 5; 185; 615.
wyd'sd'rnt Syr. *'tdmrw* : 5.
wyd'st' Syr. *ttdmrwn* : 185.

wd's Syr. *mtdmrw* : 615.
wyd's-γwny "something amazing". Syr. **ø** : 275.
wyn/wyt "to see". Syr. **ḥz'** : 65; 70; 75; 150; 165; 210; 280; 285; 385; 410; 420; 480; 485; 585; 600; 630; 635; 710; 730; 760.
wyny Syr. *ḥz'* : 75.
wynt'q' Syr. *tḥzwnn* : 410.
wyng' Syr. *'ḥz* : 420.
wynntqn Syr. *ḥzyn* : 480.
wynt' Syr. *ḥzw* : 480.
wyntqn Syr. *ḥz'* : 585.
wynmsqn Syr. *ḥz' 'n'* : 600.
wynynt Syr. *nḥzwn* : 635.
wynt'sqn Syr. *ḥzyn 'ntwn* : 485.
wynt'sqn Syr. *ḥzyn 'ntwn* : 635.
wynntq' Syr. *nḥzwn* : 760.
wyd'rt Syr. *ḥẓ'* : 65.
wyd'rm Syr. *ḥzyt* : 70.
wyd'ryšt' Syr. *ḥzytwn* : 150; 210.
wyd'rym Syr. *ḥzyn* : 280; 710; 730.
wyd'rnt Syr. *ḥz'w* : 165.
wyd'rnt Syr. *ḥzw* : 285; 385; 635.
wyd'ry Syr. *ḥzyty* : 630.
wyn'wcyq qt- "to appear". Syr. **'tḥzy** : 310; 765.
wyn'wcyq qty Syr. *'tḥzy* : 310.
wyn'wcyq qtnt Syr. *'tḥzyw* : 765.
pr wyn'wcyqy' "plainly". Syr. **gly'yt** : 440.
wyn'mnty "form, vision". Syr. **ḥzw'** : 210.
wyny : see wyn and xw.
wyny b(w)-/qt- "to receive sight". Syr. **'tḥzy** : 560; 565.
wyny qtyštyw Syr. *'tḥzy lk* : 560.
wyny qtym Syr. *'tḥzy ly* : 565.
wyny b(w)-/qt- "to receive sigth". Syr. **ḥz'** : 575.
wyny qty Syr. *ḥz'* : 575.
wyrq "wolf". Syr. **d'b'** : 330.
wyrqyšty Syr. *d'b̈'* : 330.
wyrwxš "to shine". Syr. **nhr** : 765.
wyrwxšd'rt Syr. *ṇhr* : 765.
wysp "each, every, all, ". Syr. **kl** : 420; 440; 650.
wyspw : 420; 430; 650.
wyspw 'dy "everyone, all". Syr. **klnš** : 5; 345; 370.

wyspw ’dy “each”. Syr. **’nš’** : 445.
wyspw ’dy “anyone”. Syr. **kl** : 640.
wyspw xwny ’dy “everyone”. Syr. **kl mn** : 120; 675.
wyšnt/y : see xw.
wyt’p’mnty “sunrise”. Syr. **dnḥ’** : 35.
wytwr qt “until”. Syr. **‘dm’ d-** : 575.
wytwr qw ...prm “up to, as far as, until”. Syr. **‘dm’ l-** : 40; 90; 265; 345.
wytwr qw qšy prm “until now, so far”. Syr. **‘dm’ lhš’** : 425; 485.
wyθrb “to fright”. Syr. **’trhb** : 475.
wyθrbd’rnt Syr. *’trhbw* : 475.
wyθrbnync “troubled”. Syr. **rhybty** : 530.
wyws “[day] to dawn ”. Syr. **ngh** : 535.
wywsd’rt Syr. *nght* : 535.
wyzr “true”. Syr. **šryr** : 195.
wyzrw : 195.
wyžt’ wn-/qt- “to stay”. Syr. **qw’**: 1.
wyžt’ qθ’rt Syr. *qwyt*: 1.

x-, sqw-, swq-/m’t “to be”. Syr. **hw’** : 5; 15; 40; 45; 55; 60; 80; 155; 160; 165; 175; 185; 195; 200; 205; 210; 220; 225; 230; 235; 240; 245; 250; 255; 260; 270; 275; 280; 295; 300; 315; 370; 380; 395; 445; 475; 480; 485; 495; 520; 530; 550; 555; 560; 565; 575; 580; 590; 595; 600; 605; 610; 630; 635; 660; 670; 675; 700; 705; 725; 730; 775.
xcy Syr. *hẉ* : 5; 15; 185; 195; 235; 250; 280; 565; 575; 590; 595; 600; 610.
xcy Syr. *ø* : 250; 550.
xcy Syr. *hy* : 40; 530.
xcy Syr. *-w* : 60; 80; 165; 580; 630; 635; 775.
xnt Syr. *-yn* : 160.
xnt Syr. *’nwn* : 230.
xnt Syr. *ø* : 275.
sty Syr. *’yt* : 175; 205; 210; 485; 675.
sty Syr. *hẉ* : 255; 555.
m’t Syr. *hwt* : 15.
m’t Syr. *’yt hw’* : 155; 660.
m’t Syr. *’yt* : 160.
m’t Syr. *hw’*: 200; 260; 270; 275; 300; 380; 395.
m’t Syr. *’ytyh hwt* : 560.
m’t Syr. *ø* : 520; 550.
m’t wy’ Syr. *’yt hwt l-h* : 520.

m'tym Syr. *hwyt* : 495; 700; 705; 725; 730.
m't' Syr. *hwt* : 80.
'ym Syr. *'n'* : 45; 475; 480; 670.
'ym Syr. *hwyt* : 445.
'ym Syr. *'yty*: 45.
'ym Syr. *ḥnn* : 610.
'yš Syr. *'nt* : 45; 45; 605; 665.
'yš Syr. *'ytyk* : 55.
'yštyw Syr. *'nt*: 220; 225.
'yšt' Syr. *'nwn* : 245.
'yšt' Syr. *hwytwn* : 315.
'yšt' Syr. *'ntwn* : 370.
swqy Syr. *nqw'* : 295.
nyst "is not". Syr. **lyt** : 85; 240; 315; 350; 485.

x' : see xw.

x'n' "house". Syr. **byt'** : 20; 155; 220; 355; 520.
x'ny : 20; 155; 355; 520.
x'nyt : 220.

x'nt : see xwny and xyd.

x'nycyq "relative". Syr. **bny byt'** : 355.
x'nycyqty Syr. *bnÿ byt'* : 355.

xnt : see x-.

xr "donkey". Syr. **ḥmr** : 505.
xry : 505.

xrt : see xyr.

xrycq "prostitute". Syr. **znyt'** : 150.
xrycqt Syr. *znÿt'* : 150.

xšp- "night". Syr. **lly'**: 265.
xšp': 265.

xšywnqy' "(earthly) kingdom". Syr. **mlkwt'** : 760.

xšywny "king". Syr. **mlk'** : 330; 695; 715.
xšywnyty Syr. *m̈lk'* : 330.

xw "he". Syr. **hw** : 75; 140; 275; 290; 300; 430; 515; 550; 565; 585; 590; 595; 635; 775.
wyny Syr. *-h* : 15; 30; 40; 50; 55; 70; 75; 110; 130; 140; 145; 160; 165; 170; 185; 190; 210; 220; 225; 295; 355; 390; 395; 440; 505; 510; 520; 525; 560; 675.
wyn Syr. *–h*: 400.
wyny Syr. *-hy* : 105; 280; 440; 540.
wny Syr. *-h* : 550; 555; 590; 595; 600; 605; 620; 630; 635; 655; 665;

670; 675; 690; 695; 720; 770; 785; 790; 795.
wny Syr. *-lh* : 585.
wny Syr. *-hy* : 560; 585; 590; 605; 625.
wny Syr. *-why* : 675; 690; 720; 760; 765.
wny Syr. *-ywhy* : 795.
wnyy Syr. *lhw* : 560.
šy Syr. *-hy* : 150; 160; 165; 270; 290; 300; 630.
šy Syr. *-h* : 155; 550; 625.
šy Syr. *-ḣ* : 115; 520; 745; 750.
šy Syr. *-ywhy* : 790.
wy' Syr. *l-ḣ* : 415.
wy' Syr. *-ḣ* : 115; 415; 525; 530.
x' Syr. *-lḣ* : 520.
x' Syr. *ø* : 525.
pryw "of whom, on him, about him, of him". Syr. *'lwhy* : 65; 75; 75; 505; 515; 570; 575.
pryw " of whom, on him". Syr. *bh*: 155.
wyšnt "they". Syr. **hṇwn** : 310; 465; 475; 520; 605; 670; 730.
wyšnt Syr. *–hwn* : 10; 30; 55; 110; 135; 145; 160; 165; 175; 245; 290; 300; 340; 355; 380; 390; 445; 460; 470; 475; 480; 490; 495; 500; 550; 555; 565; 575; 595; 615; 645; 650; 675; 695; 760; 775.
wyšnt Syr. *–hnwn* : 720.
wyšnt Syr. *ø* : 230; 275.
wyšnty Syr. *-hwn* : 10; 165; 220; 230; 295; 300; 305; 330; 335; 380; 395; 475; 500; 535; 545; 765; 780.
wyšnty Syr. *l-hwn* : 85.
wyšnty Syr. *'nwn* : 135; 170; 385; 540; 680; 690; 760; 785.
šn Syr. *'nwn* : 210; 345; 680.
šn Syr. *'ylyn* : 30; 45; 175; 195; 365.
wyšnt Syr. *'ylyn* : 50 ; 170; 190; 360.
wyšnty Syr. *'ylyn* : 35.

xw xcy "he is". Syr. **hwyw** : 635.
xw'qry' wn-/qt- "to gain". Syr. **'tgr** : 650.
xw'qry' qθ'rt Syr. *'ttgr* : 650.
xw'r "sister". Syr. **ḥt'** : 520; 525.
xw'rnt "right". Syr. **ymyn'** : 460; 695.
xwny "that one". Syr. **'yn'**: 90.
xwny "that". Syr. **ḣw** : 145; 210; 215; 345; 610; 620; 630; 795.
xwnyy : 610.
x'nt "those" Syr. **hṅwn** : 135; 170; 210; 540.

x'nt Syr. *l-hnwn* : 680.
x'nt Syr. *-hwn* : 785.
x'nt Syr. **hnwn 'ylyn** : 785.

xwny 'dy "that one who, the person who, he who(m)". Syr. **ṁn** : 75; 115; 125; 195; 235; 365; 375; 405; 615; 745.

xwny 'dy "that one who, the person who, he who(m)". Syr. **'yn' d-** : 75; 345.

xwny 'dy "that one who, the person who, he who(m)". Syr. **hw** : 675.

xwr/xwrt "to eat". Syr. **'kl** : 490; 700.
xwrd'rt Syr. *'kl*: 490.
xwrt Syr. *m'kl*: 700.

xwrwny "adultery". Syr. **znywt'** : 120.

xwrwny wn-/qt- "to commit adultery". Syr. **g'r** : 120.
xwrwny wn't Syr. *tgwr* : 120.
xwrwny wntyq' Syr. *g'r* : 120.

xwsnty' "joy". Syr. **ḥdwt'** : 410; 420; 425; 485.

xwšp'ny "shepherd". Syr. **r'y'** : 690.

xwštr "chief". Syr. **rb'** : 140; 270.
xwštrt Syr. *rbÿ* : 140.
xwštr Syr. *r̈by* : 270.

xwštrt "elder". Syr. **qšÿš'** : 270.

xwšty "teacher". Syr. **rb'** : 350.

xwštyq numeric indicator. Syr. **ø** : 510.

xwšw "six". Syr. **št'** : 760.

xwt'w "Lord (referred to Jesus)". Syr. **ø** : 65; 175; 245; 250; 265; 285; 325; 380; 385; 395; 445; 455; 475; 480; 515; 525; 535; 545; 560; 625; 630; 645; 740; 760; 765; 770.

xwycq q'ry pwsty "deed of repudiation". Syr. **ktb' d-dwll'** : 115.

xwycq b(w)-/qt- "to be opened". Syr. **'tptḥ** : 5; 300; 550.
xwycq qty Syr. *'tptḥ* : 5.
xwycq qtnt Syr. *'tptḥ* : 300.
xwycq qtnt Syr. *'tptḥ* : 550.

xwycq wn-/qt- "to open". Syr. **ptḥ** : 560; 570; 585; 600; 615; 620.
xwycq qθ'rt Syr. *ptḥ* : 560; 570; 585; 600; 615.
xwycq wnwty Syr. *ptḥ* : 620.

xwycn'q "sick". Syr. **kryh'** : 700; 710; 725.

xwysm b(w)-/qt- "to take care" Syr. **'tbṭl** : 505.
xwysm b' Syr. *'tbṭl* : 505.

xwysm br "to be concerned, be anxious, take care". Syr. **yṣp** : 335; 510; 530.

xwysm brt' Syr. *t'ṣpwn* : 335.
xwysm br' Syr. *yṣp* : 510.
xwysm brync 'yš Syr. *yṣypty* : 530.

xwysm x-, sqw-, swq-/m't "to worry". Syr. **bṭl** : 525.
xwysm nyst Syr. *l'bṭyl* : 525.

xyd "that, he". Syr. **ḣw** : 60; 65; 325; 395; 420; 430; 515; 540; 545; 630; 660; 680.
xyd Syr. *-hy* : 175; 530.
prywnt Syr. *-hwn* : 35.
prywnt Syr. *bhyn*: 400.
prywnt Syr. *'lyhyn* : 505.
dywnt Syr. *hnwn* : 535.
xyd 'dy̤y̤"that who". Syr. **hw** : 575.
x'nt 'dẏt qt "those who" Syr. **'ylyn d-** : 305.

xypθ "his, its, own". Syr. **-h** : 15; 20; 25; 30; 110; 120; 165; 215; 290; 340; 350; 385; 445; 505; 520; 585; 645; 685; 745; 750; 760; 790; 795.
xypθ Syr. *-hy* : 140; 145; 155; 325; 340; 385; 455; 485; 535; 560; 585; 745; 755.
xypθ Syr. *-ḣ*: 520.
xypθ "their, own". Syr. *-hwn* : 170; 245.
xypθ Syr. *ø* : 335; 570; 610.
xypθ Syr. *dyl* : 370; 510.

xypθ'wnt "sir, owner, master, lord". Syr. **mr'** : 145; 170; 215; 220; 225; 240; 350; 355; 385; 395; 520; 525; 630; 635; 650; 655; 660; 675; 780; 790; 795.
xypθ'wnt': 145; 525; 630; 635; 650; 655; 660; 675.
xypθ'wnty : 220; 355; 395; 520; 780.

xyr/xrt "to go, go out, go away". Syr. **'zl** : 140; 145; 280; 555.
xrt Syr. *'zl* : 140; 145.
xrtnt Syr. *'zlw* : 280.
xrtym Syr. *'zlt* : 555.

xyr/xrt "to leave". Syr. **ḥzq** : 155.
xrt Syr. *ḥẓq* : 155.

y'nt : see 'yny.

y'ty "flesh". Syr. **bsr'** : 485.

yγqwb "Jacobs". Syr. **y'qwb** : 540; 760.

yhwd "Judea". Syr. **yhwd** : 10; 545.
yhwdy : 10.

yhwd' "Judas". Syr. **yhwd'** : 545.

ysr'yl "Israel". Syr. **'ysryl** : 15; 70; 275.
ysr'ylyq "Israelite". Syr. **'ysryl** "Israel": 40; 350.
ysr'ylyqt : 40.
ysr'ylyqty : 350.
yšwγ "Jesus". Syr. **yšw'** : 175; 245; 250; 285; 325; 380; 385; 395; 445; 455; 475; 480; 515; 525; 535; 545; 560; 625; 630; 740; 760; 765; 770.
yw "one". Syr. **ḥd/ ḥd'** : 130; 155; 240; 520; 530; 600; 690; 775.
yw-'dy : 440.
yw ywtr : 650.
ywy Syr. *l-ḥd* : 240.
yw Syr. *ø* : 365; 520; 565; 765; 775.
yw Syr. *–why* : 495.
yw ywtr "one by one". Syr. **ḥd ḥd** : 220.
yw'r "but". Syr. **'l'** : 75; 125; 190; 195; 275; 315; 410; 430; 450; 550; 615.
yw'r "but". Syr. **brm** : 680.
ywc/ywxt "to teach". Syr. **mlp** : 625.
ywcyq' Syr. *mlp 'nt* : 625.
ywntsnw "eleven". Syr. **ḥd'sr** : 305.
ywp'tqy "utter". Syr. **ø** : 625.
ywx'y/ywxst "to separate". Syr. **prš** : 690.
ywx'ytq' Syr. *nprš* : 690.
ywx'yt Syr. *mprš* : 690.
ywtr cn "one of". Syr. **ḥd' mn** : 365; 395.
ywḥnn "John". Syr. **ywḥnn** : 5; 40; 55; 65; 70; 80; 150; 205; 540; 760.
ywḥnn-'y: 40.
ywny "immediately, at once". Syr. **mḥd'** : 5; 300; 785.

z'rcnwq "merciful". Syr. **ø** : 30.
z'rcnwqy' "mercy". Syr. **ḥnn'** : 20.
z'ry'wy "punishment". Syr. **tšnyq'** : 740.
z'ry sy/sy't "to show mercy". Syr. **'trḥm** : 515.
z'rysy'd'rt Syr. *'trḥm* : 515.
z'rysy'mnty "goodness, kindness". Syr. **rḥm̈'** : 35.
z'rysy'mnty Syr. *rḥm̈'* : 35.
z'ty "son, Son, child". Syr. **br'** : 165; 180; 185; 340; 415; 545; 580; 630; 685; 775.
z'tyy Syr. *l-br'* : 165; 340.
z'ty "son". Syr. **ø** : 145.
z'wr θbr/θbrt "to help". Syr. **'dr** : 525.
z'wr θbr't Syr. *m'dr'* : 525.

z'wrqyn b(w)-/qt- "to become strong". Syr. **'tḥyl** : 35.
z'wrqyn b'sq Syr. *mtḥyl* : 35.
z'y "land, ground". Syr. **'r‘'** : 320; 370.
z'y "earth". Syr. **ø** : 130.
zb'q "tongue". Syr. **lšn'** : 5.
zkry' "Zechariah". Syr. **zkry'** : 15.
zmpy "shore". Syr. **ø** : 455.
zn "to give birth". Syr. **yld** : 415.
zn't Syr. *yld'* : 415.
znd'rt Syr. *yldt* : 415.
zn'mnty "(child) birth, delivery". Syr. **mwld'** : 415.
znwq "cheek". Syr. **pk'** : 130.
zprt "holy". Syr. **qdyš** : 20; 25; 690.
zprt Syr. *qdÿš'*: 20.
zprt Syr. *qdÿšt'* : 25.
zprt w't "Holy Spirit". Syr. **rwḥ' dqwdš'** : 15; 75; 390.
zprt w't. Syr. *rwḥ'*: 40; 75.
zpry'q wn-/qt- "to be devoted, honour". Syr. **yqr** : 240.
zpry'q wnty Syr. *nyqr* : 240.
zrync/zrγt "to deliver, redeem". Syr. **prq** : 25; 275.
zrγtyt bym Syr. *ntprq* : 25.
zryncy Syr. *nprqyw* : 275.
zw "I". Syr. **'n'** : 45; 55; 60; 70; 130; 175; 190; 195; 200; 215; 230; 315; 325; 350; 375; 390; 405; 410; 420; 430; 435; 465; 475; 480; 510; 575; 635; 665; 670; 735; 785.
mn' Syr. *-y* : 60; 70; 75; 140; 145; 165; 190; 195; 205; 215; 220; 225; 335; 345; 370; 375; 385; 400; 410; 420; 425; 430; 445; 465; 480; 495; 525; 555; 630; 635; 650; 655; 660; 695; 700; 715; 720; 725; 730; 735; 745; 750.
mn' Syr. *-ly* : 85; 205; 215; 485; 525; 665.
mn' Syr. *‘ly* : 215.
mn'yy Syr. *-ly* : 310.
mn'y Syr. *-ly* : 320.
mn' Syr. *ø* : 435; 565.
m'x "we" Syr. **ḥnn** : 270; 435; 595; 610.
m'x Syr. *–n* : 20; 25; 30; 105; 175; 225; 275; 280; 295; 300; 305; 385; 520; 580; 585; 675; 705.
m'xy : 20; 35.
m'x Syr. *ø* : 275; 280; 710.
m'xy Syr. *ln* : 625; 770.

zw'rt/zywst "to return". Syr. **hpk** : 305.
zywstnt Syr. *hpkw* : 305.
zwrt "to come back". Syr. **pn'** : 780.
zwrtq' Syr. *npn'* : 780.
zwrt "to come back". Syr. **hpk** : 510.
zwrtm Syr. *hpk 'n'* : 510.
zwyrt "to turn". Syr. **'pn** : 130.
zwyrt Syr. *'pn'* : 130.
zy'm "to spend". Syr. **tpq** : 510.
zy'my Syr. *tpq* : 510.
zywst : see zw'rt.

ž'y "to speak, talk, say". Syr. **mll** : 10; 20; 300; 340; 425; 430; 440; 585; 610; 635; 770; 775.
ž'tyt byq m'tnt Syr. *mtmlln hwy* : 10.
ž'yq m't Syr. *mmll* : 300.
ž'ẏt'q' Syr. *mmllyn* : 340.
ž'ẏt'q' Syr. *mmll'*: 340.
ž'ynq' Syr. *'mll* : 430.
ž'ysq Syr. *mmll 'nt* : 440.
ž'ẏṭ Syr. *nmll* : 585.
ž'ytqn Syr. *mmll* : 635.
ž'yntqn Syr. *mmllyn* : 770.
ž'ysq Syr. *mmll* : 775.
ž'd'rt Syr. *ṃll* : 20; 610.
ž'd'rm Syr. *mllt* : 425.
ž'y "to say". Syr. **'mr** : 450.
ž'd'rm Syr. *'mrt* : 450.
žγnt "messenger". Syr. **ml'k** : 720.
žγntt Syr. *m̈l'k* : 720.
žγrt "quickly". Syr. **b'gl** : 225.
žγyr/žγyrt "to cry out, summon, call". Syr. **qr'** : 50; 220; 355; 540; 575.
žγyrt Syr. *qr'* : 50.
žγyrd'rt Syr. *q̣r'*: 220; 540.
žγyrd'rnt Syr. *qrw* : 355; 575.
žγyrty b(w)-/qt- "to be called, be invited". Syr. **'tqry** : 30; 85; 260; 535.
žγyrty byq' Syr. *ttqr'*: 30.
žγyrtyt qtnt Syr. *'tqryw* : 85.
žγyrty bwt Syr. *'ttlmd hw'* : 260.
žγyrty bwt Syr. *mtqr'*: 535.

žmn "time, season". Syr. **zbn'** : 155; 170; 795.
žmnw : 155; 170; 795.
žw/žw't "to live, survive". Syr. **ḥy'** : 345.
žwytq' Syr. *nḧ'* : 345.
žw'n "life". Syr. **ḥ̈y'** : 30; 185; 190; 210; 740.
žw'ny : 30; 190.
žwγm'ny "severe". Syr. **qšy'** : 670.
žwnty "alive". Syr. **ḥy** : 280.
žwxšq "disciple". Syr. **tlmyd'** : 135; 325; 350; 385; 440; 465; 475; 535; 545; 605; 610; 740.
žwxšqt' Syr. *tlm̈yd'* : 325; 385; 440; 475; 605; 610; 740.
žwxšqy : 350; 465; 610.
žwxšqt'(y) Syr. *tlm̈yd'* : 135.
žwxšqt'y Syr. *l-tlm̈yd'* : 535.
žwxšqt'y Syr. *tlm̈yd'* : 545.
žwxšqt' Syr. *ø* : 305.
žy'wr "heart". Syr. **lb'** : 10; 250; 300; 420; 480.
žy'wrt Syr. *lbẅt'* : 250; 480.
žyšty b(w)-/qt- "to be hated". Syr. **sny' hw'** : 345.
bwt'q' žyštyt Syr. *thwwn snÿ'yn* : 345.
žyšty d'r "to hate". Syr. **sn'** : 240.
žyšty d'rt Syr. *nsn'* : 240.
žyšty ny's/ny't "to hate". Syr. **sn'** : 315.
žyšty ny'd'rt Syr. *ṣn'* : 315.

INDEX OF SYRIAC WORDS ATTESTED IN THE SYRIAC PARTS OF THE GOSPEL LECTIONARY E5

y “10” : 250.
-y “my” : 685; 740; 745.
yb “12” : 740.
yhẅdy’ “Jews” : 250.
ywḥnn “John” : 65; 95; 250; 375; 450.
ywm’ “day” : 65.
yẅmt’ “days” : 535.
yṭ “19” : 685.
ylydwt’ “birth” : 40.
yšw‘ “Jesus” : 125; 250; 325; 455; 740; 800.

kd “when” : 380; 470.
-kwn “you” : 325.
knwn qdym “Kānūn qədēm” : 40.
knÿšyn hww “they were gathered” : 470.
kn̈š’ “crowds” : 250.
ktb’ “book” : 40.

l- “to, for” : 65; 250; 325; 455; 645; 740.
lwq’ “Lukas” : 530.

m’ d- “when” : 685.
mdm “anything” : 800.
mwd̈yn’ “Easter” : 325.
mḥd’ “immediately” : 475.
mtl’ “parable” : 645.
ṁn “who” : 745.
m‘ly “opening, beginning” : 800.
mr’ “lord” : 685; 740.
mšdr’n’ “(I) send” : 325.
mty “Matthew” : 40; 325; 685; 740.

n’t’ “to come” : 745.
nkpwr “let him deny” : 745.
npš’ “soul” : 455; 745.

srgys “Sergius” : 740.

‘bd “to do” : 800.

BIBLIOGRAPHY

Aikhenvald, A.Y. - Dixon, R.M.W., eds. (2001) *Areal diffusion and genetic inheritance: problems in comparative linguistics*, Oxford.

Alfieri, L. - Barbati, Ch. (2010) "Su alcuni aspetti della storia del neopersiano: nascita ed evoluzione della diglossia", in C.G. Cereti (ed.) in collaboration with Ch. Barbati, M. De Chiara and G. Terribili *Orientalia Romana*, 11, pp. 23-52.

Ashurov, B. (2015) "Inculturation matérielle de l'Élise d'Orient en Asie centrale: témoignages archéologiques", in P.G. Borbone - P. Marsone (eds.) *Le christianisme syriaque en Asie centrale et en Chine*, *Études syriaques*, 12, pp. 161-183.

Asmussen, J.P. (1962) "Das Christentum in Iran und sein Verhältnis zur Zoroastrismus", in *Studia Teologica*, 16, pp. 1- 22.

Asmussen, J.P. (1983) "Christians in Iran", in *The Cambridge History of Iran*, vol. 3(2), Cambridge, pp. 924-948.

Asmussen, J.P. (1984) "The Sogdian and Uighur-Turkish Christian Literature in Central Asia before the Real Rise of Islam", in *Indological and Buddhist Studies. Volume in honour of Professor J.W. de Jong on his sixtieth birthday*, pp. 11-29, Delhi, (2nd edition; 1st edition Canberra, 1982).

Auer, P. (1998) *Code-switching in Conversation: Language, Interaction, and Identity*, London.

Bachmann-Medick, D. (2004) "Übersetzung als Medium interkultureller Kommunikation und Auseinandersetzung", in F. Jaeger- J. Straub (eds.) *Handbuch der Kulturwissenschaften*, 2, Weimar, pp. 449-465.

Bachmann-Medick, D. (2009) "Translational turn", in *Cultural Turns. Neuorientierungen in den Kulturwissenschaften*, Reinbek bei Hamburg, pp. 238-283.

Balicka-Witakowska, E. (1998) "Remarks on the Decorations of the Syriac gospel, British library add. 7174", in *Symposium syriacum VII, Uppsala University, Departement of Asian and African languages, 11-14 August 1996, Orientalia Christiana Analecta*, 256, pp. 642-659.

Barbati, Ch. (2010) "The Christian Sogdian manuscript *C 5* as an example of *translation literature*", in M. Macuch- D. Weber and D. Durkin-Meisterernst (eds.) *Ancient and Middle Iranian Studies. Proceedings of the 6th European Conference of Iranian Studies, held in Vienna, September 18-22. 07*, *Iranica*, 19, pp. 1-10.

Barbati, Ch. (2013) "The Christian Mediaeval Iranian Codicology: an Unexplored Territory", in *Comparative Oriental Manuscript Studies Newsletter*, 5, pp. 7-9.

Barbati, Ch. (2014) "Notes on Christian Sogdian terminology with special references to the Sogdian gospel lectionary C5", in M. Bais- M.C. Benvenuto and C.G. Cereti (eds.) *Nāme-ye-Irān-e Bāstān, International Journal of Ancient Iranian Studies*, 12/1-2, pp. 105-120.

Barbati, Ch. (2014a) "The Emergence of the Allographic Phenomenon within the Christian Sogdian Tradition", in J. den Heijer- A.B. Schmidt and T. Pataridze (eds.), *Scripts beyond Borders. A Survey of Allographic Traditions in the Euro-Mediterranean World*, in *Publications de l'Institut Orientaliste de Louvain*, 62, Louvain-la Neuve, pp. 257-278.

Barbati, Ch. (2015) "Syriac into Middle Iranian: A Translation Studies Approach to Sogdian and Pahlavi Manuscripts within the Church of the East", in A. Keidan (ed.) *Translation Techniques in the Ancient and Oriental Cultures*, *Open Linguistics*, 1, De Gruyter Open, pp. 444-457, http://degruyteropen.com/ttaoc/.

Barbati, Ch. (2015a) "La documentation sogdienne chrétienne et le monastère de Bulayïq", in P.G. Borbone - P. Marsone (eds.) *Le christianisme syriaque en Asie centrale et en Chine*, *Études syriaques*, 12, pp. 89-120.

Barbati, Ch. (2015b) "The northern-central group of the Iranian Central dialects: an areal and diachronic perspective", in A. Krasnowolska- R. Rusek-Kowalska (eds.) *Studies on the Iranian World: Medieval and Modern. Proceedings of the 7th European Conference of Iranian Studies (Cracow 2011)*, Cracow, pp. 13-22.

Barbati, Ch. (forthcoming) "Mitteliranisch-christliche Manuskriptologie", in L. Paul (ed.) *Handbuch Iranistik*, 2, Wiesbaden.

Baum, W. - Winkler, D.W. (2003) *The Church of the East*, London-New York.

Baumstark, A. (1915) "Neue soghdisch-nestorianische Bruchstücke", in *Oriens Christianus*, 4, pp. 123-128.

Baumstark, A. (1921) *Nichtevangelische syrische Perikopenordnungen des ersten Jahrtausends*, Münster.

Baumstark, A. (1922) *Geschichte der syrischen Literatur*, Bonn [repr. 1968].

Baumstark, A. (1927) "Neuerschlossene Urkunden altchristlicher Perikopenordnung ostaramäischen Sprachgebietes", in *Oriens Christianus*, 3/1, pp. 1-22.

A. Bausi- P.G. Borbone- F. Briquel Chattonet- P. Buzi- J. Gippert- C. Macé-

M. Maniaci- Z. Melissakis- L.E. Parodi- W. Witakowski (eds.) (2015) *Comparative Oriental Manuscript: An Introduction*, Hamburg.

Benveniste, É. (1955) "Études sur quelques textes sogdiens chrétiens I", in *Journal Asiatique*, 243, pp. 297-337.

Benveniste, É. (1959) "Études sur quelques textes sogdiens chrétiens II", in *Journal Asiatique*, 247, pp. 115-136.

Benveniste, É. (1964) Le vocabulaire chrétien dans les langues d'Asie Centrale. In *Atti del convegno internazionale sul tema: l'Oriente cristiano nella storia della civiltà*, Roma, pp. 85-91. Reprinted in *Id.* (1979), *Études sogdiennes*, Wiesbaden, pp. 308- 314.

Berruto, G. (2009) "Confini tra sistemi, fenomenologia del contatto linguistico e modelli del code switching", in (a cura di) G. Iannaccaro-V. Matera, *La lingua come cultura*, Torino, pp. 3-34; 212-216.

Berti, V, (2006) "Cristiani sulle vie dell'Asia tra VIII e IX secolo. Ideologia e politica missionaria di Timoteo I, patriarca siro-orientale (780-823)", in *Religioni per via*, *Quaderni di Storia religiosa*, pp. 117-156.

Berti, V. (2009) *Vita e studi di Timoteo I Patriarca cristiano di Baghdad*, *Studia Iranica. Cahiers de Studia Iranica*, 41.

Berti, V. (2011) "Idéologie et politique missionaire de Timothé Ier Patriarche syro-oriental" in in C. Jullien (ed.) *Itinéraires missionaires. Échanges et identités*, *Cahiers de Studia Iranica*, 44, pp. 71-110.

Bielmeier, R. (1989) "Yaghnōbī", in R. Schmitt (ed.) *Compendium Linguarum Iranicarum*, Wiesbaden, pp. 480-488.

Bivar, A.D.H. (1983) "The history of Eastern Iran", in *The Cambridge History of Iran*, vol. 3(1), Cambridge, pp. 181- 231.

Bogaert, P.M. (1999) "Ordres anciens des évangiles et tétraévangile en un seul codex", in *Revue théologique de Louvain*, 30, pp. 297-314.

Borbone, P.G. (2006) "I blocchi con croci e iscrizione siriaca da Fangshan", in *Orientalia Christiana Periodica*, 72/1, pp. 167-187.

Borbone, P.G. (2013) "Les églises d'Asie centrale et de Chine. État de la question à partir des textes et des découvertes archéologiques. Essai de synthèse", in F. Briquel-Chatonnet (ed.) *Les églises en monde syriaque*, *Études syriaques*, 10, pp. 441-465.

Borbone, P.G. (2015) "Les «provinces de l'extérieur» vues par l'Église-mère", in P.G. Borbone- P. Marsone (eds.) *Le christianisme syriaque en Asie centrale et en Chine*, *Études syriaques*, 12, pp. 121-159.

Borbone, P.G.- Briquel Chatonnet, F.- Balicka-Witakowska, E. (2015) "Syriac codicology", in Bausi- Borbone- Briquel Chattonet- Buzi-Gippert- Macé- Maniaci- Melissakis- Parodi- Witakowski (eds.) *Comparative Oriental Manuscript: An Introduction*, Hamburg, pp. 252-

266.
P.G. Borbone- P. Marsone (eds.) (2015) *Le christianisme syriaque en Asie centrale et en Chine*, *Études syriaques*, 12.
Bosworth, C.E. (1992) *Central Asia IV. In the Islamic Period up to the Mongols*, in E. Yarshater (ed.) *Encyclopaedia Iranica*, 5, Costa Mesa, pp. 169-172.
Briquel Chatonnet, F. (2013) "Les églises dans les textes", in F. Briquel Chatonnet (ed.) *Les églises en monde syriaque*, *Études syriaques*, 10, pp. 11-40.
Brock, S. (1975) "Some Aspects of Greek Words in Syriac", in *Synkretismus im Syrisch-persischen Kulturgebiet. Bericht über ein Symposion in Reinhausen bei Göttingen in der Zeit vom 4. bis 8. Oktober 1971*, Göttingen, pp. 80- 108.
Brock, S. (1992) "Chronicle of Edessa", in E. Yarshater (ed.) *Encyclopaedia Iranica*, 5, Costa Mesa, pp. 549-550.
Brock, S. (1996) "The "Nestorian" Church: a lamentable misnomer", in *Bulletin of the John Rylands University Library of Manchester*, 78/3, pp. 23-35.
Brock, S. (2006) *The Bible in the Syriac Tradition*, Piscataway.
Brock, S. (2006a) *La spiritualità nella tradizione siriaca*, Roma.
Brockelmann, C. (1928) *Lexycon Syriacum*, Halle.
Brown, L.W. (1956) *The Indian Christians of St. Thomas. An account of the Ancient Syrian Church of Malabar*, Cambridge.
Burkitt, F.C. (1904) *Evangelion da-Mepharreshe I-II. The Curetonian Version of the Four Gospels, with the Readings of the Sinai Palimpsest and the Early Syriac Patristic Evidence* (*I. Text; II. Introduction and Notes*),Cambridge, repr. 2003, Piscataway.
Burkitt, F.C. (1923) "The Early Syriac Lectionary System", in *Proceedings of the British Academy*, 10, Oxford, pp. 301-338.
Burkitt, F.C. (1925) *The religion of Manichees*, Cambridge.
Cadonna, A. (1992) *Turfan and Tun-Huang. The Texts: Encounter of Civilizations on the Silk Route*, Firenze.
Campbell, L. (1985) "Areal linguistics and its implications for historical linguistic theory", in J. Fisiak (ed.) *Proceedings of the Sixth International Conference of Historical Linguistics*, Amsterdam, pp. 25-56.
Campbell, L. (1997) "Typological and Areal Issues in Reconstruction", in J. Fisiak (ed.) *Linguistic Reconstruction and Typology*, Berlin, pp. 45-72.
Cereti, C.G. (2003) "Le croci di San Tommaso e la letteratura cristiana in lingue medioiraniche", in M.V. Fontana- B. Genito (eds.) *Studi in onore*

di Umberto Scerrato per il suo settantacinquesimo compleanno, 1, Roma, pp. 193-206.

Chiesa, P., ed. (2011) *Guglielmo di Rubruk, Viaggio in Mongolia*, Fondazione Lorenzo Valla, Milano.

Christensen, A. (1936) *L'Iran sous les Sassanides*, Paris.

Ciancaglini, C.A. (2006) "L'origine delle locuzioni verbali con *'bd* in siriaco", in M. Tosco- P. Borbone- A. Mengozzi (eds.) *Loquentes linguis: studi linguistici e orientali in onore di Fabrizio A. Pennacchietti*, Wiesbaden, pp. 173-184.

Ciancaglini, C.A. (2008) *Iranian Loanwords in Syriac*, Wiesbaden.

Ciancaglini, C.A. (2011) "The Formation of the Periphrastic Verbs in Persian and Neighbouring Languages", in M. Maggi – P. Orsatti (eds.) *The Persian Language in History*, Wiesbaden, pp. 3-21.

Dahl, Ö. (2001) "Principle of areal typology", in M. Haspelmath- E. König- W. Österreicher- W. Raible (eds.) *Language typology and language universals: an international handbook*, 2, Berlin, pp. 1456-1470.

G. Dagron- P. Riché- A. Vauchez, eds. (1994) *Bischöfe, Mönche und Kaiser (642-1054)*, Freiburg-Basel-Wien.

Dauvillier, J. (1956) "L'expansion de l'église syrienne en Asie centrale et en Extrême-Orient", in *L'Orient Syrien*, 1, pp. 76-87.

Dauvillier, J. (1957) "Guillaum de Rubrouck et les communautés chaldéennes d'Asie centrale au Moyen Age", in *L'Orient syrien*, 2, pp. 237-238.

Debié, M. (2010) "Livres et monastères en Syrie-Mésopotamie d'après les sources syriaques", in F. Jullien (ed.) *Le monachisme syriaque, Études Syriaques*, 7, pp. 123-168.

Desreumaux, A. (1996) "Les lectionnaires syro-palestiniens", in C.B. Amphoux - J.P. Bouhot (eds.) *La lecture liturgique des Épitres catholiques dans l'Église Ancienne*, Lausanne, pp. 87-103.

Dickens, M. (2009) "The Syriac Bible in Central Asia", in E.C.D. Hunter (ed.) *The Christian Heritage of Iraq. Collected papers from the Christianity of Iraq I-V Seminar Days*, Piscataway, pp. 92-120.

Dickens, M. (2009a) "Multilingual Christian Manuscripts from Turfan", in *Journal of the Canadian Society for Syriac Studies*, 9, pp. 22-42.

Dickens, M. (2009b) "Syriac gravestones in the Tashkent History Museum", in D.W. Winkler - Li Tang (eds.) *Hidden Treasures and Intercultural Encounters*, Wien-Berlin, pp. 13-69.

Dickens, M. (2013) "The importance of the Psalter at Turfan", in Li Tang – D.W. Winkler (eds.) *From the Oxus River to the Chinese Shores. Studies on East Syriac Christianity in China and Central Asia*, Berlin, pp. 357-

380.
Dickens, M. (2013a) “Scribal Practices in the Turfan Christian Community”, in *Journal of the Canadian Society for Syriac Studies*, 13, pp. 3-28.
Dickens, M. - Savchenko, A. (2009) “Prester John's Realm: New Light on Christianity between Merv and Turfan”, in E.C.D. Hunter (ed.) *The Christian Heritage of Iraq. Collected Papers from the Christianity of Iraq I-V Seminar Days*, Piscataway, pp. 121-135.
Dickens, M. - Zieme, P. (2014) “Syro-uigurics I: A Syriac Psalter in Uyghur Script from Turfan”, in J. den Heijer- A.B. Schmidt and T. Pataridze (eds.), *Scripts beyond Borders. A Survey of Allographic Traditions in the Euro-Mediterranean World*, in Publications de l'Institut Orientaliste de Louvain, 62, Louvain-la Neuve, pp. 291-328.
Dinkler, E. - v. Schubert (1974) “Kreuz” in *Lexicon der christlichen Ikonographie*, 2, Rom, pp. 562-590.
Diettrich, G. (1909) “Bericht über neuentdeckte handschriftliche Urkunden zur Geschichte des Gottesdienstes in der nestorianischen Kirche”, in *Nachrichten von der Königlichen Gesellschaft der Wissenschaften zu Göttingen*, pp. 160-218.
Doerfer, G. (1992) “viii. Turkish-Iranian Language contacts”, in E. Yarshater (ed.) *Encyclopaedia Iranica*, 5, Costa Mesa, pp. 481-484.
Dresden, M. (1983) “Sogdian Language and Literature”, in *The Cambridge History of Iran*, 3(2), Cambridge, pp. 1216-1229.
D. Durkin-Meisterenst- S. Raschmann- J. Wilkens- M. Yaldiz- P. Zieme, eds. (2004) *Turfan Revisited- The First Century of Research into the Arts and Cultures of the Silk Road*, Berlin.
D. Durkin-Meisterernst- Ch. Reck- D. Weber, eds. (2009) *Literarische Stoffe in mitteliranischer Gestaltung und ihre Zeit. Colloquium anlässich des 70. Geburtstages von Werner Sundermann*, *Beiträge zur Iranistik*, 31.
Durkin-Meisterernst, D. (2004) *Dictionary of Manichaean Middle Persian and Parthian*, Turnhout.
Durkin-Meisterernst, D. (2006) “The Pahlavi Psalter Fragment in Relation to Its Source”, in *Studies on the Inner Asian Languages*, 21, pp. 1-19.
Durkin-Meisterernst, D. (2007) “The use of Parthian ’h’z and related forms in Sogdian and Bactrian”, in *Festschrift für Christoph Koch zum 65. Geburstag*, München, pp. 31-44.
Durkin-Meisterernst, D. (2008) “Aspects of the Organization of Manichaean Books”, in *Gazette du livre médiéval*, 52-53, pp. 1-15.
Durkin-Meisterernst, D. (2009) “Khwarezmian”, in G. Windfuhr (ed.) *The Iranian Languages”*, London-New York, pp. 336-376.
Durkin-Meisterernst (2012) “Translation Features in Sogdian Texts

translated from Middle Persian and Parthian: Some Observations" in *The History behind the Languages. Essays of Turfan Forum on Old Languages of the Silk Road*, Shanghai, pp. 32-40.

Durkin-Meisterernst, (2013) "Mitteliranisch", in L. Paul (ed.) *Handbuch der Iranistik*, Wiesbaden, pp. 239-257.

D. Durkin-Meisterernst- M. Friedrich- O. Han- A. Helmann-Ważny- R. Nöller- S. Raschmann (2015) "Scientific methods for philological scholarship: Pigment and paper analyses in the field of manuscriptology", *Journal of Cultural Heritage*, (http://dx.doi.org/10.1016/j.culher. 2015.06.004).

Emmerick, R.E. (1968) *Saka Grammatical Studies*, Oxford.

Emmerick, R.E. (2009) "Khotanese and Tumshuqese", in G. Windfuhr (ed.) *The Iranian Languages*, London- New York, pp. 377-415.

Fragner, B. (2006) "Das Persische als Hegemonialsprache in der islamischen Geschichte: Überlegungen zur Definition eines innerislamischen Kulturraums", in L. Johanson - Ch. Bulut (eds.) *Turkic-Iranian Contact Areas. Historical and Linguistic Aspects*, Wiesbaden, pp. 39-48.

Frye, R.N. (1992) "Central Asia III. In Pre-Islamic Times", in E. Yarshater (ed.) *Encyclopaedia Iranica*, 5, Costa Mesa, pp. 164-169.

Gershevitch, I. (1954) *A Grammar of Manichean Sogdian Sogdian*, Oxford.

Gershevitch, I. (1985) *Philologia Iranica*, Wiesbaden.

Gharib, B. (1974) "An Old Persian-Sogdian Isogloss", in *Mémorial Jean de Menasce*, Louvain, pp. 389- 398.

Gharib, B. (1995) *Sogdian Dictionary. Sogdian-Persian-English*, Tehran.

Gharib, B. (2006) "Present and Past Perfect Transitive in Sogdian and its Comparative Similarities with some New Iranian Dialects", in A. Panaino - A. Piras (eds.) *Proceedings of the 5th Conference of the Societas Iranologica Europaea held in Ravenna, 6-11 October 2003*, Milano, pp. 437-444.

Gillmann, I. - Klimkeit, H.J. (1999) *Christians in Asia before 1500*, Richmond.

Gignoux, Ph. (1969) "L'auteur de la version pehlevie du psautier serait-il nestorien?", in *Mémorial Mgr Gabriel Khouri-Sarkis*, Louvain, pp. 235-244.

Gignoux, Ph. (1991) *Les quatre inscriptions du mage Kirdīr, Cahiers de Studia Iranica*, 9.

Gignoux, Ph. (1995) "The Pahlavi inscription on Mount Thomas Cross (South India)", in Z. Zevit- G. Gitin- M. Sokoloff (eds.) *Solving Riddles and Untying Knots. Biblical, Epigraphic, and Semitic Studies in Honor of Joans C. Greenfield*, Winona Lake, Indiana, pp. 411-422.

Gignoux, Ph. (2001) "Une croix de procession de Hérat inscrite en Pehlevi", in *Le Muséon*, 114, pp. 291-304.

Gignoux, Ph. (2001a) "L' apport scientifique des chrétiens syriaques à l'Iran sassanide", in *Journal Asiatique*, 289/2, pp. 217-236.

Gnoli, Gh. (2003) *Il Manicheismo*, Fondazione Lorenzo Valla, Milano, pp. 35-40.

Golden, P.B. (2006) "Turks and Iranians: A Historical sketch", in *Turkic-Iranian contact areas. Historical and linguistic aspects,* L. Johanson-Ch. Bulut (eds.), *Turcologica*, 62, pp. 17-38.

Grenet, F. (1996) "Les marchands sogdiens dans les mers du Sud à l'epoque preislamique", in *Cahiers d'Asie centrale*, 1-2, pp. 65-84.

Gropp, G. (1970) "Die Pahlavi-Inschrift auf dem Thomaskreuz in Madras", in *Archeologische Mitteilungen aus Iran*, pp. 267-271.

Gulácsi, Z. (2005) *Mediaeval Manichaean Book Art*, Leiden-Boston.

Gusmani, R. (1993) *Saggi sull'interferenza linguistica*, Firenze.

Gyselen, R. (2006) "Les témoignages sigillographiques sur la présence chrétienne dans l'empire sassanide", in R. Gyselen (ed.) *Chrétiens en terre d'Iran: implantation et acculturation*, *Cahiers de Studia Iranica*, 33, pp. 17-78.

Hage, W. (1978) "Einheimische Volkssprachen und syrische Kirchensprache in der nestorianischen Asienmission", in G. Wiessner (ed.) *Erkenntnisse und Meinungen*, 2, Wiesbaden, pp. 131-160.

Hage, W. (1987) "Das Christentum in der Turfan-Oase", in W. Heissig - H.J. Klimkeit (ed.) *Synkretismus in den Religionen Zentralasiens*, Wiesbaden, pp. 46-57.

Hage, W. (1988) *Syriac Christianity in the East*, Kottayam.

Hage, W. (1995/1996) "Crosses with Epigraphs in Medieval Central and East Asian Christianity", in *The Harp*, 8-9, pp. 375-382.

Haig, G.L.J. (2008) *Allignment Change in Iranian Languages. A Construction Grammar Approach*, Berlin- New York.

Hamilton, J. - Sims-Williams, N. (1990) *Documents turco-sogdiens du IX-X siècle de Touen-houang*, *Corpus Inscriptionum Iranicarum*, London.

Hansen, O. (1941) "Berliner sogdische Texte I", in *Abhandlungen der Preußischen Akademie der Wissenschaften*.

Hansen, O. (1955) "Berliner soghdische Texte II", in *Abhandlungen der Preußischen Akademie der Wissenschaften und der Literatur in Mainz*, 15.

Hansen, O. (1966) "Über die verschiedenen Quellen der christlichen Literatur der Sogder", in *Iranian Studies. Presented to Kaj Barr on his seventieth birthday, June 26*, Copenhagen, pp. 95-102.

Hansen, O. (1968) "Die christliche Literatur der Sogdier", in *Handbuch der Orientalistik, Iranistik*, Leiden, pp. 91-99.

Hansen, V. (2012) *The Silk Road. A New History*, Oxford.

Hatch, W.H.P. (1946) *An Album of Dated Syriac Manuscripts*, Boston.

Henning, W.B. (1936) "Ein manichäisches Bet und Beichtbuch", in *Abhandlungen der Preussischen Akademie der Wissenschaften*, [repr. 1997] *Selected Papers*, in *Acta Iranica. Hommages et opera minora*, 5, pp. 3-143.

Henning, W.B. (1945) "Sogdian Tales", in *Bulletin of the School of Oriental and African Studies*, [repr. 1977] *Selected Papers*, in *Acta Iranica. Hommages et opera minora*, 6, pp. 465-487.

Henning, W.B. (1958) "Mitteliranisch", in *Handbuch der Orientalistik*, Leiden-Köln, pp. 20-130.

Heston, W.L. (1976) *Selected problems in Fifth to Tenth Century Iranian Syntax- A Dissertation in Oriental Studies*, University of Pennsylvania.

Hunter, E.C.D. (1989-91) "The Conversion of the Kerait to Christianity in A.D. 1007", in *Zentralasiatische Studien*, 22, pp. 142-163.

Hunter, E.C.D. (1996) "The Church of the East in Central Asia", in *Bulletin of the John Rylands University Library of Manchester*, 78/3, pp. 129-142.

Hunter, E.C.D. (2009) "The Persian contribution to Christianity in China: reflections in the Xi'an Fu Syriac inscriptions", in D.W. Winkler – Li Tang (eds.) *Hidden Treasures and Intercultural Encounters*, Wien-Berlin.

Hunter, E.C.D. (2012) "Syriac, Sogdian and Old Uyghur Manuscripts from Bulayïq", in *The History behind the Languages. Essays of Turfan Forum on Old Languages of the Silk Road*, Shanghai, pp. 79-93.

Hunter, E.C.D. - Dickens, M. (2014) *Syriac texts in the Berlin Turfan Collection*, Stuttgart.

Hutter, M. (2013) "Minderheitenreligionen im Iran: Buddhismus, Judentum, Christentum, Baha'itum", in L. Paul (ed.) *Handbuch Iranistik*, Wiesbaden, pp. 206-221.

Jenner, K. (1997) "Development of Syriac lectionary systems", in *The Harp*, 10, pp. 257-286.

Jenner, K. (2001) "The relation between Biblical text and Lectionary systems in the Eastern Church", in A, Rapoport-Alber and G. Greenberg (eds.) *Biblical Hebrew, Biblical Texts*, Sheffield, pp. 376-411.

Jeremias, É. (1995) "Some Grammatical Problems of Early New Persian Syntax: Pronominal Clitics in Persian", in B. Fragner- Ch. Fragner- Gh. Gnoli- R. Haag-Higuchi- M. Maggi and P. Orsatti (eds.) *Proceedings of the Second European Conference of Iranian Studies held in Bamberg, 30th September to 4th October 1991, Serie Orientale Roma*, pp. 325-334.

Jinshi, F. (2010) *The Caves of Dunhuang*, The Dunhuang Academy in collaboration with London Editions, Hong Kong.

L. Johanson– B. Utas (eds.) (2000) *Evidentials: Turkic, Iranian and Neighbouring Languages (Empirical Approaches to Language Typology)*, 24, Berlin- New York.

Jullien, C. (2004) "Contribution des actes des martyrs perses à la géographie historique et à l'administration de l'empire sassanide", in R. Gyselen (ed.) *Contribution à l'histoire et à la géographie historique de l'empire sassanide*, Paris, pp. 141-169.

Jullien, C. - Jullien, F. (2002) "Aux frontières de l'iranité: <nāsrāyē> et <krīstyonē> des inscriptions du *mobad* Kirdīr: enquête littéraire et historique", in *Numen*, 49/3, pp. 282-335.

Jullien, F. (2006) "Le monachisme chrétien dans l'empire iranien (Ive-XIVe siècles", in R. Gyselen (ed.) *Chrétiens en terre d'Iran: implantation et acculturation*, *Cahiers de Studia Iranica*, 33, pp. 143-184.

Jullien, F. (2011) "Stratégies du monachisme missionaire en Iran", in C. Jullien (ed.) *Itinéraires missionaires. Échanges et identités*, *Cahiers de Studia Iranica*, 44, pp. 49-70.

Kannookadan, P. (1991) *The East Syrian Lectionary. An Historical-Liturgical Study*, Rome.

Kessel, G. - Sims-Williams, N. (2011) "The Profitable Counsels of Šem'ōn D-Ṭaibūtēh" in *Le Muséon*, 124 (3-4), Leuven, pp. 279-302.

Klein, W. (2004) *Syrische Kirchenväter*, Stuttgart, pp. 152-167.

Klein, W. - Reck, Ch. (2004) "Ein Kreuz mit sogdischer Inschrift aus Ak-Bešim/Kyrgyzstan", in *Zeitschrift der deutschen Morgenländischen Gesellschaft*, 154, pp. 147-156.

Klimkeit, H.J. (1979) "Das Kreuzessymbol in der zentralasiatischen Religionsbegegnung", in *Zeitschrift für Religions und Geistesgeschichte*, 31, pp. 99-115.

Klimkeit, H.J. (2000) "Manichaeism and Nestorian Christianity", in *Religions and religious movements- Part two*, in *History of Civilizations of Central Asia*, 4, Paris, pp. 69-81.

Kotsifou, C. (2012) "Bookbinding and Manuscript Illumination in Late Antique and Early Medieval Monastic Circles in Egypt", in J.P. Monferrer-Sala- H. Teule- S. Torallas Tovar (eds.) *Eastern Christians and their Written Heritage: Manuscripts, Scribes and Context*, Leuven, pp. 215-244.

Lala Comneno, M.L. (1995) "Cristianesimo nestoriano in Asia centrale nel primo millennio: testimonianze archeologiche", in *Orientalia Christiana Periodica*, 61, pp. 495-535.

Lazard, G. (1978) "Remarques sur les style des anciennes traductions persanes du Coran et de la Bible", in *Bullettin d'études orientales. Mélanges offerts à Henri Laoust*, 30, Damas, pp. 45- 49.

Le Coz, R. (2010) *Histoire de l'Eglise d'Orient*, Paris.

Lemaire, J. (1989) *Introduction à la codicologie*, Louvain-la Neuve.

Lenzi, G. (2000) "I vangeli siriaci", in *I vangeli dei popoli*, Città del Vaticano, pp. 37-45.

Lerner, J.A. (1977) *Christian Seals of the Sasanian Period*, Leiden.

Lerner, J.A. (1992) "Christianity II. In Pre-Islamic Persia. Material Remains", in E. Yarshater (ed.) *Encyclopaedia Iranica*, 5, Costa Mesa, pp. 528-530.

Leroy, J. (1958) *Moines et monastères du Proche-Orient*, Paris.

Leroy, J. (1964) *Les manuscrits syriaques à peintures conservés dans les bibliothèques d'Europe et d'Orient. Contribution à l'étude de l'iconographie des églises de langue syriaque*, Paris.

Lewis, A.S. (1910) *The Old Syriac Gospels*, London, repr. 2005, Piscataway.

Lieu, S.N.C. (2007) "The Luminous Religion (Ch'ing-chao, i.e. the Church of the East or Nestorianism) in China: a Historical Survey", in A. Mustafa- J. Tubach- G.S. Vashalomidze (eds.) *Inkulturation des Christentums im Sasanidenreich*, Wiesbaden, pp. 307-324.

Litvinsky, B.A. (1996) "Christianity, Indian and local religions. Religions and religious movements II", in *History of Civilizations of Central Asia*, 3, Paris, pp. 421-431.

Lyon, J.P. (1994) *Syriac Gospel Translations: A Comparison of the Language and Translation Method Used in the Old Syriac, the Diatessaron, and the Peshitto*, Louvain.

Maclean, A.J. (1894) *East Syrian Daily Offices*, London.

MacKenzie, D. N. (1970) "Christian Sogdian notes", in *Bulletin of the School of Oriental and African Studies*, 33, pp. 116-124.

Macomber (1967) "The Chaldean Lectionary system of the Cathedral Church of Kokhe", in *Orientalia Christiana Periodica*, 33, pp. 483-516.

Maggi, M. (2003) *New Persian Glosses in East Syriac Texts of the Eighth to Tenth Centuries*, in L. Paul (ed.), *Persian Origins. Early Judaeo-Persian and the Emergence of New Persian*, Wiesbaden, pp. 111- 145.

Maggi, M. (2005) *A Syro-Persian version of Matthew 23.29-35*, in M. Bernardini – N.L. Tornesello (eds.) *Scritti in onore di Giovanni M. D'Erme*, Napoli, 1, pp. 637- 658.

Maggi, M. - Orsatti, P. (2011) "Two Syro-Persian Hymns for Palm Sunday and Maundy Thursday", in M.Maggi and P. Orsatti (eds.) *The Persian language in history*, Wiesbaden, pp. 247-285.

Maniaci, M. (2002) *Archeologia del manoscritto: metodi, problemi, bibliografia recente*, Roma.

Marshak, B.I.- Negmatov, N.N. (1996) "Sogdiana", in *History of Civilizations of Central Asia*, 3, Paris, pp. 233-280.

Mersmann, B. (2004) "Bildkulturwissenschaft als Kulturbildwissenschaft? Von der Notwendigkeit eines inter- und transkulturellen Iconic Turn", in *Zeitschrift für Ästhetik und allgemeine Kunstwissenschaft*, 49/1, pp. 91-109.

Messina, G. (1951) *Diatessaron Persiano*, Roma.

Meyers-Scotton, C. (2002) *Contact linguistics. Bilingual encounters and grammatical outcomes*, Oxford.

Mingana, A. (1925) "The Early Spread of Christianity in Central Asia and the Far East: A New Document", reprinted from *The Bulletin of the John Rylands University Library of Manchester*, 9/2, pp. 297-371.

Moffet, S.H. (1998) *A History of Christianity in Asia, Vol. 1: Beginnings to 1500*, Maryknoll.

Moule, A.C. (1931) "The Use of the Cross among the Nestorians in China", in *T'oung Pao*, 28, pp. 78-86.

Müller, F.W.K. (1907) "Neutestamentliche Bruchstücke in soghdischer Sprache", in *Sitzungsberichte der Preussischen Akademie der Wissenschaften*, pp. 260-270.

Müller, F.W.K. (1913) *Soghdische Texte I*, Berlin.

Naymark, A. (1996) "Christians in Pre-Islamic Bukhara. Numismatic Evidence", J. Elverskog – A. Naymark (eds.) *Annual Central Eurasian Studies Conference*, Bloomington.

Nida, E. (2004) "Principles of correspondence", in L. Venuti (ed.) *The Translation Studies Reader*, (2nd edition), New York- London, pp. 153-167.

Nöldeke, T. (1898) *Kurzgefaßte syrische Grammatik*, Leipzig, [reprinted with additional material ed. by A. Schall, Darmstadt, 1966].

Orsatti, P. (2003) "Syro-Persian Formulas in Poetic Form in Baptism Liturgy", in L. Paul (ed.), *Persian Origins. Early Judaeo-Persian and the Emergence of New Persian,* Wiesbaden, pp. 147- 176.

Orsatti, P. (2007) *Appunti per una storia della lingua neopersiana*, Roma, pp. 128- 147.

Panaino, A. (2002) "A proposito dell'uso dell'inchiostro rosso nei manoscritti avestici con un'appendice a cura di Werner Sundermann sull'uso dell'inchiostro rosso nei testi di Turfan", in *Quaderni di scienza della*

conservazione, 2, pp. 36-55.
Panaino, A. (2007) "The Pāzand version of the Our Father", in A. Mustafa - J. Tubach – G.S. Vashalomidze (eds.) *Inkulturation des Christentums im Sasanidenreich*, Wiesbaden, pp. 73-90.
Parker, D.C. (2012) *Codex Sinaiticus. Geschichte der ältesten Bibel der Welt*, Darmstadt [Aus dem Englischen von Tobias Gabel, London 2010].
Parpulov, G.R. (2012) "The Bibles of the Christian East", in R. Marsden-E.Ann Matter (eds.) *The New Cambridge History of the Bible*, 2, Cambridge, pp. 309-324.
Parry, K. (1996) "Images in the Church of the East: the evidence from Central Asia and China", in *Bulletin of the John Rylands University Library of Manchester*, 78/3, pp. 143-162.
Paykova, A.V. (1979) "The Syrian Ostracon from Panjikant", in *Le Muséon*, 92, pp. 159-169.
Payne-Smith (1879-1901) *Thesaurus Syriacus, I-II*, Oxonii: Clarendon, London.
Pazzini, M. (1999) *Grammatica siriaca*, Jerusalem.
Pazzini, M. (2004) *Lessico Concordanziale del Nuovo Testamento Siriaco*, Jerusalem.
Pelliot, P. (1973) *Recherches sur les Chrétiens d'Asie Centrale et d'Extrême Orient*, 1, Paris.
Peters, C. (1936) "Der Text der soghdischen Evangelienbruchstücke und das Problem der Pešiṭta", in *Oriens Christianus*, 11, pp. 153-162.
Petersen, W. L. (1994) *Tatian's Diatessaron: Its Creation, Dissemination, Significance, and History in Scholarship*, Vigiliae Christianae. Supplementa, 25, Leiden.
Piemontese, A.M. (1989) *Catalogo dei manoscritti persiani conservati nelle biblioteche d'Italia*, Roma, pp. 104-108.
Pinggéra, K. (2011) "Die Apostolische Kirche des Ostens der Assyrer", in Ch. Lange – K. Pinggéra (eds.) *Die altorientalischen Kirchen*, Darmstadt, pp. 21-40.
Pittard, W.J. - Sims-Williams, N. (2013) "Fragments of Sogdian Gospel Lectionaries: some new identifications", in Li Tang and Dietmar W. Winkler (eds.) *From the Oxus River to the Chinese Shores. Studies on East Christianity in China and Central Asia*, Münster, pp. 43-48.
Pittard, W.J. - Sims-Williams, N. (2014) "Fragments of Gospel Lectionaries", in N. Sims-Williams (ed.) *Biblical and other Christian Sogdian Texts from the Turfan Collection*, Turnhout, pp. 55-62.
Provasi, E. (2005) "Sogdian Lexicography", in C.G. Cereti- M. Maggi (eds.) *Proceedings of the Conference held in Rome, 9-11 April 2001*,

Orientalia Romana, 8, pp. 101-146.

Pusey, P.E.- Gwilliam, G.H. (1901) *Tetraeuangelium Sanctum juxta Simplicem Syrorum Versionem*, Oxford.

Reck, Ch. (2008) "A Survey of the Christian Sogdian Fragments in Sogdian Script in the Berlin Turfan Collection", in Ch. Jullien (ed.) *Controverses des Chrétiens dans l'Iran sassanide*, *Studia Iranica*, 36, pp. 191-205.

Reichelt, H. (1926) "Soghdisches", in *Zeitschrift für Indologie und Iranistik*, pp. 239-250.

Richard, F. (1981) "Un lectionnaire persan des évangiles copié en Crimée en 776H./1374", in *Studia Iranica*, 10/2, pp. 225-245.

Rouwhorst, G. (1996) "Les lectionnaire syriaques", in C.B. Amphoux-J.P. Bouhot (eds.) *La lecture liturgique des Épitres catholiques dans l'Église Ancienne*, Lausanne, pp. 105-140.

Russel, J.R. (1992) "Christianity: i. In Pre-Islamic Persia: Literary Sources", in E. Yarshater (ed.) *Encyclopaedia Iranica*, 5, Costa Mesa, pp. 523-528.

Salemman, C. (1907) "Manichaica II", in *Izvestija Imperatorskoj Akademii Nauk*, pp. 531-558.

Savchenko, A. (2008) "Urgut", available at http://www.iranicaonline.org/articles/urgut.

Schwartz, M. (1974) "Sogdian Fragments of the *Book of Psalms*", in *Altorientalische Forschungen*, 1, pp. 257-261.

Schwartz, M. (1982 rev.) *Studies in the Texts of the Sogdian Christians*, PhD dissertation, Berkeley, 1967.

Schwartz, M.- Sims-Williams, N. (2014) "A Sogdian Psalter", in N. Sims-Williams (ed.) *Biblical and other Christian Sogdian Texts from the Turfan Collection*, Turnhout, pp. 7-53.

Segal, J.B. (2003) *The diacritical point and the accents in Syriac*, Piscataway.

Shaked, Sh. (1990) "Bible iv. Middle Persian translations", in E. Yarshater (ed.) *Encyclopaedia Iranica*, 4/2, London and New York, pp. 206-207.

Sims-Williams, N. (1978) "[Review of] D.N. MacKenzie, The Buddhist Sogdian Texts of the British Library", in *Indo-Iranian Journal*, 20, pp. 256-260.

Sims-Williams, N. (1979) "On the Plural and Dual in Sogdian", in *Bulletin of the School of Oriental and African Studies*, 42, pp. 337-346.

Sims-Williams, N. (1981) "Some Sogdian denominal abstract suffixes", in *Acta Orientalia*, 42, pp. 11-19.

Sims-Williams, N. (1981a) "Remarks on the Sogdian letters *γ* and *x* (with special reference to the ortography of the Sogdian version of the

Manichaean Church history) in W. Sundermann *Mitteliranische manichäische Texte kirchengeschichtlichen Inhalts*, Berlin, pp. 194-198.

Sims-Williams, N. (1981b) "Notes on Manichaean Middle-Persian Morphology", in *Studia Iranica*, 10/2, pp. 165-176.

Sims-Williams, N. (1982) "The double system of nominal inflexion in Sogdian", in *Transactions of the Philological Society*, 80/1, pp. 67-76.

Sims-Williams, N. (1983) "Indian elements in Parthian and Sogdian", in K. Röhrborn and W. Veenker (eds.) *Sprachen des Buddhismus in Zentralasien. Vorträge des Hamburger Symposium vom 2. Juli bis 5.Juli 1981*, Wiesbaden, pp. 132-141.

Sims-Williams, N. (1983) "Chotano-Sogdica", in *Bulletin of the School of Oriental and African Studies*, 46, pp. 40-51.

Sims-Williams, N. (1985) *The Christian Sogdian manuscript C2*, Berlin.

Sims-Williams, N. (1988) "Syro-Sogdica III: Syriac Elements in Sogdian", in *A Green Leaf. Papers in honour of Professor Jes P. Asmussen*, *Acta Iranica*, 28, pp. 145-156.

Sims-Williams, N. (1989) "Baršabbā", in E. Yarshater (ed.) *Encyclopaedia Iranica*, 3, London- New York, p. 823.

Sims-Williams, N. (1989a) "Eastern Middle Iranian", in R. Schmitt (ed.) *Compendium Linguarum Iranicarum*, Wiesbaden, pp. 163-172.

Sims-Williams, N. (1989a) "Sogdian", in R. Schmitt (ed.) *Compendium Linguarum Iranicarum*, Wiesbaden, pp. 173- 192.

Sims-Williams, N.(1990) "Bulayïq", in E. Yarshater (ed.) *Encyclopaedia Iranica*, 4, London- New-York, p. 545.

Sims-Williams, N. (1990a) "Chotano-Sogdica II: Aspects of the development of Nominal Morphology in Khotanese and Sogdian", in Gh. Gnoli- A. Panaino (eds.) *Proceedings of the first European Conference of Iranian Studies. Held in Turin, September 7th – 11th, 1987. Part I, Old and Middle Iranian Studies*, Rome, pp. 275-296.

Sims-Williams, N. (1990b) "Bible. Sogdian Translation of the Bible", in Yarshater (ed.) *Encyclopaedia Iranica*, 4, London- New-York, p. 207.

Sims-Williams, N. - Hamilton J. (1990) *Documents turco-sogdiens du IX-X siècle de Touen-houang*, London.

Sims-Williams, N. (1991) "Die christlich-soghdischen Handschriften von Bulayïq", in H. Klengel- W. Sundermann (eds.) *Ägypten-Vorderasien-Turfan. Probleme der Edition und Bearbeitung altorientalischer Handschriften. Tagung in Berlin, Mai 1987, Schriften zur Geschichte und Kultur des Alten Orients*, 23, Berlin, pp. 119-125.

Sims-Williams, N. (1992) "Christianity III. In Central Asia and Chinese Turkestan", in E. Yarshater (ed.) *Encyclopaedia Iranica*, 5, Costa Mesa, pp. 530-534.

Sims-Williams, N. (1992a) "Christianity IV. Christian Literature in Middle Iranian Languages", in E. Yarshater (ed.) *Encyclopaedia Iranica*, 5, Costa Mesa, pp. 534-535.

Sims-Williams, N. (1992b) "Sogdian and Turkish Christians in the Turfan and Tun-Huang Manuscripts", in A. Cadonna (ed.) *Turfan and Tun-Huang: the texts. Encounter of civilizations on the Silk route*, Firenze, pp. 43- 61.

Sims-Williams, N. (1995) "A Sogdian version of the 'Gloria in excelsis Deo'", in R. Gyselen (ed.) *Au carrefour des religions. Mélanges offerts à Philippe Gignoux*, *Res Orientales*, 7, Bures-sur-Yvette, pp. 257-262.

Sims-Williams, N. (1996) "Deylam, John of", in E. Yarshater (ed.) *Encyclopaedia Iranica*, 7, Costa Mesa, pp. 336-337.

Sims-Williams, N. (1996a) "The Sogdian manuscripts in Brāhmī script as evidence for Sogdian phonology", in R.E. Emmerick- W. Sundermann- I. Warnke - P. Zieme (eds.) *Turfan, Khotan und Dunhuang*, Berlin, pp. 307-315.

Sims-Williams, N. (1996b) "The Sogdian Merchants in China and India", in A. Cadonna – L. Lanciotti (eds.) *Cina e Iran. Da Alessandro Magno alla dinastia Tang*, *Orientalia Veneziana*, Firenze, pp. 45-67.

Sims-Williams, N. (1996) "On the Historic Present and Injunctive in Sogdian and Choresmian", in *Münchener Studien zur Sprachwissenschaft*, 56, pp. 173-189.

Sims-Williams, N. (2004) "A Greek-Sogdian Bilingual from Bulaÿq", in *La Persia e Bisanzio. Atti del convegno dei Lincei*, 201, Roma, pp. 623-631.

Sims-Williams, N. (2007) "The Sogdian Potentialis", in M. Macuch -M. Maggi -W. Sundermann (eds.) *Iranian languages and texts from Iran and Turan*, *Iranica*, 13, Wiesbaden, pp. 377-386.

Sims-Williams (2008) "Sogdian-Turkish bilingualism and linguistic interference in 9th-10th century Dunhaung", in Z. Zarshenas – V. Naddaf (eds.) *Papers in Honour of Professor B. Gharib*, Tehran, pp. 41-51.

Sims-Williams, N. (2009) "Christian literature in Middle Iranian languages", in R. Emmerick and M. Macuch (eds.) *The Literature of Pre-Islamic Iran. Companion Volume I to A History of Persian Literature*, London, pp. 266-287.

Sims-Williams, N. (2011) "Early New Persian in Syriac script: Two texts from Turfan", in *Bulletin of the School of Oriental and African Studies*, 74/3, pp. 353-374.

Sims-Williams, N. (2011a) "A new fragment of the Book of Psalms in

Sogdian", in *Bibel, Byzanz und christlicher Orient: Festschrift für Stephen Gerö zum 65. Geburstag, Orientalia Lovaniensia Analecta*, 187, Leuven, pp. 461-465.

Sims-Williams, N. (2011b) "Differential object marking in Bactrian" in A. Korn- G. Haig- S. Karimi- P. Samvelian (eds.) *Topics in Iranian Linguistics*, Wiesbaden, pp. 23-38.

Sims-Williams, N. (2012) *Iranian Manuscripts in Syriac Script in the Berlin Turfan Collection*, Stuttgart.

Sims-Williams, N. (2013) "A Christian Sogdian Hymn in Sogdian script", in *In Fond Memory of Gregory Bongard-Levin, Monumentum Gregorianum*, Moscow, pp. 172-177.

Sims-Williams, N. (2013a) "A Sogdian Fragment of the Martyrdom of Cyriacus and Julitta, in F. Pál (ed.) *More modoque: Festschrift für Miklós Maróth zum siebzigsten Geburtstag*, Budapest, pp. 235-240.

Sims-Williams, N. (2014) "An early source for the Life of John of Dailam. Reconstructing the Sogdian version", in M. Bais - M.C. Benvenuto - C.G. Cereti (eds.) *Nāme-ye-Irān-e Bāstān, International Journal of Ancient Iranian Studies*, 12/1-2, pp. 121-134.

Sims-Williams, N. (2014a) *Biblical and other Christian Sogdian Texts from the Turfan Collection*, Turnhout.

Sims-Williams, N. (2015) *The Life of Serapion and other Christian Sogdian Texts from the Manuscripts E25 and E26*, Turnhout.

Sims-Williams, N. (forthcoming 2016) "The Sogdian Lectionary *E5* and the text of the Syriac Gospel", in *Oriens Christianus*.

Sims-Williams, N. (forthcoming 2016a) *A Dictionary of Christian Sogdian*.

Skaff, J. (2005) "Documenting Sogdian society at Turfan in the seventh and eighth centuries: Tang Dynasty census records as a window on cultural distinction and change", in Vaissière de la- Trombert (eds.) *Les Sogdiens en Chine*, Paris, pp. 331-341.

Skjærvø, P.O. (1983) "Case in Inscriptional Middle Persian, Inscriptional Parthian and the Pahlavi Psalter", in *Studia Iranica*, 12/1, pp. 69-94; 2, pp. 151-181.

Skjærvø, P.O. (1996) "Aramaic Scripts for Iranian Languages", in P.T. Daniels- W. Bright (eds.) *The World's Writing Systems*, New York, pp. 515-535.

Skjærvø, P.O. (2009) "Middle West Iranian", in G. Windfuhr (ed.) *The Iranian Languages*, London- New York, pp. 196-278.

Soden von, H.F. (1913) *Die Schriften des Neuen Testaments. Text und Apparat*, Göttingen.

Sokoloff, M. (2009) *A Syriac Lexicon*, Winona Lake-Piscataway.

Spuler, B. (1961) "Die nestorianische Kirche", in *Handbuch der Orientalistik*, 1/8, 2, Leiden, pp. 120-169.

Standaert, N. (2001) *Handbook of Christianity in China, vol.1 (635-1800)*, Leiden.

Steingass, F. (1973) *Persian-English Dictionary*, New Delhi.

Stilo, D.L. (2004) "Iranian as a Buffer Zone between the Universal Typologies of Turkic and Semitic", in É.Á. Csáto- Bo Isaksson- C. Jahani (eds.) *Linguistic Convergence and Areal Diffusion. Case studies from Iranian, Semitic and Turkic*, London, pp. 35-63.

Stilo, D.L. (2006) "Circumposition as an areal response: The case study of the Iranian zone", in L. Johanson- Ch. Bulut (eds.) *Turkic-Iranian Contact Areas. Historical and Linguistic Aspects*, Wiesbaden, pp. 310-333.

Sundermann, W. (1968) "Christliche Evangelientexte in der Überlieferung der iranisch- manichäischen Literatur", in *Mitteilungen des Instituts für Orientforschung*, 14, Berlin, pp. 386-405.

Sundermann, W. (1974) "Nachlese zu F.W.K. Müllers „Soghdischen Texten I", 1.Teil", in *Altorientalische Forschungen*, 1, pp. 217-255.

Sundermann, W. (1974a) "Einige Bemerkungen zum syrisch-neupersischen Psalmenbruchstück aus Chinesisch-Turkistan", in Ph. Gignoux- A. Tafazzoli (eds.) *Mémorial Jean de Menasce*, Louvain, pp. 441-452.

Sundermann, W. (1975) "Nachlese zu F.W.K. Müllers "Soghdischen Texten I", in *Altorientalische Forschungen*, 3, pp. 55-90.

Sundermann, W. (1981) "Nachlese zu F.W.K. Müllers "Soghdischen Texten I", in *Altorientalische Forschungen*, 8, pp. 169-225.

Sundermann, W. (1981a) *Mitteliranische manichäische Texte kirchengeschichtlichen Inhalts*, Berlin.

Sundermann, W. (1983) "Lo studio dei testi iranici di Turfan", in *Orientalia Romana*, Roma, pp. 119-133.

Sundermann, W. (1994) "Byzanz und Bulayïq", in P. Vavroušek (ed.) *Iranian and Indo-European Studies. Memorial Volume of Otakar Klíma*, Praha, pp. 255-264.

Sundermann, W. (2004) *Turfan expeditions*, in E. Yarshater (ed.) *Encyclopaedia Iranica* http://www.iranica.com/articles/turfan-expeditions-2, last update July, 20, 2004.

Thackston, W.M (1999) *Introduction to Syriac. An Elementary Grammar with Readings from Syriac Literature*, Bethesda, Maryland.

Tedesco, P. (1922) "Ostiranische Nominalflexion", in *Zeitschrift für Indologie und Iranistik*, pp. 94-166.

Telegdi, S. (1938) "Notes sur la grammaire du sogdien chrétien", in *Journal*

Asiatique, 230, pp. 205-233.

Thomason, S.G. - Kaufman, T. (1988) *Language contact, creolization and genetic linguistics*, Berkeley.

Thomason, S.G. (2001) *Language contact: an introduction*, Edinburgh.

Thordarson, F. (2009) *Ossetic Grammatical Studies*, Wien.

Tremblay, X. (2001) *Pour une histoire de la Sérinde*, Wien.

Uray, G. (1983) "Tibet's connection with Nestorianism and Manicheism in the 8th-10th centuries", in Steinkellner, E. - Tauscher, H. (eds.) *Contributions on Tibetan Language, History and Culture*, Wien, pp. 399-420.

Vaissière, É. de la (2005) *Sogdian Traders. A History*, Leiden-Boston.

Vaissière, É. de la - Trombert, É. (2005) *Les sogdiens en Chine*, Paris.

Vergani, E. (forthcoming 2016) "Il canone siriaco", in E.G. Farrugia, S.J. (ed.) *Il canone biblico nelle Chiese orientali. Atti del convegno tenuto a Roma nel giorno 23 marzo 2010*, Facoltà di Scienze Ecclesiastiche Orientali, Pontificio Istituto Orientale, Roma.

Walker, J.T. (2006) *The Legend of Mar Qardagh. Narrative and christian heroism in late antique Iraq*, Berkeley-Los Angeles-London.

Walker, J.T. (2010) "Ascetic Literacy: Books and Readers in East-Syrian Monastic Tradition", in H. Börm- J. Wiesehöfer (eds.) *Commutatio et contentio: Studies in the Late Roman, Sasanian, and Early Islamic Near East: In Memory of Zeev Rubin*, Düsseldorf, pp. 307-345.

Watson, W. (1983) "Iran and China", in *The Cambridge History of Iran*, 3(1), Cambridge, pp. 537-558.

Weinreich, U. (1953) *Languages in Contact*, New York.

Wendtland, A. (2011) "The emergence and development of the Sogdian Perfect", in A. Korn- G. Haig- S. Karimi- P. Samvelian (eds.) *Topics in Iranian Linguistics*, Wiesbaden, pp. 39-52.

Wilmshurst, D. (2000) *The Ecclesiastical Organization of the Church of the East, Corpus Scriptorum Christianorum Orientalium*, Lovanii,582, pp. 1318-1913.

Windfuhr, G. (1992) "Cases" in E. Yarshater (ed.) *Encyclopaedia Iranica*, 5, Costa Mesa, pp. 25-37.

Windfuhr (1996) "Dialectology" in E. Yarshater (ed.) *Encyclopaedia Iranica*, 7, Costa Mesa, pp. 362-370.

Windfuhr, G. (2006) "Language change and modeling modal axes: Irano-Turkic convergence", in L. Johanson- Ch. Bulut (eds.) *Turkic-Iranian Contact Areas. Historical and Linguistics Aspects*, Wiesbaden, pp. 252-282.

Windfuhr, G. (2009) "Dialectology and Topics", in G. Windfuhr (ed.) *The*

Iranian Languages, London- New-York, pp. 5-42.

R. Wodak – B. Johnstone – P.E. Kerswill, eds. (2010) *The SAGE Handbook of Sociolinguistics*, New York.

Wright, W. (1901) *A Catalogue of the Syriac Manuscripts Preserved in the Library of the University of Cambridge*, 2 vols., Cambridge.

Yoshida, Y. (1980) "On the dialectology of Christian Sogdian", in *Oriento*, 23, pp. 83-93.

Yoshida, Y. (2009) "Sogdian", in G. Windfuhr (ed.) *The Iranian languages*, London- New-York, pp. 279-333.

Yoshida, Y. (2009a) "Turco-Sogdian features", in W. Sundermann - A. Hintze and F. de Blois (eds.) *Exegisti monumenta. Festschrift in Honour of Nicholas Sims-Williams*, *Iranica*, 17, pp. 571-585.

Zieme, P. (1974) "Zu den nestorianisch-türkischen Turfantexten", in *Sprachen, Geschichte und Kultur der altaischen Völker*, Berlin, pp. 661-668.

Zieme, P. (2000) "The search for knowledge through translation: translations of Manichaean, Christian and Buddhist literature into Chinese, Turkic, Mongolian, Tibetan and other languages", in *The development of education: maktab, madrasa, science and pedagogy. Part two*, in *History of Civilizations of Central Asia*, 4, Paris, pp. 43-51.

PLATES

Manuscripts:
Depositum of the BERLIN-BRANDENBURGISCHE AKADEMIE DER WISSENSCHAFTEN in the STAATSBIBLIOTHEK ZU BERLIN – Preußischer Kulturbesitz, Orientabteilung.

Manuscript photographs marked with an asterisk (*):
NIEDERSÄCHSISCHE STAATS- UND UNIVERSITÄTSBIBLIOTHEK GÖTTINGEN, bequest of Carl Friedrich Andreas.

The captions contain only the *E5* numbers according to N. Sims-Williams' new classification and the shelf numbers (starting with *n*) as in the Digital Turfan Archive. See also: Chapter 2.3 *The signatures of E5. A list of concordances.*

E5/5 = n166 [part]
E5/6a-b = n497 + n166 [part]*
E5/19 = n149
E5/21a-b = n413d + n498*
E5/23 = n150
E5/28a-b = n151 + n409
E5/34 = n152
*E5/38 = n499**
*E5/41 = n500**
E5/48 = n153
E5/51 = n154
*E5/65 = n501**
E5/72 = n156

E5/73 = n 157
E5/75-76 = n158 + n413a
E5/78 = n413b
*E5/79 = n502**
*E5/80 = n503**
*E5/83a-b = n159b + n504**
E5/91 = n162
E5/100-101 = n160+n161
E5/109 = n163
E5/125-126 = n 505-n506**
E5/127a-c = n164
E5/130a-b = n165+n413c

E5/5 = n166 [part] *recto*

E5/5 = n166 [part] *verso*

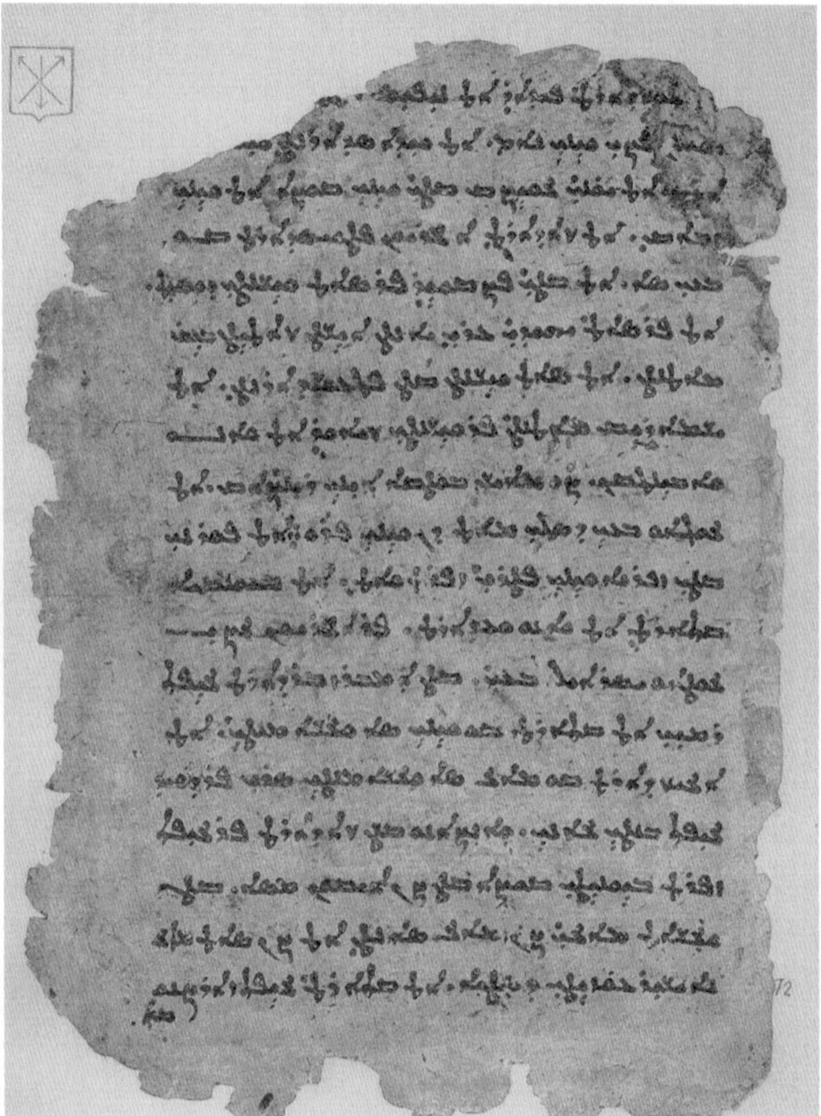

E5/6a = n497* *recto*

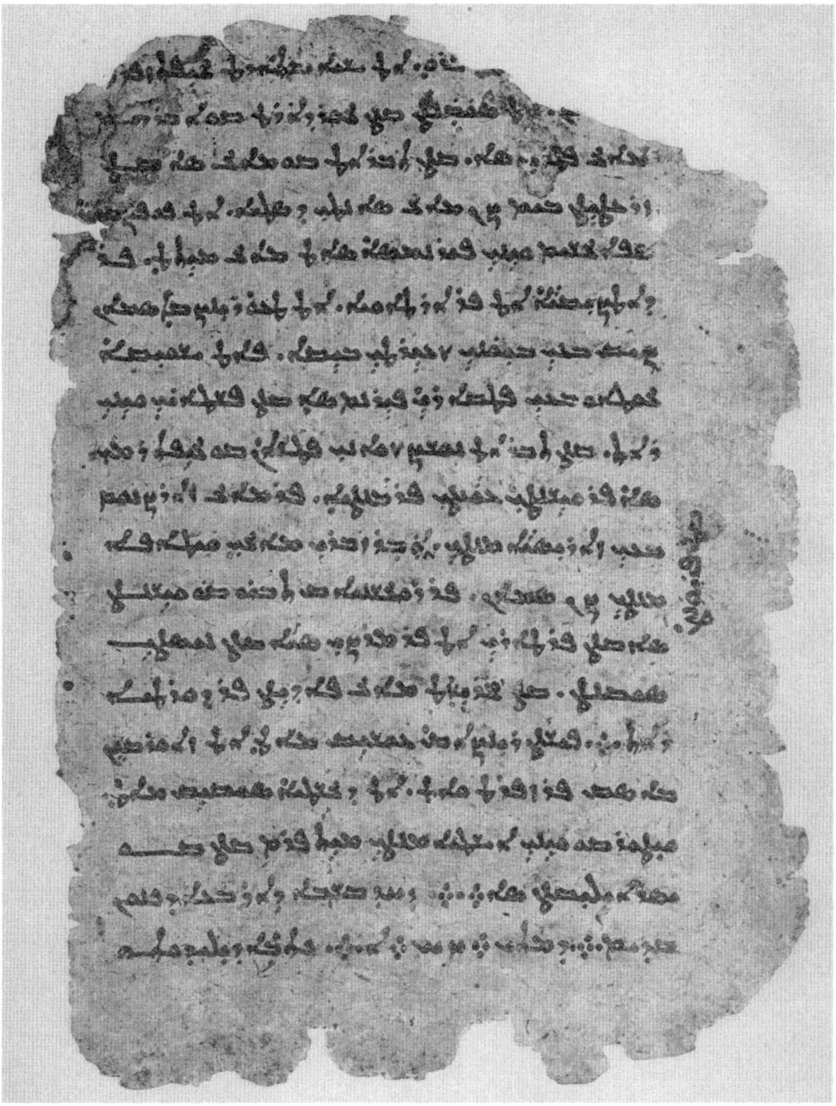

E5/6a = n497* *verso*

E5/6b = n166 [part] *recto*

E5/6b = n166 [part] *verso*

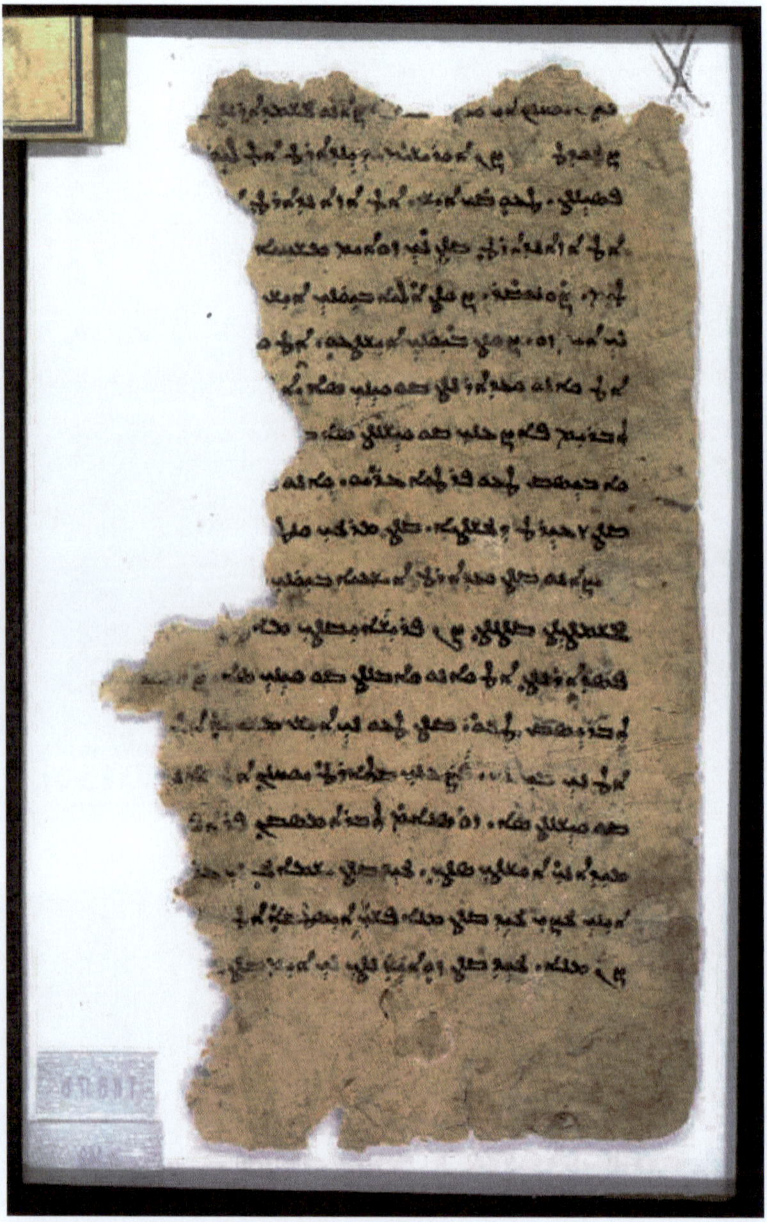

E5/19 = n 149 *recto*

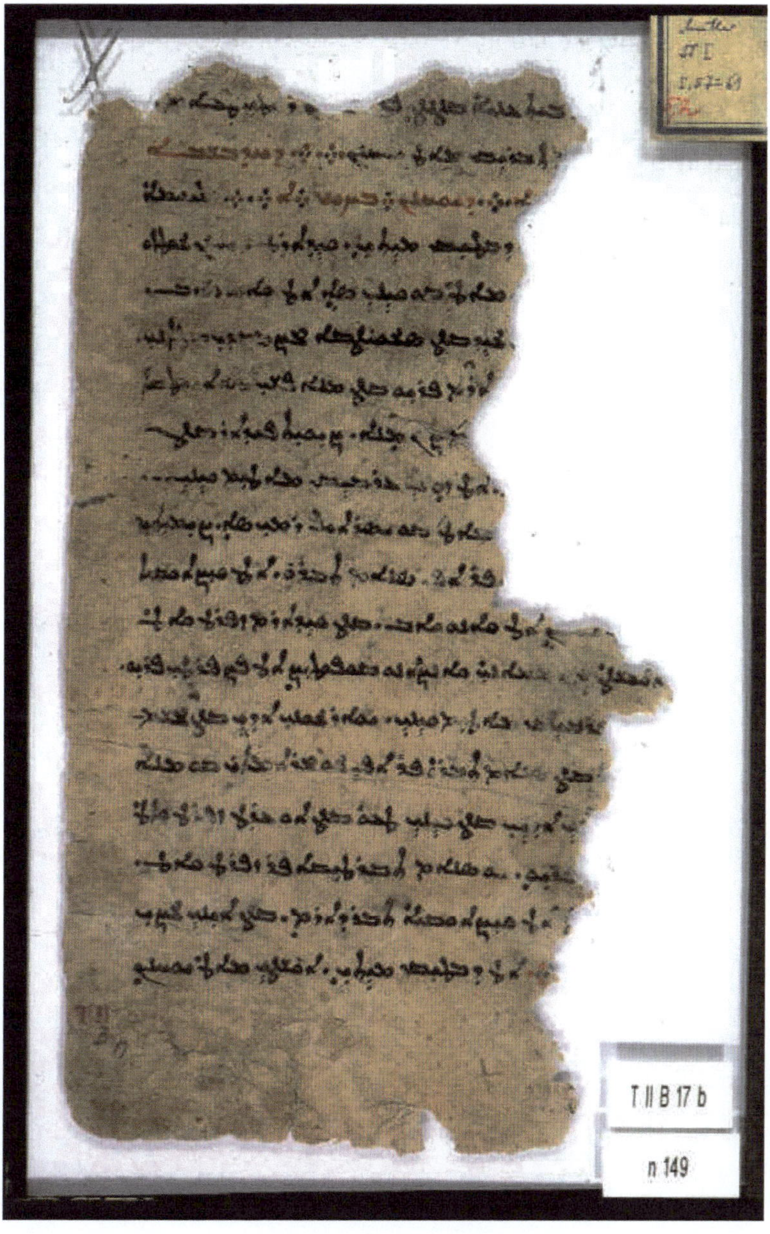

E5/19 = n 149 *verso*

E5/21a = n413d *recto*

E5/21a = n413d *verso*

n 498*

E5/21b = n498* *recto*

n 498*

E5/21b = n498* *verso*

E5/23 = n150 *recto*

E5/23 = n150 *verso*

E5/28a = n151 *recto*

E5/28a = n151 *verso*

E5/28b = n409 *recto*

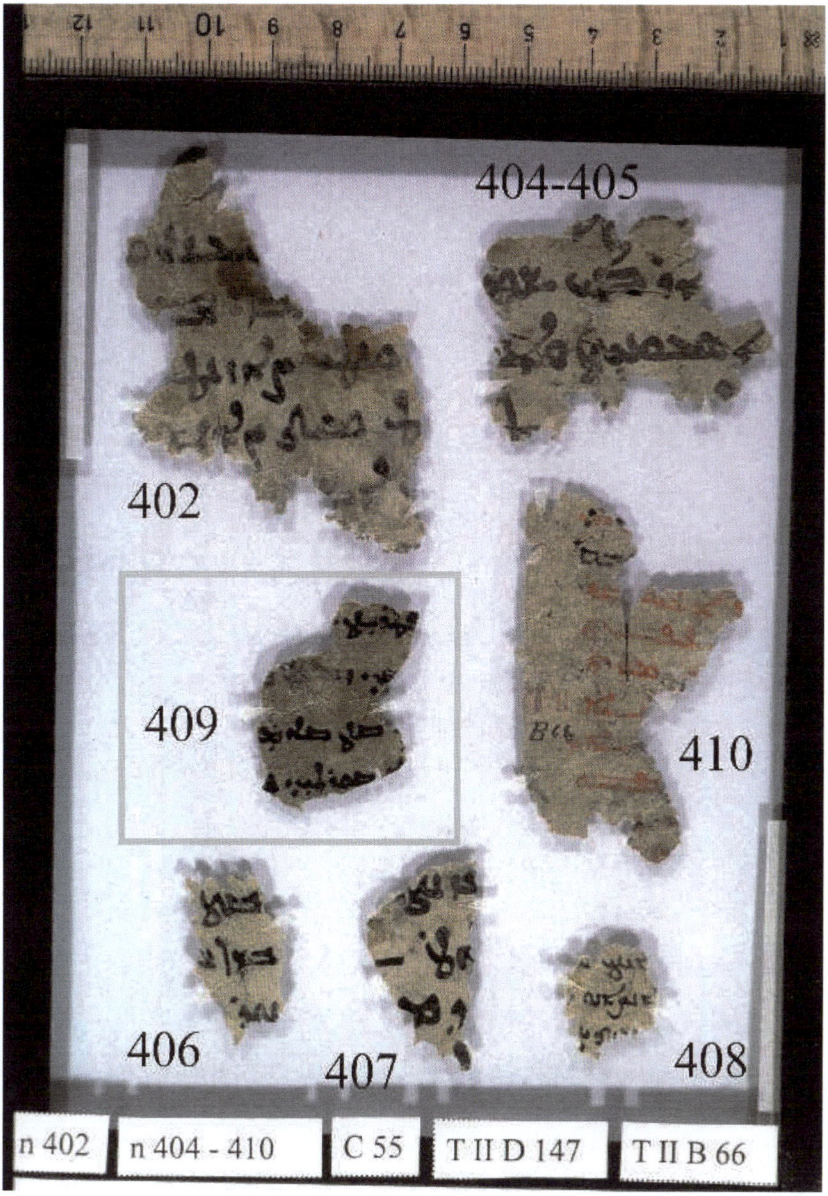

E5/28b = n409 *verso*

E5/34 = n152 *recto*

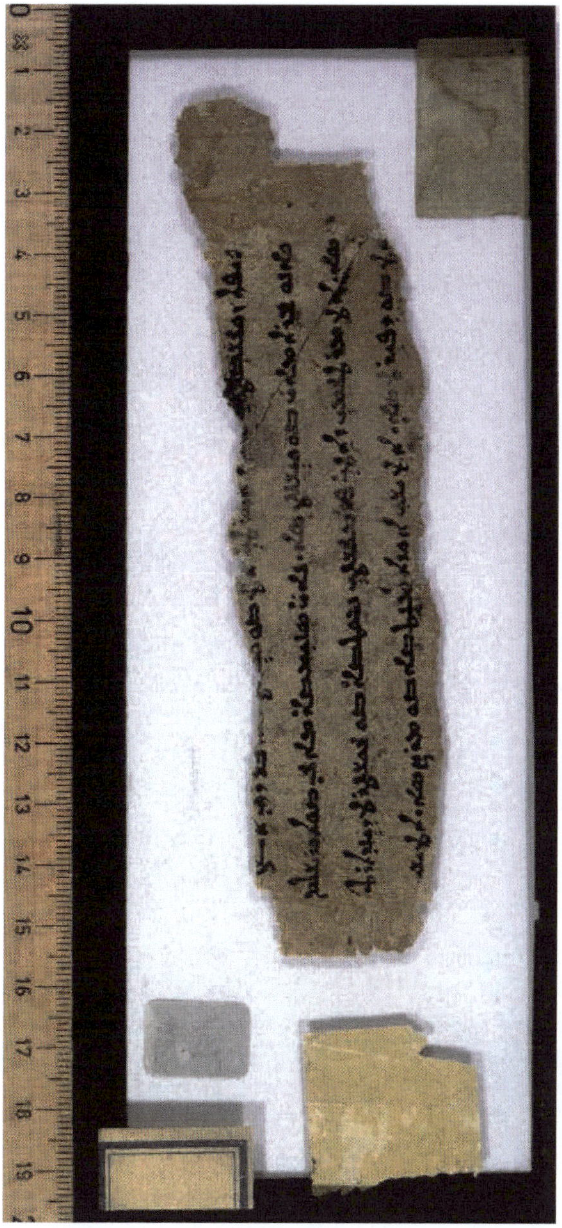

E5/34 = n152 *verso*

E5/38 = n499* *recto*

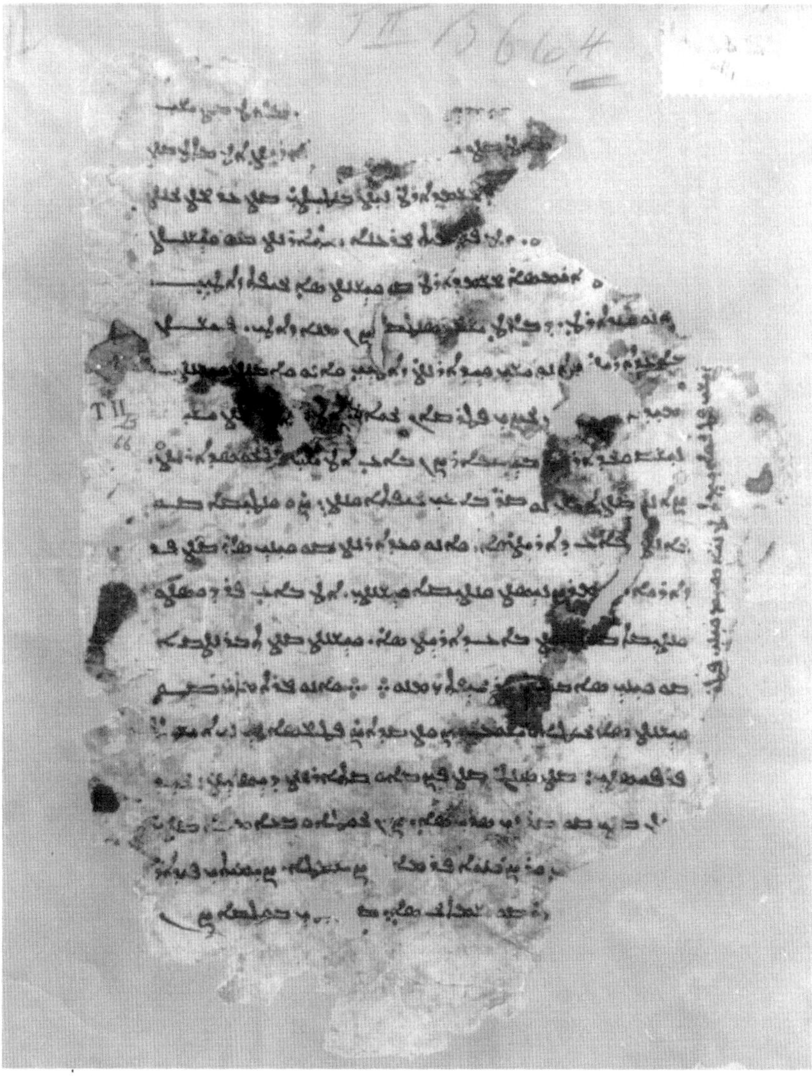

E5/38 = n499* *verso*

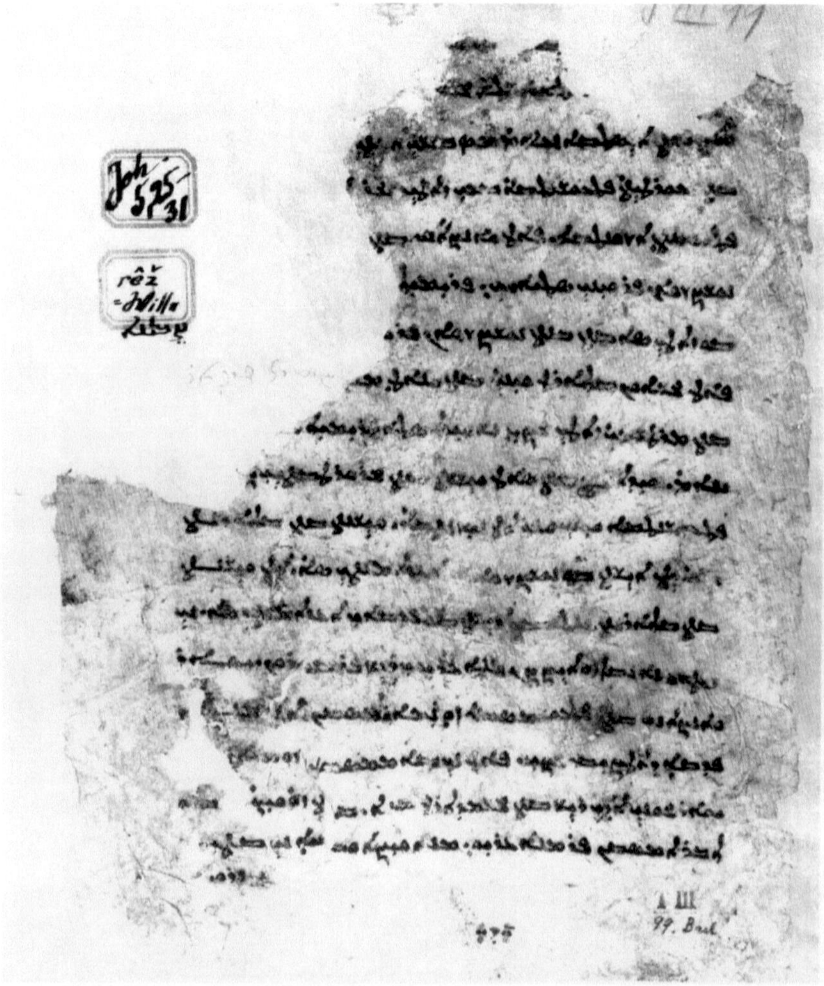

E5/41 = n500* *recto*

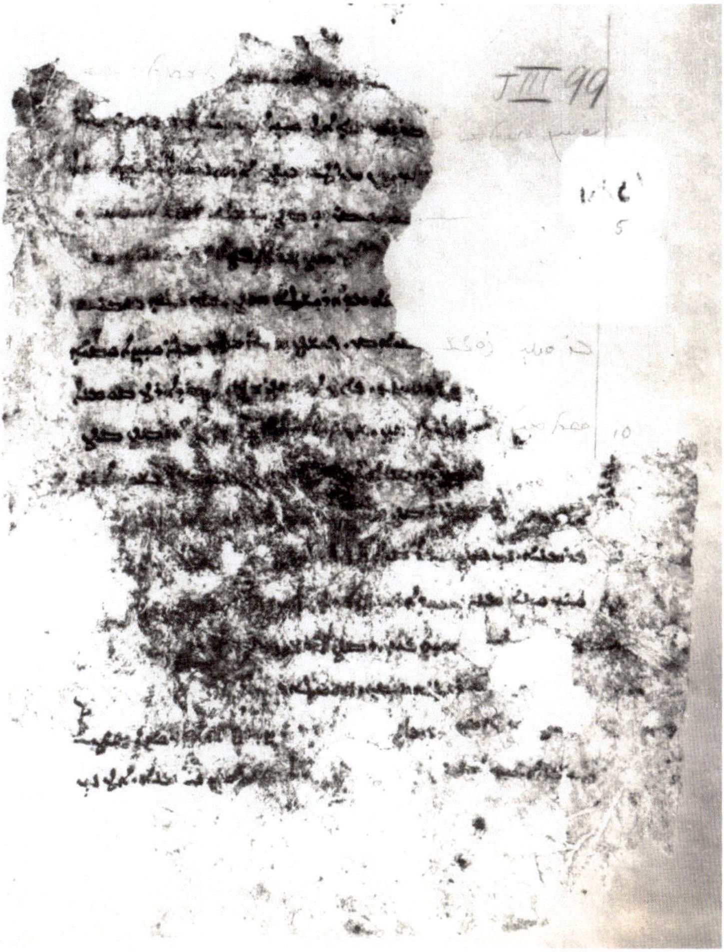

E5/41 = n500* *verso*

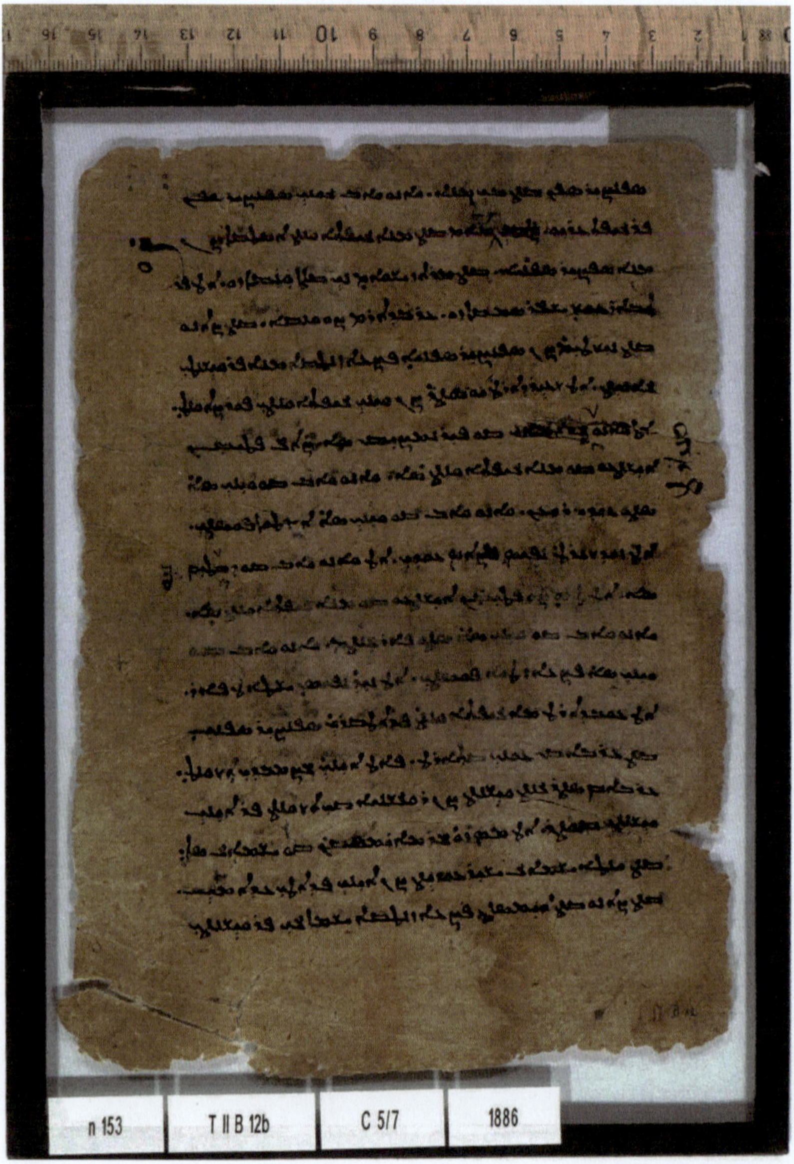

E5/48 = n153 *recto*

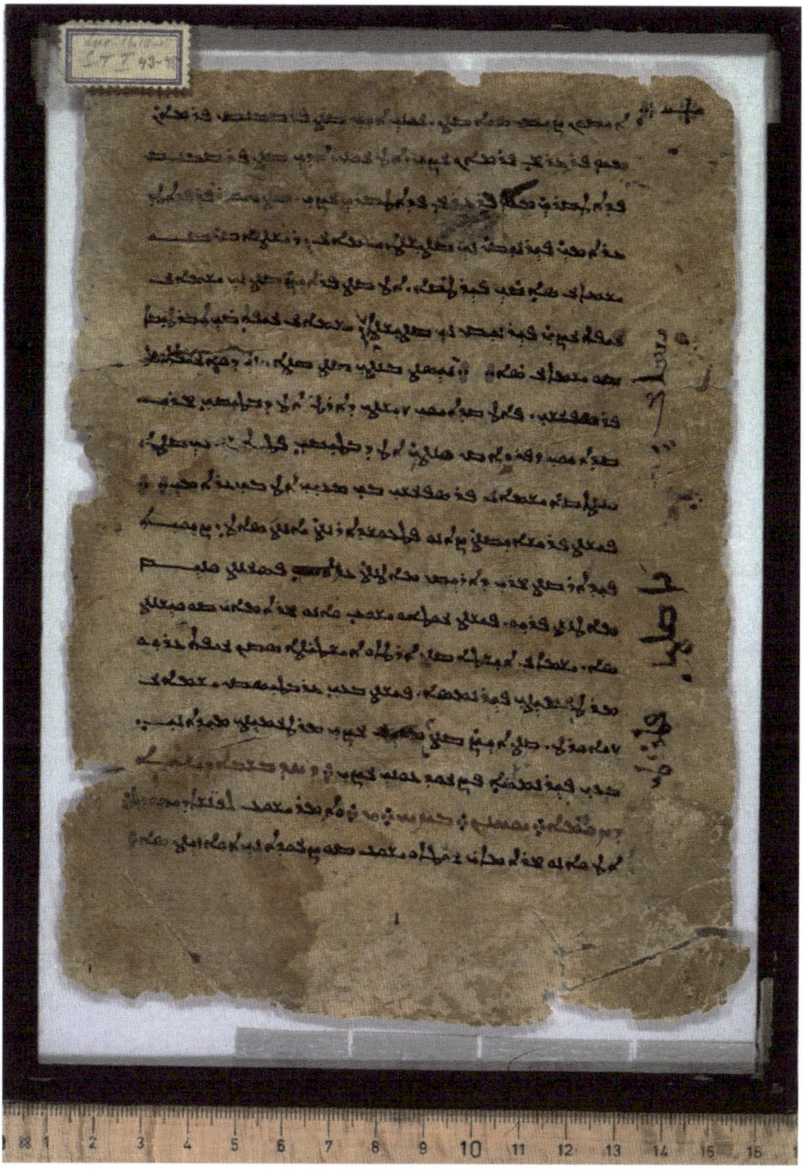

E5/48 = n153 *verso*

E5/51 = n154 *recto*

E5/51 = n154 *verso*

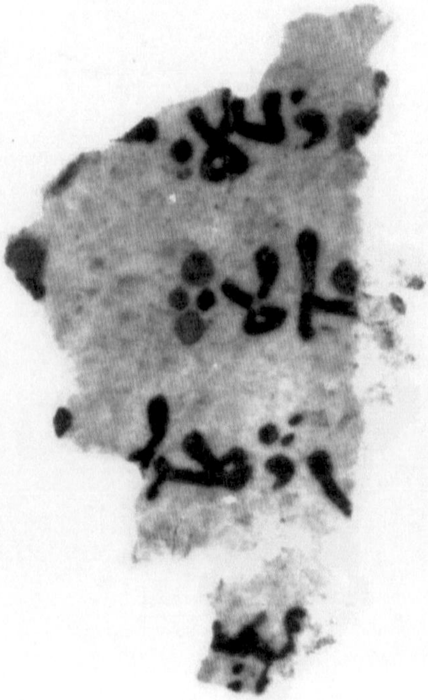

E5/65 = n501* *recto*

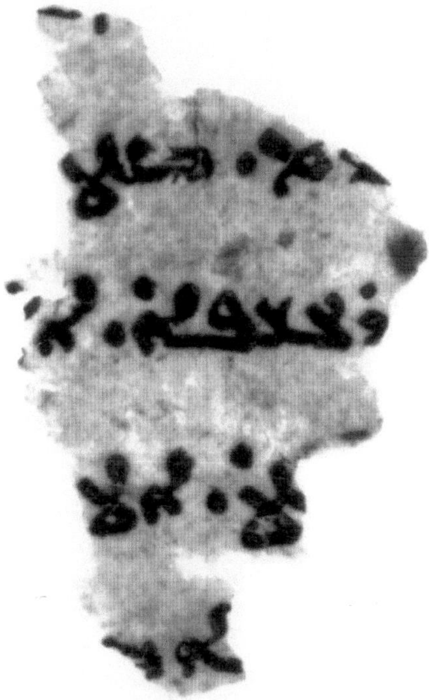

E5/65 = n501* *verso*

E5/72 = n156 *recto*

E5/72 = n156 *verso*

E5/73 = n 157 *recto*

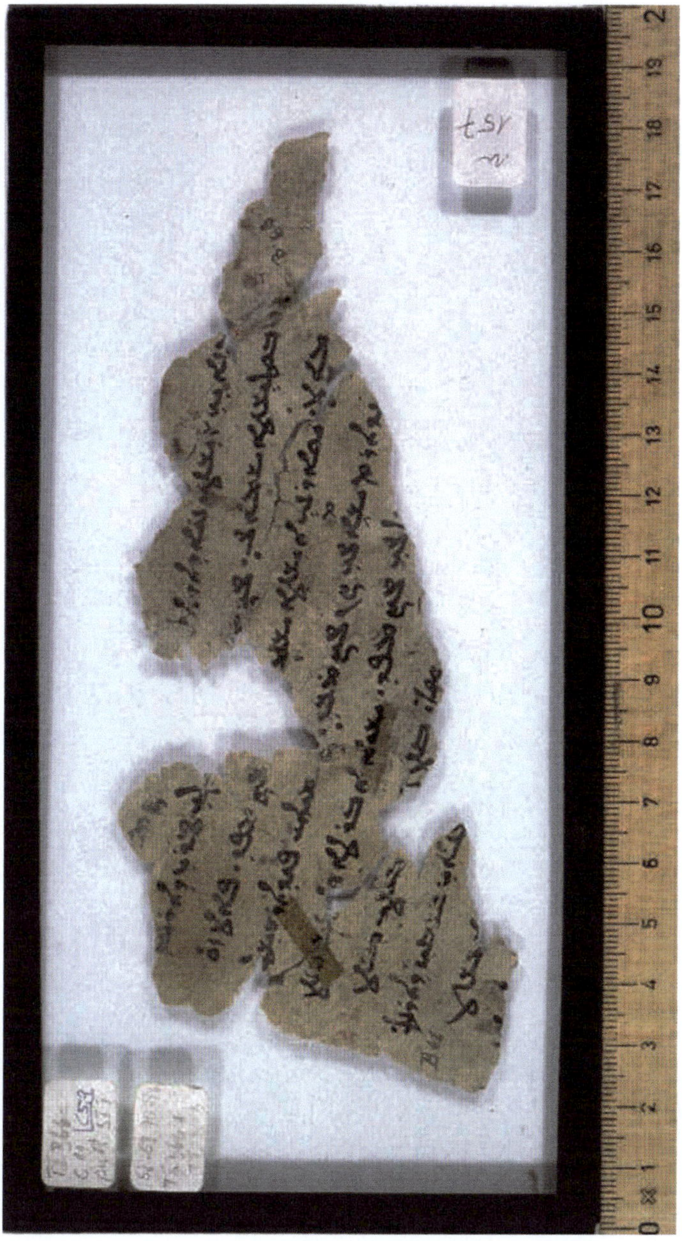

E5/73 = n 157 *verso*

E5/75-76 = n158 *recto /I/ + n158 verso /II/*

E5/75-76 = n158 *recto /II/ + n158 verso /I/*

E5/75-76 = n413a1 *recto /I/ + n413a2 recto /II/*

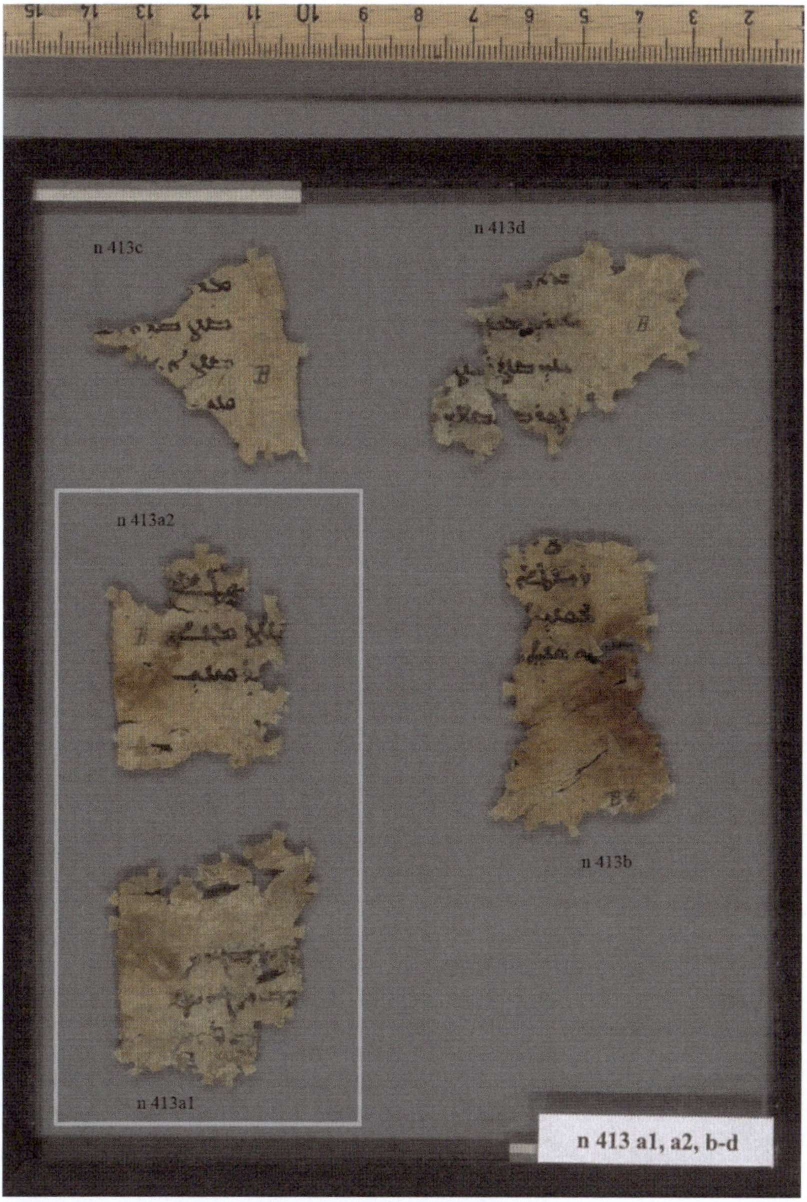

E5/75-76 = n413a1 *verso /I/ + n413a2 verso /II/*

E5/78 = n413b *recto*

E5/78 = n413b *verso*

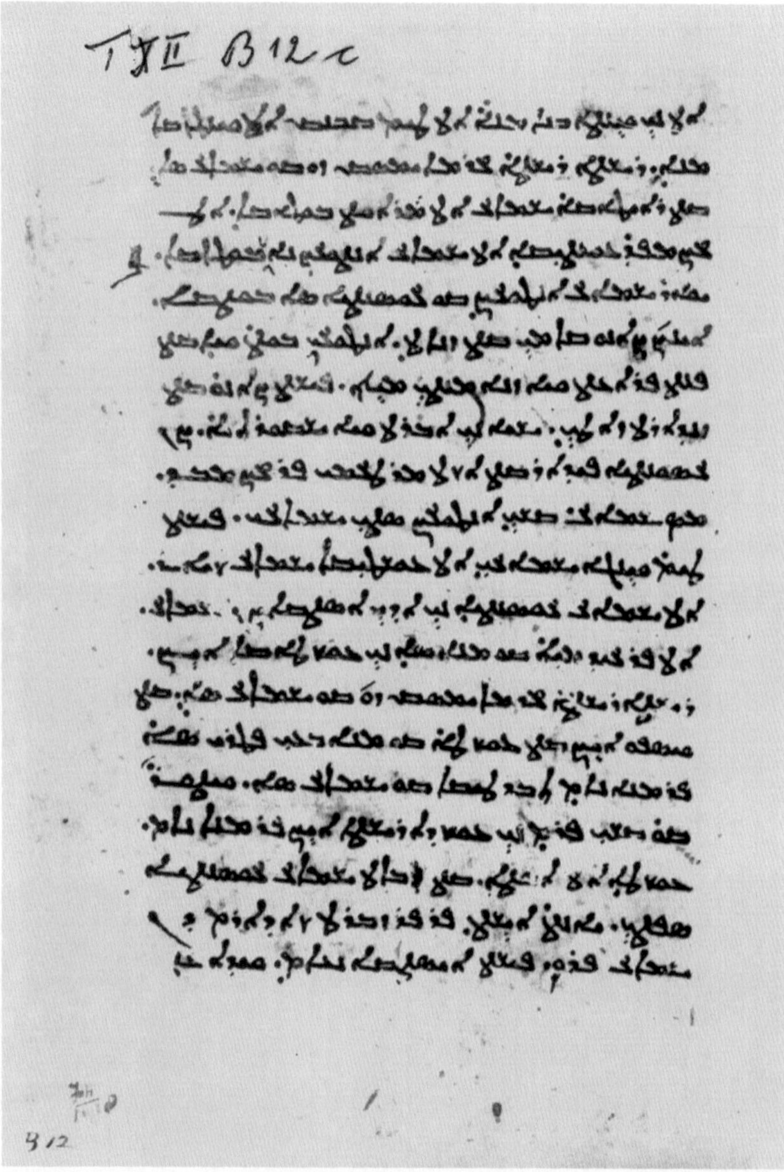

E5/79 = n502* *recto*

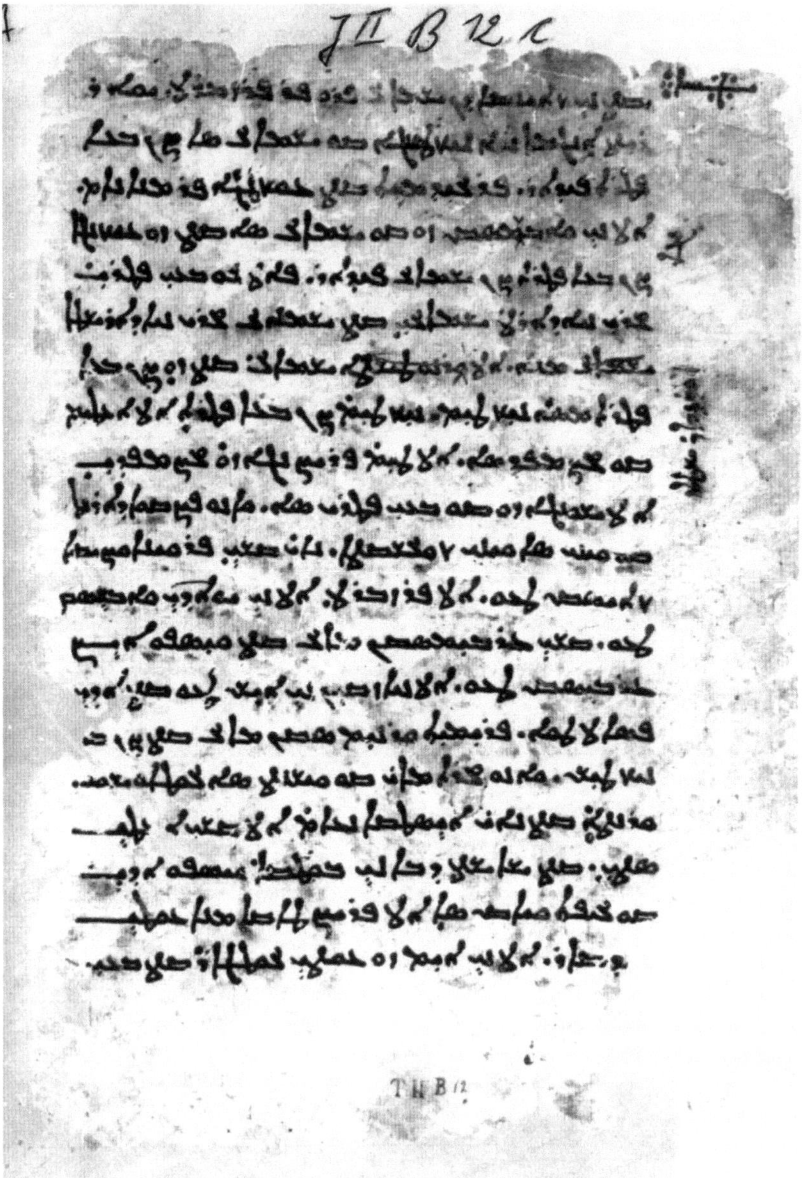

E5/79 = n502* *verso*

E5/80 = n503* *recto*

E5/80 = n503* *verso*

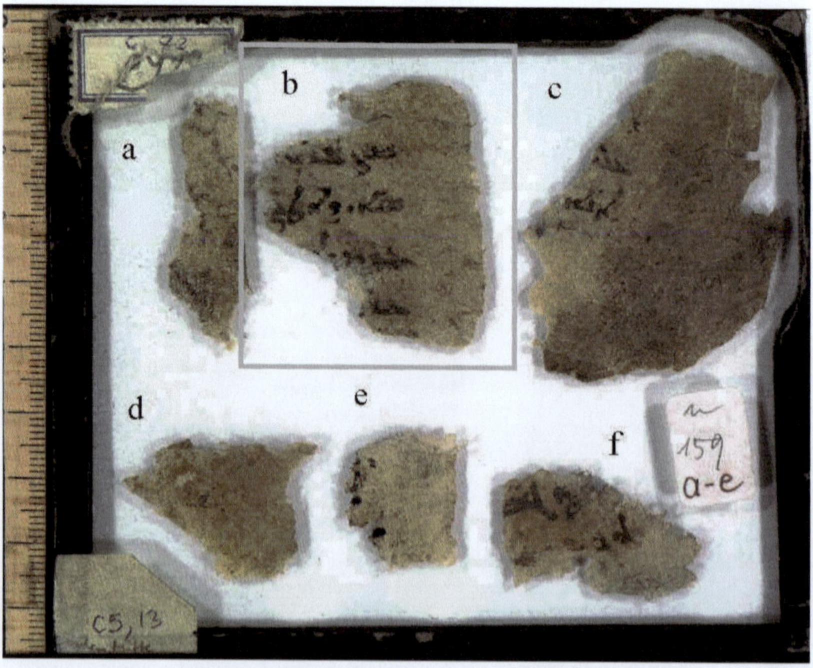

E5/83a = n159b *recto*

E5/83a = n159b *verso*

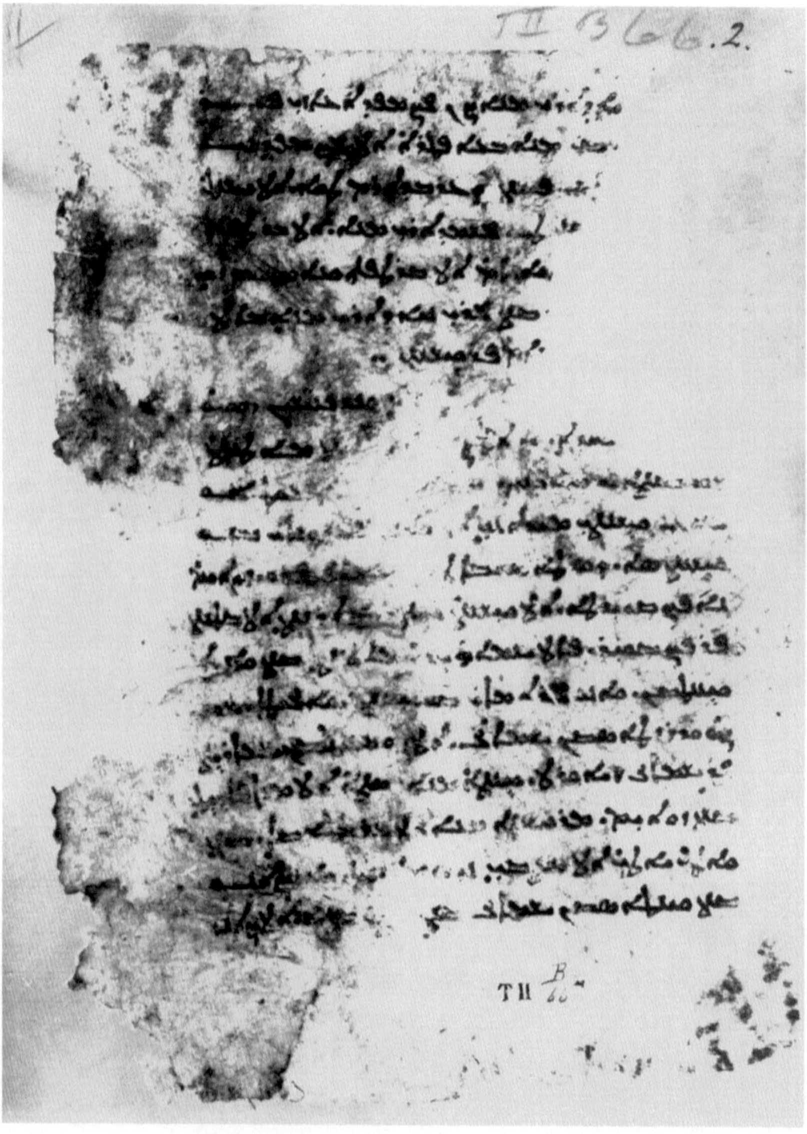

E5/83b = n504* *recto*

E5/83b = n504* *verso*

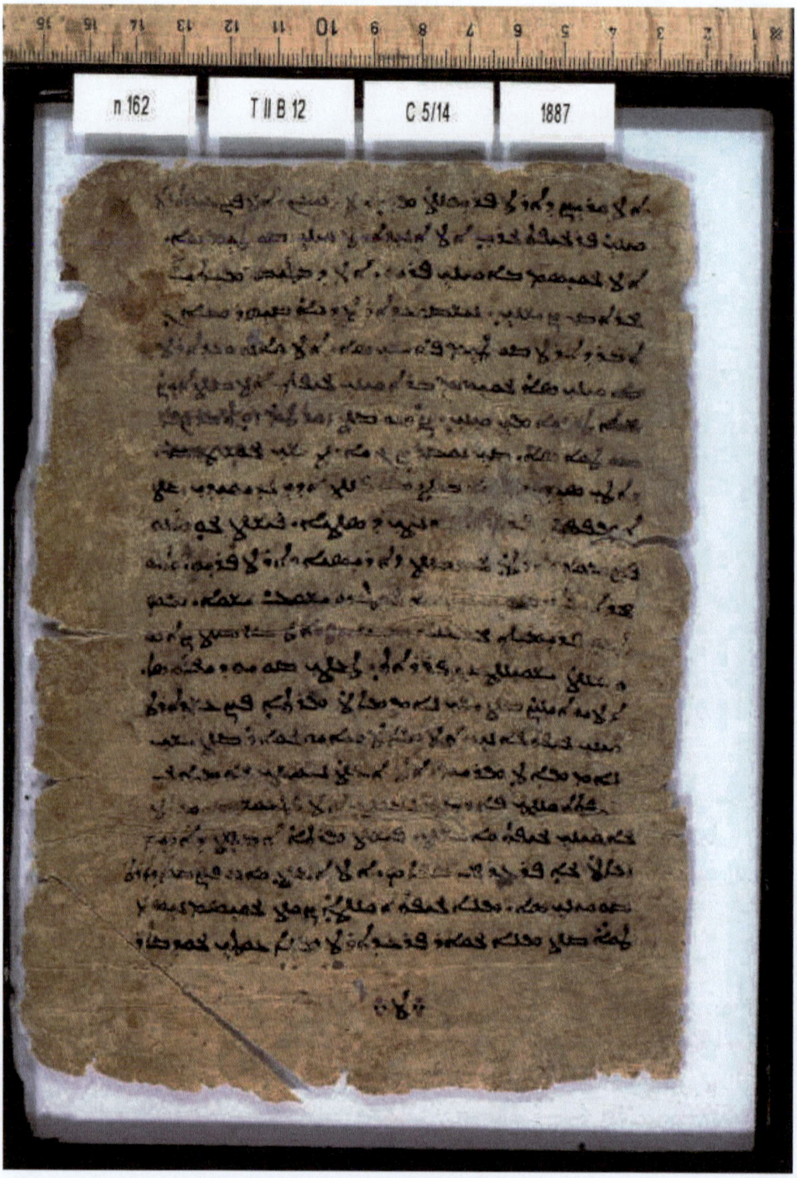

E5/91 = n162 *recto*

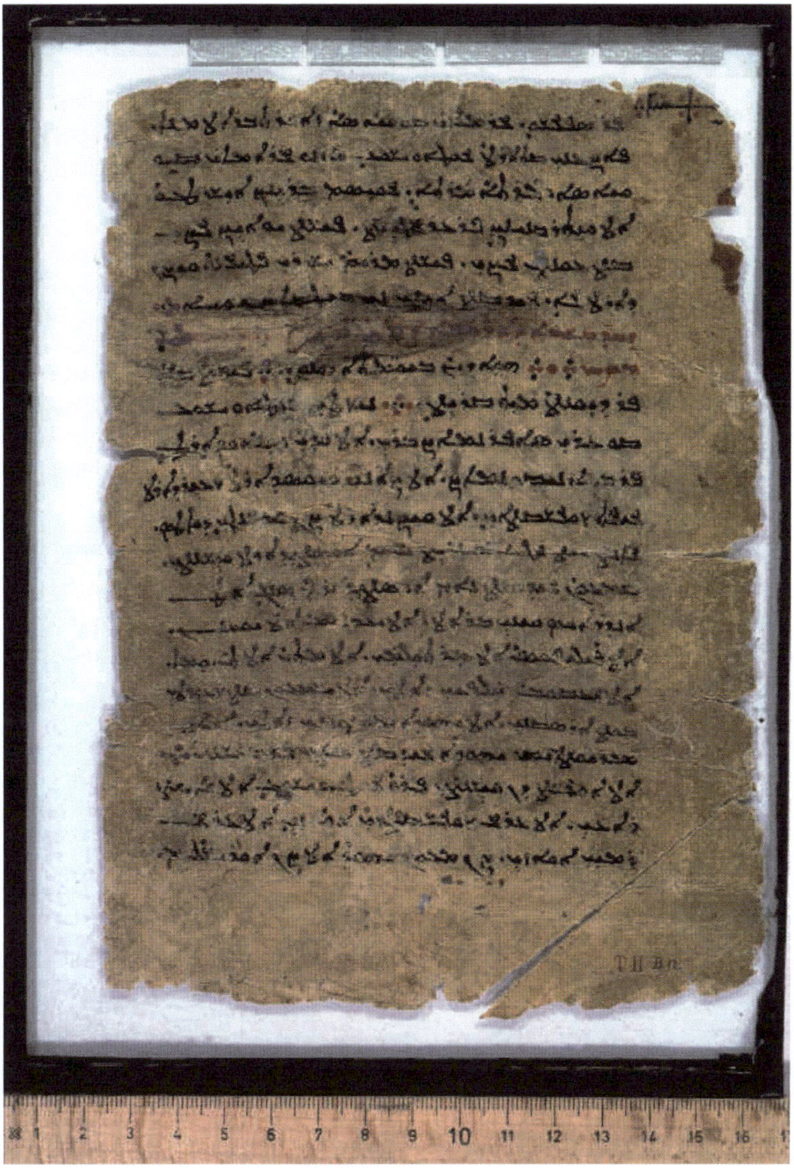

E5/91 = n162 *verso*

E5/100 = n160 *recto* /I/

E5/100 = n160 *verso /I/*

E5/101 = n161 *recto /II/*

E5/101 = n161 *verso /II/*

E5/109 = n163 *recto*

E5/109 = n163 *verso*

E5/125 = n 505* *recto /I/*

E5/125 = n 505* *verso /I/*

E5/126 = n506* *recto /II/*

E5/126 = n506* *verso /II/*

E5/127a-c = n164 = *recto*

E5/127a-c = n164 *verso*

E5/130a = n165 *recto*

E5/130a = n165 *verso*

E5/130b = n413c *recto*

E5/130b = n413c *verso*

VERÖFFENTLICHUNGEN ZUR IRANISTIK

HERAUSGEGEBEN VON BERT G. FRAGNER UND FLORIAN SCHWARZ

(Nr. 1–21: Veröffentlichungen der Iranischen Kommission,
Nr. 22–29: Veröffentlichungen der Kommission für Iranistik,
Nr. 30–31: Herausgegeben von Bert G. Fragner
Nr. 32–68: Herausgegeben von Bert G. Fragner und Velizar Sadovski)

Nr. 1: Manfred Mayrhofer, Onomastica Persepolitana. Das altiranische Namengut der Persepolis-Täfelchen. Unter Mitarbeit von János Harmatta, Walter Hinz, Rüdiger Schmitt und Jutta Seiffert. 1973 (SBph, 286. Band)

Nr. 2: Karl Jahn, Die Geschichte der Kinder Israels des Rašīd ad-Dīn. 1973 (Dph, 114. Band)

Nr. 3: Manfred Mayrhofer, Zum Namengut des Avesta. 1977 (SBph, 308. Band, 5. Abhandlung)

Nr. 4: Karl Jahn, Die Frankengeschichte des Rašīd ad-Dīn. Einleitung, Übersetzung und Kommentar. 1977 (Dph, 129. Band)

Nr. 5: Ronald Zwanziger, Zum Namen der Mutter Zarathustras. (Sonderdruck aus Anzeiger, 114/1977)

Nr. 6: Rüdiger Schmitt, Die Iranier-Namen bei Aischylos. (Iranica Graeca Vetustiora. I). 1978 (SBph, 337. Band)

Nr. 7: Manfred Mayrhofer, Supplement zur Sammlung der altpersischen Inschriften. 1978 (SBph, 338. Band)

Nr. 8: Karl Jahn, Die Indiengeschichte des Rašīd ad-Dīn. Einleitung, vollständige Übersetzung, Kommentar und 80 Texttafeln. 1980 (Dph, 144. Band)

Nr. 9: Oswald Szemerényi, Four Old Iranian Ethnic Names: Scythian – Skudra – Sogdian – Saka. 1980 (SBph, 371. Band)

Nr. 10: Rüdiger Schmitt, Altpersische Siegelinschriften. 1981 (SBph, 381. Band)

Nr. 11: Kaikhusroo M. JamaspAsa, Aogəmadaēcā. A Zoroastrian Liturgy. 1982 (SBph, 397. Band)

Nr. 12: R. E. Emmerick and P. O. Skjærvø, Studies in the Vocabulary of Khotanese I. 1982 (SBph, 401. Band)

Nr. 13: Manfred Mayrhofer, Lassen sich Vorstufen des Uriranischen nachweisen? (Sonderdruck aus Anzeiger, 120/1983)

Nr. 14: Reinhard Pohanka, Zu einigen Architekturstücken von Tell-e Zohak bei Fasa, Südiran. (Sonderdruck aus Anzeiger, 120/1983)

Nr. 15: Wilhelm Eilers, Iranische Ortsnamenstudien. 1987 (SBph, 465. Band)

Nr. 16: Reinhard Pohanka, Die Masdjed-e Djoume in Darab, Südiran. (Sonderdruck aus Anzeiger, 121/1984)

Nr. 17: R. E. Emmerick and P. O. Skjærvø, Studies in the Vocabulary of Khotanese II. 1987 (SBph, 458. Band)

Nr. 18: Wolfgang Felix, Antike literarische Quellen zur Außenpolitik des Sāsāniden-staates. Erster Band (224–309). 1985 (SBph, 456. Band)

Nr. 19: Reinhard Pohanka, Burgen und Heiligtümer in Laristan, Südiran. Ein Surveybericht. 1986 (SBph, 466. Band)

Nr. 20: N. Rastegar und W. Slaje, Uto von Melzer (1881–1961). Werk und Nachlaß eines österreichischen Iranisten. 1987 (SBph, 477. Band)

Nr. 21: Ladislav Zgusta, The Old Ossetic Inscription from the River Zelenčuk. 1987 (SBph, 486. Band)

Nr. 22: Wolfram Kleiss, Die Entwicklung von Palästen und palastartigen Wohnbauten in Iran. 1989 (SBph, 524. Band)

Nr. 23: Nosratollah Rastegar, Zur Problematik einiger handschriftlicher Quellen des neupersischen Namenbuches. 1989 (SBph, 525. Band)

Nr. 24: Dorit Schön, Laristan – eine südpersische Küstenprovinz. Ein Beitrag zu seiner Geschichte. 1990 (SBph, 553. Band)

Nr. 25: Rüdiger Schmitt, Epigraphisch-exegetische Noten zu Dareios' Bīsutūn-Inschriften. 1990 (SBph, 561. Band)

Nr. 26: Jost Gippert, Iranica Armeno-Iberica. Studien zu den iranischen Lehnwörtern im Armenischen und Georgischen. Band I–II. 1993 (SBph, 606. Band)

Nr. 27: R. E. Emmerick and P. O. Skjærvø, Studies in the Vocabulary of Khotanese III. 1997 (SBph, 651. Band)

Nr. 28: Xavier Tremblay, Pour une histoire de la Sérinde. Le manichéisme parmi les peuples et religions d'Asie Centrale d'après les sources primaires. 2001 (SBph, 690. Band)

Nr. 29: Rüdiger Schmitt, Die iranischen und Iranier-Namen in den Schriften Xenophons. (Iranica Graeca Vetustiora. II). 2002 (SBph, 692. Band)

Nr. 30: Rüdiger Schmitt, Meno-logium Bagistano-Persepolitanum. Studien zu den altpersischen Monatsnamen und ihren elamischen Wiedergaben. Unter redaktioneller Mitwirkung von Velizar Sadovski. 2003 (SBph, 705. Band)

Nr. 31: Antonio Panaino, Rite, parole et pensée dans l'Avesta ancien et récent. Quatre leçons au Collège de France (Paris, 7, 14, 21, 28 mai 2001). Edité par Velizar Sadovski, avec la collaboration rédactionnelle de Sara Circassia. 2004 (SBph, 716. Band)

Nr. 32: Roman Siebertz, Die Briefmarken Irans als Mittel der politischen Bildpropaganda. 2005 (SBph, 722. Band)

Nr. 33: Rüdiger Schmitt, Iranische Anthroponyme in den erhaltenen Resten von Ktesias' Werk. (Iranica Graeca Vetustiora. III). 2006 (SBph, 736. Band)

Nr. 34: Heiner Eichner, Bert G. Fragner, Velizar Sadovski und Rüdiger Schmitt (Hrsg.), Iranistik in Europa – gestern, heute, morgen. Unter redaktioneller Mitarbeit von Hannes Hofmann und Vera Giesen. 2006 (SBph, 739. Band)

Nr. 35: Uto v. Melzer, Farhangnevīs. Materialien zu einem Persisch-deutschen Wörter-buch. Hrsg. von Nosratollah Rastegar. Band I–IV. 2006 (Dph, 339. Band)

Nr. 36: Manfred Mayrhofer, Einiges zu den Skythen, ihrer Sprache, ihrem Nachleben. 2006 (SBph, 742. Band)

Nr. 37: Siegfried Weber, Die persische Verwaltung Kaschmirs (1842–1892). Band 1–2. 2007 (SBph, 754. Band)

Nr. 38: Farhangnevīs. Datenbank zu Uto von Melzers lexikographischen Materialien: Persisch-Deutsch/Deutsch-Persisch. Hrsg. von Nosratollah Rastegar. 2007 (CD-ROM)

Nr. 39: Rüdiger Schmitt, Pseudo-altpersische Inschriften. Inschriftenfälschungen und moderne Nachbildungen in altpersischer Keilschrift. 2007 (SBph, 762. Band)

Nr. 40: Thamar E. Gindin, The Early Judaeo-Persian Tafsīrs of Ezekiel: Text, Translation, Commentary. Vol. I: Text. 2007 (SBph, 763. Band)

Nr. 41: Antonio Panaino und Velizar Sadovski, Disputationes Iranologicae Vindobonenses, I.: Antonio Panaino, Chronologia Avestica. Velizar Sadovski, Epitheta und Götternamen im älteren Indo-Iranischen. 2007 (SBph, 764. Band)

Nr. 42: Helmut Slaby, Bindenschild und Sonnenlöwe. Die Geschichte der österreichisch-iranischen Beziehungen bis zur Gegenwart. Nachdruck. 2010 (SBph, 770. Band)

Nr. 43: Tommaso Gnoli, The Interplay of Roman and Iranian Titles in the Roman East (1st–3rd Century A.D.). 2007 (SBph, 765. Band)

Nr. 44: Thamar E. Gindin, The Early Judaeo-Persian Tafsīrs of Ezekiel: Text, Translation, Commentary. Vol. II: Translation. 2007 (SBph, 766. Band)

Nr. 45: Thamar E. Gindin, The Early Judaeo-Persian Tafsīrs of Ezekiel: Text, Translation, Commentary. Vol. III: Commentary (*in Vorbereitung*)

Nr. 46: Bert G. Fragner, Ralph Kauz, Roderick Ptak und Angela Schottenhammer (Hrsg.), Pferde in Asien: Geschichte, Handel und Kultur / Horses in Asia: History, Trade and Culture. 2009 (Dph, 378. Band)

Nr. 47: Giorgio Rota, La Vita e i Tempi di Rostam Khan. Edizione e traduzione italiana del Ms. British Library Add 7,655. 2009 (SBph, 790. Band)

Nr. 48: Fridrik Thordarson, Ossetic Grammatical Studies. 2009 (SBph, 788. Band)

Nr. 49: Rüdiger Schmitt und Gerhard Brugmann (Hrsg.), Aus Karl Brugmanns Jugend-erinnerungen. Eingeleitet und mit Anmerkungen versehen von Rüdiger Schmitt. 2009 (SBph, 786. Band)

Nr. 50: Velizar Sadovski, Untersuchungen zu Sprache und Stil des ältesten Indo-Iranischen (Veda und Avesta). (Stilistica Indo-Iranica, II.) (*in Vorbereitung*)

Nr. 51: Velizar Sadovski und David Stifter (Hrsg.), Iranistische und indogermanistische Beiträge in memoriam Jochem Schindler (1944–1994). 2012 (SBph, 851. Band)

Nr. 52: Ralph Kauz, Giorgio Rota und Jan Paul Niederkorn (Hrsg.), Diplomatisches Zeremoniell in Europa und im Mittleren Osten in der frühen Neuzeit. 2009 (SBph, 796. Band)

Nr. 53: Giorgio Rota, Under Two Lions. On the Knowledge of Persia in the Republic of Venice (ca. 1450–1797). 2009 (SBph, 793. Band)

Nr. 54: Manfred Mayrhofer, Indogermanistik: Über Darstellungen und Einführungen von den Anfängen bis in die Gegenwart. 2009 (SBph, 787. Band)

Nr. 55: Ela Filippone, The Fingers and their Names in the Iranian Languages. (Onomasiological Studies of Body-Part Terms, I). 2010 (SBph, 811. Band)

Nr. 56: Olav Hackstein, Apposition and Nominal Classification in Indo-European and Beyond. 2010 (SBph, 798. Band)

Nr. 57: Geschichte Wassaf's. Persisch herausgegeben und deutsch übersetzt von Hammer-Purgstall. Neu herausgegeben von Sibylle Wentker nach Vorarbeiten von Klaus Wundsam. Band 1. 2010 (SBph, 802. Band)

Nr. 58: Gisela Fock, Die iranische Moderne in der Bildenden Kunst: Der Bildhauer und Maler Parviz Tanavoli. 2011 (SBph, 815. Band)

Nr. 59: Geschichte Wassaf's. Deutsch übersetzt von Hammer-Purgstall. Herausgegeben von Sibylle Wentker nach Vorarbeiten von Elisabeth und Klaus Wundsam. Band 2. 2010 (SBph, 803. Band)

Nr. 60: Toshifumi Gotō: The Old Indo-Aryan Morphology and its Indo-Iranian Background. 2013 (SBph, 849. Band)

Nr. 61: Yuri Stoyanov, Defenders and Enemies of the True Cross. The Sasanian Conquest of Jerusalem in 614 and Byzantine Ideology of Anti-Persian Warfare. 2011 (SBph, 819. Band)

Nr. 62: Barbara Karl, Treasury – Kunstkammer – Museum: Objects from the Islamic World in the Museum Collections of Vienna. 2011 (SBph, 822. Band)

Nr. 63: Şevket Küçükhüseyin, Selbst- und Fremdwahrnehmung im Prozess kultureller Transformation. Anatolische Quellen über Muslime, Christen und Türken (13.–15. Jahrhundert). 2011 (SBph, 825. Band)

Nr. 64: Geschichte Wassaf's. Deutsch übersetzt von Hammer-Purgstall. Herausgegeben von Sibylle Wentker nach Vorarbeiten von Elisabeth und Klaus Wundsam. Band 3. 2012 (SBph, 827. Band)

Nr. 65: Antonio Panaino und Velizar Sadovski, Disputationes Iranologicae Vindobonenses, II. 2013 (SBph, 845. Band)

Nr. 66: Geschichte Wassaf's. Deutsch übersetzt von Hammer-Purgstall. Herausgegeben von Sibylle Wentker nach Vorarbeiten von Elisabeth und Klaus Wundsam. Band 4. 2016 (SBph, 878. Band)

Nr. 67: Luke Treadwell, Craftsmen and coins: signed dies in the Iranian world (third to the fifth centuries AH). 2011 (Dph, 423. Band, gleichzeitig: Veröffentlichungen der Numismatischen Kommission, Band 54)

Nr. 69: Amr Taher Ahmed, La « Révolution littéraire ». Étude de l'influence de la poésie française sur la modernisation des formes poétiques persanes au début du XXe siècle. 2012 (SBph, 829. Band)

Nr. 70: Roman Siebertz, Preise, Löhne und Lebensstandard im safavidischen Iran. Eine Untersuchung zu den Rechnungsbüchern Wollebrand Geleynssen de Jonghs (1641–1643). 2013 (SBph, 835. Band)

Nr. 71: Walter Posch, Osmanisch-safavidische Beziehungen 1545–1550: Der Fall Alḳâs Mîrzâ. Teil 1 und Teil 2. 2013 (SBph, 841. Band)

Nr. 72: Niccolò Pianciola und Paolo Sartori (Hrsg.), Islam, Society and States across the Qazaq Steppe (18th – Early 20th Centuries). 2013 (SBph, 844. Band)

Nr. 73: Desmond Durkin-Meisterernst, Grammatik des Westmitteliranischen (Parthisch und Mittelpersisch). 2014 (SBph, 850. Band/Grammatica Iranica 1, hrsg. von Velizar Sadovski)

Nr. 74: Christine Noelle-Karimi, The Pearl in its Midst. Herat and the Mapping of Khurasan (15th–19th Centuries). 2014 (Dph, 463. Band)

Nr. 75: Bert G. Fragner, Ralph Kauz und Florian Schwarz (Hrsg.): Wine Culture in Iran and Beyond. 2014 (SBph, 852. Band)

Nr. 76: Alexander Lubotsky, Alanic Marginal Notes in a Greek Liturgical Manuscript. 2015 (SBph, 859. Band/Grammatica Iranica 2, hrsg. von Velizar Sadovski)

Nr. 77: Tilmann Trausch, Formen höfischer Historiographie im 16. Jahrhundert. Geschichtsschreibung unter den frühen Safaviden: 1501–1578. 2015 (SBph, 861. Band)

Nr. 78: Jeff Eden (transl. and annot.), The Life of Muḥammad Sharīf. A Central Asian Sufi Hagiography in Chaghatay. With an appendix by Rian Thum and David Brophy. 2015 (SBph, 864. Band)

Nr. 79: Rüdiger Schmitt, Stilistik der altpersischen Inschriften. Versuch einer Annäherung. 2016 (SBph, 875. Band/Grammatica Iranica 3, hrsg. von Velizar Sadovski)

Nr. 80: Andreas Wilde, What is Beyond the River? Power, Authority, and Social Order in Transoxania, 18th-19th Centuries. 2016 (SBph, 877. Band)

IRANISCHE ONOMASTIK

HERAUSGEGEBEN VON BERT G. FRAGNER UND FLORIAN SCHWARZ

(Nr. 1–10: Herausgegeben von Bert G. Fragner und Velizar Sadovski)

Nr. 1: Rüdiger Schmitt, Das Iranische Personennamenbuch: Rückschau, Vorschau, Rundschau (mit einer Bibliographie zur Iranischen Personennamenkunde). 2006 (SBph, 744. Band)

Nr. 2: Sonja Fritz, Die ossetischen Personennamen. (= Iranisches Personennamenbuch, Band III, Faszikel 3). 2006 (SBph, 746. Band)

Nr. 3: Ulla Remmer, Frauennamen im Rigveda und im Avesta. 2006 (SBph, 745. Band)

Nr. 4: Ran Zadok, Iranische Personennamen in der neu- und spätbabylonischen Nebenüberlieferung. (= Iranisches Personennamenbuch, Band VII, Faszikel 1B). 2009 (SBph, 777. Band)

Nr. 5: Philippe Gignoux, Christelle Jullien, Florence Jullien, Noms propres syriaques d'origine iranienne. (= Iranisches Personennamenbuch, Band VII, Faszikel 5). 2009 (SBph, 789. Band)

Nr. 6: Rüdiger Schmitt, Iranische Personennamen in der neuassyrischen Nebenüberlieferung. (= Iranisches Personennamenbuch, Band VII, Faszikel 1A). 2009 (SBph, 792. Band)

Nr. 7: Nicholas Sims-Williams, Bactrian Personal Names. (= Iranisches Personennamenbuch, Band II, Faszikel 7). 2010 (SBph, 806. Band)

Nr. 8: Pavel B. Lurje, Personal Names in Sogdian Texts. (= Iranisches Personennamenbuch, Band II, Faszikel 8). 2010 (SBph, 808. Band)

Nr. 9: Rüdiger Schmitt, Iranische Personennamen in der griechischen Literatur vor Alexander d. Gr. (= Iranisches Personennamenbuch, Band V, Faszikel 5A). 2011 (SBph, 823. Band)

Nr. 10: Rüdiger Schmitt, Manfred Mayrhofer: Leben und Werk. Mit vollständigem Schriftenverzeichnis. 2012 (SBph, 828. Band)

Nr. 11: Matteo De Chiara, Mauro Maggi and Giuliana Martini (Hrsg.), Buddhism Among the Iranian Peoples of Central Asia (= Multilingualism and History of Knowledge, Volume I. Hrsg. von Jens E. Braarvig, Markham J. Geller, Gebhard Selz und Velizar Sadovski). 2013 (SBph, 848. Band)

Nr. 12: Olav Hackstein and Ronald I. Kim (Hrsg.), Linguistic Developments along the Silkroad: Archaism and Innovation in Tocharian (= Multilingualism and History of Knowledge, Volume II. Hrsg. von Jens E. Braarvig, Markham J. Geller, Gebhard Selz und Velizar Sadovski). 2012 (SBph, 834. Band)

Nr. 13: Rüdiger Schmitt und Günter Vittmann, Iranische Namen in ägyptischer Nebenüberlieferung. (= Iranisches Personennamenbuch, Band VIII). 2013 (SBph, 842. Band)

Nr. 14: Manfred Hutter, Iranische Personennamen in der hebräischen Bibel. (= Iranisches Personennamenbuch, Band VII, Faszikel 2). 2015 (SBph, 860. Band)

IRANISCHES PERSONENNAMENBUCH

BEGRÜNDET VON MANFRED MAYRHOFER
HERAUSGEGEBEN VON RÜDIGER SCHMITT, HEINER EICHNER, BERT G. FRAGNER UND VELIZAR SADOVSKI

Bisher erschienen:

Band I: Die altiranischen Namen
Von Manfred Mayrhofer. 1979 (Sonderpublikation).

Faszikel 1, 2 und 3 in einem Band:
Faszikel 1: Die avestischen Namen.
Faszikel 2: Die altpersischen Namen.
Faszikel 3: Indices zum Gesamtband.

Band II: Mitteliranische Personennamen

Faszikel 2: Noms propres sassanides en moyen-perse épigraphique. Von Philippe Gignoux. 1986 (Sonderpublikation)

Faszikel 3: Noms propres sassanides en moyen-perse épigraphique. Supplément (1986–2001). Von Philippe Gignoux. 2003 (Sonderpublikation)

Faszikel 7: Bactrian Personal Names. Von Nicholas Sims-Williams. 2010 (SBph, 806. Band/Iranische Onomastik, Nr. 7)

Faszikel 8: Personal Names in Sogdian Texts. Von Pavel B. Lurje. 2011 (SBph, 808. Band/Iranische Onomastik, Nr. 8)

Band III: Neuiranische Personennamen

Faszikel 3: Die ossetischen Personennamen. Von Sonja Fritz. 2006 (SBph, 746. Band/Iranische Onomastik, Nr. 2)

Band IV: Materialgrundlagen zu den iranischen Personennamen auf antiken Münzen: Nomina propria Iranica in nummis

Von Michael Alram. 1986 (Sonderpublikation)

Band V: Iranische Namen in Nebenüberlieferungen indogermanischer Sprachen

Faszikel 4: Iranische Namen in den indogermanischen Sprachen Kleinasiens: Lykisch, Lydisch, Phrygisch.Von Rüdiger Schmitt. 1982 (Sonderpublikation)

Faszikel 5A: Iranische Personennamen in der griechischen Literatur vor Alexander d. Gr. Von Rüdiger Schmitt. 2011 (SBph, 823. Band/Iranische Onomastik, Nr. 9)

Faszikel 6a: Iranische Namen in den griechischen Dokumenten Ägyptens. Von Philip Huyse. 1991 (Sonderpublikation)

Band VII: Iranische Namen in semitischen Nebenüberlieferungen

Faszikel 1A: Iranische Personennamen in der neuassyrischen Nebenüberlieferung. Von Rüdiger Schmitt. 2009 (SBph, 792. Band/Iranische Onomastik, Nr. 6)

Faszikel 1B: Iranische Personennamen in der neu- und spätbabylonischen Nebenüberlieferung. Von Ran Zadok. 2009 (SBph, 777. Band/Iranische Onomastik, Nr. 4)

Faszikel 2: Iranische Personennamen in der hebräischen Bibel. Von Manfred Hutter. 2015 (SBph, 860. Band/Iranische Onomastik, Nr. 14)

Faszikel 5: Noms propres syriaques d'origine iranienne. Von Philippe Gignoux, Christelle Jullien, Florence Jullien. 2009 (SBph, 789. Band/Iranische Onomastik, Nr. 5)

Band VIII: Iranische Namen in ägyptischer Nebenüberlieferung

Von Rüdiger Schmitt und Günter Vittmann. 2013 (SBph, 842. Band/Iranische Onomastik, Nr. 13)